MILES

1884·1984

A Centennial History

About The Author

William C. Cray is a graduate of Northwestern University. After serving as a Navy officer on a landing ship in the Pacific during World War II, he worked for a publishing house in Chicago. He was director of public relations for Abbott Laboratories in the 1960s and vice-president, Public Relations, for the Pharmaceutical Manufacturers Association from 1969 until he retired in 1980. He lives in Southern Pines, North Carolina.

A Centennial History

William C. Cray

Prentice-Hall, Inc.   Englewood Cliffs, New Jersey

Prentice-Hall International, Inc., *London*
Prentice-Hall of Australia, Pty. Ltd., *Sydney*
Prentice-Hall Canada, Inc., *Toronto*
Prentice-Hall of India Private Ltd., *New Delhi*
Prentice-Hall of Japan, Inc., *Tokyo*
Prentice-Hall of Southeast Asia Pte. Ltd., *Singapore*
Whitehall Books, Ltd., Wellington, *New Zealand*
Editora Prentice-Hall do Brasil Ltda., *Rio de Janeiro*

© 1984 *by*
PRENTICE-HALL, INC.
Englewood Cliffs, N.J.

Acknowledgments

We wish to thank the following for their photography reproduced in MILES: A CENTENNIAL HISTORY:
Fabian Bachrach; Barefoot Studio; Harlan W. Bourdon & Associates; Don Brayton's Photoarts, Elkhart; Chicago
Photographers; Dominic; Roger A. Etter and Midwest Commerce; Maurice Frink, Elkhart; Steve A.
Hendrickson, Oregon, WI; Herring Studio (and especially Alex A. Tschumakow); Knapp Studio, Elkhart; The
Lattimer Studios, South Bend; Norm Lindstedt Photography, South Bend; Navarro; Richard Paul Photography;
Manuel Paz Fotografia, Mexico City; Foto Studio 3 di Michele Rubicondo, Milan; Foto Firmino Santos; Giles
Smith Photography; Thalf Associates, NY; Theatrical Chicago; Wide World Photos Inc., NY; Nick Zavalishin
Studio.

ISBN 0-13-583014-1

Printed in the United States of America

Preface

Those of us privileged to be part of Miles during its Centennial stand on a type of divide. The past year has been memorable both for the lessons that have emerged from our review of the company's 100-year development and for the exciting prospects that beckon to us in the period ahead. For me it has been a special pleasure to head Miles during this transition.

This volume describes human and corporate achievements, not just the memorable events in our history. The Miles story contains much that may be new to you, as it was to me. Certainly, Mr. Cray's account shows what human beings can accomplish through talent, good will, and dedication. That is a chronicle well worth the telling!

If the kind of effort depicted here can be projected for the years to come, I am fully confident that fresh successes will distinguish Miles and its people. So it is a keenly felt honor for me to dedicate *Miles: A Centennial History* to the employees, current and past, and their families, whose vision and efforts, preserved in this book, will remain a lasting source of inspiration for the Miles of tomorrow.

Dr. Franz J. Geks
Chairman and
Chief Executive Officer

Author's Foreword

This book, in tracking the first hundred years of Miles Laboratories, covers only what seemed to be most pertinent and engrossing.

My chief regret is that space did not permit mentioning hundreds of the able and admirable men and women who did so much in molding the company, and that many others get only brief recognition. All deserve much more.

The book was a pleasure to do, mainly because so many Miles people gave generous help and encouragement; they were most forthright in dispensing both facts and opinions.

Much of the book is grounded upon interviews with and comments from some 150 individuals, the great majority still working at Miles. A goodly number of retired executives furnished valuable insights. Taped interviews with a score of retirees, ably carried out by Bob Pattillo, added valuable anecdotal notabilia. Martha Pickrell, an experienced archivist, painstakingly researched the early years of the corporation, all of it pivotal to the first chapters. Dr. Donald Yates, corporate archivist, added significant facts and perspectives.

Research took me into a wealth of documentation, from memos and letters to such formal pieces as Annual Reports. Nothing was more beneficial than the file of *The Alkalizer*, which, through the years from the first issue, in 1936, imparted "homey"

touches, capturing the essence and spirit of Miles— along with a storehouse of facts.

I am particularly indebted to Dr. Walter Compton, who graciously granted me much time for insightful comment on the "many ages" of Miles. As chief executive officers, Theodor H. Heinrichs and Dr. Franz J. Geks provided full support. Special thanks are due a host of experts, among them Ed Bassett, Jim Murphy, Blaze Palermo, Henry Wishinsky, Dean Spence, Bob Myers, Paul Spiekermann, Adrien Ringuette, and Bayer's Christine Cromwell Hoag. Doloris Cogan, always demanding the best, gave constant and unflagging devotion to this major Centennial project. Judy Rush, in looking after a plethora of details, and Janice Casper, who typed most of the drafts, were truly indispensable.

Deep appreciation goes to the Centennial Steering Committee of Dick Kocher, president; Bob Rose, retired president; Lem Beardsley, retired senior vice president; John Gildea, vice president, administration; and Doloris Cogan, director of public relations. They read the copy seeking to assure fair-minded emphasis and interpretation within the historic framework of the company. Not a simple chore!

A final note: In writing this history, I developed an affection for Miles that, in its small way, matches that of its dedicated employees—from the storied past to the mercurial present.

Introduction

It has been a gleaming first century, by and large, for Miles Laboratories. On occasion the lights flickered low, as they do for all institutions, but at many other times they flared brightly. Taken together, they illuminate memorable achievements, manifestly worth inscribing for posterity.

Even those hundred years scurried by swiftly, encompassing but a wink of history, from Dr. Franklin L. Miles' first bottles of Nervine, to the myriad products of today's complex billion dollar corporation. The following pages tell something of how this came about. Some broad observations here will help to set that stage.

To say that able, talented, and dedicated people made it all possible merely states the obvious. Every successful collection of individuals—from the founders to the leaders who direct it today—made Miles a reality. The Miles, Beardsley, and Compton families comprise the centerpiece of this colorful mosaic.

There is a uniqueness here. It began with the acumen and dedication of Dr. Miles. It extended to one family remarkably accounting for five consecutive presidencies and a strong influence that spanned some seven decades. It included the guidance, foresight, and contributions of Walter Compton. Along with a host of other gifted men and women, they created a record that stamps "people values" as the first and most visible part of the Miles mosaic.

Without deep-seated concern for its human resources and without their diverse and competent contributions, Miles would have attained little stature in American business life. But success did come under twelve presidents, their names etched boldly in the company's chronicles—Dr. Miles, Andrew Hubble Beardsley, Arthur Lehman Beardsley, Charles Sumner Beardsley, Walter Raper Beardsley, Edward Hugget Beardsley, Walter Ames Compton, M.D., George Wells Orr, Jr., Rowland George Rose, Theodor Heinrichs, Franz J. Geks, M.D., and Richard B. Kocher. A new phase began under Heinrichs in 1979 and continued under Dr. Geks, a board of management veteran of Miles' parent, Bayer AG, of Leverkusen, West Germany, also referred to in this book as "Bayer Leverkusen" or "Bayer." Geks became chief executive officer in April 1983. Beginning in July 1984, CEO-elect Klaus Heinz Risse, Ph.D., who had been with Bayer for 28 years, would carry on.

These leaders and hundreds of others worked, and are working, diligently to forge the company characteristics, giving them substance and texture. Perhaps the first and simplest has been the plain work ethic of a small midwestern city. It was essential to overcoming early hardships and later vagaries of rapid change and mounting competition. It's a pragmatic ethic; employees have believed in an honest day's effort as a matter of course, whether on manufacturing lines, or at laboratory benches, or office desks. Both union and non-union personnel have shared this outlook without asking for special approbation.

There has also been a strong social ethic in Miles' insistence on products that help people. Dr. Miles fervently believed that his products would do just that. The concept of health care which he launched has prevailed throughout the company's first century. It will surely persist in its second. It can be found not only in such a well-known remedy as Alka-Seltzer, but in other products, notably the diagnostic line that began with the now classic Clinitest and Clinistix urine tests.

This social ethic endures in programs for diabetics. It marks educational campaigns, some of which have been pioneering, in the field of vitamins and nutrition. Even what was eventually conceded to be a commercial failure, the supplement of animal protein with vegetable protein in the human diet, has strong overtones of better nutrition goals for Americans and for people abroad as well. History ultimately may show the concept as correct—though perhaps ahead of its time.

Beyond the work and social ethics, Miles has relied heavily on science and technology; it has seldom hesitated in probing scientific frontiers. This propensity has been sharply discernible in the ingenious creation and production of Alka-Seltzer and in innovative diagnostics on down to the molecular genetics and biotechnologies pervading science today.

It's difficult to find a more trenchant example of an "interlocking" technology than Miles' use of "workhorse" enzymes, critical to such fundamental areas as citric acid, diagnostics, and cultures for cheesemaking. So-called "high-tech" endeavors are scattered across the whole corporation, from production, development, engineering, and research techniques to the pervasiveness of advanced quality assurance. The ubiquitous computers blink their messages into every corner, affecting up to one-half of all jobs. So, there are many faces to modern Miles, standing as it does on the brink of robotics and other new technologies. All of them would surely delight the energetic founders!

Another polished chunk of the century-old mosaic comes under the broad caption of marketing. It winds back to the promotional shrewdness of Dr. Miles himself. It stretches through the unusual publishing of the almanacs, calendars, and "Little Books" which helped sustain sales for so long, and which did not rumble to an end until World War II.

Marketing successes emblazoned the annals of Alka-Seltzer. Its razor-sharp and often prize-winning promotion has held classic rank for decades. Vitamins and such items as S.O.S pads and Bactine benefited, too, from superior advertising. Linked to all this was a deep-seated understanding of consumer needs. Crisp marketing research also stands as a major hallmark. Nor has promotion of professional products been of a minor magnitude. It has proceeded at a proficient pace, winning its own settings in the many-hued mosaic.

Tribute of a high order must be paid to the salesmen of Miles. Once only concerned with the consumer, the sales force has now become multi-faceted indeed, trained in many disciplines and technologies. That, too, lends an impressive dimension to modern Miles. As Charles Beardsley once proclaimed, "All honor to the man who sells things. . . ."

Global vision is another landmark characteristic. It began in the mid-1930s and has been enlarging ever since. It is Miles' philosophy that the needs of health care permeate the world and must be met; this has been no mere abstraction, but is embedded deep in the company consciousness and is expressed by action in some six-score markets around the world. The international mission is a polished stone in the mosaic.

Another characteristic of long standing has been a willingness to diversify, and, in the process, take substantial risks. A few times, failure has marred this quest, but signal successes have emerged as well, among them the acquisitions of the S.O.S scouring pad, the Marschall cheese culture business, Takamine enzymes, and the Lab-Tek labware line.

Finally, diversity might be coupled with adaptability, a factor that most assuredly erupted into dynamic play when Bayer purchased Miles in 1977. Naturally, this dramatic action raised its own set of fresh circumstances—and perplexities—but it showed, overall, how a giant European firm and an "average large" American one could mesh imaginatively for new steps tomorrow—such as an augmented thrust into the prescription drug arena, a modest part of the company story in the past but slated to be far more vital in the years ahead. Hard-driving diversity marks other advances, notably the 1983 merger with Cutter Laboratories, which bolsters the strengths and capabilities of the entire corporation.

As the Centennial clock strikes, few doubt that in the long-term, the synergism, the blending of resources, and the multinational production and marketing network can do anything except build a larger and still more flourishing enterprise. Nothing less filled the vision of management by 1984. For that matter, expected growth should make Miles' first century pale by comparison.

Has there been a single, underlying philosophy behind this chain of basic company traits? In its broadest sense, as already noted, it enfolds the high purpose of meeting human needs in the health care field, with all of its endless challenges. It's as simple—and complicated—as that. Certainly Miles' products and services, in their first century, have bestowed an endowment on society deserving of rich recognition.

Horizons are glimpsed by perceptive people, lifted by dedication, and reached by constant striving. Such is the story of the men and women of Miles. On their behalf, we proudly dedicate this Centennial book as their testimonial.

Contents

PART I

A HERITAGE
OF CARING

CHAPTER 1

The Founding Families

In the early 1880s, a country doctor in the bustling town of Elkhart, Indiana, began bottling "Restorative Nervine," his own preparation that had proven useful in the treatment of a number of chronic illnesses. He sold his medicine in small quantities at first, yet orders came from as far away as Philadelphia. For several years he managed sales out of his home office. But as his practice grew and his reputation spread, this obscure effort—known under the name of Miles Medical Company—proved to be the seedling of a corporate enterprise whose products would someday be household words.

The Founding Father

Dr. Franklin L. Miles was 38 when he founded the company that was to become Miles Laboratories, Inc. He had behind him 12 years of preparatory and

university education in the natural sciences, civil law, and medicine. Already he had established himself as a specialist in the care of eye and ear problems. Soon after commencing medical practice in Chicago in 1874, he had come to believe that the nervous system exerted much more influence on disease, both acute and chronic, than was usually supposed. He had begun a series of original investigations and subsequently kept detailed records on as many as 30,000 cases in an effort to substantiate his theories.

The newly settled physician moved his office from Chicago to Elkhart in 1875. It was 1884 when he and two businessmen founded the Miles Medical Company, and 1890 when he started "The Grand Dispensary" for treating patients by mail. Chronic bronchitis forced him to leave the company in the hands of able managers and move to Florida in the early 1900s. There, as a neighbor and friend of Thomas Edison and Henry Ford, he began a second career in horticulture. He remained active in his company business, retaining the title of president until he died in 1929. He lived to see it emerge into the modern era of pharmaceutical research. Just shortly before his death, word had reached him of a promising new effervescent medication then in preliminary tests: Alka-Seltzer.

Dr. Miles is still remembered by older Elkhart citizens. As they recall his simple home remedies, they must marvel at the leap in technology that has led Miles to the sophisticated frontiers of bioscience research, prescription medicines, and electronic diagnostic instruments.

Such advances would have delighted Dr. Miles. He was by nature inquiring, constantly applying his scientific background to new subjects and leading those around him to broader vistas.

The whole story, of course, is rooted more deeply in the past, in the very nature of the men and women who passed onto their descendants uncommon imagination, ambition, courage, and strength of character.

Not One, But Three First Families

Many companies trace their origin to a single outstanding founder. Unique in the Miles story is the presence of three families whose continuous leadership has spanned a full century.

Franklin L. Miles, George E. Compton, and Albert R. Beardsley were, in effect, co-founders of the Miles Medical Company. Their grandsons and a grandnephew—Franklin B. Miles, Dr. Walter A. Compton, and Lehman F. Beardsley—are still on the Miles board of directors. They have a combined

tenure of more than 100 years, with election of the first two taking place in the 1930s.

To the extent that genealogies can be traced, the lines of these families go back to robust forebears, who must have braved wildernesses of mind and spirit as well as of land in their search for better worlds.

The first Miles ancestor in America was Richard Miles, who crossed the Atlantic from Hertfordshire, England, sometime before 1637. A direct descendant, Charles Miles, was a Continental Army soldier who fought in the Revolutionary War.

In 1809, that soldier's son, Erastus, married Laura Carter, and they became the parents of Charles J. Miles. Charles married Electa A. Lawrence, and one of their children was Franklin Lawrence Miles, born November 15, 1845, at Olmsted Falls, Ohio, a village near Cleveland.

The Beardsleys as Early Pioneers

The Beardsley family, too, traces its roots deep into British and American Colonial history. The maternal side came from Holland. William Beardsley, a mason born in Britain in 1605, landed at the Massachusetts colony in 1635. Later he moved to Stratford, Connecticut, and became clerk at the General Court in Hartford. A devout Puritan, he was a founder of its Congregational Church. Various documents of the time refer to him as "Goodman Beardsley." He died in 1661, leaving a son, Samuel, the first native-born Beardsley. Samuel's descendants were well-known, active in medicine, law, business, and the ministry—and in resisting the unpopular measures imposed by the British Crown. They took part, evidently, in sinking vessels laden with tea, for at least one of them, Elijah (or Elisha), was reportedly an eager participant in the fabled Boston Tea Party of 1773.

In January 1777, Elijah's father, Phineas, enlisted as a captain in the Seventh Connecticut Regiment. Elijah served through the entire war, first under his father and later, as one of Washington's troopers, he endured the bitter winter at Valley Forge. He left a diary of his patriotic service.

Beardsley, Miles, and other Colonials began migrating westward after the Revolution. Elijah moved to Delhi, New York, then to Springfield, Ohio, where he died in 1826. One son, Elijah H. Beardsley, was born in 1807, the youngest of 14 children.

A wagonmaker by trade for most of his life, Elijah H. Beardsley had a son, Albert Raper Beardsley, who was born November 7, 1847, in

Downtown Elkhart around 1910.

Dayton, Ohio—the eighth generation of the family in America.

The Comptons in England and America

As with the Beardsley and Miles families, the Comptons also have roots traceable far back in English history and the earliest Colonial times.

One of the first Comptons in America was William, born about 1622 in what is now Bedford, New Jersey.

Some of his descendants in New England were, in succession, Richard Compton, Job Compton, Sr., and Job Compton, Jr. The last named served in the Continental Army. His son, Jacob, came to the East Cleveland area sometime before 1810, when the region was nothing but forest. Ezekiel, Jacob's son, putting his family and meager belongings in an oxcart, made his way over rutted roads to Osolo Township, Elkhart County, in the mid-1830s, where he raised a log cabin. A carpenter by trade, he helped build many of the houses in the area. He farmed, too, until his death in 1853.

Married to Frances Ward, Ezekiel was the father of six children who survived to adulthood. One of them was George Emmett Compton, born on August 5, 1849.

The Rugged Pioneers' Sons

Over a span of four years, 1845–1849, these rugged pioneers fathered three unusual men—Franklin L. Miles, Albert R. Beardsley, and George E. Compton—a triumvirate with varied talents. All three were to become pivotal in the creation and growth of Miles Medical.

There is evidence to suggest that the three fathers—Charles Julius Miles, Elijah H. Beardsley, and Ezekiel Compton—lived during the last part of the mid-1830s in the Elkhart area. They might have known each other and rubbed elbows without any inkling that the future would entwine their sons in the venture destined to become Miles Laboratories.

How the fortunes of the three sons converged to form the Dr. Miles Medical Company in Elkhart is a fascinating tale.

Dr. Franklin L. Miles (1845–1929), the founder, served as president from 1884 until his death.

Franklin Miles' Early Years

Franklin Miles was born in 1845 near Cleveland to Charles J. and Electa Lawrence Miles. The family had moved from Cleveland to Cincinnati when Franklin's father set out to search for gold in the Far West. The great Gold Rush started in 1849, when Franklin was only four years old. Like many men of his time, Charles Miles went west to make his fortune. Not striking it rich, he went on to Hawaii, where he stayed for five years as Surveyor and Guard of the Customs House in Honolulu. Letters home described in colorful detail the customs of the Islanders.

In 1855, Franklin's mother died, and shortly thereafter his little sister, victims of an epidemic in Cincinnati. Although sudden death from infectious disease—diphtheria, cholera, malaria, scarlet fever, smallpox, measles, typhoid, and pneumonia—was an accepted fact of life in the 19th century, this double tragedy must have devastated the young boy.

Franklin was then sent to live with relatives in Elkhart. Even though his father provided regularly and generously from his post in Hawaii, Franklin was not well treated by his uncle. Perhaps to investigate and improve those living conditions, his father returned in 1860 and opened a drugstore in Elkhart.

Franklin must have had an insecure boyhood, living without his father's guidance during his early years, suffering the loss of the rest of his family in Cincinnati, then being moved to live with virtual strangers in an unfamiliar community. Surely those experiences strengthened his courage and independence.

Pursuing an Education

Charles Miles, Franklin's father, died of pneumonia after fighting a fire in freezing weather in the winter of 1865. He was only 44. He left his 19-year old son $5,000, a rather large sum by the standards of the day. Some of it Franklin is said to have spent recklessly. But some was applied to education. That, plus the willingness to work at odd jobs enabled the young man to complete several years of higher education in some of the finest schools in the country.

Franklin entered Phillips Academy April 19, 1865, and left sometime in 1866. He then went to Williston Academy in Massachusetts, from which he was graduated that year.

Miles began his college career at Yale's Sheffield Scientific School in 1866–67. He studied law at Yale during 1869–70 and continued to pursue a legal education at Columbia in 1871.

Having decided that his stature, five feet six inches, was more befitting a doctor than a lawyer, he transferred to the University of Michigan Medical School in 1871–72 and the next year enrolled at the Hahnemann Medical College, which was associated with the Homeopathic Hospital in Chicago. He received his M.D. degree from Rush Medical College in 1874 and served his internship at the Illinois Charitable Eye and Ear Infirmary.

While in Chicago, he met Ellen Douglas Lighthall, a young lady from Elkhart who was also studying medicine as a "woman's physician." On April 4, 1873, when he was 27 and she 22, they were married.

A Zest for Living

A story in the *Elkhart Observer* in the fall of 1873 gave clues to their zest for living. The young couple traveled by boat from Elkhart down the St. Joseph River, then by steamer across Lake Michigan, in time for the start of classes. The report revealed Miles as an outdoorsman, handy with fishing rod and gun.

Soon after graduating in February 1874, Dr. Miles opened an office at 57 Blue Island Avenue, Chicago, where the two also lived. By August, Ellen's medical studies required "live in" training at the Chicago Hospital for Women and Children (now called Mary Thompson Hospital).

When Ellen finished her studies, she and Franklin gave up their life in Chicago and moved back to Elkhart, then a booming railroad town with about 6,500 inhabitants. In mid-May of 1875, the *Observer* reported that "Dr. and Mrs. Miles are pleasantly located in our city. Office and residence No. 7 Franklin St." Later that month, the paper said, "Dr. Miles and wife are keeping house in one of the coziest little cottages on Franklin Street, where the Doctor's office may also be found. While we have no doubt that Frank is capable of curing many of the ills to which the flesh is heir he will give special attention to diseases of the eye and ear. Mrs. Miles also possesses considerable medical skill."

Tragedy Strikes the Family

Over the next seven years, three children arrived in the cozy cottage—Charles (Sept. 8, 1875), Marian (July 20, 1878), and Electa (Jan. 4, 1880).

Then, in 1881, tragedy struck once again. Both parents fell ill with "typho-malaria," aggravated by unusual bronchial and lung difficulties. Franklin recovered, though he suffered from a cough and was subject to pneumonia the rest of his life. Ellen died on August 24, at Christiana Lake, their favorite summer spot, where they had gone to try to recover two weeks before.

Their life together had been all too brief. Dr. Miles, although he did not marry again for almost 15 years, kept his young family together.

During the 1880s, Dr. Miles' reputation as a physician continued to advance. Indeed, his influence spread far beyond Elkhart as he founded the Miles Medical Company in the mid-1880s and the Grand Dispensary in 1890, which for some 30 years advised and prescribed for patients through the mail.

Early products included Dr. Miles' Nervine, "for disorders of the nerves"; Dr. Miles' Heart Treatment, "a strengthening regulator and tonic"; Dr. Miles' Anti-Pain Pills, "valuable for the relief of pain"; Dr. Miles' Alterative Compound, "for impoverished or impure blood"; Dr. Miles' Tonic, "a combination of pyrophosphates with quinine and iron"; Dr. Miles' Liver Pills, "said to be efficient in constipation," and Dr. Miles' Laxative Tablets, "a new cathartic" that appealed to old and young alike. They were recommended for use singly or in combination and were believed to complement each other.

In 1893, Dr. Miles and the Grand Dispensary moved to Chicago, and in 1895 he married Elizabeth A. State, a young woman who had worked in his office almost 10 years. Elizabeth was then 29, and Franklin had hesitated in asking for her hand, thinking she might prefer someone younger. By this time, he was nearly 50, and the children from his first marriage ranged in age from 15 to 20. They knew Elizabeth well and were anxious for his remarriage.

Dr. Miles Moves to Florida

In 1902, the Grand Dispensary was moved back to Elkhart and soon placed in the hands of Franklin's son, Charles Foster Miles. Warned by doctors that he could not survive pneumonia again, Dr. Miles took his family to Florida. Two children were born to Franklin and Elizabeth. One died at birth and another, injured at birth, died at age nine. In 1908, they adopted a three-year-old daughter, Louise.

Louise Miles Bass, still living in Fort Myers, remembers with great pleasure those years when the extended family lived at least part of each year together in what was known as the Shell House in the savannah country outside Fort Myers.

"We sometimes had 16 adults, nine children, and a governess who sat down to three meals a day," she remembers, including relatives on her mother's side from Canada. "I grew up surrounded by a loving family."

Unable to remain idle, Dr. Miles soon turned to horticulture and a second career that will be described later.

A. R. Beardsley's Road to Success

Meanwhile, Albert Raper Beardsley was traveling another route that would, nevertheless, take him to the same doorway as the entrepreneurial physician.

Farm chores were assuredly a part of Albert's boyhood at "Beardsley Prairie" in St. Joseph County. At 14, he left the farm and went to live in Elkhart with his Aunt Rachel, the widow of Dr. Havilah Beardsley, who had founded the town in 1831. While attending school for three years, he earned his keep by milking his aunt's cows. To earn money for clothing, he sawed wood for neighbors at 50 cents a cord.

At 17, he went to work as a clerk in the dry goods store of John Davenport. It was a practical way to learn something of the business world, and he proved an apt pupil. In 1869, his five-year apprenticeship ended. With $250 given him by his father, he formed a partnership in a general store with J. L. Brodrick. One year later, he sold that interest to join J. L. Wolf in a clothing emporium. Within two years, he bought Wolf's interest for $11,000, with a down payment of $3,000.

Skill in Business and Politics

Albert's business survived the panic of 1873, and he continued it until 1876. In 1878, he became secretary-treasurer and sales manager of the Muzzy Starch Company in Elkhart. By about 1882, he was president of seven starch companies. His connection with the starch business lasted at least until 1890, when he became agent for a New York starch syndicate. The syndicate offered him a leading role, but because this would have forced him to move to New York City, he declined.

In these busy years, while he was honing and polishing his natural business acumen, Albert married Elizabeth Baldwin, in September 1872.

He became active in Republican politics, continuing a family tradition that went on for generations. He was elected city clerk, treasurer, and councilman, which prepared him well for his later service in the Indiana Legislature, where he served as a representative in 1899 and as a senator in 1905 and 1907. In Seed's *History of the Republican Party in Indiana* (1899), Albert Beardsley is described as "one of the most conservative and able members of that body."

Albert proved to be a prudent manager of political money as well as a sound tactician. He handled a Republican campaign in 1888, according to accounts of the time, by eschewing parades and concentrating instead on circulating literature. A substantial local victory followed.

His contributions to the fledgling company were in the same vein. He served as general manager from 1890 to 1922 and as corporate treasurer from 1891 to 1924.

George Compton's Route to Miles

George Compton's early career paralleled Beardsley's, starting with farm chores in his youth. They could not have been easy years, as his father, Ezekiel, had died when George was only three years old.

George abandoned the farm sometime in his mid-teens to become a clerk apprentice, with some of the time spent in Davenport's store in Elkhart. Later, he worked for Beardsley, then in 1874 went into the "mercantile" business with a William Meader. Three years later, George and Elizabeth "Lizzie" Price Ames were married on September 25, 1877. She was a descendant of the Samuel Ames family of Canterbury, New Hampshire.

Compton returned to the family homestead in Osolo Township in 1882 for health reasons. He moved back to town about five years later and purchased the former Voisinet Flour Mill in partnership with E. A. Jenkins. He also became associated with the Elkhart Knitting Company.

In the 1880s and thereafter, he was also active in banking, real estate, and other enterprises. In 1886–1887 his influence began to make a difference in the development of the Dr. Miles Medical Company. Several times when needed, he gave extra money to meet the company's expenses. He was corporate treasurer from 1887 to 1890.

George E. Compton (1849–1910) was the first in a line of Comptons holding important positions. He was treasurer in 1887, then vice president from 1888 to 1910.

Albert R. Beardsley (1847–1924), was general manager from 1890 to 1922 and treasurer from 1891 to 1924.

George Compton had enough iron and enthusiasm in his makeup to survive physical hardship. For example, he was seriously injured in a fall at the flour mill in 1889, in an accident that long caused him great pain. But he pursued business interests energetically for the rest of his life.

Three Converging Paths

What brought the three men together in the Elkhart of the 1880s—Franklin Miles, the physician, A. R. Beardsley, the manufacturer and merchant, and George Compton, the developer and investor? Their families were, of course, acquainted and probably had jostled against each other over several generations in the moves from New England into Ohio and Indiana, a part of the area called the Old Northwest.

George Compton, we know, invested in several Elkhart businesses with start-up funds. The Compton family, in fact, were important developers and investors throughout Elkhart's early history. Tradition has it that George Compton first convinced Dr. Miles to put the Miles business venture in the hands of capable managers, thus freeing Dr. Miles for his more important work as a physician.

Dr. Miles' office, serving as a pharmacy, was a local gathering place for Elkhart's movers and shakers. One of these, A. R. Beardsley, gradually bought into the new company with capital accumulated from the declining starch trade. He and his able nephews eventually assumed control of orders, manufacturing, and advertising.

Dr. Miles Begins His Second Career

After the early years, and with competent managers on hand, Dr. Miles took little part in the day-to-day operations of the pharmaceutical business. Nevertheless, he held the position of president until his death. In 1906, when he moved to Florida, he was suffering from bronchial complications.

He was 61 at the time, and everyone assumed he was going to retire. They were wrong. He launched a second career. As his foster daughter, Louise Bass, recalls, "He could not sit around twiddling his thumbs. He could only do so much fishing and so much hunting of the panthers, bobcats, and ducks common to the area that long ago."

Miles settled in a relative wilderness, eight miles from a riverfront village in Lee County that is now the large resort city of Fort Myers. The railroad reached town about the same time. He eventually owned over 16,000 undeveloped acres on both sides of the Ca-loosahatchee River, filled with flatwood pines and palmettos in what is now part of Cape Coral. His holdings included Shell Point, Shell Point Island, and citrus groves upriver. Thomas Edison, a neighbor, imported many strains of bamboo, which he shared with Dr. Miles. The two families often spent Sundays together.

The farmhouse Dr. Miles bought was already a landmark when he purchased it. Patterned after a chateau in France, it was a 17-room mansion built after the Civil War by a Confederate officer. Known as the Shell House, its exterior was of white stucco covered with oyster shells. He later bought a Victorian home on First Street in downtown Fort Myers. Both were destroyed by fire in 1926 and 1936, and many valuable records were lost.

Helping Local Farmers

The doctor found that farmers in the region, plagued by poor soil, subtropical heat, and insects, grew vegetables only in small patches. So he began a scientific study of these problems. He contacted growers in similar climates throughout the world and, with the aid of the U. S. Department of Agriculture, their letters were translated. Later, he went abroad to study their methods.

Along his extensive tract, Miles made hundreds of experimental plantings, studying and recording the results as meticulously as he had once observed human disease. Louise remembers row upon row of bottles containing insects.

Dr. Miles established a plantation called "Poinsettia Place" and built homes for 40 workers and their families, both black and white. There were no roads to Fort Myers. Paddle boats plied the river, bringing provisions once a week. School rooms were established, and there were church services on Sunday. Dr. Miles favored no particular religion but stressed the similarities in all world faiths.

He cultivated eggplant, green peppers, cucumbers, green beans, tomatoes, squash, sugar cane, gladioli, bananas, and citrus. He formulated his own insecticides and was the first in the region to use chemical fertilizers. His plantation had sugar mills and sawmills, a packing house for tomatoes, and a stone-crusher to smash oyster shells into fertilizer.

More and more farmers turned to him for advice, and he became recognized as an agricultural expert. He established a free "trucker's school" to pass on what he had learned. In time, he was acknowledged as the "father" of Southwest Florida's now huge vegetable-growing industry.

This stately gray residence at 403 West Franklin Street in Elkhart, built by Eber Darling Sr. around 1870, was purchased just before the turn of the century by Dr. Franklin Miles and served as the family home for many years. (Courtesy Hartzler-Gutermuth Funeral Home)

Dr. Miles was an innovator by nature. In 1926, he built a handsome Spanish-style apartment building on McGregor Boulevard in Fort Myers, so unusual that skeptics thought it would never be occupied. He considered it just another experiment "to see if people would come this far out to rent." They did.

Farsighted Innovator

Louise describes him as farsighted. "Someday," he told her, "they will build a road to Miami and bridges across the river, and when they do, you aren't going to have standing room down here." He advised her to hold onto whatever waterfront property he left her, saying "These islands (Sanibel and Captiva) are fabulous." They once built a vacation place on Captiva and then bought the old Captiva Hotel.

He was equally sanguine about medicine, predicting a lens implant. "We can't use glass," he told Louise, "but someday someone is going to discover a material suitable for inserting in the eye."

Dr. Miles died in Fort Myers on April 1, 1929, from the infirmities of age. He was 83. After services in Florida, he was brought home to Elkhart for burial in Rice Cemetery.

The *Fort Myers Tropical News* printed a glowing

tribute describing him as "a charming neighbor.... A fine man.... A pioneer of American business.... An experimenter by nature and habit.... Who left behind a heritage of valuable knowledge for the growers of Lee County." By describing his "unsurpassing devotion" to his family of six grandchildren and two greatgrandchildren as "the most striking of his personal characteristics," the editorial paid him a most suitable closing accolade.

The *Elkhart Truth* carried the news of his death under a banner headline on page 1, describing him as the founder of the Dr. Miles Medical Co. of Elkhart, "one of the most important concerns of its kind in the United States." The story of his life filled nearly two columns.

"Hub" Beardsley: A Second Father to the Company

An astute early move by Albert Raper Beardsley that would have a profound effect for several generations was the hiring of his nephew, Andrew Hubble Beardsley. Forever known in the annals of the company as "Hub," A. H. served as corporate secretary from 1891 to 1925, when he became the company's first chairman. On Dr. Miles' death in 1929, he was

Andrew H. "Hub" Beardsley (1864–1936) was corporate secretary from 1891 to 1925, chairman from 1925, and simultaneously president from 1929 until his death.

A rare Beardsley family portrait, probably taken sometime between 1910 and 1915. Standing, from left, David, Arthur L., Thomas, Andrew H., and Charles S. Seated, from left, John, Jesse Beardsley Bender, and Rachel Beardsley Miles.

Ruthmere, a splendid mansion in the French beaux-arts style, was built by A. R. Beardsley and his wife Elizabeth on Beardsley Avenue in Elkhart, facing the St. Joseph River, in 1910. It has been restored as a House Museum.

also elected president, the first of five Beardsleys to hold that post. He was both chairman and president until his death in 1936.

Born in 1864, the second of 10 children of Solomon Lehman Beardsley and Martha Foster Beardsley, Hub attended high school in Kalamazoo, Michigan, and "all but graduated" before going to work selling hay-unloading machinery, repairing farm equipment in the Dakotas, and even taking a job as a fireman for a straw-burning engine. In 1889, his uncle persuaded him to join the Dr. Miles Medical Company. There he first washed bottles and mixed medicines. But his drive and energy soon came to the fore, and by 1891 he was elected corporate secretary, the same year the company set up its own printing department.

Hub obviously had much to do with the growth of Miles in the first third of the 20th century, from the years of its early promotion to the advent of Alka-Seltzer. When he died at 72, the *Elkhart Truth* called him "Elkhart's leading citizen," noting his "public spirit without limit," his "determination and persistence when he was convinced the cause was right," his "personal popularity," and his services "generously given" to local, state, and national affairs.

Frank Blair, president of the Proprietary Association, on whose Executive Committee Hub had served since 1898, said that "everyone loved him—for his kindness, his thoughtfulness, and the great amount of good he did, but I think more particularly for his outspoken frankness. There was never any doubt as to Hub Beardsley's attitude on any subject...."

Some insight into his character can be glimpsed from the quietly mundane letters he wrote his uncle, Albert Raper Beardsley, mostly in 1912 and 1913 when A.R. was in Europe or recuperating from rheumatic attacks at Hot Springs, Arkansas. The letters make plain Hub's strong family feelings, his desire to help others, his respect and affection for his uncle, and his range of interests. He commented on many subjects, major and minor, from the illness of employees, the printing runs of calendars and almanacs, and sales trends, to the weather and family matters. Almost every letter gave sales figures and news such as, "Business is a little off this week," or, "Business is running along about so," or, "Harry thinks we will have a nice margin over this month last year."

The correspondence reflects the even keel on which Miles was running, with its traditional products holding up well, and with the "Little Books," calendars, and almanacs tumbling off the presses by the millions—the real backbone of the business in maintaining sales.

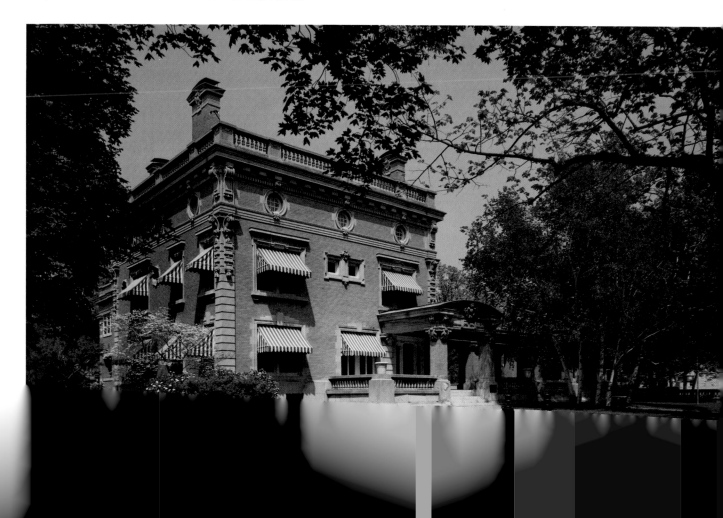

This ad appeared in 1924 and summed up the company's first 41 years.

CHAPTER 2

The Fledgling Years

The 19th century must, for all time, rank as the first "golden age" in pharmaceutical history. For in those years, many of the great drug houses in America grew out of the pharmacies of practicing physicians, who had a special interest in creating their own remedies. Others developed from professional pharmacies.

Forerunners of the Giants to Come

In 1858, with only $1,300, Dr. Edward R. Squibb set up stills in Brooklyn to make ether and chloroform—long to be the basic products of his company.

In Detroit, in 1875, Parke, Davis, & Co. started specializing in alkaloid drugs and botanicals. Perhaps a greater contribution was the machine-filled gelatin two-piece capsule which assured accurate dosages.

In 1876, a Civil War veteran in Indianapolis, Colonel Eli Lilly began preparing fluid extracts bearing such exotic names as Sea Wrack, Squaw Vine, and Black Haw. He was armed with capital of $1,400, two employees and his 14-year old son.

In 1883, in Kalamazoo, Michigan, Dr. William E. Upjohn's "Pill and Granule" Company began manufacturing "friable" (softer) pills, working at first in the attic of "W. E.'s" home.

In 1888, Dr. Wallace C. Abbott, in suburban Chicago, established the Abbott Alkaloidal Company using his own kitchen to make alkaloidal extracts of crude drugs. He got $8 in orders after his first mailing.

Dr. Miles, too, mixed his first medicines in his own home and office on Franklin Street in downtown Elkhart. An old ledger shows he was bottling Nervine for shipment to druggists as early as October 1882.

If these entrepreneurs wanted their remedies used, they had little recourse except to make them themselves. There was nobody else to do it. With his growing practice Miles had to accept the reality that he must be his own pharmacist.

Dr. Miles' America "Feeling Its Oats"

What was America like when Dr. Miles launched his rather frail operation? It was a country feeling its oats. In a mood of optimism, it was a nation on its way to greatness. Civil War veterans, in the prime of life, were prominent in business, politics, and community activity.

Exciting discoveries and advances loomed on every horizon. The telephone, only a few years old, was coming into every village, town, and city. Electric streetcars reached major metropolitan areas. Ottmar Mergenthaler patented his Linotype machine. Food processing was being transformed by the tin can. Standard Oil was refining petroleum and shipping it in railroad tank cars that looked similar to those of today. Big stores of natural gas were found in Ohio and Indiana. Iron ore was being scooped from the open pits of the Gogebic Range in Michigan. It was also the heyday of brand advertising and of extravagant claims for breakfast cereals and tonics.

In 1884, Mark Twain published *Huckleberry Finn*, which a Concord, Massachusetts, library promptly banned as "trash and suitable only for the slums." William Dean Howell's *The Rise of Silas Lapham* appeared that year—eventually to become standard reading for generations of students. The cornerstone of the Statue of Liberty was laid and the capstone placed on the Washington Monument.

Advances also marked the slow-moving field of medicine, including the first use of cocaine as a spinal anesthetic, better surgical techniques for hernia repair and breast removal, and endoscopic examination of the stomach. The Mayo Clinic was founded in Rochester, Minnesota and, at Saranac Lake, New York, the first tuberculosis sanitarium was established.

These earliest views of the inside of the Franklin Street plant from the 1890s depict a veritable temple of industry. The so-called "double profile," center, long served as the company's trademark on the letterheads and labels.

Miles Medical Is Born

In this climate of national expansion, the Miles Medical Company was founded in 1884. It did not emerge full-blown on the Elkhart scene, but appeared rather unobtrusively.

Even at the beginning, Miles' venture was as much promotional as product oriented. By April 1884, the *Elkhart Review* reported that Miles had issued his first *Medical News*, which was intended, it said, "to give an epitome of the later discoveries in certain lines of medical science, and...at the same time contain departments devoted to special topics, as The Household, The Children, etc."

"The Dr. will also use it quite largely for advertising his remedies," the paper stated. Although a small line of "restorative" medicines was being produced as early as 1882, the first recorded use of the name Miles Medical Company was on March 7, 1884, when the doctor ordered letterheads. It is this date the company has chosen to mark as Founder's Day and from which it numbers its years.

Laboratory of THE DR. MILES' MEDICAL CO., Elkhart, Ind.

From 1888 to 1892 the burgeoning company occupied this spacious building which formerly housed the Independent *newspaper.*

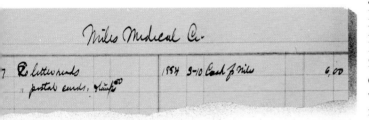

From Dr. Miles' cash book, this ledger entry of March 7, 1884 documents the first appearance of the Dr. Miles Medical Company, an order for stationery.

While the founding of the company did not pass unnoticed, it was small compared to the two starch mills, two knitting factories, three flour mills, and six paper mills that were started in Elkhart in the post-Civil War period, or the carriage-making plant that was to come soon afterward.

Incorporation in 1885

After months with virtually no sales (only 14 lots of Nervine are listed in the ledgers for 1885), Dr. Miles found two partners. One was Hugh McLachlan, a former harnessmaker who, in 1881, had opened a large dry goods store called "The Fair." The other was Norris Felt, a young associate in the store. On October 28, 1885, the three incorporated as the Dr. Miles Medical Company.

The Articles of Association said the object was "to manufacture and sell certain remedies invented and discovered by Dr. Miles, to be known as 'The Restorative Nervine,' 'Restorative Tonic,' 'Restorative Blood Purifier,' and 'Restorative Nerve and Liver Pills.'" Capital stock was set at $25,000—500 shares of $50 each, with Miles, McLachlan, and Felt as directors. The two businessmen each put in $500, with Miles receiving the remaining 480 shares for making available his formulas and equipment.

The Lean Years

The business languished in those early years. Dr. Miles himself spent most of this time with patients, his writings, and his investigations. McLachlan and Felt, immersed in their dry goods business, probably gave little time to the fragile enterprise. The ledgers for March 1886 show 13 customers with payments totaling $63.47. A year later, 19 customers bought $104.21 worth of medicines. Interestingly, the ledgers reveal George Compton putting in five $100 amounts in 1886–87, undoubtedly at times when cash was desperately needed.

The turnabout, with more assurance of survival, began on February 11, 1887. At a special stockholders' meeting, McLachlan and Felt sold their interests to George Compton and A. R. Burns, a local druggist. New stock certificates were issued, with Compton taking over as treasurer and Burns as secretary. The operation then moved into larger rented quarters.

Money may still have been scarce, but more was put into bold advertising. For example, on October 21, 1887, the *Goshen Weekly News* carried this intriguing item: "$5,000 Reward will be freely given for a better remedy for Headache, Nervousness, Sleeplessness, Etc. than Dr. Miles' Restorative Nervine, A Brain and Nerve Food. Contains no Opium or Morphine. Sold by Druggists. Sample Bottle Free." It probably was the first ad Miles placed in a local paper.

Burns traveled around northern Indiana, and perhaps farther, trying to persuade fellow druggists to carry the company medicines.

By March 1888, 81 customer payments worth $1,034 were on the books. Young ladies were hired to wrap the literature and package the bottles, which by then included a heart remedy.

Beardsley Comes on Board

In 1888, the company moved into the vacated offices of a newspaper on High Street, bought a small printing press, and stepped up its newspaper advertising. Business gradually improved.

As an early pivotal year, 1889 stands out. For in August, Albert Raper Beardsley joined the company, buying a portion of the shares owned by Burns and Compton. New stock certificates issued in November gave Dr. Miles 167 shares worth $8,350, with Beardsley, Burns, and Compton each receiving 111 shares.

Activity soon quickened. More employees were hired to increase production; the payroll, excluding salesmen, totaled 14 in October. That fall four salesmen went on the road. Forceful ads appeared in 800 newspapers, some as far away as Pennsylvania. A stream of 16-page pamphlets, a print order of 100,000 pieces in all, began flowing to the professions and the public. These "treatises" espoused the opinions and reflections of Dr. Miles, then in the full vigor of his medical advocacy.

A Strong Hand on the Tiller

With Beardsley keeping a strong hand on the tiller, customer payments climbed from 61 in March 1889 to 232 in March 1890, with a value of $4,728. Although it doesn't appear to be much today, this sum was substantial enough to hold out a promising future. In May of that year, the directors "reduced" the role of Burns to overseeing the compounding and bottling of medicines, with Beardsley assuming charge of the office, finance, books, printing, advertising, packing, and shipping. The number of wage earners in late 1890 varied from 19 to 29.

That year also saw the first real profits. What to do with them? After several meetings, it was voted to pay Burns $450 and Beardsley $600 for their services

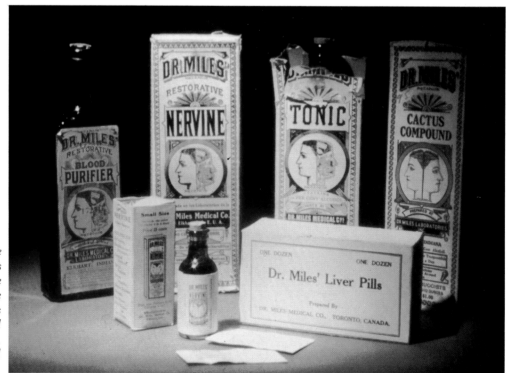

The company's first five products, all formulations of Dr. Miles: Nervine (1882–present), Nerve and Liver Pills (1884–1949), Blood Purifier (1885–1937), Tonic (1885–1938), and Heart Cure (1888–1938).

over the past 16 months. The directors recognized the contribution of Dr. Miles by providing royalties of $5 per dozen on bottled medicines and $1 per dozen on "pill" packages sold to druggists over the past three years. This arrangement helped lay the foundation for the doctor's fortune.

Showing its flair for promotion, the company decided to spread its story to the big cities, starting with an advertising campaign in Chicago. It hired A. S. Davenport to reach Brooklyn and New York City in the same way.

December 16 was another key date that year. The directors voted to acquire a lot on Franklin near Second Street for a new building. To some, this might have smacked of audacity. To the directors, however, it was an expression of confidence in the future.

More Pressmen than Chemists

For more than half its history, the printing press and bindery were as much a part of the Miles Medical Company as drug mixing vats and coating pans, and the operation needed more pressmen than chemists. The big Miehle presses rumbled on year after year; the

first foreman, in 1892, was Albert G. Wade, later founder of the Wade Advertising Agency in Chicago. The printed material dealt not only with medicine and health, but with a variety of other topics as well. Advertisements extolling products were always astutely scattered throughout the various publications.

The company's involvement in printing took on a unique facet when it manufactured and provided thousands of proof presses to small newspapers in exchange for advertising space. Castings and blankets for the cylinders were bought locally, with the machining of the parts done in Miles' own machine shop. The practice continued until about 1950. Also furnished for many decades were ink, leads, slugs, rules, type, and borders.

Calendars, Almanacs, and "Little Books"

In the first four decades of the 20th century, almanacs and calendars were the real linchpins of the publishing part of the business.

Almanacs were distributed to boxholders on RFD routes, and in small towns, and to customers through distributors on contract. Retail druggists gave

Possibly the most classic photograph that has survived to Centennial time. The office force when it occupied the new plant in 1892: from left, Emil T. Stronquist, stenographer; William B. Canis, chief stenographer; Edwin P. Kellogg, chief bookkeeper; Mrs. Edna Billington Simpson, stenographer; Mrs. Bessie Smith Burris Boylen, stenographer; William C. Johnson, advertising manager; A. R. Beardsley, chief executive and treasurer; Mrs. Florence Throop Gordon, stenographer and clerk; Mrs. Millie Myers Havourd, stenographer and clerk; E. C. Swayne, clerk; and William Gardner, office boy. Unfortunately missing, A. H. Beardsley, general superintendent.

Dr. Miles' calendar of 1904 catered to the Victorian sentiment of the day and cemented relations with drug stores and their clientele.

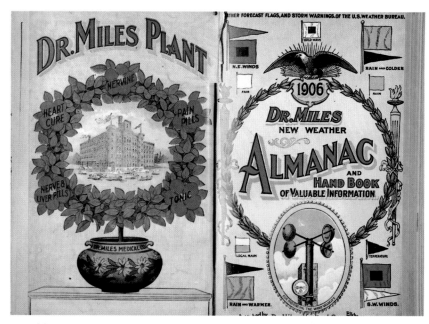

Potted history: a clever institutional ad from the turn of the century, left, shows the company's growing "plant" and its chief "product." Facing, right, the ornate cover of the 1906 Dr. Miles Almanac, with its advanced "seed catalogue" color printing.

out the calendars, receiving them in proportion to their orders for Miles' products.

Almanacs made their debut at Miles in 1902 and endured until 1942. Whoever had the idea deserves a bright star in the Miles firmament. The almanacs were popular and filled a promotional need.

Even at the end of the almanac venture, when the paper shortages of World War II brought about its demise, Miles could proudly state, "We believe that Dr. Miles' Almanac is the single biggest edition of any book in any language—20 million are printed and distributed each year." It took radio and TV to replace its long-nurtured advertising impact.

As well as a vehicle for product promotion, the almanacs were designed for the "common man," with no pretense of literary quality, as the homespun jokes and other editorial copy clearly illustrate. In a less sophisticated age, people loved them and looked forward to getting their copies year after year.

The jokes reflected a simple but hardy sense of humor:

> *Laura:* "Jack told me the other night that he was going to kiss me or die in the attempt." *Belle:* ....? *Laura:* "You haven't read his obituary, have you?"

> "Do you think the motor car will entirely supersede the horse?" Farmer replies, "I sure hope not. I depend on what I make selling hay to buy my gasoline."

> Little girl: "Poppa, when a man has two wives, it's bigamy, isn't it?" Poppa: "Yes, dear." Little girl: "What is it when he has only one wife?" Poppa: "Monotony, dear."

Weather was also of consuming interest to the predominantly rural readership of the almanacs. As early as 1905, there appeared a notice of the Dr. Miles Weather Observatory, later described in Tom Stephenson's article in the 1973 *Elkhart Truth* as resembling a "scaled down version of the lower deck of a modern rocket-launching structure." Incidentally, this bizarre rooftop room on the Franklin Street building later housed the company's first research and quality control lab and became the birthplace of Alka-Seltzer.

Big Press Runs Mirror the Company

Each issue of the almanac offered free "pictorial wall calendars" with pads, along with weather forecasts and a "trial package of Dr. Miles Anti-Pain Pills." All this in exchange for a 2¢ postage stamp!

As the almanacs rolled off the presses in large quantities (18,500,000 in 1930, for example), they mirrored the focus of the company. So it happened that in the 1930s, Alka-Seltzer became prominent in almanac advertising. The 1931 Almanac offered, in a coupon, the regular $.25 package for $.10. By 1935, the almanac was pronouncing one of the many slogans that would make Alka-Seltzer famous: "You won't dread the morning after if you take Alka-Seltzer the night before."

Even as time ran out, the almanac maintained its pungency and relevance. The 1940 edition had a feature on rainfall and the history of U.S. territorial expansion. The last edition published in 1942 listed the "Best Fishing Dates" month by month. It also offered a final household hint: "Peel onions root end up and the eyes won't be affected—as much."

The extensive Little Book series, another arm of promotion, bore such titles as *Circus Life, Buried Treasure*, and *Housekeeping, the Oldest and Greatest Industry*. Others did deal with health, such as *How to Relieve Pain*, and *First Aid to the Injured*, and some focused directly on products, such as *Dr. Miles' Nervine Brings Sweet Sleep*.

The Franklin Street Building— Evidence of Progress

The Dr. Miles Medical Company grew slowly by modern standards. Still, it grew. In 1891, a three-story brown-front-brick plant was built at 117 Franklin Street. A year later came a three-story addition to house printing equipment, and by 1897 both structures expanded. In 1903, another four-story addition testified to further growth, and a few years later a fourth story was continued across the three-story original plant. In 1928, a final four-story addition on the west side completed the structure as it stood at the advent of Alka-Seltzer manufacturing.

Officials took obvious pride not only in this material evidence of progress but also in "making things right." In 1896 the company newspaper tells of facilities where the girls worked "in snowy white caps and aprons," with "all the steel beams, posts and girders... protected with fireproof tiling." An automatic sprinkler system was installed, and from the 90-foot tank tower, 75 electric lights beamed the word "Miles" over the countryside as a "beacon light for the sick and suffering."

Late in the 19th century, as well as in the early years of the 20th, the Dr. Miles Medical Company, if it did not thrive spectacularly, did develop solidly, spurred on by a steady acceptance of its products.

Early Stockholder Meetings

Although no modern annual report appeared until 1929, a few odd and interesting scraps of information mark the earlier minutes of stockholder meetings. In 1891, the directors met on a Saturday evening. In 1892, they investigated unspecified charges against Mrs. Brussler, an employee, found her to be "a most estimable lady," and voted to retain her services. At that same meeting, they voted to go into the printing business.

Dividends, which had first been issued in 1894, had risen from $4 a share in 1895 to $10 in 1897. That

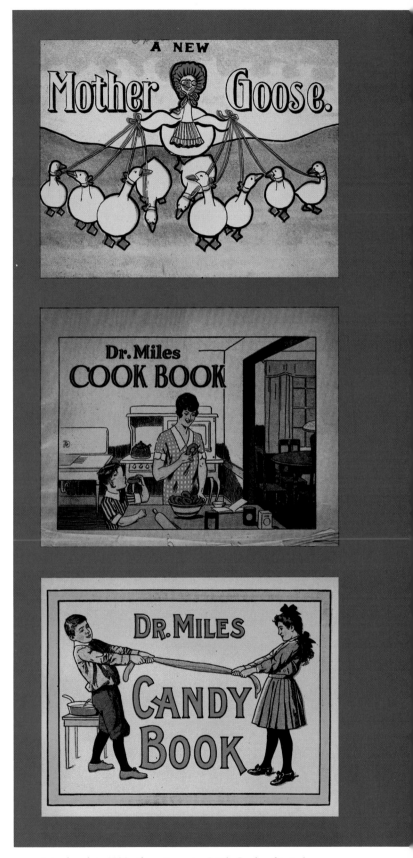

Introduced in 1890, the octavo-size Little Books of popular reading appeared several times a year and reached virtually every household in rural America.

Probably the first photo of the new building on Franklin Street just before occupancy in 1892. (Note that the front door is still boarded up.) The house to the right was one of Dr. Miles' first home offices.

All rolled up in one: treasury, sales, accounting, purchasing, general manager's office, stenographer's station, and office of the secretary, 1913. A. R. Beardsley can be seen, center, and the young Harry Gampher, foreground.

From a rare photographic essay of 1913, this shot features the steam-powered, belt-driven machinery for manufacturing pills.

same year, the directors voted to eliminate strychnine from the Nerve and Liver Pills, Nervine, and the Heart Cure.

Dividends rose to $20 a share in 1902; in 1905, they plummeted to $10 again, then rallied to $20 the following year. In 1908, the directors voted to drop the term "new cure" in favor of "remedy" in the heart medicine advertising—in compliance with the new regulations of the 1906 Pure Food and Drug Act.

In 1909, annual salaries of $40,000 were voted for Dr. Miles as president and for Charles F. Miles as second vice president, with George Compton getting $25,000 as first vice president, A. R. Beardsley $35,000 as manager and treasurer, and A. H. Beardsley $30,000 as secretary. Such salaries in those days certainly reflected a prosperous enterprise.

In 1912 the company changed its legal structure, dissolving the corporation in favor of a partnership. The company was reincorporated in 1922 as the Dr. Miles Medical Company. The name was changed to Dr. Miles Laboratories, Inc. in 1932 and to its present form in 1935.

Still Small in 1900

Miles was still relatively small around the turn of the century. In 1898, the State of Indiana's Inspection Bureau listed 102 workers—66 of them women. The number climbed to 200 in 1904.

During the first quarter of the 20th century, the company slid into a prolonged period of new product stagnation as did most other pharmaceutical firms. Pharmaceutical science chugged along at a languid pace. Some new drugs of varying significance did

Before the installation of cartoning machines, women's nimble fingers wrapped the tiny vials containing Dr. Miles' Anti-Pain Pills, introduced in 1893.

make their entry into medicine, such as phenobarbital in 1912, but none of them came from Miles. New Miles products had included Anti-Pain Pills, Laxative Cold Cure, and Restorative Nerve Plasters, among others.

By coasting sagaciously with its basic remedies, and sustained by its innovative publications and promotion, the company prospered modestly until the breakthroughs of the 1930s and 1940s spurred new, sometimes revolutionary advances in drug, nutritional, and medical therapy.

In these comfortable pre-breakthrough years, Harry Gampher occupied a colorful niche as the only non-family stockholder in the 1920s. His steady, dedicated hand was most helpful to Hub Beardsley. He was generally involved in Beardsley's business affairs, informing him, for example, that his 1929 income tax amounted to $18,100 compared to $10,514 in 1928.

An insight into their harmonious personal and working relationship can be gained from their correspondence in the late 1920s, much of it relating to marketing facts and strategies while Beardsley was away and Gampher was "minding the store" in Elkhart.

Gampher tended to be an optimist. In 1928, he wrote that "we have a wonderful demand for Aspir-Mint tablets.... Nervine tablets are going along fine.... The $1000.00 (bonus) proposition given the boys is working out nicely.... We have made a decided gain in sales and it does look as though we are going to make a clean-up.... I venture to predict that 1928 will be our banner year...."

Almanacs and Calendars, the Mainstays

Another letter from Gampher underscores the importance of promotional campaigns: "We have increased the almanacs 2,500,000... and the calendars 200,000... holding the calendars and shipping in carload lots will probably save us considerable of the extra expense which was incurred last year on account of our not sending out the calendars with the merchandise...." A mundane item, yet indicative of the attention paid to holding down costs at a time when it might not have seemed a cardinal matter.

At one point, to cut costs, Hub suggested going from four-color to two-color printing and "to get out a set of booklets devoted entirely to our medicines."

Newspaper advertising was carefully monitored. For example, in June 1929, a memo from advertising manager Herbert S. Thompson noted, "We then went to Kalamazoo and used a full page (for Aspir-Mint) for which we paid $192.50.... We received 914 inquiries, making a cost of $.20 per inquiry...." Obviously, this was judged a good return.

The Alcohol Controversy Raises Alarms

An early 20th-century controversy, with which Miles and many other medicine makers had to contend, involved the amount of alcohol used in patent medications. Clearly some formulae contained excessive amounts—enough to account for their popularity. Miles's did not.

The company defended itself with an argument that remains common currency today—"It is inconceivable that a medicinal preparation which has been largely used for many years, often 20, sometimes 30 and even 40, and by...hundreds of thousands of patients should not fairly accomplish what is claimed for it. It is possible by a lavish expenditure of advertising space to create a considerable temporary demand....But it is not within the power of money or brains to make the demand permanent...." Such

From the earliest days, Miles depended heavily on advertising, especially in newspapers. This typical ad of 1906 was aimed at Nervine's large female following.

comments still appear in varying language—perhaps none stated it as well as in that pamphlet long-ago.

In December 1905, the Proprietary Association, in which Miles was active, proposed legislation to "prevent the use of alcohol in proprietary medicines for internal use in excess of the amount necessary as a solvent and preservative." The resolutions also called for the strictest regulation "of the sale of cocaine and other narcotics" and urged its members to give "most careful scrutiny to the character of their advertising...avoiding all overstatements."

Advent of the Pure Food and Drug Act

Overstated advertising and labeling along with the alcohol content controversy had raised the ire of physicians and others. The pressures built up rapidly for legislation to curb the promotion and use of patent medicines. Leading the official fight was Dr. Harvey W. Wiley, then chief of the Bureau of Chemistry of the U.S. Department of Agriculture, and Dr. George H. Simmons, at the forefront of the American Medical Association. Journalists took up the cudgels, and their exposures, particularly in 1904 and 1905, probably had more to do with the passage of the historic Pure Food and Drug Act of 1906 than any other factor.

As Congress edged inexorably toward passage of the landmark law in 1906, apprehension mounted and allies were sought. Many legislators themselves in that conservative time did not exactly embrace the idea of stringent regulation. They saw it as an infringement on individual and business freedom, and on the right of people to buy and use what food and medicine they preferred.

It was a losing battle. With President Theodore Roosevelt himself finally demanding action, the Senate passed the Act, 63–4. The House passed it 240–17, spurred on by the revelations about bad meat in Sinclair's *The Jungle*. On January 1, 1907, the Act became law.

Dismantled July 1, 1958, the Print Shop was one of the largest private plants in the United States, producing 23,000,000 almanacs and 35,000,000 Little Books at its peak.

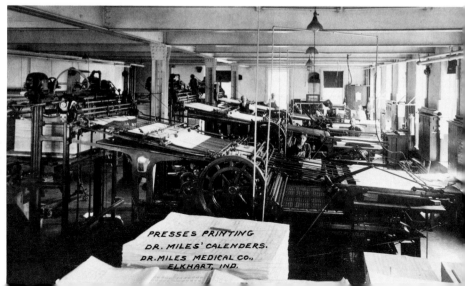

Exuberance for Nervine is reflected in this 1902 gathering of women displaying paper dolls, used to promote the product.

The Dr. Miles Medical Company did not actively oppose the action of the Congress; there is only some evidence that it shared the misgivings of its industry. The law changed the way drug firms—even the best of them—made and marketed their products. It forced them to meet standards on such things as more exacting dosage forms, and the worst of the patent medicines and their makers faded into a deserved oblivion. Thus, while the pharmaceutical industry drifted into the creative doldrums, where it would stay for years to come, the 1906 law led to a somewhat less dangerous marketplace. In fact, it was deemed so effective that the basic structure of the law remained the same another 32 years.

The Battle of Price Cutting

One aspect of Miles' history revolves around stout legal battles on behalf of its products, trademarks, claims, and prices. The company seldom backed away from its convictions.

The 1911 Supreme Court decision on vertical price fixing in the case of Dr. Miles Medical Company vs. John D. Park & Sons Company is still considered a classic case history, often studied in law

school, and referred to as late as December 1, 1983, in the *Wall Street Journal.*

Always anxious to nurture relations with its customers, the company devised a policy that became known as the Miles Plan. Designed first of all to keep pharmacists favorably disposed toward Miles and its products, it was launched in 1903.

The Miles plan simply attempted to short-circuit price cutting. It offered contracts to retail druggists under which they agreed not to sell "at less than the retail price fixed by" the company, with some exceptions.

Miles published a "creed" under the plan. It declared that "cut rates demoralize and devour the drug trade," that cutting "encourages substitution and eventually ruins the trade of the druggist by destroying the confidence of the public."

The plan did not find universal acceptance, and the company, remonstrating in print, unctuously noted that "now and then a hasty brother...takes us to task because some matter in his bailiwick is not cleared up with rapidity." At one point, in commenting on "sore cutters," promotion turned to doggerel:

> Cutter, spare that tree,
>   On every branch or bough,
> The fruit looks good to me,
>   And I can use it now.
> 'Twas Miles, with cash and sand
>   Who priced it on the spot,
> Then cutter, let it stand,
>   Your acts shall harm it not.
>   (with apologies)

What are they up to? We can't be sure, but old timers think these lads—in 1910—were grappling with a greased pig at the annual picnic.

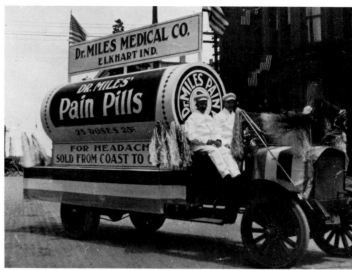

Sales manager Hal McCann, left, salesman Mart Burhans, center, and Dr. Franklin Miles, age 67, seated right, during a promotion around 1912.

The Dr. Miles Medical Co. was never reticent or shy about advertising its products, as this motorized effort on behalf of the Pain Pills shows, probably about 1920.

Miles said it spent $100,000 in putting the plan into operation, certainly a substantial sum for the time.

This subject of fair trade took on its legal turn with Miles' case against a wholesaler for refusing to sign a contract establishing minimum prices. Miles said it had contracts forbidding price cutting with some 400 wholesalers and 25,000 retail druggists. Miles also claimed the restrictions were valid because the proprietary medicines were manufactured by a secret process and that, apart from this, a manufacturer had the right to control prices for its own products.

The court spurned the first argument, contending that the question did not concern the process of the manufacture but the manufacturer's product as an article of commerce.

On the second question, the court reasoned that "because a manufacturer is not bound to make or sell, it does not follow in case of sales actually made he may impose upon purchasers every sort of restriction...nor can the manufacturer...fix prices for future sales...."

But there was a dissent from no less a personage than Justice Oliver Wendell Holmes. "I think that we greatly exaggerate the value and importance to the public of competition in the production or distribution...of an article as fixing a fair price. What really fixes that is the competition of conflicting desires...." He further wrote "Of course, I am speaking of things that we can get along without. There may be necessities that sooner or later must be dealt with like short rations in a shipwreck. They are not Dr. Miles' medicines.... The company knows better than we do what will enable it to do the best business.... We must assume its retail prices to be reasonable."

A 1928 point-of-purchase display features what might be described as the pre-Alka-Seltzer "top of the line."

CHAPTER 3

A Doctor's Mission

In hindsight, it is easy to scoff at the limited scientific knowledge of physicians of a century ago. True, some of them tended to promote miracles, all flowing from the same bottle. Armed only with the art of medicine rather than the more exact and precise data of modern medical practice, and without the modern "miracle" drugs of the past half century, too often they could offer little more than solace—a comforting hand on the brow—to the sick and the dying. Today we too easily take for granted the disappearance of such killers as lobar pneumonia, diphtheria, streptococcal myocarditis—the closing of the majority of tuberculosis sanataria—and many other health phenomena. Given the background of doctors a hundred years ago and the advances of the past five decades, it is difficult to assess the competence of physicians whose careers encompassed these past eras.

So what of Dr. Miles? He looks exceptionally good in retrospect. In the scope and diversity of his efforts, his reach was extraordinary. As a surgeon (even performing difficult eye operations), as a theorist and diagnostician, as a specialist in diseases of the eye and ear, as a prolific pamphleteer, and as a medical evangelist, he emerges as outstanding in his time and place. Today's scientific investigators would have trouble faulting his thoroughness at observation and record keeping, though they might find fault with aspects of his medical theories.

Nerves: A Key to Health

Dr. Miles' approach to medicine revolved around his opinion that the nervous system was the key to health and to overcoming disease. He believed in keeping sound, or restoring to soundness, the complex of nerves at the base of the brain. Problems existing there, he felt, abetted many ailments. So he treated the "nerves" for everything from heart palpitations to stomach disorders. He used his Restorative

Nervine (a bromide sedative syrup) for a wide variety of illnesses, many of which would be described today as psychosomatic or emotional in origin, such as insomnia, headaches, depression, and anxiety. In this prescription he may not have been far amiss.

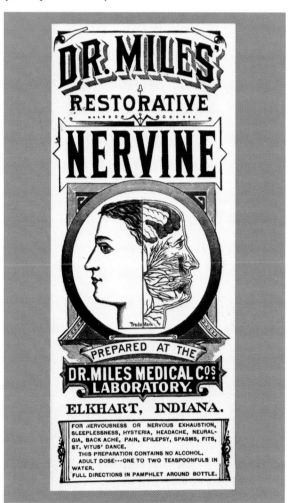

Nervine, bottled as early as 1880, was first sold to drugstores in 1882, then packaged for sale under Dr. Miles' double profile trademark in 1884.

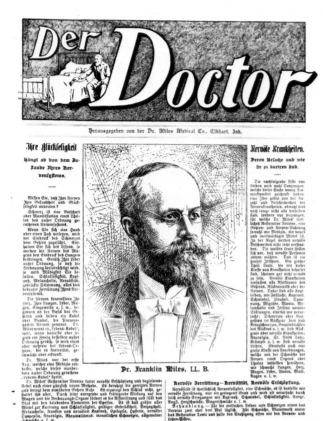

Dr. Miles' treatises were published in a multitude of languages corresponding to the immigrant groups of the 1890s, including German.

A stream of medical treatises, brochures, and promotional copy, basic to successful marketing, poured forth from the presses of the High Street factory and later the Franklin Street plant.

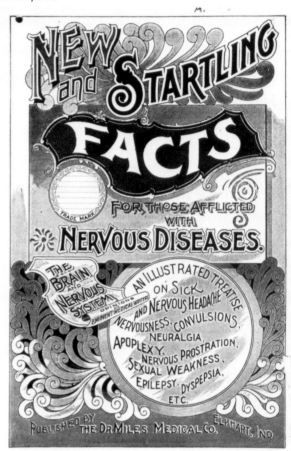

An early publication notes that nervousness, as a disease, was not recognized until 1869 and takes pride in the fact that within ten years Dr. Miles had "perfected a formula for the treatment of this very common disorder."

The publication goes on to examine the underlying causes of some of the symptoms:

> "Unless you are kept awake by pain, the chances are nine out of ten that your sleeplessness is caused by Overtaxed Nerves. Aside from the extremely trying ordeal of lying awake for hours and the 'all in' feeling the following day, Sleeplessness exhausts Nerve Force very rapidly. During our waking hours we use up Nerve Force and when we are asleep Nature restores it.
>
> To try to go on without a sufficient amount of sleep is like continually drawing checks on the bank without depositing a sufficient amount of money to meet them.
>
> Fear, Anger, Worry, Jealousy, may cause Indigestion. An unpleasant sight may make us 'sick at the stomach.' A great love or a great sorrow may cause us to lose our appetite. This is a wise provision of Nature because the Nervous System is so taken up with emotions that it lacks force to digest food if it were eaten. A fit of anger, worry or anxiety at meal time may exhaust Nerve Force and prevent digestion."

The publication continues in this vein, which is perhaps a fair picture of the clinical view of the medical area which preoccupied Dr. Miles in the last three decades of the 19th century.

Restorative Nervine

Nervine contained a genuine drug with an undisputed sedative action. That drug was bromide,

discovered in 1826 in the Mediterranean Sea. As potassium bromide, it appeared in the British Pharmacopeia in 1835, recommended for treating enlarged spleens. A few decades later it became a widespread treatment for epilepsy. In 1857, Britain's *Lancet* reported its value for insomnia. There was no longer any doubt that it had a sedative effect on the central nervous system. Given in proper doses, it caused drowsiness and induced calmness. One of its

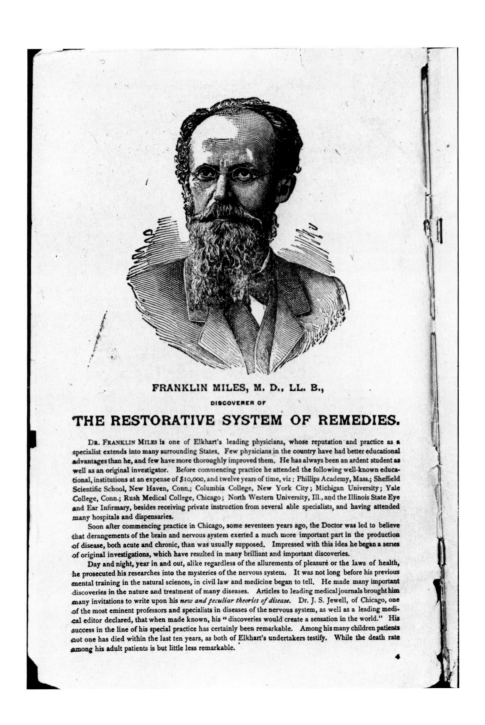

FRANKLIN MILES, M. D., LL. B.,

DISCOVERER OF

THE RESTORATIVE SYSTEM OF REMEDIES.

DR. FRANKLIN MILES is one of Elkhart's leading physicians, whose reputation and practice as a specialist extends into many surrounding States. Few physicians in the country have had better educational advantages than he, and few have more thoroughly improved them. He has always been an ardent student as well as an original investigator. Before commencing practice he attended the following well-known educational, institutions at an expense of $10,000, and twelve years of time, viz: Phillips Academy, Mass.; Sheffield Scientific School, New Haven, Conn.; Columbia College, New York City; Michigan University; Yale College, Conn.; Rush Medical College, Chicago; North Western University, Ill., and the Illinois State Eye and Ear Infirmary, besides receiving private instruction from several able specialists, and having attended many hospitals and dispensaries.

Soon after commencing practice in Chicago, some seventeen years ago, the Doctor was led to believe that derangements of the brain and nervous system exerted a much more important part in the production of disease, both acute and chronic, than was usually supposed. Impressed with this idea he began a series of original investigations, which have resulted in many brilliant and important discoveries.

Day and night, year in and out, alike regardless of the allurements of pleasure or the laws of health, he prosecuted his researches into the mysteries of the nervous system. It was not long before his previous mental training in the natural sciences, in civil law and medicine began to tell. He made many important discoveries in the nature and treatment of many diseases. Articles to leading medical journals brought him many invitations to write upon his *new and peculiar theories of disease.* Dr. J. S. Jewell, of Chicago, one of the most eminent professors and specialists in diseases of the nervous system, as well as a leading medical editor declared, that when made known, his "discoveries would create a sensation in the world." His success in the line of his special practice has certainly been remarkable. Among his many children patients not one has died within the last ten years, as both of Elkhart's undertakers testify. While the death rate among his adult patients is but little less remarkable.

most important uses was for menstrual pain and nervous tension. Mothers recommending Nervine to their daughters accounted for a large part of the product's sales.

As a bona fide sedative, Nervine occupies an unassailable niche in medical history. It was a precursor of the tranquilizers that in the 1960s became household words. Whatever controversies swirl around these newer medications, they launched a new age in the treatment of mental illness, then went on to ubiquitous use for every type of anxiety. Despite some flagrant abuse by doctors and patients, they have been a boon to millions of people. Nervine served some of the same purposes decades before.

Nervine slowly moved to the proprietary medicine sidelines, mainly because of the controversy over bromides. Late in the 1970s, the FDA removed them from the market. Miles had excised bromide from Nervine's time-honored formula shortly before, replacing it with an antihistamine. In this way, the venerable name, in new dress, quietly remains on the market.

At the time, Dr. Maurice H. Seevers, for 29 years professor and chairman of the Department of Pharmacology at the University of Michigan Medical Center, the oldest department of pharmacology in the United States, wrote: "One of the strange quirks of drug history, ending in a loss of perspective by the medical profession, concerns the bromides.... In comparison with the psychotoxic potentialities of the barbiturates and the so-called lesser hypnotics, and even the non-specific tranquilizing agents like meprobamate, the bromide ion hardly seems to deserve its current fate as a much-maligned medical discard."

But discarded it was, trampled by the newer agents of the tranquilizer age. That Nervine should have lived so long with its original formula is a striking tribute to Dr. Miles and the company he founded. Certainly, his recognition that the nerves directly affect one's state of health will stand the test of time.

Dr. Miles' Other Products

Nervine was not the only one of Dr. Miles' remedies that enjoyed a long life. Three others had a span of about a half-century each.

One of them was the Restorative Blood Purifier, later known as the Alterative Compound, made of various vegetable drugs, potassium iodide, Fowler's Solution, sugar, flavorings, and caramel for coloring. It remained on the market until 1937.

Another was the Restorative Tonic, which included iron and quinine and was 10 percent alcohol. It was discontinued in 1938.

The Heart Cure, even though it underwent name and formula changes, also persisted for many years. The principal ingredients were digitalis and fluid extract of cactus grandiflorus. This plant, found in Monterrey, Mexico, was shipped to Elkhart in large bundles wrapped in burlap. In production, a feed chopper cut the plants into one-inch pieces that were ladled into barrels containing a solution of 80 percent alcohol. After "soaking" for six months in the sealed barrels, the cactus was drained and the liquid was bottled as Dr. Miles' Cactus Compound. At that point, the liquid was 11 percent alcohol, not high compared to other medications of the day containing 80 percent. This product likewise met its demise about the time of the new Federal Food, Drug, and Cosmetic Act in 1938.

Two other stalwarts had even longer lives. One was the Nerve and Liver Pill, made primarily of powdered extracts of aloin, ipecac, and podophyllin. It did not vanish from the sales sheets until 1950, so its actual life, from an 1884 starting date, lasted 66 years.

The Pain, or Anti-Pain Pill, had its origin in 1893. These little pink pellets did not contain opiates, a point emphasized in the literature. Ingredients included methyl salicylate and acetanilid. Around 1934, controversy led by the American Medical Association arose over acetanilid. Consequently, a new formula was devised, containing aspirin, acetophenetidin, and caffeine. The Anti-Pain pills survived—alongside the companion product, Antipyn, during the 1940s and 1950s—until 1973. A longevity of 80 years was thus achieved.

Dr. Miles' Laxative had a 28-year run. Pura-Laxa was introduced in 1925 in regular and effervescent form and dropped 11 years later.

In 1927 came Aspir-Mint, soundly conceived since it consisted of 4 grains of mint-flavored aspirin, 1½ grains of phenacetin, and ½ grain of caffeine. Aspir-Mint took off reasonably well in 1928, in part because of a severe flu epidemic, but it never made a dent in the market. Phenacetin and caffeine were eliminated from the formula in 1940. It stayed on the market until 1947.

Dr. Miles as a Medical Communicator

Only reluctantly did Dr. Miles consent to advertise his remedies in the popular press, beginning around 1889. As a serious and well-read investigator with a reputation to uphold, he was eager to separate himself and his medical business from the host of notorious quacks.

The times favored a man of his talents. As Dr. Compton, retired chairman and chief executive officer, told the Rotary Club of Elkhart in 1976:

> "In many midwestern towns, in the last third of the last century, when doctors and pharmacies alike were few, with little or nothing in the way of hospitals, as we know them today, and travel always difficult and sometimes impossible, medical care rested, as indeed it had for many centuries before this, principally on what could be done within the resources of the home. A number of physicians responded to this situation, at first out of their office dispensaries, later through country stores, and finally through pharmacies, with the preparation of more or less simple remedies labeled generally for a wide variety of symptoms, but in many instances capable of providing a reasonable degree of relief...."

In the decade that preceded the formation of the company, Dr. Miles vigorously developed his medical theories and products. Study and experience reinforced his convictions, even lent them a measure of urgency. Being so well educated, he understood how to communicate better than most professionals and businessmen of his time. That knowledge formed the bedrock for the company he founded in 1884.

Dr. Miles' remedies and preparations were never just products with a florid label and a price tag. They were always accompanied into the marketplace by service, and a large part of this service behind Miles' products had to do with Dr. Miles' mission as a popular medical educator.

The doctor began publishing soon after establishing his practice in Elkhart, at least as early as 1876, with a treatise on the ear being his first. Other papers dealt with nervous diseases, a "Permanent Cure for Headache without Change of Occupation" and "Use of Spectacles in Treatment of Diseases of the Brain."

Written for the layman in forceful and fluent style, they stressed cleanliness, moderation in diet, regular bowel movements, proper clothing, and exercise. And they strongly cautioned against worry.

The doctor, with his diverse interests, did not confine himself strictly to medicine. In 1888, he disclosed his philosophy of life and his social concerns in a 20-page booklet, *Human Rights, A Quarterly Journal for the People*. There he expressed opinions on a wide array of matters, from the rights of children to the "art of prolonging life." The first page contains a flowery poem he had written, and his lead article warned that city-dwelling families would soon "become extinct" because of poor health habits.

Miles called for the "scientific" rearing of children and for the "temperate" example of parents. He criticized the schools and lashed "land pirates" and "gigantic" monopolies "for robbing the people."

Perhaps the capstone of the doctor's early popular writing was the book, *A New Era Dawning in Medical Science*, sponsored in 1895 by the Miles Medical Association he had founded in Chicago.

Here, once again, he expounded on the nerve and brain centers, colorfully comparing the brain cells to batteries, the nerve force to electricity, the nerves themselves to wires and organs to machines. He admitted that chronic disease lay beyond the skills of medicine to cure. He reiterated his belief in a common cause for disease in one or more organs. He considered the pneumogastric nerve the most important and found the "human switchboard" at the base of the brain a remarkable instrument. As always, he noted the significance of the eyes, which "probably consume more nerve force than all the large organs."

Dr. Miles was certain that "nearly every human person has certain constitutional weaknesses which predispose him to a particular class of diseases." He acknowledged that most drugs of the day "simply palliate and do not permanently cure." He looked upon many physicians as neglectful since they tended to treat the "result" of the cause instead of the cause itself.

By page 37, he was going into a series of illustrative cases dealing with heart disease, epilepsy, headache, and such vague symptoms as dullness, pressure, confusion, melancholy, smothering spells and so on, all of which he ticketed as "only different manifestations of the same central disturbance of the nervous system."

The book prints letter after letter gratefully reciting recovery from various ailments: "I never took any medicine in my life that relieved me at once as yours does," "I seem to gain strength with every dose," "Your treatment is wonderfully good," "In three months I was totally cured."

The appendix describes the detailed medical questionnaire available to patients and the doctor's rules of practice. He stressed that there should be no "false inducements.... We make few promises and guarantee no cures.... We charge reasonable fees...."

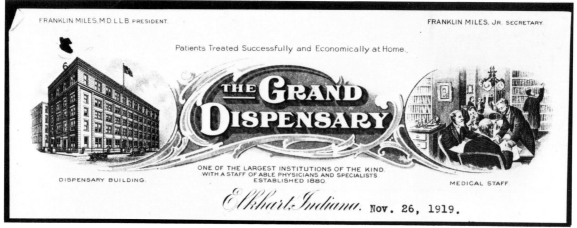

Another enterprise of Dr. Miles was the Grand Dispensary, a long-distance "diagnostic service" that answered bushels of mail sent to the famous nerve specialist of Elkhart.

He also defended practicing medicine by mail. All in all, the book remains a rather remarkable monograph, the work of a forceful intellect thoroughly dedicated to universal health care.

The Grand Dispensary

One aspect of Dr. Miles' career centers on his Grand Dispensary, which was started in 1890 and was always independent of the Dr. Miles Medical Company.

Dr. Miles called it, "The greatest medical institute in America...established for the scientific treatment of patients in their homes." "Nowhere else," the literature claimed, "do ailing people receive the same skillful treatment...for such reasonable charges."

In a sense, since Dr. Miles had assistants, the Dispensary was a forerunner of group practice as we know it today. But it was mostly a direct mail business, with the doctor's imprimatur stamped on every aspect of it. Letters and tracts went out in profusion offering consultation by mail, with the "come on" a free $2.50 supply of medicines. Elkhart physicians helped answer the mail, among them Dr. Hannah O. Staufft and Dr. C. W. Frink.

The mailings were designed to attract patients. And attract them they did. A typical appeal, brimming with confidence, offered free a complete examination chart. Patients were requested to mark the location of pains and aches on a diagram of the human body and to fill in a three-page questionnaire. In some ways, the form was more complete and solicited more specific symptoms than written inquiries used by physicians today.

"There is absolutely no risk," the pamphlets admonished. "Every disheartened sufferer should try once more."

"Remember, it may never occur again," the literature insisted. "Are you ailing? Have you been suffering for months or years with some lingering disease that has made your life a burden? This pamphlet tells you of a system of marvelously curative Neuropathic Treatments with which hundreds of hopeless cases have been cured after failure of many eminent physicians in the largest hospitals and sanitariums...."

Of course, not everybody was entranced by this method of operating. In the company archives there is the case of an attorney who, in 1920, wrote, "Dear Hub (Beardsley): It strikes me that the undertaking to cure Splenic Anaemia on the part of the old Doc is going some."

The Grand Dispensary is important to the corporate history not only because it was integral to Dr. Miles' career but also because it was a factor in an estrangement between him and the other directors. Dr. Miles wanted to incorporate the Dispensary into the structure of the company. The others demurred. The question may have become somewhat rancorous since the Dispensary was moved to Chicago in 1893, into the Masonic Temple Building, then the highest office building in the world. With that, Dr. Miles moved his residence to Chicago.

In a letter of March 17, 1894, to the directors, Dr. Miles addressed them aloofly, beginning, "Gentlemen:" After discussing some routine business, he added a cryptic postscript: "I shall hereafter expect remuneration for all work done for the Miles Medical Company. I cannot afford longer to devote my time to their service without pay, particularly as they have seen fit to charge me for all services they render." The response: "We will endeavor to arrange the matter."

Until 1902, various addresses are listed for the Grand Dispensary in Chicago. After that date, it came back to Elkhart for good, occupying part of the Bucklen Opera House and, later, a floor of the Monger Building. In 1922, medical treatment by mail became illegal. Then the venerable institution, with its partly practical and partly idealistic concept of patient care, faded into history.

Dr. Miles, the Man

What manner of man was Franklin Miles, and how does he stand as a professional in the light of history?

His adopted daughter Louise, and many others, recall him as very "outgoing," always eager to learn and to help others.

"My daddy was a little man," Louise says, "only five foot six, but he was the biggest man I ever knew. He was big in every way. You could bring your problems to him and discuss them. He never flew off the handle. Yet, he was firm and everybody knew he was in command, but gentle and kind and thoughtful. Nobody ever went to my father for help and didn't get it one way or another...."

"I never asked my father a question that he couldn't answer correctly. He knew something about everything. He was an inveterate reader."

When asked about their famous neighbors, the Thomas Edisons, Louise acknowledged that "we knew the Edisons quite well because daddy and Mr. Edison were persons who had inquiring minds. They wanted to know what made things run."

"When Mr. Edison was experimenting with trying to find filaments for the light bulb, he imported a lot of bamboo plants. He gave daddy roots and cuttings. The bamboos that grow on the river, Mr. Edison gave us. And then when he became interested in rubber, he gave daddy quite a lot of cuttings from his rubber trees."

Dr. Miles was an avid fisherman, an excellent

marksman, "president of the Rifle Club at Yale or one of the big eastern schools," Louise says, and an expert horseman.

Most of all, he is remembered as an exemplary family man. Louise recalls several "lessons for life" that he taught her as a small child. Once after a hurricane, he put his arm around her, took her to a window, and pointed to a pine tree that had broken and crashed to the ground. Then he singled out a coconut palm still intact. "You see," he said, "the tree that could not give to the storm broke, but the tree that could give and bend to the storm survived and stands upright again when the storm is past. Remember that in your life. When the storms of life hit, bend to them, and when they are gone, straighten up and go ahead."

Another time, the family was in Indiana at their summer place on Christiana Lake. "The water was placid, like a mirror," Louise recalls. "Daddy was skipping stones on the water. He skipped a big one, and the waves rocked a boat before going off to the horizon."

The things you do and say in life, he told her, travel like those waves, "so be careful what you do and say. You can hurt people you didn't intend to hurt, and your actions can travel a long, long way."

"Never turn your back on your troubles," he told her at other times. "Face them and conquer them. Life is a series of falling down, getting up again, and going on."

His grandson, Franklin B. Miles, remembers he used to lecture them on the question, "Do you want to be a race horse or a work horse?" He also told his grandchildren "to marry for intelligence, not love, and to marry tall people to improve the strain." Frank also remembers that his grandfather, bald at 27, nearly always wore a toupee.

Charles "Chuck" Miles, also a grandson and retired company executive, says the doctor taught his grandchildren to play poker and would lecture them "over their heads." He was "a stickler for discipline and courtesy, somewhat formal and almost domineering."

Whatever else this man was, he was first of all by nature and inclination a physician in the classic sense and by the standards of the time a first-rate one. He had a driving determination to make sick people well and to make healthy people live sensibly. He was more than competent in his treatment of eye and ear disorders, as newspapers of the time attest: "Dr. Miles recently performed the difficult operation of creating an artificial pupil.... Dr. Miles operated on a cross-eyed girl, 4th in five days...." *The Elkhart Review* reported on several occasions that he would treat patients unable to pay.

If he had been only a physician, even with a successful practice, which he unquestionably had, his name would be unknown. But the more captivating aspect of his career revolves around his vigorous, personal style as a communicator, partly because it was cardinal to the founding and growth of the company and partly because it presaged the marketing innovations that would make Miles, in the 20th century, one of the most resourceful of all American firms in promoting its products.

PART II

MILES IN THE MARKETPLACE

CHAPTER 4

Plop, Plop, Fizz, Fizz

A pivotal development soon to transpire would shift attention from Dr. Miles and his early medications to a new effervescent product destined to become one of the great home remedies of all time.

A Company in Search of a Product

As the company moved into the gloom-ridden 1930s, it was known and modestly successful but hardly passed for a pharmaceutical giant. The 1929 Annual Report, a concise account in 14 typewritten pages, disclosed sales of $1,600,877, a gain of almost $66,000 over 1928. Profits amounted to $149,000, a decline of $37,380 from 1928 because of "increased production, selling, and advertising expense."

The Anti-Pain Pill produced the biggest volume, with 184,000 dozen being sold. Nervine Tablets and Liquid accounted for 152,000 dozen. Then came 64,000 dozen Aspir-Mint, with much lower volume for the Tonic, the Laxative, and the Alterative and Cactus Compounds.

Figures illuminated the vital role of promotion. Some 2.5 million laxative samples and the same number of Aspir-Mint were distributed. The presses turned out 18 million Little Books, 18.5 million almanacs, and 5 million calendars. The entire promotional program consumed $848,378, or 53 percent of sales.

In 1930, sales climbed to $1,721,497, but profits slipped to $130,564. The second Annual Report (1930) mentions the deepening Depression and slashed advertising budgets because of business conditions. The nation's worst economic plummeting was yet to come in 1932.

This was Miles, then, at a turning point, almost half a century old. The outlook seemed a bit bleak—except for that spectacular new product impatiently awaiting a rendezvous with medical history.

A. H. "Hub" Beardsley got the idea for Alka-Seltzer when he and the Elkhart Truth *editor discussed how to ward off the flu.*

The Background of Alka-Seltzer

Alka-Seltzer had humble origins, although the research that led to its production and marketing is no mystery.

By the mid-1920s, Hub and Charlie Beardsley felt a need to come up with a humdinger product or two. They sensed that part of the answer would be found in effervescence.

In 1925 Miles added a powdered laxative, Pura-

Maurice Treneer, whose inventiveness made Alka-Seltzer effervesce, will forever have a lofty standing in the story of Miles.

Laxa, to its line of products—salvaged from the Grand Dispensary. Though it never did much, it was the company's first effervescent product.

In 1927 Maurice Treneer, a chemist, quietly came on stage. British-born and educated, he had been brought to Elkhart by Hub Beardsley to make Dr. Miles' Nervine more modern in appearance and to improve its formula by making it effervescent. Always forward-looking, Hub had for some time been aware of the work of Treneer. For a number of years, he had been an employee of Burroughs–Wellcome, a British-based pharmaceutical firm with a large American subsidiary. He had left their employ to engage in custom product development and described himself as "a pioneer of the effervescent tablet business in the United States." Which, indeed, he was.

Upon joining Miles, Treneer managed to put Nervine into effervescent form, and for a while it even had a new name—Bromo-Vess.

In 1927 the company brought out Aspir-Mint, a specialty mint-flavored tablet of aspirin, phenacetin, and caffeine. "It looks like the real thing," Charlie Beardsley said in 1929, and the product did stay on

Two legendary Alka-Seltzer personages: Left, Maurice Treneer, effervescence technologist, and Harry Beaver, pharmacologist, in their laboratory in 1938.

the market until 1947. But Hub had high hopes for still another product. He wrote to his brothers that Treneer was working on two new items, one of them Aspir-Vess—later to be Alka-Seltzer—and that it was going to be "a real startler."

A Most Memorable Memo

In what has to be the most memorable memo in the history of the company, Hub Beardsley himself described the origin of Alka-Seltzer as follows:

The Origin of Alka-Seltzer

When the Dr. Miles Laboratories, in 1928, were making Dr. Miles Effervescent Nervine Tablets, we had an expert chemist, especially skilled in effervescent products, making these tablets.

In December, 1928, an epidemic of colds and influenza struck our country. It was estimated that fifty percent of the population were affected, in some way or other. Although this epidemic was milder than the previous one in 1918, it was serious, nevertheless.

At the height of the epidemic, the Dr. Miles Laboratories had twenty-five percent of its employees out, at one time or another, on account of this scourge.

One morning, I went over to the office of the *Elkhart Truth*. The Managing Editor, Mr. Tom Keene, had just had a phone call from the Manager of the *News-Times* of Goshen, and had loaned him two operators or linotypists. The *News-Times* linotype operators—four in number—were all down with the flu, and they could not get out their paper. The *Truth* loaned them two operators in the emergency.

I asked Mr. Keene how they could do this, and he told me that not one of their employees had lost any time on account of the colds and flu. When I asked him why, he said that when a member of his staff showed signs of coming down with a cold, he brought him into the office and dosed him with aspirin and bi-carbonate of soda, with instructions to continue until he was free from symptoms.

When I returned from our Laboratories, I asked our chemist, Mr. Maurice Treneer, if he could make an effervescent tablet containing bi-carbonate of soda and aspirin, and he said he could. In about a week, he brought down some very satisfactory samples, using approximately the formula of Upjohn's Citro-carbonate, containing

35	grains	of	bi-carbonate of soda
24	"	"	citric acid
1	"	"	magnesia
1	"	"	calcium
1	"	"	phosphate

Added to this, was   5   "   "   aspirin.

We used these tablets around the office and the Laboratories, with very gratifying success, in January.

On January twenty-second, Mrs. Beardsley, my son Walter, and I went on a Mediterranean cruise, on the Cunard Liner, "Samaria," going first to Madeira; then to Gibralter; then on to Egypt and the Holy Land. I took with me about a gross of these tablets, and tried them out on the passengers of the good ship "Samaria." We had a very rough passage, with continuous storms, from the time we left Sandy Hook, until we arrived at Madeira.

I found the tablets were wonderful for seasickness and colds. Someone brought on flu germs, and we had an epidemic of flu on board the ship. Two of the passengers died from pneumonia. I passed out these tablets, and had many compliments for them and thanks for their use.

This is the origin of Alka-Seltzer. It was primarily used for colds, and has now become almost the universal remedy.

/S/ A. H. Beardsley
1935

Given the magnitude of the Alka-Seltzer achievement and Beardsley's part in it, the memo is somewhat understated, laconic in tone, and generous in giving anecdotal credit to Tom Keene. By the time of the memo, in 1935, the success of the product was assured, and Hub would have been forgiven for bragging, but his modesty prevailed in his brief description for posterity.

The "Recipe" for Alka-Seltzer

Deep in the Miles archives lies a crumbling notebook that contains "recipes" for making and testing Alka-Seltzer, its scrawlings in pencil. The inscriber was the company's first pharmacist, Harry Beaver, who had come to the company in 1914 from the Grand Dispensary and who was to retire in 1957 after 43 years with Miles.

In his precise directions for each ingredient, Beaver indicated that the manufacturing process was pretty much a hand operation. Perfecting Alka-Seltzer was a stubborn challenge because aspirin can be troublesomely unstable. Frances Meiser, who worked for all the Beardsleys in her 47-year career, recollects that Treneer, Beaver, and others tinkered the better part of two years before they felt the product

The Franklin Street plant in 1935.

was stable enough to be marketed with confidence. Fred Lobley, also from England, who was chief engineer and in charge of the new modern multicolor printing press, experimented with heat and humidity controls in the production area until he got them just right.

Edging Alka-Seltzer Toward Its Destiny

So Treneer and his aides, at the turn of the decade, edged Alka-Seltzer toward its days of destiny.

In 1929 Hub Beardsley wrote cautiously to his brothers that "it would be well to think about forming a . . . company . . . to market these in a small way to physicians as a tryout." This was carried out, the new company being named Effervescent Products, Inc., its formulations to be developed as medical specialties for promotion to physicians. Eventually the line consisted of five "Vess" products: Bromo-Vess, Aspir-Vess, Alka-Vess, Cinco-Vess, and Salici-Vess.

In 1931 Hub wrote, "We are getting ready to put Alka-Seltzer on the market and getting the whole organization keyed up for the promotion. We believe it is going to be a big success. . . . If it isn't, there is going to be wailing and gnashing of teeth and wearing of sackcloth and ashes. . . ."

As it turned out, of course, there was no need for penitence. Nevertheless, not everyone was so confident. Beaver, for one, was certainly a shade less assured than his boss. For example, in September 1931, he feared he had "over-bought" when he ordered five pounds of cotton to stuff into the tops of Alka-Seltzer bottles, which had to be corked and sealed in molten paraffin before screw caps were adopted in 1936.

In the story of the development of Alka-Seltzer, there are probably unsung and forgotten names. Beaver played a major role since he worked closely with Treneer, as did Fred Lobley, the engineering expert.

There is little question, however, that Maurice Treneer was the chief architect in the development of the product. He and Miles entered into an arrangement whereby he received substantial income during his lifetime. He retired in 1947 and lived in Elkhart until he died in 1968 at the age of 86.

Relief Is "Just a Swallow Away"

What was—and is—Alka-Seltzer, and why did it succeed? It had two big things in its favor: it worked, and it was superbly promoted.

Alka-Seltzer consists essentially of aspirin, citric acid, and sodium bicarbonate. Simple to use, it has only to be dropped in water, where it effervesces before the user drinks it. Dissolving the tablet in water converts the aspirin into sodium acetylsalicylate, a salt of aspirin which is safe in the stomach when highly buffered, and which is much more rapidly absorbed into the blood than is aspirin in its original form. Sodium bicarbonate and citric acid react to form sodium citrate and release carbon dioxide (bubbles). Sodium citrate with residual sodium bicarbonate and carbon dioxide forms the buffer in the solution that handles excess stomach acid.

Effervescent and fast-working, Alka-Seltzer with its high buffering action protects the stomach lining while relieving upset stomach. It is exceptionally safe since the dry tablet is too large to be swallowed. Ingestion of large quantities of dissolved Alka-Seltzer causes nausea and vomiting (because of the tablet's salt content).

This effervescent, analgesic, alkalizing tablet soon became a popular medication that exceeded all expectations. For nagging, everyday aches and pains—colds, headaches, upset stomach, various minor muscle and rheumatic complaints, painful menstruation, and over-indulgence—people found that relief was "just a swallow away."

Spreading the Word on a New Product

There was no question that Alka-Seltzer worked. Making this fact known, however, was a prime challenge. Marketing began in the spring of 1931 in Elkhart and half a dozen nearby cities. Newspaper ads, so long successful in advertising the old Miles line, invited readers to get a free drink of Alka-Seltzer at their favorite drugstore.

But the real promotion springboard turned out to be radio. The advertising department had dipped its toes into the medium, talking up Nervine on a Fort Wayne station in 1929 and 1931. Alka-Seltzer ads were christened on Chicago's WLS on January 12, 1932, on a program called "The Songs of Home Sweet Home."

Encouraged by the response, Miles went to a national chain, but this effort flopped. Next came a 13-week stint on a Columbia network program, "The Hoosier Editor." This didn't boost sales either, and spirits drooped in Elkhart. Somehow, radio no longer seemed to be the answer.

The Barn Dance Boost

Then in came WLS with an attractive offer for sponsorship of its highly popular "Saturday Night

Barn Dance." Alka-Seltzer appeared on the program for the first time on February 4, 1933.

Prices were cut and soon sales began to climb. At the end of the 13-week cycle, the WLS contract was renewed and extended to Detroit and Pittsburgh. Sales jumped. By September 1933, the Barn Dance went national on 200 stations of NBC's Blue Network. Alka-Seltzer had indeed clambered onto a sturdy radio bandwagon.

The Barn Dance cast was a "Who's Who of Radio" in the 1930s and 1940s, with such celebrities as Fibber McGee and Molly, Vic and Sade, Gene Autry, Alec Templeton, Dorothy Collins, Roy Rogers and Dale Evans, Burl Ives, Victor Borge, the Mills Brothers, Robert Benchley, Lum and Abner, and others. Some of them, including George Gobel, got their start on the Barn Dance, all under Joe Kelly, the congenial master of ceremonies.

The program fit ideally into the American mold, when simple pleasures sufficed during the unsettled years of Depression and all-out war. Such shows as the Barn Dance—not only with "hillbillies" but "city slickers," too—seemed to muster support that even the most popular of today's television shows cannot match. Few programs in advertising history have contributed so much to a single product's success.

Out of the Barn Dance came other radio hits, including "Uncle Ezra and the Hoosier Hot Shots," teaming up for the "Friendly Little City of Rosedale."

Alka-Seltzer sponsored pianist Alec Templeton and subsequently the newly-formed Quiz Kids as the

Uncle Ezra and the Hoosier Hot Shots, from the "National Barn Dance" radio show, went on to another show of their own.

Sponsorship of the "National Barn Dance" on network radio, beginning in 1933, got Alka-Seltzer off and fizzing.

Folk songs popularized by the Hoosier Hot Shots helped the growth of the National Barn Dance—and of Alka-Seltzer.

summer replacement for the Barn Dance. "The Quiz Kids" proved to be much more than a replacement. With Joe Kelly as Quiz Master, the show caught on. Slotted between Jack Benny and Charlie McCarthy, it continued on both radio and television until 1951.

"The Flower in Beardsley's Lapel"

"We kept the Quiz Kids a lot longer than the ratings justified," said Geoffrey Wade of the Wade Advertising Agency. "But Charlie Beardsley loved the show and would say he looked on it as the flower in his lapel."

The Miles' knack for getting ads on highly-rated shows persisted into World War II and long afterward. Take "One Man's Family." That really was "a dignified soap opera," Miles adman Harold J. Beeby remembers. "Millions of Americans took it to heart and considered it a real family." Alka-Seltzer ads, as well as those for other Miles products, brightened practically every network radio show of any consequence. Even "News of the World," featuring such ace reporters as Morgan Beatty, Earl Godwin, and Alex Dwyer, was sponsored by Miles products.

Radio began to retreat before the onslaught of television in the late 1940s. Miles edged, rather than plunged, into the new medium. In 1951 and 1952, it sponsored "One Man's Family" on television and other shows such as "Garry Moore" and "Ernie Ford" along with news telecasts.

Once the switch had been made, there came a great variety of sponsored shows, from "Broken Arrow" to the "Wednesday Night Fights," "The Rifleman," "Bonanza," "Laramie," "Andy Williams," "Hawaiian Eye," "Jack Paar," "Combat," "The Naked City," "Hootenanny," "The Virginian," and "The Flintstones." Nobody could argue that this was not diversity in programming.

"Break the Bank!" was another popular show sponsored by Alka-Seltzer.

A Bold and Prolific Advertiser

Miles was a bold, prolific radio and television advertiser in the first quarter century of Alka-Seltzer. Who was behind this broad and consistent effort? Certainly the company could boast of a long line of exceptionally apt advertising men, each of whom left his stamp on one or more segments of the program. Such men included the legendary Herbert Thompson, Oliver Capelle, and Charles Tennant.

Staunch support for advertising came from Hub Beardsley, right up to his death in 1936. But the most credit must go to Charles Beardsley. "Let's not beat around the bush," Harold Beeby asserts. "The man was a marketing genius. Together with Jeff Wade's

By insisting on creative and expanded promotion for Alka-Seltzer, Charles S. Beardsley earned lasting fame in Miles history.

Three generations of the Wade family guided Miles in its advertising beginning in the early 1900s. Seated: Albert G. Wade, Sr. On his lap, great grandson, Albert Geoffrey Wade, 3rd. Standing, Geoffrey Wade, 2nd, and son, Walter Albert Wade. They helped get Miles started on radio and television and originated "Speedy Alka-Seltzer."

father, he produced all the important innovations... that brought the company along as fast as it did... and it grew amazingly fast...."

"Besides that," Beeby continues, "there wasn't much going on that he didn't know about. If you were doing badly, he knew that and there was no use lying to him. He was more a friend than a boss."

"Uncle Charlie" had a unique, if unscientific, way of evaluating advertising results. "If you have the right commercial," he once told Beeby, "you can wait three weeks and go out on the loading dock and see the constructive result." "I didn't believe it," Beeby admits, "but it was true."

Spending Money to Make Money

Beardsley and Wade were convinced that you had to spend money to make money. Before World War II, Miles spent $4 to $5 million a year on advertising, most of it for Alka-Seltzer promotion; this was quite a lot of money in those days.

It rankled Beardsley that in the pre-war era, CBS would not accept advertising for a proprietary medicine. So he went to New York to see the legendary William S. Paley, the network head. Beardsley waited in an outer office for two hours, then decided that it was long enough and stomped out. He issued stern

A typical early ad for the famed remedy in the heyday of the National Barn Dance.

"Listen to It Fizz" first appeared in 1935.

orders that no one would ever be allowed to approach CBS again. The ban lasted a long time.

Throughout its history, Alka-Seltzer clearly benefited from a media program with few equals in the annals of advertising.

Strokes of Advertising Genius

Placement of advertising was one thing, the copy another. Here, too, sporadic strokes of pure advertising genius prevailed. Over the years, many slogans, themes, and lines have vanished, yet an astonishing number have survived in living memory.

Early copy flourished under few constraints, legal or medical, circumscribed only by good taste and reasonable discretion. From the start, Charles Beardsley always insisted the messages comply with what he called "pharmaceutical elegance."

Alka-Seltzer was first acclaimed in printed ads as a "new drink for health.... The new alkaline way to relieve sour stomach, colds, headaches, gas on stomach, neuralgia, rheumatism, and that tired run-down feeling." In the 1930s this expanded to the notion that systemic excess acidity fostered the development of colds and other respiratory ailments. Alka-Seltzer was glamorized in one ad with the lines—"They've had a terrible fight. He snapped at her and left.... It's all lovely now.... What caused it? Too much acidity in the body." The company's promotional staff today would cringe at such claims. But not in those days. An unforgettable slogan was: "Be Wise—Alkalize with Alka-Seltzer!"

In the radio years, a glass of water would be held next to the microphone, two tablets would be dropped into the glass, and listeners would be exhorted to "Listen to it fizz!" By 1935, other lines had made their mark, among them, "There's nothing quite like Alka-Seltzer," and "The morning after's what I hate; take Alka-Seltzer, it's great."

"The Stipulation"

Early on, Miles began toning down its advertising voluntarily. For example, the company decided it could not claim that neuritis and rheumatism were helped much by Alka-Seltzer. But through the 1930s it continued to stress the excess systemic acid theme.

That was true until 1939. Then a bombshell burst over corporate headquarters. It would not be the last to explode in the annals of Alka-Seltzer, but as the first one, it wounded egos, shattered convictions, and changed the course of Alka-Seltzer promotion.

The incident, to be forever known as "The Stipulation," brought to the forefront a man of the future Miles: Dr. Walter Ames Compton, grandson of George Compton.

Born in Elkhart in 1911, Walter attended Princeton University, where he earned a degree in chemistry. He went on to graduate from Harvard Medical School in 1937, and interned at Billings Hospital in Chicago in 1937–38. At that point, he had to make a career decision; he found the prospect of private medical practice "intriguing," but he also liked the challenges of scientific research, especially in biological chemistry.

The young doctor knew that the scientific field was wide open at Miles, so he came aboard in 1938. He had barely started to become familiar with his job as the first research and medical director when he was thrust into the controversy over the very existence of Alka-Seltzer. It was a spectacular, if chilling, way to get started.

Compromising with the FTC

The crisis erupted because the Federal Trade Commission had described Miles' advertising as "false, misleading, and deceptive" in claiming that systemic acidity caused various bodily disturbances and that Alka-Seltzer, by correcting this acidity, could relieve symptoms. Dr. Compton, a scientist by training and conviction, still recalls his reaction at realizing that the company product assertions had little or no evidence to support these medical claims, not only at Miles but in the entire scientific world. It was a situation he would soon begin to correct.

Compton visited the FTC where he managed to achieve a compromise by agreeing to drop the claims involving systemic acidity, together with stipulating that they were in fact false and misleading except where subsequent research might support them in the future. He also stated that the company would submit all advertising copy and claims to review and approval by graduate, licensed physicians.

Promotion on the Fast Track

With "The Stipulation" in effect, Alka-Seltzer promotion went back to the fast track. In spite of the controversy, advertising did not really suffer, and some observers thought it actually improved. It was not necessary to abandon all "pre-stipulation" slogans. "Be Wise—Alkalize with Alka-Seltzer" continued on radio until the late 1950s.

Rhymes became popular early: "When your tablets get down to four, that's the time to buy some more." That couplet persisted until 1954.

Other commercial jingles frequently rode the airwaves: "An extra package in the grip can come in handy on a trip"; "An extra package in the car can act just like a spare; you may not need to use it, but it's wise to have it there." Hardly Shakespearean, it was nevertheless sharp advertising. Contests, too, became part of the advertising programs, attracting millions who competed for Buicks and Zenith radios.

In 1949, the "first-aid" theme was unveiled. The year 1952 brought, "Feel better while you're getting better," which lasted for nine years and "Alka-Seltzer—for that feel-better feeling."

"Triple comfort relief" stressed stomach symptoms in 1955, as did "Action in the glass." The more famous, "Relief is just a swallow away," emerged in 1957; it would run intermittently for several years.

"Speedy Alka-Seltzer" in Person

Like all good admen, those at Miles and the Wade agency were always on the prowl for new ideas. Jeff Wade had for years wanted a cartoon character to personify Alka-Seltzer. Chuck Tennant, account representative, remembering a wartime flying buddy who had become a commercial artist, invited him to invent a "Mr. Alka-Seltzer."

So, in 1951, Robert Watkins roughed out a red-haired, blue-eyed, pink-cheeked sprite sporting a toothy grin and a magic wand, who wore an Alka-Seltzer tablet on his head. Another tablet made up his body, and Watkins was even ready with a name—Sparky.

"The drawing was right on the money," Wade remembers. "I took it to Elkhart, and Perry Shupert, then the sales manager, changed Sparky's name to Speedy."

Speedy Alka-Seltzer would reign for more than 10 years, but he wasn't recognized as a winner right away. "I took a wood carving of Speedy to Elkhart," Wade recalls. "Everybody took a look, and then the arguments started. It was about 50-50 around the table. Walter Compton was the one who finally tipped the scales."

Speedy was then rushed into print, mostly in the big circulation "shelter" magazines, and heavily promoted to the drug trade. A four-page circular about him, entitled "Miles Ahead," went to 58,000 drug retailers in early 1952.

The search then began for the right voice for radio. Scores of actors were auditioned, until the diminutive, four-foot six-inch Richard Beals, finally took a crack at it. He read the script only once and Forrest Owen of Wade on the West Coast called Elkhart immediately and announced, "I've found the voice!" Nobody else was ever used. In Latin America, Speedy became Pron-tito.

The real blossoming came on television, beginning in 1954, where Speedy's impact startled even the most optimistic. Fearing overkill, the ad people restricted him to about half the commercials. He still appeared in about 100 different versions, then was reincarnated for the 1976 American Bicentennial and the ill-fated 1980 Olympics. When the United States pulled out of the Summer Games, the spirited sprite had to go home with the athletes.

Speedy won many awards, one of them as the top commercial for the entire decade of the 1950s. Without a doubt, he buoyed sales, but was he used too long? It's a moot point. Bob Wallace, who capped his career at Miles as head of the Consumer Products Group, says, "Speedy may have somewhat overstayed his time. While sales were still rising, they may have been masked by the tremendous growth in the number of TV sets."

But in many ways, Speedy *was* Alka-Seltzer for almost a decade, waving his magic wand over the fizzing glass. He'll always be a nostalgic part of Miles' past.

One Ad Era Ends and a New One Begins

On September 1, 1963, Miles shook the drug advertising world with its terse announcement that it had appointed the Interpublic Group to handle the Alka-Seltzer account, thus ending a relationship with the Wade agency that had lasted nearly 50 years.

Interpublic's head, Marion Harper, assigned Jack Tinker and Partners, with their enviable reputation for creativity, to find new approaches for the familiar product.

In making this historic but reluctant change, Miles went directly for top talent. As Division President O. G. "Red" Kennedy explained, to do otherwise

Dick Beals, the voice of Speedy. No other voice was ever used in more than 100 commercials.

would have been an "unwarranted burden" on agencies that would have flooded Miles with speculative presentations.

The Tinker team included Mary Wells, then beginning to build her fame in advertising. She and the group dropped Speedy but came up with advertising that was spectacular by any standard—the celebrated "stomachs" commercial. The clever, funny visuals, along with lines like, "No matter what shape your stomach is in," got America's attention. This commercial, too, won many awards, including the Cleo (the TV commercial equivalent of an Oscar) and a gold medal from the Art Director's Club of New York.

The "Stomachs" Start a Trend

Advertising Age, in selecting the "Stomachs Montage" as one of the best spots of 1964, commented on "this rare collection of stomachs photographed by Howard Zieff...as particularly

The "Stomachs Montage" commercial of the 1960s started a new humorous trend and won numerous awards.

"I can't believe I ate the whole thing," from an Alka-Seltzer commercial, became part of America's everyday language.

effervescent." The ad was so successful, says Bob Wallace, because "it had hard sell couched subtly in palatable humor. It started a trend, took guts to put on TV." Marketing experts conceded it was different, even daring.

Having once broken the long link with Wade, Miles spent less time in making more changes. After five years with Tinker, it turned to Doyle Dane Bernbach, another major agency renowned for its creativity. "Groom's First Meal" was one of its first humorous slice-of-life entries. "Magadini's Meatballs," a commercial about making a commercial, was acclaimed the best TV advertising spot in 20 years by the Hollywood Radio and Television Society in 1980.

The Doyle Dane Bernbach association with Alka-Seltzer didn't last long, although that agency continues to this day to handle the company's S.O.S soap pad account. Early in 1971, Alka-Seltzer went to Wells, Rich, Greene. As Dr. Compton explained, the shift brought back "the talents of Mrs. Mary Wells Lawrence, who played a major role in the creation of our breakthrough advertising in 1965."

"Try It, You'll Like It"

Wells, Rich, Greene kept the account until September 1983, when it was transferred to McCann-Erickson, New York. Wells, Rich, Greene advertising will long be remembered for such lines as "Try it, you'll like it," and "I can't believe I ate the whole thing." The latter was picked by *Newsweek* as one of the ten best quotes of the decade. "Plop, plop, fizz, fizz" was one of the agency's most successful campaigns.

Over time, Alka-Seltzer entries have probably won more awards than those for any other single product in the history of advertising, not only in the United States but overseas as well. Consumers regularly place them in the top ten in the *New York Times'* annual poll of the most popular commercials.

Thus, everything from subway cards to high exposure TV has kept Alka-Seltzer in the public consciousness over the years. The advertising succeeded because it remained simple, direct, and attuned to the everyday speech of ordinary people. It never tried to be fancy, it stayed light and humorous, and put common ailments into understandable terms. The visuals, too, had the same simplicity and charm, and all left a great creative legacy for Miles' second century.

Coming to the Defense of Alka-Seltzer

Marketing techniques and practices continued to be fundamental to the success of Alka-Seltzer into the 1980s, as they must be to any over-the-counter medication. But the story of the product over the last 15 years is also a regulatory, legal, medical, and public relations story of substantial proportions. For, off and on during this period, Alka-Seltzer came under nearly constant fire. At times it seemed that its very existence was at stake. Company resources had to be mustered on its behalf on a major scale.

The medical defense of Alka-Seltzer has been a prime consideration since its earliest days, particularly after Dr. Compton came on the scene. The first recorded Alka-Seltzer studies started in 1935. By the early 1960s, 45 investigations had been completed. Scores of experts in some 15 medical specialties have contributed to what today is a voluminous medical profile on Alka-Seltzer.

Through the decades, the Medical Department has been a stern monitor of promotional copy. It did not like the word "stop" in advertising copy, since that implied complete relief; neither was "treatment" considered suitable. It insisted that "suffer" be eliminated and that "misery" and "distress" be used with caution. It did approve of "soothe" for acid indigestion claims.

The enactment in 1938 of the Federal Food, Drug, and Cosmetic Act also greatly strengthened federal regulation of drug labeling practices. Also, new drugs could not be marketed without a review of safety data. These "new drug" controls did not apply to older drugs, such as Alka-Seltzer, generally recognized as safe.

In 1962 amendments to the law plugged more teeth into drug regulation by requiring, before marketing, "substantial evidence of effectiveness," as well as of safety. Again, though, it had no immediate effect on most over-the-counter medications. That was to come a decade later in January 1972, when the Food and Drug Administration began a monumental review of the safety and effectiveness of all over-the-counter products. Even now, more than another decade later, this review has not yet been completed. All of the panel reports have appeared, but few have reached final monograph stage.

Gearing Up for Battle

The FDA plan made reasonable sense because panels of experts were convened to study the various categories of ingredients. Anticipating this program,

Miles had long been gearing up for battles it knew were brewing in a world moving toward the stronger regulation of medicines. The impressive evidence being collected to support Alka-Seltzer around the world would certainly be needed.

Even so, Miles faced perplexing problems. It had to confront challenges in not just one but three of the FDA Advisory Review Panels—Antacids, Analgesics, and Miscellaneous Internal Drug Products. Involved was a question of separate symptoms treated by two types of ingredients—analgesics and antacids—and the ruling of the FDA that each ingredient had to contribute to the claimed effect for both headache and upset stomach. But what if you had only one of the symptoms? Could you prove claims for each ingredient?

To satisfy the regulations, head and stomach symptoms had to be concurrent, unless you could prove that aspirin relieved upset stomach. It was clear to Miles that linking the two symptoms would be required.

The next questions: Was it rational to combine aspirin with an antacid for concurrent symptoms? Was there a need? At that time, plain aspirin was under a cloud as a potential danger to the stomach, even though it is now known that the special buffering of Alka-Seltzer makes it safe in the stomach.

Under the direction of the general counsel, Adrien Ringuette, the Alka-Seltzer Research Committee, made up of scientists from Miles and Miles consultants, was formed to arrange a long chain of submissions and to prepare for hearings.

Convincing the Antacid Panel

In March 1972, Miles submitted eight volumes of material, covering some 50 studies and 169 references to the Antacid Panel. Headed by the late Dr. Franz Ingelfinger, the distinguished editor of the *New England Journal of Medicine*, this Panel reported back to the FDA a year later. One of its conclusions: It *was* rational to combine an antacid with an analgesic for the concurrent symptoms of headache and acid indigestion. It was a vital victory, even though the Panel rejected claims for antacid use alone. But new trouble loomed.

On April 4, 1973, the FDA held a press conference to summarize—and laud—the Antacid Panel's findings. It promised to be a routine affair. It wasn't. For into the room strode representatives of Ralph Nader's Health Research Group, headed by Dr. Sidney Wolfe, long a critic of doctors in general and of the drug industry in particular. Wolfe attacked Miles for obtaining "favored treatment" for Alka-Seltzer by the use of "undue influence." He said the product was "unsafe and ineffective."

This was the opening salvo in what was to be a year-long war, with the aftermath dragging on for some time. Both the Panel and the FDA quickly sprang to their own defense. Dr. Ingelfinger called the accusation "rubbish." FDA Commissioner Alexander Schmidt flatly rejected the Health Research Group's allegations.

Dr. Wolfe entered the controversy on a formal basis, however, filing a statement on June 4 that repeated the April 4 allegations. That same day, Miles issued its rebuttal, and on July 3 released more detailed comments to counter June 6 testimony before the Subcommittee on Monopoly of the Senate Select Committee on Small Business, chaired by Senator Gaylord Nelson.

The Nelson Hearings Spark Controversy

These so-called Nelson Hearings had long been conducted in spurts by Senator Nelson (D–Wis.), an avowed critic of the drug industry. The Hearings generated negative publicity on drugs, pharmaceutical companies, doctors, and the government's handling of health matters. Senator Nelson overlooked no opportunity to denounce a drug product, so Alka-Seltzer could hardly escape his assault.

"Dr. Wolfe and Senator Nelson were going for the jugular," Ringuette recalls. "They marshalled hostile witnesses, and their testimony on June 6, while ill-founded, was still tough to counter."

Since it was not testifying, about all Miles could do was issue a rebuttal. It passed out a press release in the hearing room which said that "the relief provided by aspirin can be obtained with safety in the form of Alka-Seltzer.... More than 70 billion Alka-Seltzer tablets have been sold.... No home medication has had its safety and effectiveness more thoroughly tested in the home and in the laboratory...." Ringuette says that, "In retrospect, 1973 was a most critical year in the most critical decade for the product."

A decisive stage in the controversy came on July 27 when Dr. Wolfe sent a letter to the FDA calling for the censure of Miles for "deliberately withholding important data showing that Alka-Seltzer causes bleeding...in normal people." That accusation was rushed to the press, and though invalid, got attention.

On that very night, a Friday, a Miles team

General counsel Adrien L. Ringuette beside 650 pounds of Alka-Seltzer studies boxed for submission to the FDA.

arrived from England, pleased that for the third time it had bolstered the claims for Alka-Seltzer before British health authorities.

The Case Against Miles Crumbles

The Miles group, under Ringuette, had already planned to spend the weekend in Washington preparing for vital oral testimony before another panel, the Analgesics Panel, which was also to consider Alka-Seltzer for relief of pain. Now Ringuette's team had additional work to do, defending Miles against Wolfe's accusations.

"It was the most intensive working weekend of my life," Ringuette recalls. "We didn't have a moment to waste."

Wolfe's charge of withholding data proved baseless. It was contradicted by the investigator himself. The FDA wasted little time in replying to Wolfe. On August 7, it said, "We are unable to determine that Miles deliberately withheld data...." On November 12, 1973, the Tentative Final Order for Antacid Products was issued. Confirming the recommendations of the Antacid Panel, the FDA concluded that "there is a significant target population for which the antacid-analgesic combination provides rational concurrent therapy."

On June 4, 1974, the FDA issued its final order for antacids, clearing Alka-Seltzer for use in relieving acid indigestion when it occurs concurrently with headache or other pain. So, in the end, the Health Research Group's case against the product crumbled.

Alka-Seltzer survived, but not without damage. The Nader-Wolfe-Nelson assaults raised consumer doubts, and sales suffered. It took years for them to stabilize.

Stout Defenses in the 1970s

The stout defense of Alka-Seltzer was steadily maintained through the 1970s. On several occasions between 1974 and 1976, more Miles' evidence and testimony was submitted to the Analgesics Panel.

Through these years, the most critical problem swirled around the Analgesics Panel with its "hard line" on aspirin products. Obviously, its adamant position that no form of aspirin should be taken when stomach distress was present flew in the face of the Antacid Panel's declaration of safety in concurrent symptoms.

This running battle with the Analgesics Panel went on for several years until the panel issued its report on July 8, 1977, with Miles continuing to build its case with new evidence that Alka-Seltzer does not cause stomach bleeding.

The company filed further material with the FDA in 1977 and 1978, with a dozen medical experts supporting the Miles position. Still more data were sent to the FDA in 1979. By fall of 1983, the FDA still had not issued its Tentative Final Order for Analgesic Products. From 1980, the center of attention had switched to the highly qualified Miscellaneous Internal Drug Products Panel. That Panel undertook a third review of the scientific evidence on Alka-Seltzer. Miles submitted its initial data to this panel in February 1976, and more on April 15 of the same year, both supporting claims on overindulgence. Then, on July 17, 1980, the company handed over to the FDA and the Panel quite possibly the most comprehensive documents ever compiled in the history of the over-the-counter drug review: nine bulging sets of 400 scientific papers bound into 16 books, weighing 650 pounds. The statement and argument took 160 pages, single-spaced.

Here, for the moment at least, was the accumulated wisdom on Alka-Seltzer. On August 8–9, 1980, Miles' medical witnesses testified before the Panel. Afterwards, on October 1, 1982, the Panel recommended that the FDA again approve the famed

medication as safe and effective for the concurrent symptoms of headache and upset stomach associated with overindulgence, rejecting again the Analgesic Panel's position. Miles submitted even more data on January 28, 1983.

Miles Funds More Studies on Its Famous Product

The eventual regulatory status of Alka-Seltzer rests with science. This is why Miles has for so long given cardinal urgency to sponsoring and funding its various studies, along with symposia on pertinent areas of science.

In 1981, Miles, along with other major companies with products containing aspirin, supported the founding of the Aspirin Foundation of America. Joseph M. White, M.D., long a consultant to Miles, representing Miles on the Board, was elected chairman and serves as president of the Foundation.

Millions of people remember the familiar Alka-Seltzer Dispenser— for many years a fixture at thousands of drugstore fountains.

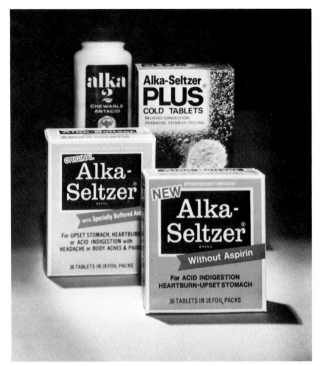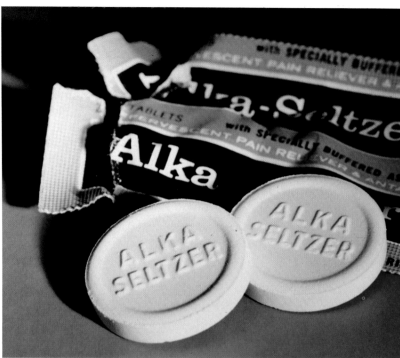

Several line extensions were added to the classic Alka-Seltzer in foil.

A worldwide network of experts constantly seeks more understanding of aspirin, whose fate has for so long been entwined with that of Alka-Seltzer. By the early 1970s, scientists began to suspect that small daily doses of aspirin in some instances might cut the risk of heart attacks. Angina pectoris is severe chest pain caused by deficient oxygen in the heart due to blocked or narrowing arteries. Unstable angina is a new or sudden worsening of the pain without increased activity.

The theory that aspirin could help prevent angina found dramatic support in a report in the August 18, 1983, issue of the *New England Journal of Medicine*. In a seven-year study of 1,266 men in Veterans Hospitals, aspirin, in the form of a daily dose of one Alka-Seltzer tablet dissolved in water, had a "highly protective effect, a 51 percent reduction, against acute myocardial infarction in men with unstable angina. The data also suggest a similar reduction in mortality."

Why was Alka-Seltzer used? In other trials, larger doses of unaltered aspirin given in tablets or capsules had caused gastrointestinal side effects, including bleeding. With the buffering action of Alka-Seltzer and the aspirin converted to water soluble sodium acetylsalicylate, the VA subjects were free of

such side effects. Alka-Seltzer emerged as the safest way to take aspirin.

The report was a notable scientific victory, a particularly agreeable one on the eve of the Centennial.

The Impact of Alka-Seltzer on Miles

From the early 1930s, the impact of Alka-Seltzer on company sales, finances, and growth was swift and profound. Miles had limped into the Depression, clinging stubbornly to its brittle and aging line of products, still flooding the country with its popular Little Books, calendars, and almanacs. With little new in the offing, it had no choice but to promote what it had. The 1931 Annual Report noted that "some items must eventually be eliminated from promotional effort, such as Cactus Compound, Tonic, Laxative Tablets, and Alterative Compounds." It was a signal that dangerous shoals lay ahead.

It is fascinating today to look at the sales charts drawn for Miles' early years, with the lines bending ever so slowly upward. Then Alka-Seltzer came on the scene with 1931 sales of $112,333. The second full year in 1933 brought volume close to $400,000. Then began what was for the times a spectacular spurt—from $2.1 million in 1934 to $8.7 million in 1937. Sales plateaued a few years, not reaching a new high until passing $9 million in 1943.

With the static nature of the rest of the line, the bulge in the charts for Alka-Seltzer was stunning, especially in a deep Depression rife with business failures, sales and profit slumps, and unemployment at frightening levels.

Caution Prevailed at First

Annual reports in the first few Alka-Seltzer years give the impression that the company hadn't yet realized what it had within its grasp. Either that, or caution prevailed. Not until 1936 does the annual report use "wonderful" and "marvelous" to describe sales. By that year, too, the strain on manufacturing facilities was severe. The plant was running two shifts of nine hours, seven days a week. The product's success forced plans for the major new building, dedicated in 1938.

Alka-Seltzer sales reached $13 million in 1946 and have grown steadily ever since, with some year-by-year dips and some loss of market share.

Diversification did not come as rapidly as the company would have liked, so by 1950, Alka-Seltzer still accounted for 73 percent of total sales. It accounted for 91 percent of all foreign volume as late as 1953. By 1975, sales amounted to $52 million in the United States alone, and as the Miles Centennial approached, world sales exceeded $100 million, with about 65 percent credited to domestic and 35 percent to foreign operations.

Even with all of Miles' diversification and growth, Alka-Seltzer remains the company's largest single product, a remarkable achievement. Resting on laurels has not been the key either: Since not everybody liked the taste of the effervescing drink, experimentation seldom lagged in seeking an even more acceptable product. Much effort went into new flavors, lemon and mint among them. The citrus-flavored formulation was test marketed as early as 1960. It probably would have added 10 percent to volume, according to A. D. Little studies, but tests through the years showed that the average user did not want to turn to another kind of Alka-Seltzer.

The Alka-Seltzer Line Grows

Meanwhile, marketers closely watched medical and over-the-counter fashions and acted accordingly. Lemon-flavored "Alka-Seltzer Plus Cold Tablets" (later changed to Cold Medicine), introduced in

A commemorative medal was struck after the 100 billionth Alka-Seltzer tablet rolled off the line in 1981, the product's 50th year.

1969, contains an antihistamine, a decongestant, and an analgesic (aspirin, of course). Alka-Seltzer Gold is for people who need, or prefer, an antacid without aspirin. In 1976, Alka-2, a tasty chewable antacid tablet, made its debut. These are without question excellent products that have bolstered the consumer line, with their volume reflecting the amount of promotion deemed affordable.

Regardless of what happens to Alka-Seltzer in the years to come, its place in the history of home remedies stands secure for all time. Few products have been around for 50 years. Fewer still have sold at the rate of two billion tablets a year. Yet, here it is, not only busily fizzing into its second half-century, but with new uses being suggested in the medical literature.

Alka-Seltzer was the making of modern Miles. For its profits funded research for other products and led the company down avenues of diversification.

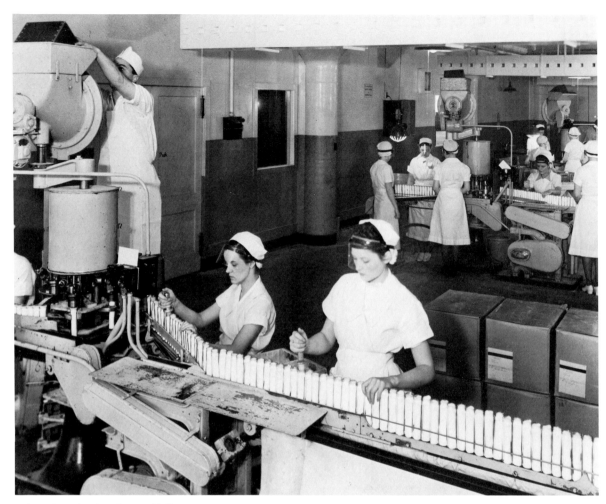

Alka-Seltzer bottling line in 1943.

CHAPTER 5

Vitamin Vim And Vigor

The proclivity of Miles Laboratories to identify a human need and then move to meet it has never been better exemplified than in the field of nutrition. The need had long been apparent. As witnesses before a Senate Committee as late as 1970 testified, the United States was still a nation of "nutritional illiterates."

In a speech in 1973, Dr. Walter Compton said:

What we began to realize in the early 1940s, and is now becoming generally understood, is the widespread incidence in our own country not only of a malnutritional lack but also of a different kind of malnutrition . . . the symptoms of relative degrees of vitamin and mineral deficiencies, of protein imbalance, and of such serious medical problems as obesity and premature cardiovascular failure.

It is in preventing this "different kind of malnutrition," mainly inadequate vitamin consumption, that Miles has had a historic role. It did not develop the very first vitamin preparation, but it did market one of the earliest and perhaps most memorable one, with a name that has survived more than four decades. It is, of course, One-A-Day.

Miles was to market other prestigious vitamin products, with names like Chocks and Flintstones and Bugs Bunny that were to lift the company to market leadership among nationally advertised brands. It would, through promotion and educational efforts, teach the public the value of vitamins and minerals to health. It would pioneer, in their manufacturing, little-understood accomplishments that were, however, of enormous importance in making vitamins easy and pleasant to take.

Ethical Leadership, Always a Miles' Goal

In the 40 years of its strong presence and supremacy in the supplemental vitamin field, it would also maintain an ethical leadership, eschewing faddism and holding, in the main, to government and scientific standards of recommended daily allowances. It paid a price in doing so, but Walter Compton and his colleagues insisted upon this policy long after many competitors abandoned it, and when others rushed blindly into formulations unsupported by evidence, medical or otherwise.

The vitamin-mineral background that preceded the invention of the classic One-A-Day vitamins in 1940 is one of the best-known stories in medical history.

In 1747, a British surgeon, Lind, demonstrated that sailors long denied fresh food recovered remarkably from scurvy when fed oranges and lemons. Thus the first clue was recognizing that a vital substance existed in certain foods—a concept verified by studies on beri-beri conducted by Nobel Prize winner Christian Ejkmann in the Dutch East Indies between 1893 and 1897.

Other data were gradually accumulated and in 1912 the Polish scientist, Casimir Funk, coined the word "vitamines"; it was later changed, of course, to "vitamins." The first actual identification of vitamin A came in 1913. That opened the gateway to discovery, first of the better-known vitamins, then, after 1940, of still others. Since then, studies have concentrated on the biochemical function of these miniscule, potent substances and their interrelationships with enzymes, hormones, and minerals, as well as with each other.

Vitamins Are a Part of Enzyme Systems

Research shows that vitamins act as part of enzyme systems and are involved with the metabolism of sugars, fats, and proteins. They are either water soluble or fat soluble, although the division is not absolute. Most burn up in the body, and must be replaced from outside sources. They have no calories.

Vitamins take part in chains of swift chemical reactions that release energy from foods, and act in various vital processes affecting organs, blood, nerves, circulation, and the mind itself.

They are essential to life. Without them all kinds of illnesses and complaints develop—from irritability and digestive disorders to the now rarely seen scurvy, rickets, pellagra, and beri-beri.

We do know quite a bit about what minute amounts can accomplish. For example, six micrograms (.000006 grams; 28.35 grams equal 1 ounce) of vitamin B$_{12}$ daily keep a pernicious anemia patient in good health. The U.S. Department of Agriculture's recommended daily allowance of 13 vitamins in a year's time would add up to only 1½ ounces.

So the need for vitamins and minerals has been established for decades. No longer can anyone question the fact that normal health is impossible without an adequate supply working busily within the body. But another question has simmered for decades: Doesn't the average person, on a reasonably balanced diet, get enough vitamins without the need for supplements? That core inquiry has never been answered satisfactorily.

A series of events surrounded Miles' decision to enter the market. The first "vitamania era" struck in the 1930s. It came on strong at first. Aided by press accounts, vitamins became popular in the health field. A few medical authorities jumped on the vitamin bandwagon, sometimes making extravagant claims. The U.S. Public Health Service reported that 40 percent of the population had inadequate diets. In 1934, the first vitamin extract began appearing on drugstore counters. Such proprietary merchandisers as Vicks and Lever Brothers introduced their "Vitamins-Plus" and "Vimms."

Making a Case for Vitamins

Part of the agenda that Dr. Compton drew up for the company when he joined it as the new medical director in 1938 called for diversification into the controversial field of vitamins. He was fortunate enough to recruit Dr. Michael A. Rafferty, associate professor of biochemistry at West Virginia University. Dr. Rafferty came from a big Irish family in Appalachia and had observed first-hand the effect of malnutrition. He received his M.D. from Rush Medical College (Dr. Miles' alma mater) in 1937.

As Miles' assistant medical director, Dr. Rafferty worked very closely with Dr. Compton toward "a total conviction that one of our major targets had to be nutrition and the combating of malnutrition." The fruits of their labors had just begun to appear on the

Dr. Michael A. Rafferty served as Miles' assistant medical director for only four years before he died on the battlefields of Europe in 1944. He and Dr. Compton worked closely on the development of One-A-Day vitamins.

market as the first multiple vitamin preparations made available to the public when, sadly, Dr. Rafferty—now Major Rafferty—was killed in action in Belgium, November 24, 1944. The young man, only 39 at the time, had captured the affections and fired the imaginations of those at Elkhart who knew him, and advertising manager Oliver B. Capelle, in a commemorative service, fittingly quoted these lines from the poet Dryden:

"Whate'er he did was done with so much ease,
    In him alone 'twas natural to please."

Even in the 1930s, there wasn't much question about what comprised an adequate diet, and the Department of Agriculture's recommendations carried much credence. In theory, anyone who stuck to such varied fare would get enough vitamins and minerals to maintain good health. But what of countervailing factors: variations in edible plants caused by differences in soil, use of fertilizer, sunlight, etc.; variations in the composition of animal meats and dairy products; and variations in the preparation and cooking of foods? Were these factors intangibles? Perhaps, but they were factors nonetheless.

Consistent Philosophy for the Decades

It seemed clear that a nutritional deficit existed quite apart from the malnutrition caused by the economic hardships of the Depression.

National eating habits centered more and more on meats and dairy products and less on cereals, fruits, and vegetables. Food faddism was popular, and nutritional intake varied from one part of the country to another. Neglect of adequate diet by the aging was a problem then as now.

In 1963 Dr. Compton reviewed the case for supplementation—a case that a stream of studies had reconfirmed.

"It is not enough to eat a diet almost adequate in almost all the vitamins," he wrote. "Each must

literally be certain he gets enough of every one of the vitamins...."

"Unquestionably, many persons get a sufficient intake of most of their vitamins...and some even manage to get all the essential ones from food...no one really knows with certainty who *does*. We can't make all the vitamins for ourselves, and even though the quantity we need is actually small, it is often hard to get this quantity. Millions of people, in fact, don't. Since many of the vitamins are water soluble, storage in the body is brief at best. Consequently, a consistent, regular intake of vitamins is essential, as well as an adequate total intake for life.

"Fortunately, an insured vitamin intake is available. It can prevent...deficiency resulting from inadequate intake or poor eating habits....Rules out danger of loss of vitamin quality in foods caused by poor storage or processing. It protects against the vagaries of appetite. It offers vitamins in a form that can be absorbed more readily...one tablet taken daily can meet total needs...while adding less than 3¢ a day to the daily cost of [one person's] food."

After World War II, this booklet was mailed to virtually every household in the United States, explaining the importance of vitamins to good health.

Compton Coaxes Miles into Vitamins

In the late 1930s, the young Dr. Compton, with his developing interest in nutrition, zestfully persuaded Miles to get into vitamins. By the time he left to serve in World War II, he had put his imprint on yet another historic venture. True, for some years profits were not easily attained in the marketing of vitamins, but eventually they would confirm Compton's vision and help make the company successful for decades to come.

Miles' first vitamin preparation, bearing the trademark One-A-Day, moved into distributor warehouses and drugstores in October 1940. Those initial soft gelatin capsules contained vitamins A and D. The capsule was standard, decreed by the technology of the time, and was supplied by outside contractors.

Aggressively advertised and promoted, One-A-Day did not just edge timidly into the market. Instead it made a bold thrust. Learning from the successes of Alka-Seltzer, One-A-Day was immediately advertised on a national radio network and on shows such as the "National Barndance," "Quiz Kids," and the "Alec Templeton Show." Commercials bore the tagline, "Look for the Big *One* on the Package." It worked well and, with modifications, lasted a long time.

Everyone a Promotional Target

Grandparents, adults, and children were all promotional targets, and, as time went on, ingenious advertising broadened from the relatively staid beginnings. As with various Alka-Seltzer ads of the period, even verse was attempted, as in this 1943 version:

> The One-A-Day vitamin twins are we,
> B Complex and A & D,
> And we're the ones, we must confess,
> Who give you more, yet cost you less.

Such concepts as "tissue starvation" also crept into the copy. Thus Miles was on its way early toward teaching the public about vitamins. It was in the vanguard that developed the entire business.

Of course, 1940 hadn't been the most propitious time to plunge into the field. Times were still grim, and a vitamin market was yet to be established. Even with substantial promotion, One-A-Day struggled for product awareness among consumers. Volume declined in 1941. But the new B-Complex tablets, introduced in January 1942, and the One-A-Day multivitamins, appearing in 1943, revived sagging sales. Success came slowly, and many talented people

had a hand in building the business in the early years. The first manufacturing aim was to propel the company beyond the soft gelatin capsule stage. It took endless experimentation, with the B-complex formula in 1942 an early success.

In 1948, sugar-coated One-A-Day multivitamins first appeared. Competition arose from such retail giants as Sears and Jewel Tea, as well as from small private label companies.

Miles adhered to the Recommended Dietary Allowances first introduced by the National Research Council in 1943. Such standards were based on a planned national study of the need and availability of nutrients in the diet. But not everybody paid them scrupulous attention, even when the FDA established its own dietary standards called Minimum Daily Requirements. Meanwhile, vitamin promotion had waned; in the late 1940s, Miles was virtually the only company trying to reach the public.

With few regulatory inhibitions marking the 1950s, specialty claims and companies proliferated, especially with the explosion in television advertising. The vitamin market flourished, reaching a high of about $350 million by the end of the decade. This was not to be exceeded for some years, perhaps because the public had become disenchanted by the advertising excesses of some manufacturers.

Miles stuck to its insurance concept, boosted advertising, and took One-A-Day vitamins into large grocery and discount chains. In 1951, it discontinued the A & D and B-Complex products, and in 1952 came out with an improved multiple tablet.

Miles' share of the market kept growing faster than the category in the 1960s, assuring continuation of One-A-Day vitamins in first place among branded vitamins, the position it still holds. The share of total market decreased, however, as single vitamins, megadoses, and unusual combinations promoted door-to-door and through health food stores propelled the category first to $1 billion in annual sales, then to $2 billion in the 1970s and 1980s. For the most part, Miles stuck to government recommended daily allowances, letting other less medically-oriented companies take the unorthodox routes. This strategy was being reviewed at Centennial time, but drastic changes appeared unlikely.

A Regulatory Victory for Vitamins

Among notable regulatory triumphs in the annals of Miles, the one on vitamins ranks high. The story began in 1966 when the FDA sought to standardize vitamin supplements. It also said there was no "scientific basis" for using them. That statement earned notoriety as "the crepe label." Miles and other parties immediately filed legal objections to the proposed regulation. Miles' general counsel John B. Buckley mustered company opposition to the "crepe label" and FDA-proposed restrictions on claims which struck at the very heart of the company's dietary supplement business.

The team recruited to defend the company's position included Joseph M. White, M.D., a Miles medical consultant; James M. Johnstone of Kirkland & Ellis, and company staff. They consulted with nationally known nutritionists, hematologists, and other scientific experts. For the first time ever, available literature on the nutritional status of the American public was assembled and reported in the *Journal of Nutrition Education*.

In hearings on the proposed regulation, Miles put in its documentary evidence the testimony of more than a dozen witnesses, among them Dr. Jean Mayer of Harvard University, and Dr. George Briggs, of the University of California. Following more than two years of hearings, the FDA in final regulations of August 1973 scrapped the "crepe label" and modified its proposed restrictions on claims. Out of this episode came full support for the Miles position embracing the "insurance concept" of daily vitamin and mineral supplementation.

As general counsel, John B. Buckley led Miles' opposition to FDA-proposed restrictions on vitamin claims in the 1960s.

Chocks: The First Tasty Vitamin for Children

Almost a quarter of a century ago, inventive people in Miles' development labs nurtured the idea that a tasty vitamin tablet for children would find ready acceptance. They gave it a lot of attention. In September 1958, product development and marketing people found a name they liked—Chocks. But creating a product for successful marketing was another matter. Tests started that year, with chocolate-coated tablets in six colors and an uncoated fruit-flavored version.

Vitamins were sold in apothecary jars, and new production lines were designed to fill them.

Automated vitamin filling operations required careful surveillance.

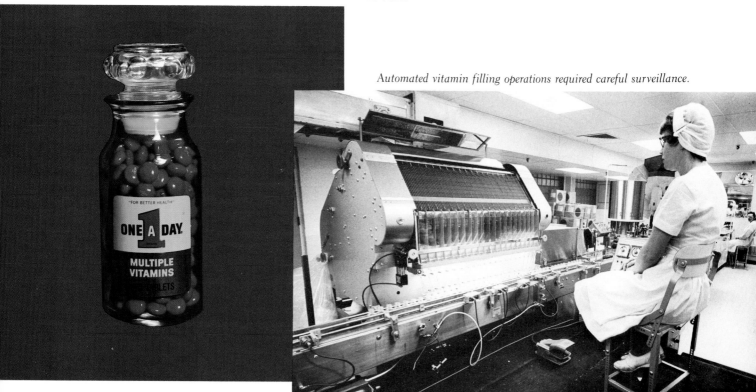

Test marketing began with a modest national introduction by the turn of the decade. It didn't go too well.

The 1960s, however, were to bring success to Chocks—introduced in 1960. Again, the key to that success was Miles' technology. It simply pulled ahead of its rivals in developing chewable vitamin-mineral combinations. With a tasteless base, many flavors could be used.

In 1962, Mead-Johnson's Vi-Sols went on the market. In the shape of animal crackers, they provided tough but no real lasting competition to the popular trapezoid-shaped Chocks. In 1963, a modified Chocks appeared—uncoated in five colors and with an improved fruit flavor. They sold well.

One-A-Day Plus Iron Boosts the Market

Now, back to adult vitamins for a moment. In 1964, iron was added to the One-A-Day formula. A heavily advertised product at the time was Geritol, aimed at the geriatric market, with a heavy emphasis on its iron content. Should Geritol be challenged directly? If so, how, and with what name? As the marketing people knew, a "flanker" product presented high risks.

Blaze Palermo, the vitamin development expert, thought the challenge of adding iron was well worth accepting but not especially for the geriatric market. He based his decision on the medical fact that women in their menstrual period need as much as 50 percent more iron than men. Bob Wallace, division president, and others enthusiastically approved the idea of meeting this market need. Thus, by 1965, One-A-Day Multiple Vitamins Plus Iron forged its way into a market where consumer awareness of the need for iron was growing. Within a few years, One-A-Day Plus Iron was outselling the regular One-A-Day.

Then came 1968—always to be a landmark year for Miles' children's vitamins. The J. Walter Thompson advertising agency suggested making the tablets in the shape of the famous Flintstones cartoon characters, and that year a contract was signed with the copyright owners. As Don Bryant, once head of Consumer Products, recollects, "This proved to be more successful than we had reason to hope. Using the characters as animated spokesmen in commercials worked well. We soon outdistanced our competitors."

Technology Makes It All Possible

Behind Miles' success in vitamins stand the twin pillars of technology and promotion. There have always been technical challenges. Take the irregularly shaped Flintstones. Manufacturing was convinced the characters would crumble and fade in the bottle. Production experts know well the challenges of assuring consistent quality. Tablet making is an art of its own, involving such factors as speed and timing of compaction; selection of additives, fillers, binders, and colors, not to mention sensitivity to moisture, thickness of coatings, and so on. Moreover, any tablet, no matter how perfectly made, is worthless unless it releases its individual ingredients properly in the digestive tract.

Even so, Palermo and his aides, George Hoss, Ron Duvall, and Larry Daher, devised formulations where the jagged shapes of the Flintstones characters survived compressing procedures and remained intact when packaged. The success of these quietly brilliant scientists should not have been surprising. After all, their combined total experience came to some 85 years by 1983!

Clearly, their achievements and those of the development laboratories as a whole rank high in Miles' history.

Children's chewable vitamins were first introduced by Miles in 1960. In 1969 they assumed the cartoon-character shapes. Miles sells more branded children's multivitamins than any other company.

Flintstones vitamins.

Cyclamate Banning Causes a Near Disaster

The 1960s did not end without a diversion—in fact, a near disaster for the chewable vitamin industry. On October 15, 1969, on the grounds that it could be carcinogenic, the FDA suddenly banned the use of cyclamate, a widely known sweetener. It was extensively used in foods, beverages, and drugs as a sugar substitute, and was a particular boon to diabetics. It was the preferred sweetening substance in Chocks and Flintstones.

Galvanized into action by what many remember as Black Friday, the development specialists worked day and night for four days to come up with a reformulated chewable tablet that included saccharin. It was a poor-tasting substitute and was eventually discarded with disdain.

Luckily, Miles knew as much about compacting sugar as anybody, and its first major accomplishment in the 1970s was perfecting its use in the chewable vitamin line. Working with the American Sugar Corporation, it developed a special form of sucrose, a compressible form of sugar. The result was a large chewable tablet that tasted better than any others. By 1972, Flintstones Vitamins, with newer flavors, made their entry in sucrose form. They thus helped restore Miles' chewables to their pre-cyclamate popularity. Each tablet, incidentally, contains less than one-fourth of a teaspoon of sugar—not much in a child's daily diet.

The Magic of Film Coating

The year 1972 was to be etched into Miles' memory for another important reason—the introduction of the film-coating system, which surpasses every other achievement in the field of tablet technology. To appreciate its magnitude, one must note how vitamins were made and coated before this development.

Compacted tablets containing the recommended daily allowance of vitamins and minerals (bitter to taste) would be ladled into large, drum-shaped rotating pans, where the 125,000 tablets in each batch would eventually be coated with sugar. This may sound simple, but it wasn't. One of the biggest challenges was to prevent moisture from migrating into the tablet itself. An intermediate cover of shellac or other impervious lacquers was used. Then the operators of the rotating pans could gradually coat the tablets with high concentrations of syrup. This drawn-out cycle lasted three full days. Near the end of the process, color was added along with wax to give the tablets a smooth, polished look.

The key to this lengthy procedure was not

Vitamins were dispensed free not only at Miles but also at the Adams and Westlake Company next door. The "vitamin lady" always dressed like a nurse.

equipment but man. Sugar coating demanded a unique sort of artistry. Through the years, when it represented the state of the art, Miles had about 40 expert coaters at any given time. This was probably the best assemblage of such artisans in the industry. At that time, sugar was relatively inexpensive, and one skilled person could operate two or three coating pans. For this reason, there was no particular outcry for change—except in Miles' development labs.

As early as the 1950s, Palermo and his experts felt that ultimately a very thin film coating involving an organic solvent system would replace thick sugar coating. Technically they knew it could be possible. The larger concern, however, was how the cost would compare to that of the sugar-coating process.

In addition, as Palermo points out, film coating had to come because new ingredients for One-A-Day formulations required larger tablets. Since any alteration had to conform with the One-A-Day image, the consumer would have to be comfortable with a familiar size, shape, color, and taste.

Uniformity and Automation Achieved

Making any change involved three problems awaiting solutions. The first was resolved with better machinery that punched out uniform tablets amena-

The bottle with a safety cap replaced the apothecary jar.

ble to thin coatings. The second demanded improvement of a film-coating principle developed at the University of Wisconsin in 1962. Miles was the first company to modify the idea and highly automate the process, helping make it a commercial success. Essentially, in this ingenious process, the tablets are sprayed with polymers and colors while being agitated by a heated air stream in long, circular glass cylinders. The whirling tablets dry as they cascade down the sides of the cylinders, while the solvents, including methylene chloride and alcohol, are "flashed" away.

But what do you do with the solvents? That was the third problem. Miles solved it characteristically by devising a system to capture the solvent vapors and ultimately reuse them. In this involved process, the material flows through a charcoal bed and into a fractionating column that separates the methylene chloride and the alcohol.

"We recover 98 percent of the material we use," Palermo notes. "So theoretically we're still using today some of the first methylene we put into the system a decade ago."

This was important, too, since the solvents did not have to be expelled into the atmosphere, thereby eliminating any possible environmental hazard.

Development felt it was ready to recommend the system as early as 1967, but it took a long time to sell the concept to others, especially skeptical manufacturing veterans. Meanwhile, a regulatory threat was hanging over vitamins that would have made it more difficult to use desired formulations. This fact spurred the arguments of the development team. Finally, after strong support from marketing and Walter Compton, who had favored the concept from the beginning, the new process came into being. Sadly, in a way, the coating artisans became obsolete. But other work in the company was found for them.

The system worked as intended: it just about wiped out the moisture problem; the cylindrical columns spewed forth stable and uniform tablets, and it was all cost effective. The old three-day cycle per batch was slashed to 70 minutes and later to even less than that. Miles believes that no one in the industry can surpass the technical finesse of its film-coating process. It certainly added more flexibility to vitamin making. For example, in 1976 One-A-Day Plus Minerals—a product containing eleven vitamins and seven minerals—bolstered the line.

The Megadose Era Builds Popularity

During the decade of the 1970s competition intensified, partly because Congress, in 1976, passed a law restricting FDA authority over vitamin regulations. This emboldened the health food industry and others to broadcast far-reaching claims and to expand and specialize. Even the most reputable of houses came out with versions of "megadose" brands. These trends stranded such firms as Miles on an ethical island.

Nevertheless, the vitamin-mineral field in the early 1980s appeared to be a fairly safe anchorage. It was rapidly expanding. Scientific evidence questioning megadoses was lacking. Without evidence of toxic reactions, the FDA expressed disinterest. Its Over-the-Counter Review Panel finally published a report on vitamins in late 1981; it got little attention, and the Panel itself was disbanded. Consumers reacted well to the new products, perhaps on the theory that more is better, and the medical profession raised few questions. The popularity of vitamins and minerals for maintaining health and even preventing disease had never been greater.

Consequently, Miles had little alternative but to broaden its lines and approaches. Its first departure from the conservatism of the past came in 1980, when greater amounts of vitamin C were added in One-A-Day Core C 500 and Flintstones with Extra C. The new Core C featured 500 milligrams of vitamin C, bonded in a single tablet with nine other essential vitamins. A reformulation of One-A-Day Plus Minerals came along, too.

Staying on Top with Chewables

Through the changing decades, Miles never did lose its market position in the chewable field. Today, six chewable dosage forms in colorful packaging embellish the vitamin counters of America and the world—Flintstones, Flintstones with Iron, Flint-

stones with Extra C, Bugs Bunny, Bugs Bunny Plus Iron, and Bugs Bunny with Extra C. (As an immortal of the cartoon world, Bugs had "joined" the team in 1971.) All these favorites have at least five flavors and six shapes.

A new adult entry, Stressgard vitamins, was launched in 1981 to compete with Lederle's StressTabs, then the leading high B-Complex product. Stressgard offered the key vitamins and high-potency B-Complex with 600 milligrams of vitamin C, plus iron, copper, and zinc. This was a lot of vitamin power indeed. Meanwhile, graphics brightened the entire multivitamin line with new packaging.

More was to come. In late 1982, Miles announced two new adult vitamins—One-A-Day Enriched Singles and One-A-Day Vitapace, the latter a uniquely engineered product designed to deliver B-Complex and C vitamins in two stages, portions of them at once and the rest gradually.

For all its strengthened formulas, Miles adheres essentially to high standards. Its branded products, with their long traditions and broad "family" concept, have an assured basis in science and nutrition. Miles continues to be "a company that cares about nutrition."

Promotion Paves the Way

As mentioned earlier, One-A-Day vitamins would not have gotten started without skillful promotion. They certainly could not have grown and been sustained without it. The vitamin story would be quite incomplete without references to the skills of company and agency people who not only made One-A-Day and the children's vitamins famous trademarks but in the process built public knowledge and awareness of nutrition.

Toward that end, the company did considerably more than consumer advertising. It supported the scientific studies of the National Vitamin Foundation, then robustly backed the work of its offshoot, the Vitamin Information Bureau. For years Miles was the biggest corporate contributor. The bureau provided educational materials to students, health professionals, and the general public. It sponsored press seminars in which clinical researchers presented studies on nutrition.

In the early years, One-A-Day vitamin ads, both in print and on radio, did not resort to much flamboyance or exaggeration. Sometimes, in fact, they lacked the off-beat zest of Alka-Seltzer commercials. Clearly, the intent was to be simple and factual,

with such lines as "You will find A & D (or later B-Complex) easier to take—less expensive—a single tablet daily is all you take."

Marketing acumen was vital. For example, in the late 1940s, it was decided to hitchhike vitamin commercials onto every Miles program. This meant tacking 35-second commercials at the end of programs Miles sponsored on behalf of other products. Thus saturation radio advertising began on such shows as "Saturday Night Round-Up" (the successor to the "National Barn Dance"), "The Quiz Kids," "News of the World," and "Lum 'n Abner." In 1949, One-A-Day vitamins finally reached television, and the advertising-to-sales ratio, as an old internal monograph noted, "began to take a favorable turn."

Ads That Educate

In the years since TV became the lodestone of modern advertising, One-A-Day vitamin commercials may not have achieved the fame or awards of Alka-Seltzer, but they have often had as much charm and cleverness.

In the late 1960s some TV series closed with the slogans, "The world's most trusted vitamin," "family vitamin insurance," "double coated for double protection just to be on the safe side," and "the pill for people who don't know what they're missing." Ad after ad pounded away on a basic point: "We snack more and you can't be sure what vitamins you're getting in today's processed foods"; "Experts worry that Americans are eating more empty calories"; "Fad diets...never enough time...you don't have to be poor to eat poorly."

The ads didn't hesitate to say boldly, "If you're one of those people who knows he eats well-balanced meals every day, forget our product...." They spoke as well of the "nutrition recession."

Promotion did a particularly convincing job with One-A-Day Plus Iron in catering directly to the requirements of women for iron supplementation. Some typical ad lines: "You never forget your outside makeup. Well, don't forget your inside makeup. Your One-A-Day Plus Iron," or "Just because you're a woman, your evenings are 50 percent more glamorous. You solve 50 percent more tragedies, make 50 percent more executive decisions. And, for most of your life, you need 50 percent more iron than that big male animal...." Some ads referred to this product as "the other pill," thus piggybacking on wide publicity given at the time to birth control pills.

With variations, sometimes using music and

singers, these kinds of spots interlaced TV programs in the 1960s and 1970s. They unquestionably helped maintain the company's foothold in a vitamin market pervaded by not only small and not always reliable producers but by the pharmaceutical giants as well—Abbott, Upjohn, Parke-Davis, Squibb, Roche, Eli Lilly, and so on. With changes in FDA regulations, Miles' adherence to government standards offered no advantage, and without expert marketing, Miles would have been submerged by its rivals.

Meeting the Competition Head On

By the early 1980s, Miles was no longer hesitant in meeting the competition head on. One TV spot noted that Theragran had 16 vitamins and minerals, Myadec 17, and Centrum 21. Miles claimed victory at that particular moment in the numbers game, with 24 vitamins "in a more complete formula." Ads for Stressgard dueled with claims of competitors, too, with such copy as "physiological wear and tear, long hours, and hard work that can deplete C and B-Complex vitamins, water-soluble vitamins your diets may not replace... make sure you get them back and more...."

Advertising for children's vitamins conveyed a flair of its own, both in print and on TV, building on such points as, "A Government survey has shown that among pre-schoolers, nine out of ten didn't get the recommended levels of iron," and, "five out of ten... the recommended amounts of vitamins A and C."

Some spots featured Flintstones characters in situations such as a dinosaur race; others often blended humor with the rationale for vitamins. (Fred Flintstone: "I'm the world's funniest-looking authority on kids.") Children, of course, have been used appealingly in many ads—even though the messages have been aimed carefully at mothers.

In one ad, youngsters are shown with Flintstones mugs (offered free with proof of purchase and $.50 postage). One child remarks that he's "smug" about his "mug," another that this has been a "plug for Flintstone mugs."

Maintaining Technological Leadership

Maintaining technological leadership in vitamins still gets top priority. "You are never anywhere near satisfied or finished," Palermo once stressed. The problem with minerals in chewable vitamins is a case in point. Minerals taste bitter and astringent, so

this calls for new technology. At the start of this decade, Miles embarked on a basic program, especially studying calcium and magnesium. The worst-tasting minerals besides these two are zinc, copper, and manganese; none in their natural state can possibly please the palate.

However, as in the past, Miles found the answer in innovative technology. Larry Daher and George Hoss spearheaded a concentrated research effort that finally provides these essential minerals in a tasteless yet readily absorbable form. This new discovery was the development laboratory's crowning achievement in the area of chewable tablets and resulted in the marketing of Flintstones Complete with Iron, Calcium, and Minerals. In 1983, it was the only chewable vitamin-mineral tablet containing calcium, which is perhaps the most vital mineral for growing children.

Meanwhile, Palermo says even better vitamin formulations will come. He rates the "bridge" formulas out there now as very good, and is sure that Miles' specialists can concoct any formula Marketing thinks it can sell. That's confidence!

Self-Medication—A Highly Favorable Trend

Confidence, too, certainly isn't lacking with George Davy, the dynamic head of the Consumer Products Group. He sees the trends toward self-medication and preventive medicine as highly favorable to vitamins. "The relative lack of training and interest in nutrition among doctors, recognition of changing life styles as people live longer, plus general consumer awareness, all point toward vitamin supplementation as a daily ritual," says Davy. "It will be a flourishing market for years to come."

Scientifically, the field may still be in its infancy, in contrast to the pharmaceutical area. But eventually much more will be learned. "Meanwhile, we have a special responsibility to keep claims as accurate and formulations as supportable as we can," Davy adds. "And we will do just that."

Indeed, self-medication is founded upon the principle, embodied in the 1938 Federal Food, Drug, and Cosmetic Act, that the public has a right to purchase medicines safe for use, without the intervention of health professionals, on the basis of labelling on the packaging. Miles has stoutly defended this principle, both as a leader in the Proprietary Association and directly on its own. The dedication of the company to this concept is amply demonstrated by its resistance to FDA's 1963 legal action to limit Decholin, a drug then marketed by Ames, to prescription use. The Legal Department, under John B. Buckley, enlisted the aid of Joseph M. White, a medical consultant, and as trial counsel Bruce Brennan, who later became general counsel of the Pharmaceutical Manufacturers Association. The case was one of first impressions and the Government was forced to back down after a federal district court in Detroit firmly endorsed the legal basis for self-medication.

George Davy, president of the Consumer Products Division in the 1970s, oversaw extension of the vitamin line.

CHAPTER 6

To Help Heal The Hurt

The project tag, XM472, sounded like the code number for a plane or missile, but in Miles' Production Research Laboratory in 1947, it denoted an assignment to develop a "household antiseptic germicide for topical application."

Dr. Compton laid down the specifications, calling for a "painless, stainless, and colorless compound that would also not interfere with healing." Richard S. Nicholls, son-in-law of Maurice Treneer, and Dale E. Fonner, took on the project.

Another Famous Name

Within a few years, XM472 would become a product called Bactine—and Miles would have introduced another famous name soon to be found in virtually every medicine cabinet in America.

As the research team began its quest for an improved, safer, and gentler family antiseptic, perhaps the surprising thing is that nobody had done this previously. After all, man had been applying tars, balsams, and aromatic substances to torn skin since ancient times. In 1870, Lister won lasting fame with his theory of antisepsis, which led quickly to the use of agents to retard the growth of microorganisms in wounds. Carbolic acid (phenol) was the first. Lister used it himself in 1867.

Many others followed: citric acid, hexachlorophene, silver nitrate, boric acid, hydrogen peroxide, and so on, some of them still used decades after their initial discovery.

Possibly most familiar to the average person—in the pre-Bactine era—were iodine and mercurochrome. Iodine stung and stained. Mercurochrome may have stung less but it stained, too. So the field was wide open for a better product.

Aware of this, the Miles researchers probed the field of germicides, disinfectants, bacteriocides, and fungicides. They set high objectives: not only a stingless and stainless chemical, but one that would

Dr. Walter Compton guided development of Bactine antiseptic as the addition to "Miles' Family of Products" following multivitamins.

be aromatic or at least odorless, cooling, greaseless, and, of course, safe, effective, and easy to use. Nothing that good was on the market.

Their search centered on quaternary ammonium germicides, surface active agents, whose biological effects had aroused interest with the advent of a so-called "new class" of disinfectants around 1935. That such compounds could fight bacteria and "germs" was indisputable; just how they did it wasn't at all clear.

It didn't really matter. Exhaustive testing resulted in the right dilutions. Other ingredients were worked into the developing preparations over several years of effort. The exact formula remains a trade secret.

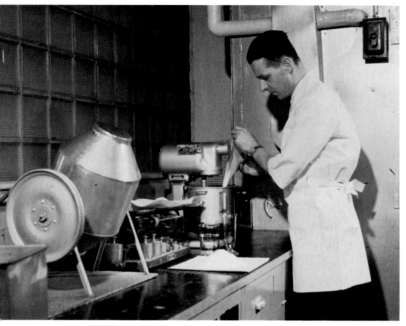

R. S. Nicholls helped develop and refine Bactine products.

"Germ-Killing. . . . Only a Small Part of the Story"

The effectiveness and success of Bactine, ultimately, as a 1964 monograph on the product states, was "due to the formula as a whole. . . . The germ-killing action is important but this is only a small part of the Bactine story." For what the research team finally perfected, the monograph laconically stated, "went considerably beyond their expectations."

It did indeed. The pharmacology of Bactine was impressive from the beginning. It demonstrated an ability to inhibit the growth and multiplication of bacteria. With that established, it was not surprising that Bactine found uses across the entire spectrum of topical medicine.

The substance proved it could relieve mild pain and itching caused by everything from mosquito bites to poison ivy. It could cleanse, soothe and cool, attack the fungi responsible for "athlete's foot," even in the contaminated socks causing it, and it could make water "wetter." It deodorized, removing garlic and onion odors from the hands, and disinfected scalpel blades, glass syringes, needles, and thermometers. Possibly better than the standard surgical scrub as a hand disinfectant, it could also numb the discomfort in minor burns.

Tests showed all this could be accomplished

without irritating the skin, and the compound wasn't really harmful, even if swallowed accidentally—a safety-in-the-home factor of some consequence.

With these characteristics, all documented by research, enthusiasm grew and marketing plans were rushed. Batches of the first liquid form went into test marketing in 1949. Consumer research unveiled promising results, and Bactine, as a medicated, spray-on first-aid "for cuts, scratches, scrapes, sunburn, minor burns, acne, and pimples" went into drug stores nationally in May 1950.

Wise Marketing Is the Key

The company knew instinctively that it had an excellent new consumer item, superior to anything else then available, so wise marketing was the key to success.

It took time and experience to find that formula. The first decision was to present Bactine to the general public and the medical profession simultaneously. Both popular magazines and medical journals ran the first printed ads, and eight radio shows began running commercials. Initial spots appeared on the TV version of the "Quiz Kids."

The first advertising stressed the multiple uses. While the claims were accurate, listeners apparently found them too good to be true. Sales in 1951, 1952, and 1953 hovered around $450,000 a year, hardly a satisfactory level. Another factor emerged: A bottle of Bactine would last a long time, so "repeat" business lagged.

In 1953, Walter Beardsley told his staff, "Either get this product going or take it off the market," Charles Reed recalls. "They made me the first product manager. I revamped the package. I was also instrumental in putting it in aerosol. We took the product from a plateau of $850,000 to $3 million in five years."

A turning point in marketing came after Dr. Ernest Dichter's study, in August 1953, found that Bactine claims were too general, leaving feelings of disbelief. So the advertising appeal was narrowed, emphasizing Bactine as a pleasant-to-use germicide for cuts, scratches, and abrasions, with secondary value in treating minor burns, sunburn, and itching from insect bites.

Direct the Message to Mom

The new focus helped. Perhaps bolstering the effort even further was the decision to direct the message to mothers—a practical approach that has

Emmett Manley checks the packaging of Bactine in 1954, along with Harry Beaver. On the line: Lois Eckhart, Manley, Bertha Long, Beaver, Irene Felthouse, Theresa Cataldo, and Mabel Spurling.

been followed right into the 1980s. By June 1954, sales began rising, and in 1955, they reached the $2 million mark.

The new ads carried such lines as, "When a little helper gets a burn," "To clean away the dirt and help heal the hurt," "When an elbow hits the dust," and "When tender skin gets too much sun"—all concluding with "Mom reaches for Bactine." In the 1960s an animated spokeswoman, Doreen, won popularity by singing a ditty that ended with "Down go the mean old germs." The Tatham, Laird & Kudner ads worked, and ever since, sales have proceeded modestly but steadily upward.

A Bactine Skin Cream was put on the market in 1965. Within a few years, however, not enough advertising support could be provided, and it was discontinued.

Taking the Number 1 Spot

Meanwhile, Bactine Aerosol continued on a steady course, becoming the largest branded skin-wound cleanser in the country. A big boost came in late 1980, when the FDA permitted hydrocortisone to be sold in topical over-the-counter products. Miles entered the market in 1981 with Bactine Hydrocortisone Skin Care Cream for skin irritation, rashes, and eczema. Bactine Hydrocortisone is even effective in reducing swelling. Also, Bactine Skin Wound Cleanser was reformulated in 1982 to contain lidocaine, thought to be a better anesthetic. It "foams away pain," a 1982 print ad said.

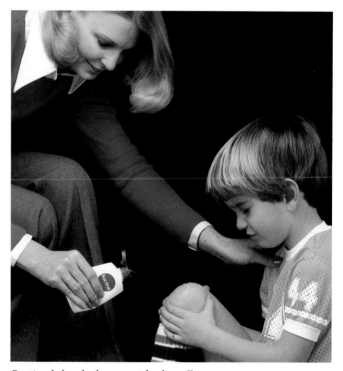

Bactine helps the hurt start healing. For many years, it has been the leading branded skin wound cleanser in the U.S.

"These improvements give us a greatly expanded franchise," explains Gordon Compton, director of marketing for Bactine. "Given the long brand-name awareness, and the trust and confidence consumers have placed in them, we see Bactine products growing steadily, perhaps even rapidly. Something a lot better will have to come along to challenge them. And how do you improve on a classic?"

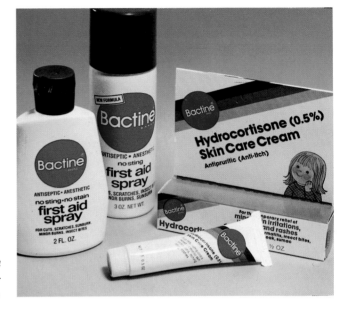

Hydrocortisone went from a prescription drug to an over-the-counter medication in 1982.

CHAPTER 7

From S.O.S To Insect Repellent

It may not be glamorous, but the S.O.S Steel Wool Soap Pad is as practical an item as ever squished its way into the work-a-day world. Housekeepers in North America use more than two million a day to scour pans, pots, and kettles.

Miles acquired S.O.S via one of those quick opportunities that sometimes confront management. In this instance, surely, no time was wasted. Bob Rose, then vice president of finance recalls well the day in September 1968, when he, Walter Beardsley, and Walter Compton strode into Citibank in New York at four o'clock on a Friday afternoon and briskly announced that in order to buy S.O.S they needed a check for $55 million—and not on Monday morning, but right away. A few of the bank officials blanched, but they promptly complied.

Dr. Compton acclaimed the acquisition "a major step in establishing a position in the household products market," and in helping Miles to diversify. Such a foothold had a lot of attraction at the time.

Since then, S.O.S has been entrenched, according to one observer, as "probably one of the top 10 grocery brand names in the U.S." It dominates a relatively small but profitable market. A truly classic product, it can be found in some 32 million U.S. households at any given time.

What Does S.O.S Stand For?

Curiously, no one seems to know what the acronym S.O.S really stands for other than one of America's best-known trademarks. (Note that no period is used after the second "S.") An *Alkalizer* article said that "no proof of its meaning exists" so far as is known by either General Foods or Miles. It apparently has no connection with the well-known international distress signal—although it can be argued that a housewife without S.O.S would indeed be in distress!

One legend has it that the inventor's wife coined

S.O.S steel wool soap pads are the largest selling household cleaning aid in their category in both the U.S. and Canada, with steady consumer loyalty.

the term to stand for "Save Our Saucepans." True or not, the origin of the pad has never been in doubt, and it fits squarely into U.S. and Miles' entrepreneurial traditions.

In 1917, a door-to-door salesman in San Francisco named Edwin Cox became aware that aluminum cookware he was selling was hard to keep clean and shiny, so he devised and patented a pad containing soap and steel wool. He began making it with a hand-dipped method, and it caught on.

Cox needed capital for production, so he sold his

71

patent rights on a geographical basis, first in 11 western states in 1919, then in the Midwest in 1920. Small plants were built in San Francisco and Chicago.

Sales Grow Even in the Depression

Even in the depressed 1930s, sales expanded encouragingly. While World War II curtailed the availability of steel for household items, volume still grew. The company also produced steel wool for army use as camouflage. In 1954, operations were consolidated in two leased plants on a 15-acre site in Bedford Park, a Chicago suburb.

Sales quadrupled between 1947 and 1957, with some of the credit going to early use of television advertising.

On January 1, 1958, the business was sold to General Foods. In 1963 the Federal Trade Commission ordered divestiture. General Foods fought back, but a U.S. Court of Appeals upheld the FTC decision. In May 1967, the U.S. Supreme Court refused to review the case, and the final FTC order to divest became effective May 1, 1968. At this point, the opportunity for Miles to purchase the business arose. The sale was completed September 3,1968.

By that time, other products had joined the original pad: S.O.Ettes, which had a sponge to back up the steel wool soap pad, and Tuffy, a plastic scouring ball, along with the metal cleaners, Copper-Kleen and Silver-Kleen. Tuffy, with its bright colors, soon became the leading mesh ball product. It was designed for light-duty scouring of non-stick cookware.

The S.O.S line includes supplementary items, such as Tuffy, with its sunshine colors, popular for scouring Teflon.

For the food service industry, special heavy-duty items were added. In 1980 came a two-sided medium-duty scrubber, one side containing soap, the other a gentle sponge, with a brand name of S.O.Ezy.

A Billion Pads a Year

More than six decades after Cox peddled his first pads door-to-door, S.O.S continues to grow handsomely. The Bedford Park plant, with a work force of some 325, is a model of mass production efficiency, turning out so many pads that in 1983 close to a billion of them tumbled from giant dryers.

To keep up with demand, the plant has been operating in three shifts for some years. A smoothly functioning distribution network, largely through a food broker system, assures adequate stocking in some 35,000 key supermarkets, besides providing a base for other pending products in the household field.

While S.O.S items can be found in stores doing 90 percent of all grocery volume in the United States, there are always new goals ahead. There can be no resting on past laurels. In what is only a $150 million a year industry (1982 figures), there are some 125 competing brands, yet none have dented the front-running position of S.O.S.

Canadians like the product as much as Americans do; by the 1970s S.O.S and a second brand called Jets had garnered a dominant share of the Canadian market. This contributes 15 percent to total volume in the division. Overseas, Miles inherited no franchises from General Foods, but the European market is relatively small. S.O.S is sold abroad only through a joint venture in Japan (Miles-Kyowa) that was started in 1977. There, in the tradition of founder Edwin Cox, it is peddled door-to-door.

Nothing Beats S.O.S

Why the remarkably successful span for such an "old" product? "Nothing better has come along," says Division President John Grant. "And we make every effort to find something better."

S.O.S protagonists insist that the product's carefully woven texture, long-lasting soap, and quick grease-cutting formula, are simply superior. Final processing, for example, fashions the pad in such a way that it can be effective regardless of the direction in which it scours. Rival products don't have that advantage.

The market appears to validate every S.O.S claim, and it remains popular for more than just pots and pans. Aluminum screens, whitewall tires, metal

Robert J. Wallace headed the new Household Products Division in 1968 and proudly assembled the able staff that administered the Chicago plant and office.

Among the General Foods executives who joined Miles after the S.O.S purchase in 1968 was John W. Grant. He has been president of the division since 1972.

Ed Gustafson became vice president of marketing in the Household Products Division.

sports equipment, barbeque grills, tools, and all kinds of other equipment can be restored to pristine condition by the scouring action of S.O.S products.

A key to success, also, has been turned by advertising. Stressing humor—and at times bluntly using comparison approaches—television spots have featured such lines as, "It's crazy to cook without it," and, "We deserve every dirty pan we get."

In 1972 *Time* magazine, in discussing the new trend of comparison advertising, mentioned the S.O.S–Brillo rivalry as its lead example. The Doyle-Dane-Bernbach advertising agency has conjured up S.O.S television commercials since 1968. In the tradition of Alka-Seltzer, they have won a number of "best" awards.

Other promotion has helped, too. In 1979, 250,000 copies of the "S.O.S Outdoor/Indoor All-Purpose Cleaning Book" were distributed through home economics teachers.

A Legacy of People Builds a Division

Finally, a legacy of fine people, mostly from General Foods, enriched the company—from scores of dexterous craftsmen to able and personable John Grant, whom Bob Wallace, then division president, hired from General Foods as vice president of marketing. Wallace also brought in Henry Fitts, an expert in marketing; scientist Dr. Thomas Welsh to head up research and development; and Edward Gustafson,

Ads for S.O.S were practical and convincing.

At the Bedford Park, IL plant, about a billion S.O.S steel wool soap pads are produced annually for the homemakers of America.

then a management trainee with the Union Division, in addition to regional sales managers and others. This skillful recruiting virtually certified the further growth of S.O.S. About 33 percent of its personnel boast more than 20 years of service; about 20 percent have more than 25 years.

Miles built adeptly with these people and carefully developed the skeletal systems it got from General Foods. The net result since the acquisition is that the S.O.S market share—and it's a tough market—had, by 1983, climbed more than 10 percent and profits had increased by even more. On occasion, S.O.S has been referred to as the "cash cow" of Miles.

The Production Process Never Stops

In the bustling Bedford Park plant, intricate machinery created years ago, and perfected over time, largely by the ingenuity of the people running it, shaves thin threads from coils of steel wire (each spool is 17 miles long) and spins them into the famous pads. The process never stops.

More cunningly contrived machinery spews forth the completed pads, ready for impregnation with a "secret" soap prepared in giant kettles in 40,000 gallon batches. Detergents, sodium bicarbonate, perfume and blue dye are added. Rushed into steam-heated dryers, the pads then tumble onto conveyor belts for automatic packaging. Each day, five or six rail cars jammed with the division's products rumble from the Bedford Park sidings, on their way to every outlet from remote country stores to big-city supermarkets.

New Household Products

Will the current S.O.S products be the end of the line? Not if the division has its way. It is expected that infusions of Bayer AG's chemical technology in the 1980s will lead to more household specialties for the U.S. market. As Grant, named division president in 1972, told a management meeting in 1982, "Areas of promise include polyurethane surfactants for such products as all-purpose cleaners, fragrances, and fragrance-delivery systems." Also, he explained, Bayer's basic organic research "may culminate in better sanitizing agents for various markets."

By 1982 the division was testing several new household products, one a totally new oven-cleaning pad designed to compete with aerosol oven-cleaning systems that have problems of their own, such as annoying fumes. Early testing in 1983 looked most promising, and the pad went national in September 1983. Plans call for at least one new product introduction each year over the next five years.

"We're looking for product superiority in no uncertain terms," Grant says, "and with Bayer's technology and our own research and development here, we think we will find those products. If successful, we will more than double the sales and profitability of the business by 1986. This is an ambitious goal but one that can be achieved."

An "Incredibly Effective" Insect Repellent

One reason this goal could well be reached is the ever-growing synergism of Miles' operations. For example, with the Cutter merger pending in 1982, Grant and his division managers were asked to take over the marketing of Cutter's widely known insect repellent.

That product has interesting origins. Lloyd Lund, a scientist in Cutter research, developed the original formula, and it was field tested by several members of the Cutter family, all of them avid sportsmen. They felt it was superior to anything on the market. So in 1960 Cutter's insect repellent was introduced to outdoorsmen through sporting goods outlets. Word spread rapidly that it was "incredibly effective." It went into drugstores, too, and by 1970 was the leading brand in both drug and sporting goods stores and remains so today. The Household Division intends to make it a leader in grocery outlets as well.

Sound technology, products that have stood the test of time, coordinated research with Bayer, marketing acumen and experienced people—all appeared to be combining at the 100-year mark to brighten the 1980s for this confident sector of Miles.

Cutter Insect Repellent, a long-time favorite of outdoorsmen, joined the Household Products Division in 1983.

An Altruistic Foray into Food Technology

In the 1970s the company mounted a bold foray into a new field—the textured vegetable protein market. In doing so, it struck an altruistic note in American corporate life. But as hindsight observers now can so easily say, it was 10, 20, or even 40 years ahead of its time.

Nevertheless, at some future date, historians looking at demographics and food technology are bound to marvel at the innovation that accompanied this daring effort to carve out a new domain in the food industry, as well as a philosophical base for expanding the food supply of the world.

The interest stemmed in part from Miles' record in nutrition; it was a natural follow-up to success with vitamins. The venture took real root in March 1970, with the purchase of Worthington Foods, already a pioneer in the production of textured vegetable protein foods and beverages. With it a large measure of technology was acquired, and a primary goal, more access to the food business, was achieved.

The concept had an intellectual appeal to many, among them Walter Compton, and he gave eloquent expression to it, especially in annual meetings of shareholders in the early 1970s. As he explained in 1970, "Much of the conventional world food supply is short of protein...and scientists, population experts, and international leaders are vitally interested in developing new foods which can correct that deficit....The world population is exploding with the energy of an unchecked nuclear reaction."

In the early 1970s, Miles set out to perfect the technology of its fascinating new line. It invested in research, expanded facilities, and developed the Morningstar Farms line of products that looked and tasted much like ham, sausage, and bacon. It seemed as if Miles had found a lane to some of the foods of the future—foods that would be nutritiously superior, inexpensive, and abundant.

In seminars, speeches, articles, and on television, Miles expertly promoted the Morningstar Farms line. Unfortunately, all of Miles' expertise could not bring the products to where the tasters wanted them. "The real problem," as Ed Gustafson, then division vice president of marketing, said, "was not texture technology, but meat flavor technology."

Miles knew as much about flavor as anybody, since it had set up its own flavor department in 1970. By 1974, it was supplying meat flavors for the protein food lines. Although the department went on to produce flavors for other industries at a good profit (it had about 100 major accounts by 1978), its experts

Morningstar Farms textured vegetable protein products were developed as meat substitutes for those watching their cholesterol intake.

could find no quick magic for the Morningstar Farms items.

Sound promotion developed a steady market among heart attack-prone people watching their cholesterol intake, but it couldn't create booming sales. The 1976 Annual Report acknowledged that "Consumer sales of plant protein food products still have not reached our expectations... partially due to substantially lower promotional support as the line has moved out of the introductory stage."

The Decision to Divest

In mid-1982 the decision came to get out of the vegetable protein food business entirely. In December 1981, the plant at Schaumburg, Illinois, had been closed. In the fall of 1982, the Worthington facilities and the Morningstar Farms line were sold.

This does not mean that the soybean is withering in the field. Of necessity, it will become increasingly important in tomorrow's world. "It has to, for both economic and health reasons," Dr. Compton insists.

CHAPTER 8

Dip And Read Diagnostics

The hope that prescription drugs in effervescent form would not only be an advance in drug delivery but win acceptance from both physicians and patients gave birth to the Effervescent Products Company, the forerunner of what became Miles' Ames Division.

Fresh out of Yale University, Charles F. Miles, grandson of the founder, was asked in 1931 to detail, or sell, Aspir-Vess, Cinca-Vess, Bromo-Vess, Salici-Vess, and Alka-Vess to doctors. Unfortunately, these products never really appealed to the majority of physicians, mainly because they were associated by both their physical appearance and mode of action with home remedies. At that time, the demarcation between prescription and over-the-counter drugs was even more clearly marked than it is today. As a result, the Effervescent Products Company never did get off the ground.

However, Miles still held fast to its hopes of getting into prescription drugs. It set up a pharmaceutical research department early in the post-war period, and in 1945 it purchased from the Alien Property Custodian of the United States assets of Riedel-de Haen, a German company. This added a line of biliary tract products under the Decholin trademark. Later, in 1955, some pediatric and dermatological products came with purchase of the Ernst Bischoff Company of Ivoryton, Connecticut. Somewhere, thought Miles' executives, should be found the "wonder drug" that would open the gate to a flourishing business in prescription drugs.

The genesis of the story of Ames, however, requires a return to 1938. That year, Dr. Walter Ames Compton joined Miles. As an intern at Billings Hospital, he had become aware of the inadequacy of the routine tests for determining the chemical constituents in a patient's urine.

Testing for sugar consisted of adding an equal quantity of urine to blue liquid (Benedict's reagent) in a test tube, which was then heated to a boil over a Bunsen burner. If sugar were present, the color of the

Charles F. Miles, one of the three grandsons of Dr. Franklin Miles, joined Ames in 1930, while a senior at Yale. For a few years, he was the entire sales force. He was elected to Miles' Board of Directors in 1934, and made president of Ames in 1947. In 1959, he added Dome Chemicals, Inc., to his responsibilities. Before retiring in 1967, he also served as corporate director of public relations.

solution went from blue through yellow to orange (if indeed boiling steam had not emptied the tube's contents before this could occur). The extent of the color change could be observed and permit one to estimate the presence and the amount of sugar in the urine.

Dr. Compton thought the procedure was messy, slow, cumbersome, and not very accurate. It led him to thinking about the whole field of clinical chemistry and pathology. When he became head of research and development at Miles, he raised the question of whether something couldn't be done about making laboratory tests more convenient. He enlisted the skills of a consultant chemist, Jonas Kamlet, and Maurice Treneer, the in-house expert on effervescence. In this case, "We had a really tough problem," Dr. Compton recalls. "We wanted to put all of the reagents into one effervescent tablet that could be dropped into a test tube of urine to determine the presence and hopefully the amount of sugar."

This meant the tablet had to contain the color-producing chemicals and be a source of heat as well. In theory, this was pharmaceutically impossible, but these innovative scientists managed to achieve it. They had an effervescent tablet ready for marketing in 1941 and introduced it with little fanfare the same year, under the trademark Clinitest.

Clinitest Spearheads a New Industry

Whether or not they had an inkling of where Clinitest would lead Miles, they had in essence started a whole new industry—convenient and accurate *in vitro* diagnostic testing.

The new product was promoted to the medical profession, to hospital laboratories, and in health care journals. It was also promoted through doctors for diabetics, who could benefit from this kind of testing. Needing no prescription, it was sold in pharmacies on the advice of physicians.

Clinitest quickly caught on, even though it was much more expensive than the old standard Benedict test. Clinitest, in fact, proved to be an historic product

in the chronicles of the company and of medicine itself. It shifted the crude course of urine chemistry toward its current level of technological excellence. It was really the first in a long chain of convenience products that are now routine in medical practice.

"If the clinical test volume of today had to be done with the methodology of the early 1940s," Ames vice-president James Murphy notes, "clinical laboratories would be multistory buildings housing many thousands of people. Clinitest tablets began the process that has led clinical chemistry into an essential adjunct to the practice of medicine."

Effervescent products were the link between Dr. Miles Medical Company and Ames.

Ames: The New Name

By 1944, Miles decided that the old name of Effervescent Products had outlived its modest usefulness and no longer described the company. That year "Chuck" Miles suggested the name change to Ames. It was the maiden name of Walter Compton's grandmother, and it was felt that doctors would feel more comfortable with a short family name.

During the late 1940s and early 1950s, the Ames Division persisted in marching along two pathways. On one of them, Clinitest advanced with a number of other tablet tests for the clinical laboratory and doctor's office. Along the other, the prescription drug business moved sluggishly.

Charles Owens, later to head the division, describes what went on in those days as "schizophrenic," and few would dispute him. Miles still had a strong faith that it would come up with drugs from its own research and development. For this reason, it worked to improve its "detailing" skills, selling the moribund drug lines obtained from Riedel-de Haen and Bischoff.

Growth, however, was mainly in diagnostics, which instead of being "detailed" were "sold." "The

Clinitest tablets, the classic effervescent urine test that started it all, still sell well more than 40 years after their introduction in 1941.

more you called, the more you sold, and call-backs were not needed, unlike physician detailing." Owens recalls. This dichotomy of marketing caused difficulties that were not really resolved until the early 1960s.

By 1951, sales had reached only about $1.5 million, with about two-thirds coming from Clinitest and related tests, and almost all the remainder from Decholin. Efforts to "crank out" new prescription drugs kept failing.

George Orr, the First "Outside" Professional Manager

Nevertheless, 1951 was a signal year because George Orr, a Duke University graduate and a Richardson-Merrell veteran, joined Ames as general sales manager. He has often since been described as the first "professional manager" to be hired by Miles from outside the founding families. In the years to come, he would play a vital role in building Ames into the major component of the corporation that it is today.

With the help of Charlie Owens, then a fast-rising young manager, Orr's first accomplishment was forging an effective field sales organization. It soon grew to 85 people, many of whom later became senior executives.

Even with its "schizophrenic" outlook, Ames by the mid-1950s was well-organized, forward-looking, and eager.

About this time came a diversion, which in this instance might be termed reverse serendipity. Company researchers had come up with a new chemical entity that seemed promising as a tranquilizer. This molecule was exciting because clinical tests showed it to be free of the side effects of meprobamate, which at that time was a relatively new and spectacularly successful product known to the public by its trademarks of Miltown and Equanil.

Nostyn, a New Therapeutic

Unfortunately, this discovery swung the balance of the two product lines of Ames toward the therapeutic side. With the enthusiastic urging of a number of respected clinicians, Ames quickly won FDA approval for a product called Nostyn and plunged into the extremely competitive tranquilizer market. Enthusiasm ran high, and backed by expert detailing, sales boomed.

The first thing anxiously watched for in a new, widely marketed drug is a serious side effect that

George W. Orr, Jr., right, and James Williams encouraged the company to go into medical electronics with the purchase of the Atomium Volemetron in 1963. Orr joined the Ames Company in sales in 1951 and was elected president in 1956. He served in that capacity until 1967 when he was elected group vice president of Professional Products. In 1973 he became the eighth president of Miles, the first to hold that office outside the founding families. He retired in 1976 after 25 years with Miles and 40 in the pharmaceutical industry.

Charles V. Owens, Jr., joined Ames in 1951. During the next 16 years, he progressed through increasingly responsible sales and marketing positions; president of Ames in 1967, in 1971 group vice president of the Professional Products Group, and in 1977 executive vice president in charge of international operations. He retired in 1982.

hasn't shown up in clinical trials. Nothing like this happened with Nostyn. Instead, doctors began grumbling about a lack of activity. Nostyn had no "muscle." Adult patients had little or no awareness of taking a drug; it did nothing for them. Before long, management realized it owned too gentle a tranquilizer, which might have had some success if promotion had only been limited to pediatrics. But the "big market" wasn't there. The advertising line "the power of gentleness" became a mockery. Nostyn failed to create the long-hoped-for prescription drug business.

In a way this was fortunate for the long-range future of Ames; it dispelled visions of quick success in drugs and fostered concentration on the growing field of diagnostics.

Clinistix—The First Dip-and-Read Strip Product

Clinistix reagent strips proved to be the next research triumph. A dip-and-read test for urine sugar, Clinistix did not provide as quantitative an answer as Clinitest Tablets, but made testing even more simple and convenient.

Clinistix was developed by a strikingly creative team headed by Dr. Alfred Free. They were seeking to perfect an elongated filter paper strip impregnated on the end with a complex enzymatic chemical system.

This was truly a challenge. These resourceful investigators could only try crude approaches since modern laboratory instruments did not exist. For example, the group used ordinary scissors to cut the strips, and they stapled them together matchbook style. Free and his cohorts realized such a handmade operation could never become a volume-manufacturing process, so they devised a way to put die-cut sheets of filter paper into wooden racks with only an inch of space separating each sheet. The filter-paper end of the rack would be hand-dipped into the reagent solution and shoved into a kiln for drying. (Polished, mounted, and framed by Dr. Chauncey Rupe, one of these original racks still hangs for posterity on a wall in the Charles S. Beardsley Research Building.)

This process was used for the first few years of stripmaking. The packaging resembled oversized matchbooks. Eventually, the paper-impregnated material was glued onto a plastic-strip backing—a much more automated and sophisticated manufacturing process.

In any event, the Free team's historic paper strip worked beautifully. Dipped into urine, the end impregnated with the reagent produced a color change in 10 seconds if glucose was present. Clinistix was

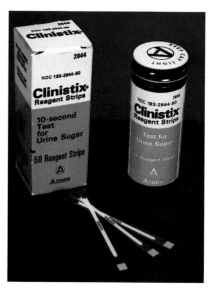

Clinistix Reagent Strips, for detecting sugar in urine, were the first in the long line of Ames dip and-read tests.

specific for glucose, an advantage to the diabetic, since Clinitest, by contrast, may react with any sugar or reducing substance.

Ames and Lilly in Competition

Clinitest had given Ames an important head-start in convenience-testing for urine sugar. However,

Dr. Alfred H. Free and his wife Helen, also a chemist, made landmark contributions to the field of diabetes by perfecting the first dip-and-read strip product—Clinistix. With great skill, Free applied his intuitive scientific judgment to the Ames line for 32 years before retiring in 1978 and becoming a consultant.

a different kind of market situation was to prevail for Clinistix. It's an intriguing story, for the door to success that Clinistix swung open proved, at first, to be only slightly ajar.

During the development period, in 1956, a New York scientist named Albert Keston strode into the Miles lobby and said he had invented a way to test for urine sugar using impregnated paper and enzymes. He demanded $50,000 just to show that he had succeeded. Miles thought it already had a similar or better testing system on the brink of success and so declined the offer to examine Dr. Keston's ideas. He then rushed to Indianapolis, where Eli Lilly, with its large stake in insulin, decided to take a chance and pay the $50,000. It more or less adopted the Keston plan.

The research and development staffs of both companies, encouraged by marketing, pushed ahead as rapidly as possible. Clinistix and Lilly's Tes-Tape were marketed within one day of each other. The legal and patent situation on these two products was not settled for years. Eventually Miles and Lilly cross-licensed each other.

Needless to say, Lilly was tough competition. Not only did it have a 15 to 1 advantage in sales manpower, but as the major producer of insulin and many other drugs, it was known and generally respected by physicians, especially those interested in diabetes.

"Tes-Tape was really a blessing in disguise," George Orr commented later. "It stimulated our own people." The competition matured the young Ames salesmen, making them confident that they could compete with one of the giants of the health-care industry. Eventually, Clinitest and Clinistix won back their market share, especially in doctors' offices, hospitals, and independent laboratories. Severe diabetics returned to Clinitest for reliability and accuracy, and the stand taken by Ames and bolstered by scientific papers earned it the respect of critical clinical lab personnel.

Albustix: Another Achievement

After Clinistix, Ames waited barely a year to record another achievement on behalf of convenience diagnostics. It originated Albustix reagent strips, a dip-and-read test for urine protein. Until that time, protein had usually been detected either by boiling the urine until the protein coagulated and could be seen, or by adding a strong acid to bring about the coagulation.

The researchers on Albustix, studying a little-

An Ames laboratory, about 1962, just when the Ames Division was beginning to surge and giving signs that it would go far.

known phenomenon called "the protein error of indicators," evolved a unique chemical system to detect the protein. Ames now had dip-and-read systems for the two most common urine tests.

This success led to another historic concept: that of combining reagents on one strip to further enhance convenience for the user. A small team of engineers and scientists, headed by Dr. John Rebar, a pharmacologist who had been hired by Miles to study new drugs, was formed to work on the problem. This team succeeded in devising a methodology for separating two reagents on the same strip. It sounds simple, but it required unique machinery to provide a water-impervious barrier between the reagents on the paper so that there wouldn't be runover from one to the other, causing aberrant results.

From Single to Multiple Tests

Surprisingly enough, the idea evoked a great deal of soul-searching, even up to the Board of Directors level. The single strip advocates thought it would be better for users to pick and choose, and that single strips would bring more income. Others, Dr. Compton and George Orr among them, felt that the customer would pay the same for two tests on a single strip as for two single strips, and that profits would

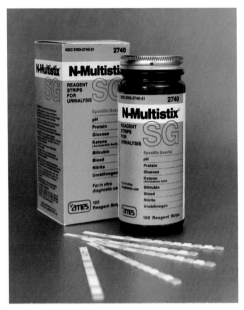

Nine urine tests can now be performed simultaneously using one Ames reagent strip.

increase because it would be less expensive to make and package multiple-test strips. Ultimately, the second idea prevailed and proved to be correct. True, over the years a new reagent formulation was usually first marketed as a single strip, but as soon as technically feasible, it was added to existing multiple forms.

The original two items have now proliferated into more than 25 separate strips of various numbers and combinations. Putting together the first two reagents opened a rich diagnostic vein, out of which came, strip by strip, famous trademarks that became familiar in every laboratory across the country, as well as around the world, such as Albustix, Combistix, Hemastix, Labstix, and Phenistix. These strips really got Ames surging, with sales approaching the $10 million mark by the mid-1960s.

Complicated Reagents, But They Work

Because of the inherent difficulty in devising stable chemical formulations in dry form, it took enormous scientific effort to make these convenience products possible. Combining multiple tests on a single strip was even harder because of reagent incompatibilities in the bottle shipped to the customer. Yet Miles' scientists managed to solve these problems and provide "simple" tests for users.

Each of the reagent areas on a multiple test strip contains a complex mixture of chemicals, including

enzymes, that bring about a color change in the presence of the substance being tested. The degree of color indicates the relative amount of substance present.

In the 20 years after 1956, Ames developed and manufactured reagents for a whole range of substances found in urine: ketones, blood, bilirubin, urobilinogen, glucose, ascorbic acid, protein, nitrates, and pH (alkalinity and/or acidity.)

Even this impressive list did not satisfy marketers and researchers. They had long dreamed of injecting into multiple colorimetric strips a capability to read specific gravity. This indexes the amount of solids in urine and defines to a certain degree the ability of the kidney to concentrate urine. An important test, it had always been done routinely by a method that resembles measuring the antifreeze level in an automobile radiator—using a "bobber" in a tube.

In 1981, Ames transformed that rather crude system, and added it to its N-Multistix reagent strips. At the time N-Multistix SG was the ultimate strip, with nine separate areas, including not only the new one for specific gravity, but another new one for detecting bacteria in urine.

In 1982, N-Multistix SG was named a winner of the prestigious IR-100 Award, presented annually by *Industrial Research & Development* magazine. Accepting the award were Dr. Robert Boguslaski, Ames vice president, research and development; Dr. Alan Burkhardt, supervisor, urine chemistry laboratory; Katharine Johnston, who was the principal developer of the product, and Dr. Joseph Wang, research scientist.

In the Forefront of Strip Technology

This kind of progress has not gone unnoticed in a competitive world. As Ames patents ran out, rivals sprang up, particularly in Germany and Japan. So it has been vital to stay at the forefront in strip technology, in such factors as speed of webbing, fiber penetration, reagent sensitivity, rate of chemical deterioration, stability, and many others that determine how swiftly and accurately the strips reveal information. Probably, nobody knows more about these technical elements than the people of Ames. An unusual level of customer service has helped maintain market share.

High technology extends to production, too. For instance, the reagent tapes before final cutting for packaging are dried in a giant tunnel where they are literally floated on an air stream using the airplane wing principle.

ucts evolved from research in a joint venture with Hebrew University in Israel.

These tests required isotope-counting technology. Fortunately, this had been acquired with the purchase of the Atomium Corporation, and George Orr's feeling that Ames should get into the hardware business was more than amply justified. These thyroid-testing products were sold extensively worldwide. Using the antigen/antibody reaction and radioisotopes, they propelled Ames early into the almost explosively growing area of immunology testing.

In the early 1970s, under Dr. Henry Wishinsky's direction, a great deal of innovative research was carried out in this area. It led to a number of significant patents. A team headed by Dr. Robert Boguslaski was convinced that immunology assay techniques would be most useful for monitoring concentrations of drugs in the body. The need for such evaluation had become more critical with the advent of new and more potent pharmaceuticals. Toxic side effects have been the bane of some of these products, often giving the physician a tough choice over whether benefits would outweigh risks of malpractice. Sensitive tests to swiftly measure the range between toxic and therapeutic levels, often small and difficult to determine, would be a boon to doctors and patients.

Robert C. Boguslaski, Ph.D., who joined Ames in 1967, was named vice president of research and development in 1981. He has directed some of Ames' most innovative research, such as projects in immunology that led to replacing the less desirable radioactive chemicals with fluorescence in therapeutic drug assay systems.

Dr. Henry Wishinsky, (center), vice president, scientific and regulatory affairs, Professional Products Group and longtime head of Ames research, is shown here on the occasion of the American Association of Clinical Chemists/Ames Award for outstanding contributions to clinical chemistry, an Ames tradition since 1952, together with Dr. and Mrs. Irving Sunshine (left) and Dr. and Mrs. Ralph E. Thiers. Sunshine, a professor of Toxicology at Case Western Reserve University, was recipient of the award in 1973, when Thiers, the 1972 recipient who was responsible for much of the laboratory screening for Ames' multiple tests, was AACC President.

It should be noted that in many cases we are talking of minutely small amounts of substance to be measured—in some cases, nanograms and picograms (a millionth of a gram and a billionth of a gram). However, it was felt that a way must be devised to develop these needed tests using immunologic techniques, to be sure, but without the difficult-to-handle radioactive isotopes.

Other therapeutic drug assay systems have now come on the market, but Ames naturally believes in the simplicity and superiority of its own. For one thing, it does not rely on the aforementioned radioactive chemicals with their disposal problems, but on fluorescence. The degree of fluorescence is proportional to the concentration of the drug in the patient's serum, measured after a series of reactions involving the drug, the patient's serum, immunologic reagents and in some cases enzymes. Readings are obtained by

measuring fluorescence in a number of Ames-fluorocolorimeters—Fluorostat, Clinistat, Optimate.

Ames and Drug Monitoring

Boguslaski's team first succeeded in perfecting tests for three related antibiotics: gentamycin, tobramycin, and amikasin. Gentamycin, for example, is highly toxic but extremely effective for fulminating infections. With precise measurement of blood levels, dosage can be adjusted to be within the narrow therapeutic-toxic parameters. Other tests have been perfected and marketed for a line of anti-convulsants, as well as for anti-asthmatic drugs. In 1982, the Ames TDA fluorescent immunoassay system was selected as one of the 100 most significant technological advances of the year by *Industrial Research & Development* magazine. Dr. Richard Falb, Ames president, and Dr. Carol Miller, senior project manager, accepted the award.

Annual growth for this rapidly expanding field of drug monitoring is expected to be in the 20 percent range in the 1980s.

The Best in Ames Technology

The Ames Therapeutic Drug Assay System exemplified the best in Ames technology at the turn of the decade and was in the vanguard of mounting demand for better management of drug therapies through accurate, rapid, simple analyses. Ames capped its achievements in this area in 1982 by marketing the Optimate instrument, which reads Ames TDA immunofluorometric tests and regular wet chemistries as well, to provide a complete automated system. It was developed in cooperation with the Gilford Instrument Company of Oberlin, Ohio. The Optimate also won an award from *Industrial Research and Development* magazine.

Still another advance deserves notice. After strenuous effort and not a few false starts, the first immunologic assay for a drug has been reduced to a system that can be impregnated into a strip and subsequently read on an instrument. This completes the circle from complex chemical reactions that partially measure substances in urine to extremely accurate systems that measure minute amounts of substances in blood, all based on Ames' dry chemistry, or strip technology. This means that, even more than in the past, Ames products in the future can be expected to make further contributions in the war against disease.

As Dr. Boguslaski, now Ames' vice president of

In one flexible system, the fully automated Optimate instrument performs 23 liquid-reagent blood tests and nine fluorometric therapeutic drug assays.

research and development, says, "It's not enough just to maintain the state of the art; you have to make continual advances, bridge all the chemical and engineering and biological sciences, and in our case new methods of measurement, to secure the future. We can handle all kinds of variables as long as we maintain an intuitive sense and cognitive ability. I think we have managed to combine both in a lot of things at Ames."

Ames Is a Major Contributor to Sales and Profits

From the beginning, Ames leadership has been internally generated by scientists and marketing people willing to take new concepts to physicians and laboratory personnel. The result has been a major contribution to corporate sales and earnings, both in the United States and overseas. Ames has grown from a fledgling to a segment of Miles' business that competes with all of the other segments and, in many cases, outranks them in relative profitability.

The very building that houses Ames reflects stability and growth. Developed under the direction of Bob Schlegel, then president of Ames, it is a handsome structure architecturally. The building has expanded three times since 1974, and nobody believes that the latest will be the last such expansion.

A Glittering Technology Probes the Future

Once, all Ames' products were manufactured in the main building in Elkhart. Today, instruments are developed, engineered, and produced in a former Naval Ordnance plant in nearby Mishawaka. There, Hugo Gauss presides over what can be described as a glittering technology. Some 400 liquid reagents are manufactured in South Bend. More recently, the production of strips moved from the main building in Elkhart to a completely automated high-speed plant several miles away.

Ames will continue to probe those frontiers where its special background, skills, and experience offer advantages and can achieve useful medical gains and convenience for doctor, patient, laboratory, and hospital. It will continue to reinforce Dr. Compton's original concept of convenience of almost half a century ago.

As Dr. Klaus Hartmann, a newer scientist in

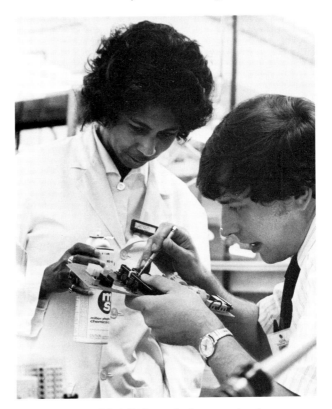

Mary Garner and Bob Eichorst check out a printed circuit board in the Ames Instrument Plant in Mishawaka.

Ames, stresses, "The physician doesn't care whether it's an instrument or a reagent, or how complicated is the internal working of a system. He likes to have a black box into which he can put the patient's body fluids or tissues and get out clinical results."

The frontiers for advancement are there. As knowledge grows, so will Ames. For example, instruments may be able to pick up disease patterns through measuring various protein levels, leading to better prevention techniques. The antigen/antibody reaction continues to be refined, particularly in connection with newer genetic engineering and monoclonal antibodies. These exquisitely sensitive systems may be able to measure as yet unknown things in patients that will forestall or ameliorate a host of ailments, from infections to cancer. The first 50 years of Ames may prove to be inordinately modest, compared with what could pour through its scientific floodgates in the next half-century.

Ames offices and laboratories are housed in this modern building in Elkhart, completed in 1980.

CHAPTER 9

Making Lab Life Easier

Along the intricate pathways of research, the bench scientist works with highly specialized materials and equipment. Most of the names are meaningless to the layman, others vaguely familiar, some—such as interferon and antibodies—almost commonplace, as they have spouted from newspaper headlines.

They are the accoutrements of the scientific trade, and one arm of Miles Scientific makes a host of them. It's a relatively low-volume business, but extremely important to the researcher. Moreover, it has for a generation closely linked Miles to the scientific community in general—to clinical laboratories, to medical and academic research institutions, and to both human and animal health-care companies worldwide.

It takes a 112-page catalog to list and describe this exotic parade of biochemicals and immunochemicals without which much research would stumble.

The Place of Immunochemistry

The catalog mirrors first of all the exalted place of immunochemistry in life-science research. Twenty pages cover that section alone, offering as it does such on-the-frontier items as monoclonal antibodies and classical antisera. Miles was one of the first companies to develop and market the antibodies, and it is the largest supplier of antisera. The catalog lists seven other types of products under the headings of lectins, blood proteins, polypeptides, nucleic acids, recombinant reagents, enzymes, and companion reagents. It is updated with additions about four times a year while assorted types of direct mail go to scientific customers.

The genesis of this arcane venture began in 1964, when Walter Compton noticed that it wasn't always easy to obtain materials for research, especially biological substances. He concluded that scientists elsewhere must be having the same frustrations, and proposed that Miles start making its own and at the same time provide them to others. As a result the program got started, with a potpourri of biochemicals primarily originating from the Chemical Division.

Compton had another purpose in mind, too. He thought such an effort would enhance the reputation of Miles in the scientific world, build relationships with scientists and science-based firms, and in the process aid recruitment of researchers and provide clues for research and even for products. He was right.

Miles began supplying biochemicals to the scientific research community worldwide as a service. The service became a business, with more than 1,000 products in the company's catalog. Here, a technician prepares to pour a Pentex lipoprotein cholesterol solution into a sample handler to determine blood cholesterol levels.

Trudy Dickinson, left, and Jean Thomas, right, owners of Pentex, stayed with Miles in key positions long after the acquisition.

Research Products Division Takes Shape

The operation moved quickly in three directions: to fill Miles' own biochemical research needs, to meet those of individual outside scientists, and to create sales in larger quantities—a sort of mini-bulk biochemical business for diagnostic and pharmaceutical companies. A Research Products Division was established with Jack Carlin as its first president.

Carlin substantially expanded the product line with some 200 items through a joint marketing program with Yeda Research and Development Com-

The number of products for sale was greatly augmented with the purchase of Pentex, Inc., of Kankakee, IL, in 1968.

pany in Israel (1966). Miles got even more serious about this new business in 1968, when Carlin pushed the acquisition of a small but innovative enterprise, Pentex Incorporated in Kankakee, Illinois, for about $1.4 million in stock.

Pentex had been founded in 1953 by two energetic young women, Trudy Dickinson and Jean Thomas, and three businessmen. Both Dickinson and Thomas had worked at Armour as protein chemists. As Armour de-emphasized its fine biochemical business, Dickinson and Thomas decided that they could prepare purified proteins just as well on their own. They also held the belief that scientists should not be wasting time preparing their own raw materials.

The founders chipped in $200 apiece, since that was all the capital needed to incorporate in Illinois. Almost as a hobby, and with a very small staff, they began furnishing items through their scientific contacts. In 1960 they built their own modest plant, and their venture grew steadily. By 1968, when they found the Miles offer attractive as a way to expand, they had 35 employees. It was apparent that common business philosophies and shared identifiable opportunities existed. The final decision to sell didn't take long; it was a "spur-of-the-moment one over lunch," Dickinson recalls.

By this time, too, Pentex was producing several hundred biochemical products of animal origin, such as bovine albumin and its derivatives, other blood proteins, enzymes, and substrates.

To broaden the biochemical line, Carlin identified Seravac Laboratories of Capetown, South Africa, which was acquired by Miles in 1969. Seravac had a marketing and distribution system in Europe and also manufactured enzymes from plant and animal sources, among them peroxidase, derived from horseradish. In fact, nobody else produces as much of it, and it is still widely used today as a diagnostic enzyme.

Pentex at the Core of a New Division

Pentex remained at the core of what became the Research Products Division, so formed and renamed in 1978 after having become a department of Corporate Research in 1971 under the able direction of Dr. Earl Dearborn. During this period, the solid basis for the operation was laid and continued (Dearborn died in 1973) under Dr. Roland Beers until the division was reestablished in 1978. By this time it embraced research biochemicals from many parts of the world.

The research substances that Miles makes, many of them customized for the special needs of purchasers, go to scores of countries in a steadily increasing volume. Although many of its customers are competitors, Miles' proprietary interests are considered first. Products researchers develop may be sold to competitors only after this in-house interest is taken into account.

Research Products was for many years headed by an Elkhart native, the chemist Dale Stauffer, an energetic Ph.D. who came to Miles in 1948. "The major thrust continues to be related to diagnostic enzymes from microbial sources," he said in late 1982.

"The kinds of products that we deal with— natural biological products—are getting more and more attention both in diagnostics and therapeutics," he stressed. "We haven't anywhere near exhausted ways of getting these natural products, whether from animal or human blood fractions, in which Cutter is also deeply involved. Progress could come, for example, by taking Cutter by-product fractions and by using our very similar technology, isolating special substances into products for investigation. We will continue to grow just by keeping pace with technology."

Lab-Tek: The Other Arm

The other arm of the division called Miles

Pentex was expanded in 1979. Most of the staff turned out for the groundbreaking.

Dale Stauffer, Ph.D., piloted the Research Products effort for many years.

Scientific is Lab-Tek. In the world of labware, the name has stood proudly for a quarter of a century. From petri dishes to ingenious systems that identify and store tissue specimens, it is highly recognized throughout the health care system, especially with tissue culturists.

The first Lab-Tek items may have had little of the sophistication common to many other Miles products, but the company moved quickly from single-use plastic-molded products into advanced laboratory instruments. Today, the division catalogs items that exemplify substantial research and manufacturing technology, and high technology at that.

Lab-Tek Plastics Company came into the Miles fold in August 1964, in exchange for $3.2 million. It had 110 employees in two plants in Westmont, Illinois. It had been founded in 1953 by a practicing pathologist, J. B. McCormick, who perceived a marketing need for pre-sterilized culture media dishes and analysis systems for clinical, pathological, and industrial laboratories.

It had, from the beginning, products that would supplement the Ames line and eventually help to broaden its leadership in diagnostics.

McCormick did not remain with Lab-Tek after the purchase. Instead he has been a consultant and continues in that role. He is, in the words of Robert Myers, former marketing vice president, a great idea man. "I can recall him years ago sketching an idea for a culture tissue slide on a napkin at lunch, and that item is still on the market today," Myers said.

The company had started in a small, 24,000 square-foot building. It was almost a "cottage" operation, even though it was making 30 million petri dishes a year. Miles obviously felt it had a lot of promise.

When in a few years the Westmont facilities became totally inadequate, a 100,000 square-foot building replaced them on a 20-acre site in Naperville, Illinois. A surprising number of employees stayed on, even though they continued to live in the Westmont area.

Division Grows Under Kalt

By 1967, Lab-Tek split from Ames and became a separate division. As executives of Ames, George Orr, then Charlie Owens and Bob Schlegel had given it strong support. When an Ames veteran, Charles J. Kalt, wrote a persuasive position paper on the operation, Orr told him to take it over. He did. He became the new division's first president.

At the time when Kalt took charge, Lab-Tek sales hardly exceeded $1 million; in the next 10 years, with such developments as Tissue-Tek, Kalt had a lot to do with raising them to $10 million. He retired in 1977 after 36 years with Miles.

Lab-Tek was first a creature of the plastics age. Before the advent of plastics, petri dishes were made of glass. Today they are made with crystalline polystyrene. The raw material flows from huge hoppers into machinery that melts and molds them with strict

Lab-Tek Plastics Company, Woodmont, IL, was acquired in 1964.

Charles S. Kalt, Ph.D., Ames' advertising manager, became president of Lab-Tek Division in the 1960s and built it tenfold before he retired in 1977 after 36 years with Miles.

precision. These complicated machines, designed and perfected by Lab-Tek over the years, can produce one million plastic piece parts in 24 hours.

Quality assurance is, and must be, impeccable. Giant sterilizers—twice as tall and as wide as a man— force ethyleneoxide gas through shipping cartons and through the products. The containers are then quarantined while quality control tests are completed.

Thus, the giant, high-speed injection molding machines turning out a dozen versions of petri dishes along with related disposable products such as tubes, containers, cups, and cytology bottles and mailers, comprise in a sense the "simple" part of the line.

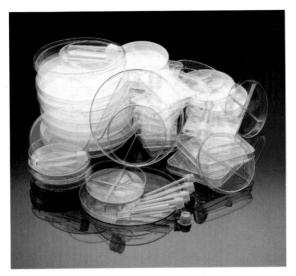

Lab-Tek petri dishes and tubes are turned out in great volume.

New injection molding machines for making labware were installed when Lab-Tek moved to Naperville, IL.

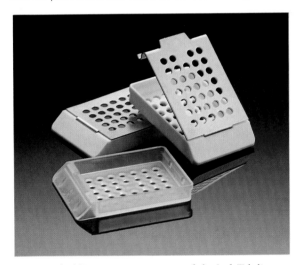

Tissue-embedding cassettes are part of the Lab-Tek line.

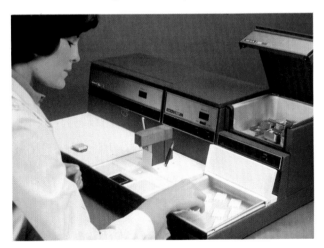

Lab-Tek is best known for its sophisticated laboratory instruments, such as this Tissue-Tek III Embedding Console, used in biopsies and autopsies.

As early as 1974, Lab-Tek had attained a new level of development with its perfected paraffin embedding specimen system. That system had a long history. Just a little more than a century before, something called the Naples Bar had been invented, and many devices had come along, from complicated medical molds to paper boxes. What was needed was a technique for handling human tissue specimens and that method was found in paraffin embedding.

The Tissue-Tek Breakthrough

The system that Lab-Tek designed in the early 1970s, called Tissue-Tek (another well-coined trademark), did, and still does, work very well in the histology laboratory.

Technology never stands still, so soon after came Tissue-Tek II, a further automatic simplifying of the procedure, with the addition of embedding cassettes and a vacuum filtrator to ensure the absence of air voids in a "start to storage" system.

Various accessories provide a complete system, such as the microtome cryostat used to mount, freeze, and precisely cut surgical sections. A biopsy Uni-Cassette and a Mega-Cassette for larger specimens, such as bones, eyes, and teeth were designed, as Miles says, to make "your lab life a little easier." Nothing is overlooked, not even disposable microtome blades called Accu-Edge, which eliminate tedious sharpening.

By 1980, Tissue-Tek III added embedding consoles in dispensing, thermal, and cryo forms and uniquely designed cassettes in colors to aid in identifying variables.

"It Miniaturizes Your Costs, Too"

A tissue culture chamber slide attests to the diversity and completeness of the Lab-Tek line. It starts, incubates, fixes, stains, examines, and stores eight separate tissue cultures. It's done in miniature and, as a promotional piece explains, "It miniaturizes your costs, too."

Wherever specimens of body fluids and body tissue are collected, transported, and tested, Lab-Tek is on the spot with its advanced labware systems—all part of a total, safety-first system of modular components and products designed to work together for the safety of specimens.

Dr. Charles F. Nielsen became president of the division in early 1978. Nielsen and Myers got busy expanding internationally from just Canada and Japan to all of Europe, parts of Asia, and Brazil. Within three years, the business tripled in volume.

In 1980, Miles purchased a small, innovative firm, Lux Scientific Corporation of Newbury Park, California. Founded by Rudy Lux about 1968, its some 100 employees had become experts in first-rate tissue culture plasticware. Its products augmented the division's culture and container line. In 1983, this California operation was phased out and tranferred to Naperville.

When Nielsen went off to head Miles' operations in the United Kingdom, V. M. "Vic" Esposito, Ph.D., succeeded him as president. Esposito skillfully blueprinted the next organizational step—the logical merging of Lab-Tek and Research Products into a new division aptly named Miles Scientific.

That step, taken in late 1982, put into one division the 1,000-plus biochemicals of the former

Under V. M. "Vic" Esposito, Ph.D., Lab-Tek and Research Products were merged into the new Miles Scientific Division.

Research Products Division and the array of Lab-Tek devices, instruments, and reagents in general, all staples in the fields of hematology, histology, cytology, and immunological-based diagnostics.

Beyond Tissue-Tek systems, exotic and advanced as they are, other fields offer promise. Take, for example, cellular diagnostics, not of great commercial value in 1983 but of dynamic import down the road, since it could lead to tools that would measure, monitor, and even treat diseases at or close to their source—at cellular levels. No more exciting concept exists in science today. And Miles is engaged in the research that could bring that concept to fruition.

CHAPTER 10

More Than Just Lemon Juice

"Citric acid is not an invention of man... it is a gift from Nature." So proclaimed a booklet issued by Miles in 1974. "[It] occurs in all living cells that depend upon carbon compounds for energy... the sweeping range of Nature's wonders: animal tissues, milk and other dairy products, trees and plants—and most notably citrus fruits."

Today, citric acid is produced by a high technology that represents decades of sophisticated research. Yet by industrial standards, it is an old product, first isolated from lemon juice two centuries ago by Carl Wilhelm Scheele.

The British first made it from calcium citrate brought in from Italy in 1860. By 1880, the French and Germans were doing the same thing, and so was Pfizer, the first American company to produce a product already widely used in foods, medicine, and soft drinks.

Miles and Pfizer: A Tale of Two Companies

For that matter, the U.S. story was almost exclusively that of Pfizer until Miles edged into production in 1952 in order to have its own source of citric acid for Alka-Seltzer. From then on in the U.S. it became a tale of two companies. A snappy industrial rivalry developed in both research and sales with Miles technology in particular making advances to enlarge already varied applications.

That, however, was a long time coming. Pfizer learned how to produce citric acid by fermentation techniques, using the black bread mold, *Aspergillus niger*. It continued to build its citric business in both the pre-war and post-war years, with virtually no competition in a steadily expanding market.

Meanwhile, Miles had long been a close observer, with an interest in citric acid fermentation going back at least to 1940. Its scientists didn't think much of the only method for producing it at the time, that is, through surface fermentation using large pans that had to be loaded manually or mechanically.

A youthful scientist at Miles, Ray Snell, worked on the process until he went into military service in 1942. Then, John Woodward and others took over, dabbling with all kinds of ideas, including submerged fermentation—a technique that appeared to be the coming thing since it had been achieved with penicillin. When he got back from service in 1947, Snell was joined by Alex Batti, also back from World War II (both had been Sanitary Corps officers in the Philippines), and experimentation resumed in earnest.

Compton Pushes for Citric Acid Research

Many Miles employees have played important parts in the citric acid story. With his talent for far-sightedness, Dr. Compton had pushed the development unrelentingly, both before and after the war. Guidance came from such experts as Dr. "Dutch" Schweiger, Dr. "Whitey" Croxall, and Merrick Shepard. Through the years, Dr. O. G. "Toby" Wegrich, who retired in 1981 as head of Operations, engineered so many improvements that he earned the sobriquet of "Mr. Citric Acid." Paul Francis, Bernie Streets, and John G. Parker, among others, made various contributions, as did Rodney Saddler, the first plant manager at the Dayton, Ohio, facility.

The two bench scientists most instrumental in bringing citric acid to efficient production levels were the dissimiliar Snell and Batti—the former calm, thorough, analytical; the latter quick, intuitive, and outspoken. Between them, they probably acquired more detailed knowledge of the field than any duo anywhere. They explored many an avenue and byway, unravelled many a mystery, often on weekends and late at night. (Both retired, full of Miles' honors and respect, in 1982.)

It Only *Looks* Simple...

To the layman, citric acid might appear to be a relatively simple product that is easily produced. Not

Ray Snell   *Alex Batti*

Miles would have found it difficult to go into citric acid manufacturing, or to stay there, without the persistent ingenuity of scientists Ray Snell, left, and Alex Batti. Both retired in 1982, their contributions deeply etched into the annals of Miles.

A vintage photo, 1937, shows quality control manager Lloyd Johnson sampling purchases of citric acid, one of the main ingredients in Alka-Seltzer. It took some prodding, especially from Dr. Compton, before Miles developed its own citric acid source.

so. A tricky technology comprises its legacy at Miles alone, going back to the time Batti and Helen Ketchum sought out microorganisms in batches of twigs, soil, and dead leaves. Helen hit the jackpot: a wild grape leaf, picked up west of town, from which the scientists isolated the famed *Aspergillus niger*.

In the first years after World War II, Miles researchers worked with cultures in glass-columned fermenters topped by agitators. "It was mostly frustration for a long time," Batti admits. "Some mornings I would actually kick those pilot fermenters to get them started again."

They tried all kinds of things to get rid of trace elements and to find varieties of *Aspergillus niger* to improve yields. They did nutrient balance studies and probed various chemical treatments. One experiment finally produced an abundance of the desired spores, which led to the first practical production from the pilot plant.

The objective all along, of course, had been to find ways to get efficient yields of citric acid from large-scale fermenters. Processing the sugar source and recovering the citric acid was one thing, curtailing trace element contamination quite another. The steel fermenters needed special linings, and many kinds had to be tried before an ingeniously contrived synthetic coating proved to be the most suitable.

Changing the Basic Raw Material

Another chain of change rattling through the years related to the basic raw material. At one time, as Snell remembers, "We latched onto Cuban high-test molasses, then switched to the Dominican Republic after Castro came to power in Cuba. But it was an inferior syrup because the cane was being grown on land that had been reclaimed from saltwater flats."

Extensive testing went into corn sugars, an improvement "but still leaving much to be desired," Snell says. After the purchase of Takamine, with its experts on enzymology, progress came faster, especially with the enzyme conversion of starch to glucose.

The truly revolutionary improvement didn't come until Miles began producing citric acid from corn. One of several sources that could be used, it was chosen because it was the most economical. For another thing, it ended uncertainty over sources of supply. Through the deep tank process, corn soon assured a product of purity and consistency.

Luck Played a Part, Too

Luck—and serendipity—played their roles. As Snell recollects, on one occasion, an operator put an excessive amount of one ingredient into an already going fermenter instead of one about to be started. Normally, that might have been a frightening mistake, but the unexpected result was a nice boost in production.

Improvements did not come dramatically but incrementally, first by tests in the laboratory, then in development, but always doubtful until proven in large-scale manufacturing. For example, Snell recalls that, when first starting production, "we were fermenting rather low sugar concentrations and thought we were doing fine. Then Batti managed to build the concentrations to increase productivity."

"When you look back, it's difficult to visualize what we went through," Batti says. "Our people were ready to go, gung-ho. They didn't know what was involved, so they got into all kinds of trouble. But they learned."

So various strides—some of them virtually forgotten—successfully sent the company down the citric acid road. Work on enhancing the *Aspergillus niger* and other related cultures never ceased. Process changes kept improving the yields.

The original intent of producing citric acid for Alka-Seltzer alone was abandoned in the late 1950s, and with good reason. It appears to be beyond

Until he retired in 1982 after 22 years of service, O. B. "Toby" Wegrich engineered so many improvements in production that he became known as "Mr. Citric Acid."

question that Miles had gotten a technological jump on the competition—one that many people believe holds true today.

If the company could produce high-grade, low-cost citric acid for its own products (and at first it was its own best customer) it could also profit from selling it for the products of others. So the modest plant at Elkhart was expanded. It has since undergone 11 expansions, with the first fermenters long since superseded by circular stainless steel towers that can hold several times more fermenting brew.

Expansion was not only confined to Elkhart. A highly modern plant was built in Dayton, Ohio, in the mid-1970s and its capacity doubled in 1979.

Much earlier, in 1961, Miles went international, entering into a joint venture at Cuernavaca, Mexico, with a citric plant that has since seen eight expansions. (There was a slight problem in the early years: built close to a lagoon, the building would be invaded by coral snakes. Seeking warmth, they would wind themselves around pipes and valves.)

Other plants were constructed in Cali, Colombia, in 1974, and in Brazil in 1980. The Latin American plants use sucrose as a supply source because it is less costly than corn.

Publications Help Marketing

No attempt will be made here to define in any technical detail the chemical and physical properties of citric acid. That kind of information is abundant, of course, in Miles literature. For example, in 1979,

Ray Snell, right, presents to Ed Beardsley, then general manager, a five-pound sample of Miles citric acid from the Elkhart plant when it first opened in 1952.

In this plant late in 1952, Miles began producing citric acid in Elkhart using the deep-tank fermentation process developed in-house. This scientific breakthrough launched a new business destined to become second only to Alka-Seltzer in volume of sales.

Doug Green, left, and John Parker handled the old liming operations in 1964.

Jim Kavas takes a citric acid sample sometime in 1964.

Gary T. Blair and Mitchell E. Zienty of the Citro-Tech Division published *Citric Acid: Properties and Reactions, a Technical Discussion of How the Substance Acts and Interacts with Other Agents.* With Philip W. Staal they also wrote an extensive pamphlet on *Citric Acid in Creative Chemical Cleaning,* first released in 1981. It describes citric acid properties, handling, and storage, along with concepts of application and investigation to improve uses.

Citric acid production, embracing as it does unique technology, journeys through a world of its own. Visually, it's a vast and complex labyrinth of tanks, tubes, pipes, valves, motors, columns of glass and metal, giant drums, dryers, pumps, evaporators, centrifuges, heat exchangers, water softeners, and other equipment, all silently or noisily engaged in turning corn products into citric acid.

Unloading Is the Simple Part

It all starts each morning with railroad hopper cars and trucks unloading corn flour into glass-lined silos. (The Elkhart plant uses the corn supply of a large farm in a single day.) Unloading is the simple part. After that a long, complicated, and continuous operation, the culmination of 40-odd years of technology, transforms the raw material into the final solid or liquid forms of citric acid.

Man is almost absent from the whole sophisticated procedure. Few are to be seen in a twisting metal and glass maze the size of a football field. Yet there are along the sidelines operators, technicians, maintenance experts, clerks, and supervisors. They know exactly what is going on as they intently trace curving or jagged lines on the gauges and graphs of complex, computer-controlled panels. Here the pulse of the operation beats 24 hours a day, dictating what has to be done in each processing stage. Alarm panels flash quick warnings at any sign of trouble.

The Key—"Deep-Tank" Fermentation

The key to making citric acid is "deep-tank" or submerged fermentation. As the 1976 Annual Report said, harnessing it is "a technology older than recorded history and modern as biochemistry."

It is certainly modern at Miles. Simply stated, special enzymes treat the carbohydrate source, thus triggering the conversion of corn starch to dextrose. Then, in the giant fermentation tanks, other unique microorganisms go to work to produce the citric acid.

All this involves a series of tightly controlled steps taken under such esoteric names as liquefaction,

saccharification, and crystallization. Another is filtration, which yields "waste" that isn't waste at all; it's sold as animal feed. As the process continues, specialized equipment gradually removes all impurities and the citric acid emerges in large crystal granules for fine forms, or else as a concentrated liquid, ready for final packaging.

For all its reliance on intricate apparatus, the making of citric in a sense is still a "hands-on art," division president Bob McGrath notes. "Our specialists will take the organism out of the fermenter, look at it under a microscope, then decide what adjustments to make that day. It takes time to develop that sort of sixth sense, but we have lots of people who are good at it," he says.

A veteran marketing and production expert, Robert McGrath headed Biotechnology operations, including citric acid and enzymes at Centennial time.

Fructose Syrup, A New Sweetener

From success in processing corn came a bonus in the late 1970s—high fructose syrup, an entirely new corn-based sweetener. It, too, relies on dextrose. The trick here is to push the dextrose through a column containing fixed isomerase enzymes. It then undergoes purification and other steps similar to those that produce citric acid. High fructose syrup quickly found favor in the food and beverage industries.

Here at the new citric acid plant in Dayton, technicians developed a liquid extraction process that increased yield and eliminated calcium sulphate, an undesirable by-product.

This feat of interlocking technology led to an important joint venture with Cargill, Inc., experts in the grain commodity business. At Dayton, Cargill operates a wet corn milling facility. The dextrose made there from corn starch slurry is converted into citric acid, or by a separate process, into the high fructose syrup. The joint venture aspect was abandoned a few years later, but the Cargill operation fills the raw material needs of the Miles plant next door.

The Calcium Sulphate Problem

Of all technical successes—small and large—that have strewn the trails of citric acid development, perhaps the most visibly spectacular involves calcium sulphate, a bulky off-shoot of manufacturing. With the advent of environmental concerns and mounting controversies over the handling of industrial waste, Miles long wrestled with this problem; and for years, it had little choice except to landfill the calcium sulphate, innocuous as it is, at various sites around Elkhart—tons of it every working day.

Again, technology came to the fore, scoring a victory not only for the company but for the community as well. The Israeli Mining Institute, along with Miles researchers, in the mid-1970s worked out a liquid extraction method for eliminating solid calcium sulphate. It was first extensively tested and then installed at the Dayton plant in 1977. The process became a reality at Elkhart in early 1981. The need for landfill operations stopped—to the relief of both Miles and local citizens. The method also lowered

the biological oxygen demand, thereby reducing pressure on the Elkhart sewage treatment plant. Finally, the system saved millions of dollars.

From Fruit Juice to Rust...

Citric acid hardly rates with the top glamour products on the industrial scene. It has been pretty much taken for granted, and its virtues get little attention. It has been in short supply (1974, 1976, 1978), although not in recent years. New uses slip routinely or mundanely into various products and processes, rarely with much fanfare. And those uses are plentiful, indeed, since it is nontoxic, highly malleable to all kinds of situations, and stable to light and air. It prevents oxidation, reacts in desirable ways with many chemicals, forms complex salts with other metals and makes an excellent starting material in manufacturing processes. Astonishingly, it is mild enough to be used in fruit juices, yet harsh enough to expunge rust from metal.

As already mentioned, citric acid's sole inaugural use at Miles was as an acidulant for Alka-Seltzer. In reacting with sodium bicarbonate to form carbon dioxide and sodium citrate, it created the quick effervescence needed for a refreshing drink. From that original captive role, applications proliferated into the food, industrial, and pharmaceutical fields.

A Variety of Uses in Food

High on the list are beverages since citric acid offers tartness and natural taste, and cuts excessive sweetness in finished beverages and syrups. It acts as a preservative, and slows browning in white wines.

As a flavor enhancer and preservative, the product is widely used in canned fruits and vegetables. It helps retain flavor, appearance, and consistency. It is particularly valuable in counteracting spoilage in canned, whole-pack tomatoes.

Candies, especially hard varieties, benefit from the tartness of citric acid. Its flavor not only improves taste, but assures the setting qualities of gelatin desserts. It does the same for jellies, jams, and preserves, enabling pectin to bring about proper jelling. The product has many other food usages, such as in meat and frozen fish, where it prolongs shelf life and forestalls discoloration. Wherever it will add to the tang of taste and preserve flavor, from baby formulas to sherbets, it plays its pleasant role.

Industrial Usage Growing

Citric acid use in foods and beverages may have been peaking by the late 1970s. On the other hand, industrial usage and opportunities abound and are growing. As a chemical cleaning agent, it fights with the much stronger and classic hydrochloric acid, which is less expensive but in this grade far more toxic to man.

Citric acid's first recorded victory of any consequence in this rivalry came in 1957 when the Philo station of the American Electric Power Corporation used it for pre-operational cleaning of a large new steam generator. Citric acid alone did not prove to be the final answer, but when combined with ammonia it came close. Since then, hundreds of steam generators at utilities and industrial plants have found ammoniated citric acid preferable in removing corrosive deposits and mill scales. As much as three-fourths of the time needed for cleaning has been saved. Applications apply to nuclear as well as conventional steam-operated power plants.

No acid other than citric offers the same fine lemonlike flavor, refreshing tartness, and high solubility to foods and beverages.

Another blending of ammonia with citric acid opened a portal to expanded use, ranging from tests for automobile radiators to better recovery of oil in the petroleum industry. The modified product dissolves rust and scales from various metals. It strips rust and deposits away from copper alloys, leaving behind lustrous surfaces—a major use. It has even largely solved the problem of rerusting.

This benign acid goes on to serve as a catalyst system to prevent wrinkling in wash-and-wear fabrics and as a retardant in flame-resistant materials. It aids in the tanning of white leather, and prevents the formation of hard-water scale in bottle washing compounds. It is ideal for descaling procedures in seawater evaporators. Still another industry, printing, employs it to stabilize the materials used in making diazo papers.

It even has a role in weight reduction—but for building blocks rather than human beings. With other ingredients it liberates gas from pockets in the blocks, thus cutting their weight substantially.

One of the more interesting applications is in reducing sulphur dioxide emissions from coal-burning power plants, metal refineries, and chemical operations. The partially neutralized citric acid solution absorbs the sulphur dioxide from the stack gas—a somewhat heroic role given the environmental anxieties of the times!

Pharmaceutical Applications

Finally, citric acid has pharmaceutical application. Its effervescence provides eye appeal, unique flavoring, and swift solution time. When an acidic taste is desirable in syrups and elixirs, it does the job admirably. It helps stabilize ascorbic acid and lotions, and is used to prepare citrated whole human blood.

As Miles forged into the fourth decade of its citric acid annals, it forged its way with optimism. The capacity for growth was there, especially after the Dayton plant doubled its capacity in the late 1970s. Division president McGrath was pushing hard toward more standard industrial uses. As a result, the number of customers in a few years had grown from a dozen to more than a hundred.

Safe for Processes and People

Marketing vice president Harold Stalter points to a glowing attribute of citric acid—its safety for both processes and people.

"You can say it helped to put the walleyes back in Lake Erie," he says. That's an apt illustration.

Concern over phosphates had made their replacement by citric acid an environmental must. Because of its marked safety, a principal use of citric acid is in laundry detergents.

The non-toxicity of the product has bolstered its standing in the chemical world. Both the Food and Drug Administration and the United Nations Expert Committee on Food Additives have never found it wanting in its effects on health and safety. It can even be incinerated and discharged into the atmosphere with no toxicity problems.

In exploring frontiers for new uses, authors Blair, Staal, and Zienty underscored such potential gains as reduced down time for cleaning, methods that will cut damage to construction metals, better copper deposit removal, eradication of hard dense deposits, and improved environmental disposal systems.

Citric Acid New Enough for Current Challenges

Old and familiar as it may be, citric acid is new enough for the most current challenges. Take nuclear power reactors: their radiation levels increase with operating life. "If chemicals (such as citric) and their implementation can be sufficiently developed," the Miles' threesome states, "system decontamination could provide significant reduction in radiation." A likely result: improved maintenance and shorter downtime.

Miles' own research never flags. "We know what we are looking for," Alex Batti says. Or, as scientist Ron Hart explains, "We are studying many organisms other than *Aspergillus niger,* some of them related to it, and some totally unique. We are trying genetically to engineer organisms of the future that could produce citric acid like crazy...."

So better cultures and better yields from refined techniques still challenge the scientists of Miles. They want not only to invigorate concepts in known uses (there are at least 150 now), but to find still additional applications for a compound that is so safe, versatile, and adaptive.

As a commodity, citric acid is now abundantly available worldwide. Miles has long been the world's lowest-cost producer. "Europe presently has an excess capacity," Stalter notes, "so the United States, of course, is a prime target, and in the hard times of the early 1980s foreign producers stepped up their selling efforts. But here our product excellence, service, and reliability stand us in good stead. We remain strong and are working to become even stronger."

*Fermentation technology gives Miles
a winning edge.*

Andy Ruffin bags citric acid in the Elkhart plant in the 1970s.

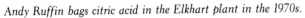

Regardless of what the coming decades may bring, Miles' development of citric acid already stands as a major achievement. In fact, in any Hall of Fame for technology, Miles' pioneering would rate three niches: one for its work in perfecting "deep-tank" fermentation, a second for using corn as the basic raw material, and a third for developing the liquid extraction process. Beyond those accomplishments, it should be noted that the company in the early 1950s filled an urgent internal need, then went on energetically to create markets both at home and abroad that have brought distinct benefits to mankind. That's quite a record!

CHAPTER 11

Enzymes—Nature's Catalysts

If any one factor stitches together the technology of Miles, it is the ubiquitous enzyme. One strand of the story winds back to the youthful Dr. Compton. Working in an Eli Lilly lab one summer while still a medical student, he became aware of the importance and promise of enzymes in understanding life and science.

Soon after he joined Miles in 1938, he helped to spark an interest in these natural catalysts, particularly in fermentation. This was significant, because another of his early goals was to make the company independent of outside suppliers for the citric acid so basic to Alka-Seltzer.

Thus enzymology, and its role in fermentation, took on research significance at Miles as far back as the 1940s. Since then, few companies have contributed more to the field, or know more about it, than Miles. Enzymology became fundamental not only to fermentation and citric acid but also to diagnostics and a host of applications in food, agricultural, and other industrial processes. Now, in the early 1980s, these substances, which have been called "the sparks of life" and the "workhorses of creation," remain a focal point for research and development.

Where will all this lead the company in its second century? Certainly it will lead to some visible goals, and perhaps to others not yet within reach.

Enzymes have been used by man since ancient times, even though he didn't know they were making possible his cheese and wine. In 1833, Duclaux introduced the custom of naming them after the substrate on which they function, followed by "ase" as the ending. This practice still prevails.

Historically, the producers of beer, wine, bread, cheese and so on had to rely on enzymes derived from plant and animal sources. Today the standardized enzymes that emerge from controlled fermentation processes are, of course, much superior to the old, variable, naturally occurring products.

Locked into Life Itself

Few substances in nature surpass the magic of enzymes, for they appear to be locked into the very secrets of life itself. "Enzymes are nature's own tools to transform one substance into another, and every chemical reaction that goes on in any living organism is dependent upon them," Dr. Compton wrote in 1976. Few have put the definition more clearly. A Miles publication once put it another way: "Enzymes recycle the earth's basic elements, replenish the soil and thus nourish the profusion of life as we know it." Or, as Miles' Al Blaze says, "It's like putting a key into a lock and turning it to open a door."

Perhaps, above all, enzymes are catalysts, and highly sophisticated ones, which react precisely and predictably within their own molecular configurations and with their environment. Their "workhorse" character stems from a catalytic power to enhance the rate of reaction factors a thousandfold. Moreover, they do the job with great specificity, acting on only one substrate (substance), one type of bond, or one compound. With this characteristic, especially in industrial processes, they create high yields of desired products.

The Shadow of Takamine's Genius

The Miles legacy in enzymes can be vividly traced to their greatest innovator, Dr. Jokichi Takamine. He died at the age of 67 in 1922, some 38 years before the small company he founded became a part of Miles. Yet the long shadow of his genius still lingers over the field in which he excelled. His life story is the stuff of fiction, except that it was real and still glows with charm six decades after his death.

As a company brochure explained in 1974, "It is unusual for any company to become sole trustee of a particular scientific heritage.... When Miles acquired the Takamine Laboratories in 1956, we be-

This Takamine plant, in Clifton, NJ, purchased in 1956, was the origin of more than 75 specialty enzymes now marketed by Miles.

In 1886, Dr. Jokichi Takamine (1854–1922) developed the first fermentation enzyme to find industrial use. In his lifetime, he patented 50 more yet found time to help build better American-Japanese relations and in 1912 to instigate Japan's gift of 3,000 cherry trees to Washington, D.C. Planted around the Tidal Basin, they still attract tourists in vast numbers at blossom time.

came the heirs of a tradition of innovation in commercial enzymology."

Born into a Samurai family in Japan, Takamine was educated in Scotland, wooed and won the daughter of a Confederate Army Colonel while visiting New Orleans, returned to Japan to encourage reluctant farmers to use phosphate as a fertilizer. All the while he was experimenting with enzymes. In 1886, he developed the initial industrial fermentation enzyme, Takadiastase, the first of about 50 for which he obtained patents in his lifetime. Virtually all of his innovations led to improvements in the food processing industries, and especially in distilling and baking.

As if his eminence in enzymes weren't enough, Takamine earned international renown by isolating the elusive hormone, adrenaline, in a pure, stable form. It was, in its way, the first wonder drug.

With the wealth this discovery generated, Takamine expanded his laboratories and small plant in

Clifton, New Jersey, which he had established in 1898. When it was purchased by Miles in 1956, it had about 85 employees and was making enzymes from both surface and deep-tank fermentation processes.

Miles' Interest in Enzymes Takes Off

Miles' avid interest in enzymes more or less "took off" with the acquisition of Takamine, under the tutelage of an exceptional group of enzymologists—Leland Underkofler, Walt Windish, Richard De-Senna, Al Blaze, Andy Lauria, Edward Bassett, Robert Charles, and William Ferracone. Takamine's expertise in enzymes and industrial fermentation dovetailed neatly with Miles' need in citric acid technology, boosted its diversification program and opened up research and marketing opportunities. In the ensuing years, all three areas proved to be most rewarding.

An early project was the large-scale production of glucose oxidase, which Ames needed for its test strip products. One reason it was vital: Ames and Lilly were both trying to develop and market the strip concept for glucose testing in urine and blood. Eventually, a competitive patent situation was resolved amicably so both companies could proceed along their own pathways.

Other Takamine-produced enzymes took on historic dimensions. Two of them, Tenase and Diazyme, were not only sold to corn processors worldwide, but also were captively consumed in the production of dextrose from corn flour in the processing operation for citric acid. That advance came in the early 1960s.

Leland A. Underkofler, Ph.D., a pioneer in microbiology, came to Miles with the Takamine Laboratory in 1956. His book, "Industrial Fermentation," published in 1955, is still considered a classic.

The basic Miles strategy was to concentrate on industrial enzymes as specialty products, especially those requiring high technology and expert technical service. It was a wise decision, still fully justified into the 1980s, as growth in enzyme sales so handsomely attests.

Siebel's Brewing Excellence

That decision led down many avenues, for example, brewing. Miles worked with the Jan Deckker Chemical Division of Naarden to develop enzymes that would act on barley grain directly, thus improving on the natural malt enzyme system for making beer. Naarden succeeded. Still, Miles had need for more expertise in brewing technology and servicing, so it purchased the J. E. Siebel & Sons Company of Chicago in 1971.

Founded in 1872, Siebel had a unique reputation in high technology service to brewing firms, as well as in such products as enzymes to prevent chill haze, enhance foam, and maintain the flavor and stability of beer.

Beyond that, Siebel stood preeminent in the world of brewing for its Institute of Brewing Technology, a school that has trained more than a thou-

Miles supplies enzymes to brewers the world over.

The Enzymology Research Laboratory in Elkhart was a busy place in 1962.

Specialty enzymes are still made in the enzyme plant in Clifton, NJ.

Behind this workaday exterior is the ultimate in enzyme production. Completed at Elkhart in 1982, it features the latest in fermentation technology.

sand brewmasters, many of them now ranked as world leaders in a craft requiring its own distinctive skills. Siebel also sponsored laboratory, educational, and technical services, as well as workshops and seminars.

Although Miles sold Siebel back to the principals in 1982, it retained a strong marketing and technical service relationship designed to provide the most effective enzymes for brewing.

The Joint Venture Route

Early on, Miles had seen the potential of the worldwide market for enzymes. But it had no excess capacity in the United States with which to supply the foreign markets. So it turned to the joint venture route.

This was a fortunate choice. Not only was the venture about to be described a success, it also illustrated the depth and diversity of Miles' talent in enzymology.

The timing was again good in 1971 when Kali-Chemie in Nienberg, West Germany, found itself with a new enzyme production plant and not a great deal of use for it because of the collapsing detergent market.

The venture began with Dick Kocher and Dean Spence evaluating the market in Europe and the potential synergism between Miles and the German company. Merrick Shepard headed manufacturing plans with Dick DeSenna, Bob Fiederer, and Walt Windish working on the actual transfer of technology. Harold Stalter and Windish relocated to Germany to guide the venture. The first managing directors were Stalter and Hans Geyer, who had started the Miles Kali-Chemie joint venture from scratch. Windish later became one of the managing directors when Stalter returned to the United States.

At about the same time, another joint venture which already existed with Aranguren y Cia in Mexico was extended to enzymes. The name was changed to Enmex and a new enzyme fermentation facility was built by 1973. Two expansions came later for the rapidly growing Mexican market. A similar joint venture was made with Arcor, S.A.I.C., in Arroyita, Argentina. A wholly owned Miles plant also produces enzymes at Vinay, France.

Elkhart Becomes the Domestic Enzyme Center

By the late 1970s, the need for a larger, more modern enzyme plant in the United States had become critical. At this time, too, Bayer AG looked

favorably on the future of industrial enzymes, and it supported plans for a new facility at Elkhart. Miles' long-range planners recommended this location after studying almost 50 others in the Midwest.

The $20 million production plant, opened in early 1982, is a symbol of Miles' continued commitment to leadership in enzymology. Designed by Miles' own experts, among them DeSenna, John Denton, and former division president Nevin Meyer, it is computer-controlled and runs entirely on the metric system.

As with citric acid, enzymes are produced by fermentation, but each enzyme has its own unique process. The operation starts with fermentable raw materials in liter-sized flasks to get the microbial seed growth under way. From there the mixture goes to seed tanks, then to huge fermenters so large that SCUBA divers checked them for leaks prior to production runs. Holding tanks next receive the mixture before it flows to a filter system that functions very much like the human kidney.

The final product ultimately emerges from a maze of pipes, tanks, and tubes, ready to be sent to customers in pails, drums, and tank trucks.

Computerized "Fingers" Trace Each Step

Again, high technology makes it all possible, with a central control point, in an area not much bigger than the large living room of an ordinary home. The only furniture here is a massive desk where a single operator monitors an impressive array of computerized panels mounted along every wall, whose "fingers" trace each step in production and flash warnings at the first indication of trouble.

The system adjusts and measures fermentation variables and purification procedures, solves process problems and provides information to boost yields and better utilize raw materials. The first control room operator in the new plant was Dorothy Suggs who had worked on production line jobs for 18 years. With a few months' training, she had mastered the intricacies of the control room panels.

The new Elkhart plant was built for large volume production to achieve economies of scale—and in a "horseshoe" configuration that can be readily expanded. The major customers are corn millers and industrial alcohol producers. Two enzymes, along with the glucose isomerase enzyme, are used to make high fructose syrup, which is as sweet as sugar but not as expensive, a fact that explains its growing use in beverages.

Meanwhile, the Clifton, New Jersey, plant concentrates on providing a number of smaller volume specialty enzymes that go into some 75 compounded and blended items serving a wide assortment of industries.

A Legion of Enzyme Uses in Food

Uses for enzymes continue to proliferate, many of them in the food industry. Enzymes increase the yields of fruit juice, clarify juices and wines, and remove pectin that causes premature thickening during processing of jams and jellies. Other enzymes take out oxygen that can affect flavor in bottled and canned goods. Still others break down fats, make proteins soluble, and release flavors in any number of widely known processed foodstuffs.

Enzymes are indispensable to corn processors, converting starch to crystalline dextrose and glucose and fructose syrups. Bakers use them to control the final properties of dough and to reduce mixing time, and they improve crackers, cookies, and even pizza. They are active ingredients for tenderizing meat, while salad dressings, cereals, milk, beverages, baby formulas, eggs, snacks, and many other food items subject to deterioration benefit from protected enzyme action.

Industrial Applications Abound

Industrial uses abound. Enzymes are employed in everything from oil-well drilling to septic tank cleaning, to bringing about smoother grain leather, to removing the gelatin coatings for silk screens to film stripping, to assuring uniform dyeing in textiles and furs. Especially promising are ventures into agriculture, including animal feeds, silage, and seed germination.

The enzyme business into which Miles moved aggressively after the Takamine purchase was still quite small—perhaps a $10 to $20 million market, with many small specialty end users. By 1967 it had tripled, in good measure because the corn wet milling industry found increased bulk usage for specialty syrups and dextrose. Meanwhile, research had improved enzyme quality yields and lowered costs.

When a big usage surge came in the late 1960s with the demand for alkaline protease enzymes in detergents, volume soared, only to plummet when

Immobilized glucose isomerase is used in the making of high fructose corn syrup.

concern arose over possible allergic reactions. The market eventually rebounded. More important to Miles, though, was its decision to continue focusing—during a period of market flux—on the growing high technology applications of enzymes for food and industrial uses.

By the early 1980s the world market had gone well above the $100 million mark. The transition from small developmental concepts had ended by the mid-1970s; the enzyme business had become big business and, seemingly, it could do nothing but mushroom in the foreseeable future, perhaps to as much as half a billion dollars a year by the late 1980s. Happily, Miles' portion had been climbing even faster than the roughly 12 to 15 percent annual growth rate for the industry.

Along salients of enzyme research, production, and marketing, then, Miles carries on the legacy of the legendary Jokichi Takamine. His faith in enzymes knew no bounds. As one observer nostalgically notes, "He thought you could run the world with enzymes." Given their present and potential end uses, he may not have been that far off!

CHAPTER 12

Bringing Culture To Cheese

All the world loves cheese. As old as civilization, cheese tempts the palate with its delightful subtleties and adds to the gustatory joys of life.

The Marschall Division of Miles Laboratories has been of enormous help to cheesemakers with contributions that go back more than 75 years. It's one more story of triumphant technology in the annals of the company.

A Danish Founder Named Marschall

It all began obscurely at the turn of the century when a Danish immigrant, Adolph J. Marschall, a pharmacist by training, worked for a firm in New York that made cheese ingredients. Cheesemakers always had problems, he felt, because their cheese starters and often their processes varied from batch to batch. Like many of his countrymen, Marschall ventured west, to Dane County, Wisconsin. It was a fortunate choice, for if there was an area where the dairy industry was developing in the United States, Dane County was it. It is the hub of the cheese-makers' wheel today.

Integral to cheesemaking at the time was something called rennet extract, made from the stomachs of calves. It was neither standardized nor reliable, but Marschall thought he could make it so. For several years he prepared five gallons of rennet each week, then pushed a wheelbarrow with the containers to the railroad station in Madison for shipment to a handful of customers.

In September 1906, with $5,000 in the bank, he founded the Marschall Dairy Laboratories, Inc. That year, total sales amounted to only $641. Marschall confidently built his business, partly because he could speak German, Danish, Swedish, and French to the immigrant farmers of the area. He had learned English himself by studying a Sears, Roebuck catalog.

World War I cut off the rennet supply from

Europe. Marschall, finding a way to preserve calf rennets by "salting them down," helped to make up the shortage. He had only 10 employees at the time.

Marschall was an individualist and a perfectionist. Always bent on product and technology improvements, he worked closely with professors at the neighboring University of Wisconsin. He never stopped experimenting.

A generous as well as a practical man, in 1936 he set up a stock distribution plan for employees based on performance and length of service. In his later years, he traveled widely to establish sales and distribution offices. He died in 1957 at the age of 88.

For decades, with insistence on standardization and quality control somewhat advanced for its day, the company did a respectable business in supplying reliable rennet as well as colors to cheesemakers. Still, it remained a modest enterprise, with sales hovering around $1 million annually through the 1950s.

During these years, cheesemaking was never easy. Not until new technology evolved, buttressed by improved enzymes, did it edge into a new era with better products and expanded markets.

Research Brings New Cheese Starters

The big change at Marschall began in the mid-1950s with the hiring of "new blood" that would really get the company going. The key men were Richard Kocher, a studious and inventive scientist; capable Verle "Chris" Christensen, a scholarly and personable cheese industry expert; talented Douglas Pangier, a quality control and product specialist; and enthusiastic V. G. "Viv" Rowley, who would revitalize sales and marketing. They knew at once that new keys to better cheesemaking could be found through research and through working very closely with the cheesemakers themselves.

For more than 25 years, Division president Chris Christensen, left, and marketing vice president Viv Rowley have been an indefatigable duo.

When a shortage of calf stomachs began developing in the late 1950s, Marschall developed a better technique for making the rennet extract and soon dominated the market. "We were the only producer for a while," Christensen recalls. "In fact, we more or less saved the Wisconsin cheese industry."

Marschall's contributions to the world of cheese rest largely on the achievements in the early 1960s of three proficient researchers—Kocher, later to be president of Miles; Christensen, later to be president of Marschall; and Harold Rasmussen, supervisor of the microbiological laboratory, who retired in 1981.

What they created were Marstar starter media and Marstar concentrated cultures, once described as "probably the most important changes of this century for the cheesemaker." This new system did two vital things. The starter media inhibited something called bacteriophage, long a deadly enemy in making cheese since it destroys starter cultures, and they provided for more consistent growth and proper acid development. The concentrated cultures helped produce cheese of consistent quality.

About the time that the new technique was first successfully tested at Iowa State in 1966, Miles moved onto the scene. With its enzyme technology, Miles had originated a microbial rennet in the early 1960s, but had no practical way to market it. Miles approached Marschall with an offer to purchase the company, and board chairman Arthur Benner liked it. So the company was bought in December 1966 for $1.67 million. Miles thus entered a new field that would prove to be fascinating from the standpoint of technology, highly significant to the cheese industry, and profitable as well.

Superstart Cultures Save Time

Miles quickly sensed that Marschall's teamwork had opened the portals to a new phase in cheesemaking. Soon the pilot plant at Elkhart was producing bulk-set cultures.

This was only a stopgap, for Dr. Les Bluhm had found a way to improve culture concentrations, and there was no way the old plant on Proudfit Street could handle the business that appeared to lurk on the horizon. In 1968, a new plant was built on a 55-acre site in the Madison countryside; and in April 1969, it turned out its first products. The building had to be expanded two years later.

By 1973, cultures and starter media were being made on a continuous operating schedule. In 1976, the first Superstart cultures, improved versions of the bulk cultures, were produced. By 1980, 18 different culture strains had been developed. The number of blends for cheese and other foods had burgeoned to more than 50—a far cry from just rennet extract and vegetable colors. Meanwhile, the staff had quadrupled since 1969, and sales volume for all cultures had multiplied 22 times in a decade.

Nowhere is quality assurance more precise than in the preparation of the Superstart concentrated cultures, hallmark products developed by Marschall.

Management Encourages Research and Development

In 1977, when Marschall was made a division, its first president was top Miles veteran Merrick Shepard, who had made major contributions in citric acid and enzymology. He set a fast pace.

Building on the Marstar system over the past 20 years, Marschall has refined and expanded its products, operations, and services as a major supplier of microbial coagulants, cultures, and processing aids to the dairy industry. It has also applied its expertise to vegetable proteins, beverage processing, and the brewing industry. Its wide range of specialized starter media goes into more than cheese, including sausage-type products, sourdough bread, pickles, sauerkraut, even Bantu beer in South Africa.

All this has required extensive reliance on research and technology, from enzyme studies to final manufacturing.

In looking for superior cultures, Marschall researchers have always displayed a high degree of inventiveness. For example, they would take seed cultures from top cheesemakers, package them in vials, then flash freeze and store them in liquid nitrogen. At each transfer of the seed culture, there would be plate counts, activity tests, and measuring of gas production. Next, further field testing would proceed, followed by tests in actual cheesemaking before final commercial approval.

Researchers made things pretty easy for the manufacturer. In using a Marstar concentrated culture, the manufacturer simply thaws the two-and-

As Marschall Division president, M. W. Shepard helped guide the destiny of products and employees in the 1970s.

one-half or five-ounce can with tap water and chlorine, opens the "pull-top," and pours the contents into the bulk tank. Such direct-to-vat cultures have the advantage of eliminating the need for "mother" and intermediate cultures, thereby sharply cutting the risks of contamination.

Marschall's Shipping Ingenuity

For all their success with starter media, technicians still had to solve the problem of how best to get

Innovative methodology has made Miles a leader
in the production of cheese cultures.

Technology Changes Production

Nowhere does the technology prevail more than
in the actual production of the line, built as it is
around a long excellence in fermentation enzymology and freeze drying. Take the Proudfit Street
plant: in one operation, rennets and rice hulls are
blended in large cypress tanks and undergo percola-
tion, not unlike that of coffeemaking, to extract
desired enzymes for cheesemaking.

In other operations, flavors are extracted from
cultures for direct application to both processed and
imitation cheese. Still other enzymes are engendered
from the ground-up gullets of kid goats, lambs, or
calves and custom-packaged especially for Italian
cheesemakers.

The Proudfit Street plant also produces the
familiar Marschall annatto colors, in use now for
more than six decades. The raw material comes from
the Caribbean—from the seed of the Bixa Orellano
tree. A million pounds of seed are shipped to Madison
each fall. Color pigments are removed from the
surface of the seeds and mixed with oil and water to
produce a wide range of edible colors—from pale
lemon to deep red-orange. They go not only into
cheeses but into bakery goods, ice cream, yogurt,
butter and margarine, sausage casings, and the aforementioned Bantu beer.

them to customers. Ingenuity prevailed here, too.
Patterned on an American Breeder's Association system, Marschall began, as early as 1963–64, to ship its
concentrated cultures in liquid nitrogen cryogenic
tanks. Shipments also went in insulated boxes containing dry ice so they could be transferred to
freezers.

Marschall has gone on with improvements to
assure better dairy products. Marzyme, a microbial
rennet first introduced in 1972, earned wide acceptance. New processing techniques evolved under
Doug Pangier's direction also helped. Various special
cultures were conceived for cheddar, bleu, and colby
cheese and for buttermilk, sour cream, cream cheese,
and yogurt. Marschall has always been close to Italian
cheesemakers in the United States, one result being
improved lipase powders and rennet paste for its
specialized products.

"We literally revolutionized the whole cheese
culture industry," Christensen says, "and we got a
great part of the business."

Growth led to this culture
plant at Madison, WI, which was completed in 1976.

Manufacturing Sophistication

A major thrust for manufacturing sophistication came with the bulk set and Superstart programs. Look at just one piece of the action at the culture plant: one process begins in batching tanks containing skim milk and other nutrients needed for culture growth. The whole fermentation procedure can be accomplished overnight (in contrast to the six to eight days required for citric acid and enzymes).

When a culture is ready for "harvesting," automatic valves pour the thick liquid into sterilized aluminum cans. The cans are automatically steam-sterilized and capped. Baskets of "sleeves" (four cans to a sleeve) are then trundled into huge freezers where liquid nitrogen maintains a temperature of more than 300° F below zero.

There the products stay in quarantine for a few days during quality assurance tests. Once cleared, they go into storage freezers, ready for shipment to customers. Dry ice in the shipping containers keeps temperatures at 80° to 90° F below zero. Dry ice works exceedingly well, yet researchers constantly look for an even better method.

Cheese Production Is Booming

Cheese production continues to boom. In the 1970s, per capita consumption rose 60 percent. In 1983, Marschall was no more resting on its technology—or on its lofty niche in the pantheon of cheesemaking—than it was when the Kocher team got cracking on the Marstar system.

There are still goals to be attained. As one researcher puts it, "What we are looking for is the development of age characteristics in a shorter time—usually in six months to a year—to develop the strong flavor that you associate with cheese. With the addition of enzymes, we are seeing that we can age cheese in approximately half the normal time. There is a very definite cost ratio per pound per month for aging cheese, and if you can get a nine-month cheddar in three months, there's a six-month saving."

So the quest continues for better cultures, for an accelerated cheese-ripening system, for improved microbial coagulants, even for a genetically engineered calf rennet to be derived by fermentation. Also sought in the early 1980s was a quick test to screen antibiotics in milk. It would be of value to farmers, milk haulers, and milk receiving stations.

The Annual Italian Cheese Seminar, started by Stan Ferris, became an institution, drawing hundreds of cheesemakers to Madison. Stan, at right, is shown with the 1973 Marschall Honorary Award Winners— Anthony Russo, Louis Russo, Filippo Candela, and Thomas Chellino, (seated).

New Cultures for Animal Feed

"The dairy product business is bound to keep growing," predicts Dan Wessley, Ph.D., culture plant manager. "But even greater growth is likely to come in agri-business. This will require a large volume of specialty cultures. So this is where our field research is largely concentrated."

Wessley points out that delivery to and keeping cultures frozen on farms still pose physical and economic problems. Hence some of Marschall research has been aimed at dry forms of cultures, once thought to be quite impractical.

Moving beyond cheese, Marschall is examining basic animal nutrition, seeking ways to supply microorganisms that can inhibit pathogenic organisms and improve nutrient absorption in feed. Even inoculating silage for dairy cows could prevent excess fermentation. As Wessley points out, better animal health means weight gains, lower costs of feeding and less livestock medication—all worthy goals and emi-

nently reachable within the specialized province of Marschall research.

Given the universality of cheese, expansion overseas was an early goal of the resurgent Marschall several decades ago. A plant was built in 1969 at Epernon, France, to provide cultures for the typical high-moisture French cheeses, and for the rest of the European market (five times larger than the United States). It has been most successful under the guidance of such people as Jean Bernard, Miles general manager; Roger Farrow, John Bonavita, and Michael Sponcet. Another plant in Guatemala has enabled marketing expert Mario Font to build demand for cultures in Central and South America.

So around the world, wherever body, texture, and flavor count in cheese, the Marschall line resourcefully serves industry and the consumer. As a streamer proclaimed at the 20th Annual Italian Cheese Seminar in 1983, "It Pays to Be Partial to Marschall."

CHAPTER 13

Prescription Drugs In The Vanguard

On September 30, 1980, Miles Pharmaceuticals submitted to the FDA a new drug application on Mezlin (mezlocillin sodium), an injectable broad spectrum antibiotic, the first of a new generation of semisynthetic penicillins developed by Bayer AG scientists.

Miles' documentation, in 130 two-inch volumes, covered 51 clinical trials. The FDA approved it, in near-record time for an antibiotic, on September 21, 1981, and it soon began appearing on the formularies of many leading hospitals.

A closely related and even more potent drug, Azlin (azlocillin), aimed in hospital situations at life-threatening bacteria called Pseudomonas, followed Mezlin onto the market in late 1982. It, too, had moved smoothly toward approval, in a year, under the FDA's rigorous scrutiny.

These antibiotics helped solidify the company's growing position in prescription drugs. There was no longer any question that a new era had begun, that a new entity of Miles Laboratories was now firmly in place.

The Bayer AG Pipeline

The basis was the Bayer AG pipeline which had been funneled into West Haven, and with commendable speed.

Near the end of 1977, Bayer had dissolved Delbay Pharmaceuticals, a joint research and marketing venture with Schering Corporation, and in doing so retained marketing rights for clotrimazole, the first broad spectrum anti-fungal agent. Bayer AG had sold this product outside of the United States as Canesten since the early 1970s, and under the trademarks Mycelex and Mycelex-G it became Miles' first Bayer-based product line.

Successful detailing of Mycelex began in the spring of 1979, with a sales force swiftly doubled to

180 people. They had new marketing tools as well, everything from new product information bulletins to audio messages that physicians could put in their car tape players.

In 1981, the field force was increased to 250 representatives and an exciting new concept incorporating laser videodisc techniques—the Miles Learning Center—was set up in 250 leading hospitals.

Bayer AG Research Leads to Anti-Infectives

Mycelex, Mezlin, and Azlin came from a rich heritage going back to 1916, when the first drugs to fight sleeping sickness and malaria were developed in Elberfeld, Bayer AG's research laboratories. Research led, in time, to the sulfonamides and the Nobel Prize-winning work of the company's own Gerhard Domagk, and it led, of course, to antibiotics.

For decades Bayer AG has been pushing toward the farthest frontiers of anti-infective therapy. It also explores newer horizons; as its elaborate 1980 booklet dedicated to Domagk said, "The development of therapy for viral diseases has only begun...and remains virtually unsolved." So its virologists are probing ever deeper into this enigmatic field, with its puzzles and promises.

All this is bound to enrich the mission of Miles, since, with the acquisition, Miles had inherited not just products but an enormous background in chemotherapy, the traditions of 70 years of anti-infective research, and the resources of a giant company.

Not surprisingly, then, Miles had no hesitation in proudly proclaiming itself "A New Force in Therapeutic Progress," which was the title of a 1981 promotional piece. It explained that the firm was now "part of one of the largest pharmaceutical manufacturers in the world...that combines a century of

This was essentially the entire Dome line of dermatological products when Miles acquired the company in 1959.

In its 75th year, Miles purchased Dome Chemicals from Irving B. Wershaw and his wife, Lona Duval. With them, at left, is Walter Beardsley.

health care technology in the United States with one hundred years of research in ethical drugs by its parent company, Bayer Aktiengesellschaft in Germany."

The Backdrop to Dome

The road that led to this broad new avenue in the final years of Miles' first century had some novel twists and turns. For Miles Pharmaceuticals has another legacy, a rather uncommon one of modest dimensions, but fascinating nonetheless. It dates from October 1, 1959, when Miles bought Dome Chemicals for $7.5 million in cash.

The year 1959 was the 75th in Miles' history and the beginning of one of the company's peak periods. The Annual Report from that year revealed a new record for worldwide sales of over $72 million, up 15 percent from 1958, enough to achieve listing for the first time among the *Fortune* 500 companies. Heavy expenses made it impossible to carry as much of the increased sales through to profit as management had hoped, but the year ended with a net income of over $4.3 million, equal to $3.62 per share, compared with $3.30 per share the previous year, an increase of 10 percent.

The increased costs had been spread pretty much across the board, but were particularly burdensome in starting up a $4.1 million addition to the citric acid plant in Elkhart and in establishing new plants in Paris and Buenos Aires. Of course, the citric acid addition would enable Miles to double production and enter the open market besides meeting its own growing needs for citric acid in Alka-Seltzer. The two foreign plants would add potential for expanding international operations, but, for the moment, they represented heavy outlays.

Another expense during the year had been the purchase of property in Elkhart as the site of a new research building. The British Research and Administrative Headquarters was simultaneously being developed on the outskirts of London.

Employment rolls stood at 2,631 and employees were described in the Annual Report as "your team...accelerating Miles' pace of progress" and "safeguarding Miles' watchword, 'quality'...."

President Walter R. Beardsley and Chairman Charles S. Beardsley wrote, "The degree of our success will be measured by how well we execute our plans for growth and diversification through research, development, acquisitions, organization, and improvement in operations." As the events of the next decade would document, they measured up very well.

This, then, was the backdrop against which the purchase of Dome Chemicals, Inc. would be set. The purchase was described as "the most important single event of the year." Dome was known as a leading producer of dermatologicals for the medical profession, and the acquisition was seen as a step in diversification that would "strengthen our whole corporate family."

Dome had been founded in New York in 1940 by Irving B. Wershaw, a pharmacist, chemical engineer and crack salesman, and his wife, Lona Duval, a skin products designer and industrial technologist.

Dome started its rise with Wershaw's development of a modern Burow's solution, universally used in the initial treatment of inflammatory skin conditions regardless of cause. Insect bites, poison ivy, swelling, bruises, and athlete's foot were among the most common indications.

Domeboro Improves on Burow's Solution

What Wershaw had done was make a simplified medication of the classic Burow's solution by creating what he called a Domeboro tablet. Until this improvement, pharmacists had had to compound daily batches because of the instability of the lead-salt ingredients. Wershaw replaced the lead with a calcium salt. So when a Domeboro tablet was dropped into water, a Burow's solution formed at once. Poured on a bandage, it provided a soothing wet dressing. The product came out just in time to be widely used during World War II, and to establish a lasting market among military physicians. Domeboro powder packets and tablets are still popular with both military and civilian physicians.

Wershaw had sensed a need to cater to the dermatologists, and he and his chief aide, Eric Zwerling, proceeded to do so with a measure of personal attention that still looks astounding today.

Wershaw had Bachrach Studios make portraits of them, which he mailed to their offices and hung in his own. Eventually, 2,000 of these portraits lined the walls at Dome headquarters. He wrote notes and letters to these doctors by the thousands, sponsored lectureships in the field, detailed them assiduously. Those close contacts had much to do with Dome developing a line that numbered about 50 products by 1959. Dome then accounted for more than a third of all sales in the field of topical hydrocortisone products.

With Domeboro tablets firmly established, Wershaw developed another item, Acid Mantle Creme, that became the mother of still another whole family of products. Hydrocortisone, tar, neomycin, estrone, and antiseptics, added to Acid Mantle, produced a series of improved medications. They included Cort-Dome Creme and Lotion for treatment of inflammatory dermatoses and Neo-Cort-Dome Creme and Lotion for dermatoses complicated by secondary infection.

Injectable Allergens Bolster the Line

Dome took a strong step toward diversification in 1962 with a unique series of injectable allergenic preparations. The scientific staff was increased, and a new allergy laboratory was established under Margaret Strauss, shown in the 1963 Annual Report evaluating results of the new Allpyral allergen extracts.

These products required fewer injections than usual in the treatment of allergic conditions and they reduced the frequency of shots, diminishing patient discomfort due to reactions. For this reason, they represented a significant advance in the treatment of

Dermatologists and allergists visiting New York City were invited by Dome Chemicals president Irving B. Wershaw to view themselves among the 1600 photographs (many by Fabian Bachrach) in the "Hall of Fame" or on the "Wall of Fame" located in the elegant Dome Club reception room on the seventh floor of the office building at 125 West End Avenue.

allergies and soon had a strong following among patients both here and abroad.

The first Allpyral products offered relief from allergies caused by house dust and pets in addition to pollens and molds. By 1966, Dome had an insect allergen formulated to protect patients susceptible to severe reactions from bee sting. By that time the extracts were also being produced in England, France, Canada, and Mexico City.

With approximately one out of every 10 people estimated to be suffering from a form of allergy, the eventual growth potential for the Allpyral line was thought to be sizable. In the 1970s, these products were responsible for nearly half of Dome's sales and perhaps 80 percent of its earnings. Basic to the Dome system of allergy diagnosis and treatment is an office kit of aqueous Allergen Scratch Diagnostic Tests containing 45 extracts of the most frequently encountered allergens.

Dome Moves to West Haven, Connecticut

At the time of the 1959 purchase, Dome occupied a Hudson River site in New York City that housed 99 employees and 67 field salesmen. Wershaw continued as president and became board chairman in 1963, but died suddenly that year at the age of 61.

J. W. Beal, Jr. was then elected president and chief executive officer. He had been executive vice president since 1960.

Leo Thompson, far left, Robert Reisch, and Bernard Brusseau prepare products used in dermatology shortly after Dome was moved to Connecticut in 1969.

Under the aegis of Miles, Dome's growth had not been especially rapid, but it was apparent that its future lay outside Manhattan. So, in 1965, a 51-acre hilltop site was purchased next to the Connecticut Turnpike in West Haven. On May 12, 1966, ground was broken for a handsome building of 288,000 square feet, supplemented by a 225,000-square-foot warehouse. In the summer of 1968, some 230 employees abandoned the big city to work in the Connecticut countryside.

In 1970, the Connecticut plant was selected by *Modern Manufacturing* magazine as one of the top 10 plants of the year. Expansion followed, and in 1983 the company purchased an additional 32 acres to assure plenty of land for the next century.

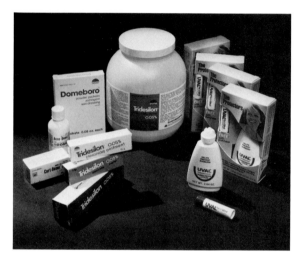

Important Dome products as of 1974.

Physical planning could be done deliberately, but product planning was more evanescent. Through the 1960s and early 1970s, Dome left few indelible marks in the field of therapeutics. Even by 1978, U.S. sales volume lagged at around $15 million. The division simply had not come up with any big pharmaceutical winners. Its dermatological and allergenic lines maintained some durability but enjoyed little growth, and there had been a lack of research dollars necessary to assure breakthrough drugs.

Therapeutic Research Steps Up

Serious therapeutics research had nevertheless been intensified during the 1960s. It included the search for more effective non-narcotic analgesics, nonsteroid anti-inflammatory compounds, psychoactive drugs, anti-hypertensive, and other car-

Here the large attractive complex in West Haven, CT, is shown with the New England Thruway on one side and Long Island Sound on the other.

diovascular agents. Even then, particular effort was directed to the stimulation of immune response and to the development of what later became known as interferon, a naturally occurring host-resistance factor that may prove to be important in the prevention and control of virus infection and certain types of cancer. Pioneering forays in the nucleic acid area led to a research program in molecular biology.

This heightened research began to bear fruit in 1971 when a new drug application was filed for Tridesilon (desonide), a non-fluorinated, corticosteroid used in the treatment of many skin conditions. It was introduced in Mexico in 1971, and in the United States in 1972, and is still one of the company's leading dermatological products.

Dacarbazine to Fight Cancer

An even more important field was entered in October 1973 when Dome was selected by the National Cancer Institute for the marketing of dacarbazine, a newly discovered drug often useful in treating a frequently fatal form of skin cancer. Selection was influenced in part by Dome's success in moving Tridesilon through the FDA. A New Drug Application (NDA) was filed for Dome-DTIC (dacarbazine), and Dome began marketing it within two years. Later, it was also approved for treating Hodgkin's disease and sarcoma.

Mithracin (mithramycin), obtained from Pfizer Corporation, was introduced for the treatment of

Tridesilon, introduced for the treatment of skin conditions in 1971, was a leading Dome product when Bayer AG acquired Miles in 1978.

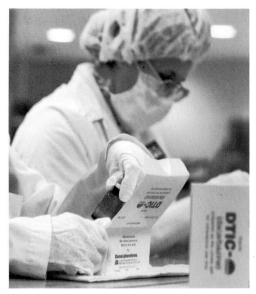
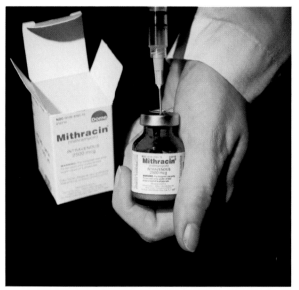

Dome entered the field of oncology a quarter of a century ago with Stilphostrol, used to treat prostate cancer. In 1975 Dome DTIC (dacarbazine) was introduced to combat skin cancer. Then in 1978 came Mithracin for treating testicular tumors. In the 1980s, Bayer AG and Miles researchers were rigorously seeking other anti-cancer agents.

tumors of the testis in 1978. For more than 20 years by that time, Dome had been marketing Stilphostrol (diethylstilbestrol diphosphate) for advanced cancer of the prostate gland.

The Dome Division at Acquisition Time

By 1977, when Bayer AG made its tender offer for Miles stock, U.S. sales of the Dome Division barely exceeded $15 million. Not great but several times larger than when purchase from the Wershaws was made in 1959. Among the many individuals who had brought Dome along was John Paolo, who became the division's third president, succeeding J. W. Beal, Jr., in 1970 and who remained in the position until 1979.

Dome Given Separate Status for Its Long-Range Potential

The long-range potential of the division was recognized early in 1978. The sales force was doubled to 180 men and women that year, and a $5 million expansion of research and development facilities and administrative offices was authorized.

A key change came in August of 1979 when Rolf W. Buell was appointed president of the division which was renamed Miles Pharmaceuticals after the integration of Delbay and Dome. Buell had been with

Guiding Miles Pharmaceuticals in its first years after the merger with Bayer were John Paolo, above, a Miles veteran who had helped to build Ames and sustain Dome, and Rolf W. Buell, a 25-year Bayer Pharma Sparte executive.

the Bayer Pharma Division since 1953, serving in many management functions over the past 26 years.

The importance of research was underscored with the integration of the Delbay Research Corporation into Miles Pharmaceuticals. Headed by Paul H. Spiekermann, M.D., with Bayer AG since 1960, the group had been investigating new Bayer drugs for introduction into the U.S. market under a joint venture with Schering Corporation. They would continue this work under the aegis of Miles. In 1979, five Investigational New Drug Exemptions (IND's), four NDA's, and four supplemental NDA's were submitted to the FDA, giving some indication of things to come.

The first Bayer AG pharmaceuticals to clear the regulatory hurdles, as mentioned earlier, were Mycelex and Mycelex-G (clotrimazole). Mycelex, which is effective in treating several topical forms of fungus infections including athlete's foot, was introduced to dermatologists, general practitioners, and podiatrists. Mycelex-G, for vulvo-vaginal candidiasis, took Miles' sales representatives into the offices of obstetricians and gynecologists for the first time.

The Institute For Preclinical Pharmacology

Early in 1980, Yale University and Miles jointly announced an agreement under which the university would rent space to the company in one of its science buildings, where Miles would set up an Institute for Preclinical Pharmacology. This was a unique arrangement for Yale. Around the turn of the decade, scientists in many institutions showed an interest in more formal and financial support from industry, partly because of government cutbacks. Universities began to consider cooperation and no longer shied away from research agreements with corporate giants.

The Miles presence at Yale was relatively small but significant. Finding itself short of research facilities at the manufacturing complex about 10 miles away, Miles worked out a contract with the university to renovate 4,500 square feet of deteriorating basement space in the 70-year-old Osborn Building. The contract, running through August 1982, was then renewed for two years. When it terminates, Yale plans to use the space for its own teaching and research programs in biology.

Strengthening the Ties Between the University and Private Industry

A highly respected scientist, Alexander Scriabine, M.D., a specialist in cardiovascular pharmacology, became the Institute's director. Before joining Miles,

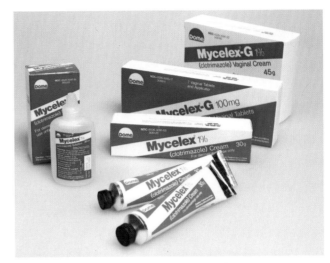

The first Bayer AG products to be marketed by Miles Pharmaceuticals (then still Dome) were the antifungals, Mycelex and Mycelex-G.

he held research posts at Wyeth Laboratories and at the Merck Institute of Therapeutic Research.

In this new position, Dr. Scriabine directed all preclinical pharmacological research and development with compounds selected for development by Bayer AG, including studies that are performed by outside contractors and universities. By 1983, he was supervising 50 projects in about 35 universities. His work is of enormous benefit since it involves assessing the benefits of a candidate compound and its safety before it is given to people.

Dr. David Taylor, principal research scientist, noted, in 1982, that "Yale's people have been surprised by the level of basic research being done by a corporation. Miles' staff benefits, too, since we have valuable contacts with the cellular biology group and with the medical school as well."

Bayer AG and Molecular Diagnostics

One of the outgrowths of the contact with Yale was the acquisition, in the fall of 1982, by Bayer AG of a majority share in Molecular Diagnostics, formed in 1981 to develop new specialized diagnostic tests and procedures by utilizing recent advances in molecular biology. To consult exclusively for Bayer AG, the company had enlisted the services of three Yale University professors: Donald M. Crothers, Ph.D., Professor of Chemistry and Molecular Biophysics; Vincent T. Marchesi, Mc.C., Ph.D., chairman of the Department of Pathology at the School of Medicine; and Francis A. Ruddle, Ph.D., chairman of the Department of Biology. Headed by Gordon P. Polley, a venture capitalist, the group subsequently established research facilities in the Miles Pharmaceuticals complex in West Haven.

The Research Link Solidly Forged

The role of research, then, had been solidly forged by Centennial time. As Dr. Spiekermann, now head of Corporate Medical Affairs reflects, "We don't want 'me-too' drugs. We expect to get valuable medications in every field we have targeted: cardio- and cerebrovascular diseases; infections; oncology; and the metabolic area, including diabetes. We must accomplish in a few years what others have accomplished over long periods of time. The company will continue to stress a regulatory philosophy that is aimed at working as closely as possible with the FDA, seeking scientific rapport. Moreover, our data are expected to apply worldwide for Bayer drug registrations."

By 1982, a research staff of 120 was working smoothly. Three NDA's made their way through the FDA, enabling Miles to tie with the Upjohn Company for leadership of the U.S. drug industry in the number of new chemical entities sanctioned that year.

Distinctive Contributions to Medicine

In addition to Azlin, the other two agents approved were Niclocide (niclosamide), the drug of choice for treating tapeworm infestation, and Biltricide (praziquantel), the first drug effective against all forms of schistosomiasis (snail fever). Both had wide applications in tropical countries but were also in demand in the United States as a result of travel by immigrants, military personnel, and overseas visitors found to be infected. Both were truly distinctive contributions to medicine.

As in so many other areas, the computer is now vital in the collecting, arranging, and filing of the exhaustive documentation required in a New Drug Application. Coordinated by such experts as Dr. Charles Ingram, director of statistics and data systems, the information is forwarded to the giant computer room at Elkhart. Researchers lean heavily on the data from sources of science around the world. Under Mary Jackson, the library at West Haven has established direct channels with the Bayer AG library in Germany and the Miles library in Elkhart.

The Leading New Drugs

When in 1981 FDA approved Mezlin (mezlocillin sodium), the medical profession had a new broad

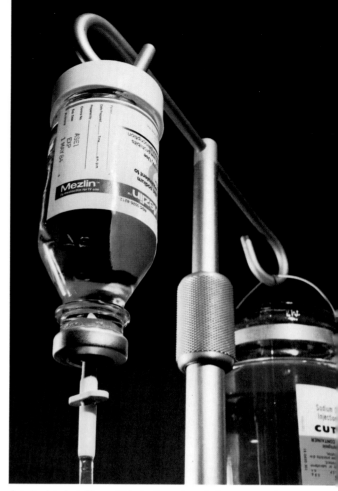

A potent injectable antibiotic for serious infection, Mezlin emerged from the Bayer pipeline in 1981 as the first semisynthetic penicillin to be marketed by Miles Pharmaceuticals.

spectrum semisynthetic penicillin for use as an intravenous injectable in lower respiratory tract, urinary tract, skin and intra-abdominal infections. To maximize the product's potential, about 60 hospital representatives specializing in antibiotics were added to the already expanded sales force. In 1982, its first full year of marketing, Mezlin became the Pharmaceutical group's leading product.

Still another drug, nifedipine, an oral calcium antagonist for the treatment of angina pectoris, was approved in 1981 for marketing in the United States and Canada. Miles Canada began detailing it under the Bayer AG trademark used in most of the world, Adalat. Sales soared. Prior to the Bayer AG acquisition of Miles, the U.S. rights had been licensed to Pfizer, which began selling it most successfully as Procardia.

With Miles' big initial stake in antibiotics, such assets as a microbiological service laboratory assume more than usual value. That lab can and does identify organisms for hospitals lacking a wide range of identification procedures. More than that, it can do synergy

Sharon Brown and Dr. Franz J. Geks stand beside the 127 volumes covering 51 clinical trials that documented the safety and effectiveness of Mezlin prior to FDA approval.

might come from Bayer AG or from its own expanded research. The autoclaves, vacuum dryers, dry heat sterilizers, laminar-flow equipment, tablet presses, filling machines, packaging lines, and all the other paraphernalia of manufacturing mean that the plant is ready for the decade ahead.

Moving Rapidly into State-of-the-Art Manufacturing

"We are moving rapidly into more state-of-the-art manufacturing—fluid-bed drying, vacuum drying, fluid-bed granulating, and so on," says Jim Crocicchia, director of production. Manager of the move out of New York in 1968, Crocicchia has witnessed all the important changes and undertaken additional training to keep himself in the vanguard of technical innovations.

Perhaps the new antibiotic plant completed in 1982 exemplifies the future as much as anything. "There's nothing better anywhere," Ralph Galustian, vice president of technical operations, asserted. "Now, we can compete with anyone." Mary Jo Hampson, first manager of the plant, pointed out that the facility is so automated that it is run by a crew of fewer than

studies of both Miles' and competitors' antibiotics to determine combinations for optimum use. An exotic new microscanning device can measure the growth of organisms and concentrations of antibiotics. As Dr. Charles Woodruff, division director of product development, explains, "This device shakes, incubates, scans, and stores the data, then plots them out for you in one automated unit." It provides a continual scan of 96 chambers, with readouts and the rates of growth on every one. Such an apparatus establishes dosages for various antibiotics. It demonstrates how Miles intends to stay at the forefront of pharmaceutical technology.

Other labs evaluate formulations sent from Bayer AG and then produce them for clinical investigators. This is exacting work, too, since parallel stability studies must be run to assure that what is produced at West Haven is precisely equivalent to what is produced in Germany. About 600 different compounds are now being shipped to clinicians annually.

Poised to Manufacture New Drugs in the Decade Ahead

Manufacturing is also fully geared for everything from hand-filling operations on small runs of ointments, lotions, and creams, to the most advanced equipment for handling sterile products. Miles is poised to make any of the sophisticated new drugs that

Going on stream in late 1982 at West Haven, CT, this sterile antibiotic plant represented the latest state-of-the-art manufacturing, with relatively few people needed to run its highly automated operations.

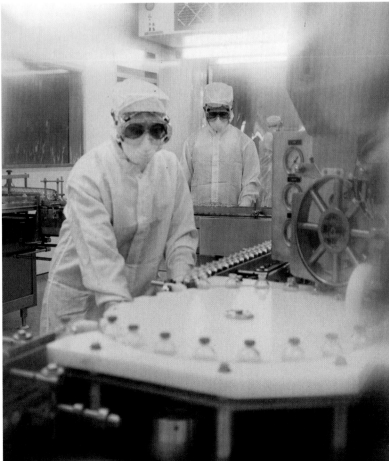

20 antibiotic specialists on a one-shift basis, but designed so it can easily operate with two or three shifts a day. The plant enabled the company to go from contract packaging to complete handling of the sterile filling of its new-generation penicillins. Azlin was approved by the FDA just three months before completion of the plant.

Management Change

Meanwhile, another management change came in late 1983. Buell returned to Leverkusen as a senior executive in the Bayer Health Care sector. Horst Wallrabe, head of Bayer Pharma in the U.K., who had been with Bayer since 1962, succeeded Buell as president at West Haven.

There could be no doubt about Miles gearing up for stronger thrusts into prescription drugs. It looked as if the company would finally achieve its founder's dream of becoming an important producer of life-saving medicines.

Horst Wallrabe, a 20-year Bayer employee who rose to be chief executive of the Bayer Pharma Division in the United Kingdom, became president of Miles Pharmaceuticals Division and an executive vice president of Miles in September 1983.

Hollister-Stier allergen extracts became a new line of Pharmaceuticals Group medicinals when Cutter merged with Miles in 1983. Hollister-Stier is the largest manufacturer of allergen extracts in the U.S.

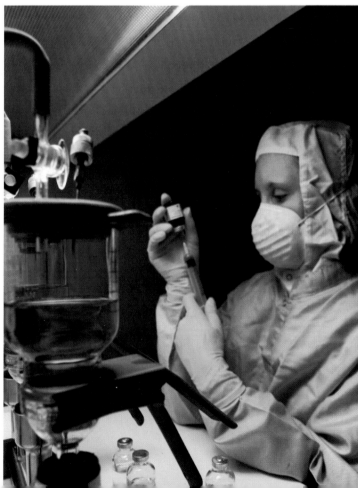

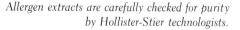

Allergen extracts are carefully checked for purity by Hollister-Stier technologists.

CHAPTER 14

Miles Away

The far horizons beckoned slowly and hazily to the pharmaceutical industry in America. Many companies retained a provincial attitude through their early decades, content to promote standard remedies in local, regional, and national markets, with little thought given to the potential beyond United States' borders.

Miles, with its aging and modest line, had little reason or incentive to cross the oceans. All that changed with the advent of Alka-Seltzer.

In the pattern of other drug firms, Miles moved cautiously into foreign markets. The 1935 Annual Report first discusses the matter, noting that the Export Department began operations December 1, 1935, with Board of Health licenses applied for in 10 countries.

"We have also been careful in the selection of agents," it said, "feeling that it is better to go slowly and thoroughly investigate demand...than to rush...." But after four months, sales were proceeding in 20 countries, and negotiations were going on in a score of others. They involved Alka-Seltzer only; upset stomachs and headaches belonged to all mankind, not just to Americans!

This is where William E. Koerting enters the picture. Born in Yokohama, Japan, to an Austrian exporter-importer, he was educated in Switzerland and spoke fluent German and Spanish.

While at Squibb and Company in October 1935, he was interviewed for the new job of export manager by Walter, Arthur, and Charlie Beardsley. Walter later asked him if he had called his wife to tell her they were moving to Elkhart. "This was the first idea I got that I was hired," Koerting recalled.

When Koerting first moved to Elkhart, he rented a house from president Arthur Beardsley's nephew, Ed. "Winter came along and we didn't know how to fire the furnace," Koerting remembered. "So, lo and behold, at 6 or 7 o'clock in the morning, Uncle Art would stop by and say, 'You kids don't know how to handle this,' and he would stoke the furnace."

Joining Miles at the same time was another

Bill Koerting, hired in 1935 as export manager, opened more foreign markets than any other Miles man. He had a knack for picking the right partners.

"Manny" Perez, far right, worked closely with Bill Koerting to build the Latin American market. Here he is with Robert Otto, left, head of their advertising agency in New York, and Walter Beardsley, then president, visiting Rio de Janeiro in 1955.

Squibb veteran, Manuel J. Perez, who would be Koerting's chief aide for years to come and who would later serve as general manager for all of Latin America.

The Agent Was the Focal Point

As the 1935 Annual Report stressed, the focal point of marketing in those days was the agent. It was this system that got Miles—and typically other drug companies—into overseas markets. Agents either acted as sole distributors, buying the products and reselling them to others, or they obtained them from wholesalers. Or, as in Cuba, the agent bought the merchandise and resold it entirely to wholesalers.

(Cuba was an excellent market for Miles and other American companies until the Castro ascension to power in 1960. Manny Perez safely visited Havana just after Castro took over, seeking ways to "save" a very good business. He couldn't. Skeptical Miles treasurer Robert L. Grant advised the company to retrieve its receivables, valued at $1 million. It did, losing only about $100,000 before that market shut down completely.)

It was a sort of "swashbuckling" age in the 1930s, with success more or less riding on personal relationships with agents. Deals were struck "man to man." "You had to pick your agents on the basis of experience, trust, and financial responsibility," Koerting remembered. "They had to be really interested in the product."

Some of them must have been most enthusiastic. "Our sales in Costa Rica per inhabitant, for many years, were larger than in any other place in the world," Koerting recollected. "We had a crack distributor there, Eduardo Moreno, and he fired up his salesmen." Other pioneers helped to get Miles moving, among them Francisco Garraton in Puerto Rico, Jose Alvins in Venezuela, Luis Bernabo in Argentina, and Robert Wilson in Brazil.

In Mexico, the key was Don Luis Aguilar, a "fantastic man," Koerting says, who built a city of 100,000 outside of Mexico City but still had time to put Alka-Seltzer on the map.

Another distributor, Don S. Momand, started the British market in the late 1930s with more than ordinary skill. In fact, he did so well that when Miles decided to start its own operation, Momand was hired as general manager and headed the British company for 21 years. In World War II, with the business "dead" in England, he served as U.S. Commissioner of the Red Cross in Europe.

Foreign Investment Begins Slowly

Investing outside the United States began formally with Miles Laboratories, Ltd., in Toronto, Canada, on May 14, 1936. The small plant began making Alka-Seltzer in January 1938 to supply British as well as Canadian needs.

The first few years abroad were hardly auspicious from a profit standpoint. In 1936, sales came to $155,300, and in 1937 they climbed to $358,000, but start-up advertising expenses crippled any opportunity for earnings. Nevertheless, products were going to 43 countries by 1937, auguring the future of a worldwide network. Curiously, one of the countries was China "where the war affected our business," as was stated in an Annual Report.

Sales outside America rose to $410,600 in 1938, but heavy advertising again resulted in losses that were cut considerably on a volume of $478,300 in 1939. Despite the outbreak of war, foreign sales finally showed a profit for the first time in 1940, but on a sharply reduced volume of $293,000.

World War II created tough problems for a fledgling operation—exchange controls, shipping shortages, rigid licensing systems, and actual embargoes on nonessentials. The Luftwaffe bombed a ship carrying Alka-Seltzer up the Thames River, and it's assumed that the shattered tablets, in protest, effervesced in the water. At any rate, supplies of the product ran out in November 1940, and what had

The Toronto work force in March, 1943—or at least most of it! Left to right, front row, Hannah Mills, Violet Baker, Rita Campbell, Irene Brown, Mary Thomson, Gay Mileham, and Dora McDonald. Back row, left to right, Walter Taylor, Andy Kennelly, Ida Cann, J. M. Rogers, Jean Saunders, Ida Edgar, Bob Cadwell, and Pat Walsh.

been a promising business in England (1939 sales were close to $200,000) ceased for the duration.

Even with the wartime difficulties, the Export Division built sales from $418,000 in 1942 to well above $1 million by the end of 1945—no small achievement. Real expansion, of course, had to await the silencing of the guns.

The United Kingdom Chapter— A Colorful One

In any recounting of the Miles experience overseas, the United Kingdom chapter has to rank as perhaps the most colorful. First of all, unlike other operations existing or to come, it had to be given a second birth. Before the war, Alka-Seltzer had won enough favor in England to convince Miles management that it could be restored rather quickly afterward. So, in the fall of 1945, a Miles team that included Ed Beardsley and Frank Miles investigated possible building sites.

It wasn't the best of times in war-prostrated Britain, and good structures were hard to find. The team settled on an abandoned ordnance plant at Bridgend in South Wales, 120 miles from London. Fred Lobley and R. S. Nicholls went there, and by April 1947, overcoming shortages of every kind and with 30 employees, they had Alka-Seltzer tablets tumbling off conveyor lines. Miles was back to stay in the United Kingdom.

Among the achievements of John Bunce was establishing the Ames line in Britain, often against tough odds. He also boosted Dome's allergen line in some European markets, and helped to build the business in Australia.

John Bunce, later to head the operation, said in 1946, "One wonders how we ever survived. Everything was scarce;.... We had to rent the two top

In 1979, fire destroyed much of historic Stoke Court, administrative and research headquarters in the United Kingdom. By 1980 its Tudor grandeur had been fully restored. It is probably in this mansion that Thomas Grey created all or part of perhaps the most famous poem in the English language, "Elegy Written in a Country Churchyard." Grey spent summers at Stoke Court from 1742 to 1750, so it seems certain that in its rooms and gardens he labored over his celebrated masterpiece.

floors of a private house for an office; we could not find trained secretaries...." Fred Eckloff, chief engineer, recalls that in 1948, "We lived from hand to mouth.... One day we had no coal, then we had 100 tons stacked against the wall.... We expected electricity cuts every day."

An Old Mansion for a New Entity

The second, more romantic site of Miles in the United Kingdom is at Stoke Court in Buckinghamshire, 20 miles from London. A crumbling Tudor mansion built in the 17th century, it was purchased in 1959 and fully restored for use as research laboratories and sales administration headquarters. For many years the imposing structure had been owned by John Penn, a grandson of William Penn, founder of Pennsylvania.

The U.K. operation at Bridgend progressed steadily from the beginning, spurred exclusively at first by the growth of Alka-Seltzer. Miles U.K. became almost a miniature of Miles U.S.

Stoke Court was once again almost lost to England—and Miles—on January 6, 1979, when fire gutted the most historic sections of the stately building; only prompt work by fire brigades saved the new Compton wing. Fortunately, it was found that reconstruction would be practical from both economic and esthetic standpoints, and by late 1980 employees returned to a totally refurbished building.

Clinitest Meets the Need for Diversity

A need to diversify was expressed as early as 1947. John Bunce happened to see a Clinitest set and at once got the feeling that it—or some adaptation of

134

it—could revolutionize urine testing in hospitals. "From that moment on," he confesses, "I am afraid I devoted most of my time to developing Ames in the U.K."

He did, indeed. It's the story of what was at first largely a one-man crusade to sell a concept to the British medical profession. It was tough going, not only for Clinitest but for other diagnostics that followed.

"Getting the medical schools interested in a new product was an essential," Bunce said. "Out of that effort came one of the most important things that exists today, Ames teaching services.

"Many of the teaching staffs wouldn't believe the Clinitest at first, but they didn't want to be behind the times," Bunce recalls. "We just kept hammering away until we were accepted. Then we had to convince the matrons, too, and finally, the Ministry of Health for the new National Health Service, which approved Clinitest on July 8, 1948."

The battle wasn't over. A British drug house came out with an item called Glucotest, which was a good copy of Clinitest, but not as good in practice. "We had a real fight on our hands," Bunce declared, "but we beat them into the ground in the field (with five men against 28), even though we had to go back and get reinstated in some hospitals."

Bunce went on to other things, such as helping to launch the Australian operation in 1957. Once, when Compton, Koerting, and Walter Beardsley went to England, they persuaded him to introduce the Volemetron, which could accurately calculate blood volume in surgery.

Next, Compton wanted him to take over the Dome products for Europe, in 1964. He did, even though little new was emerging from a rather stagnant line. He began contacting top allergists, first in Scandinavia, then elsewhere, establishing a relatively small but significant business that still had impressive acceptance into the 1980s.

Thomas C. Black—Another Stalwart

Another stalwart of the overall effort in the U.K. was Thomas C. Black, who retired in 1978 as vice president of international operations. A pharmaceutical chemist, he first concentrated on the Ames business under managing director Morgan Thompson. Black also helped develop the allergy products, with the aid of a sharp selling crew headed by Nick Plunkett, and despite the competition from Beecham, which some people thought could not be

International veteran Don Sutherland, after ten years in Australia, headed operations in the United Kingdom from 1967 to 1982, when he returned "home" to once again manage the Australian company.

overcome. "We even managed to find a way to maximize our prices," Black recalls. "It worked."

Within a decade of the refounding of Miles U.K., it had outgrown the original munitions plant and an extensive addition arose. Don Sutherland, a veteran of Miles in Australia, became general manager in 1967. Under his leadership the company continued to flourish, and by its 25th anniversary in 1971, it was using money and manpower to develop business in Europe, Asia, Africa, Australia, and New Zealand. By then, products from Bridgend (400 million Alka-Seltzer tablets, 150 million reagent tablets, 200 million reagent strips annually) flowed to some 100 countries. Employees numbered 550. Sales of diagnostics had increased ten-fold in 15 years, abetted by the Ames twin goal of providing quality products plus responsive service. For example, Miles mounted the first large-scale effort in Britain to discover hidden diabetics.

The United Kingdom—No Easy Market

With its economic hardships, the restraints of national health insurance and stringent regulations, the United Kingdom has been no easy market for Miles. Quite the opposite. Several times, Alka-Seltzer came under fire. It was successfully defended before the Committee on Review of Medicine, April 28,

1978, when the Miles team assailed the report of the Analgesics Advisory Committee in the United States for linking Alka-Seltzer to stomach ulcers and gastrointestinal hemorrhaging. On May 21, 1980, the United Kingdom Licensing Authority approved the product for the concurrent symptoms of stomach upset and headache, with no contraindication in the labeling. It was a sharp victory.

Not so incidentally, Miles has had to parry other thrusts against Alka-Seltzer around the world. It has been successful in Australia, Austria, Belgium, France, Greece, Italy, Portugal, Spain, and Switzerland, and less so in Holland, although final victories may be a long time coming.

In any event, the U.K. operation has persisted as the largest and strongest outside the United States—except for Canada. It eventually melded into its functions virtually all of the Miles line.

U.K. sales and contributions to earnings have grown steadily. In 1983, sales came to more than $41 million. Meanwhile, the notable Sutherland era ended in early 1982, when he agreed to return to Australia to build a stronger market there.

The Canadian Business, Always Solid

Less romantic but surely as solid was the early founding and largely unswerving growth of the Canadian business. Like England, it has been for decades more or less a microcosm of Elkhart operations. It has vied with England through the years for leadership as the largest non-U.S. operation. By 1969, it had outgrown the old plant in Toronto and expanded to a suburban site 20 miles away. This is still the main manufacturing facility with 175 employees. At another Toronto suburban site, some 75 employees turn out S.O.S and other steel wool soap pads at a rate of many millions a year.

The personnel reflect the ethnic and cultural diversity of Canada. Most workers at this second plant are of Italian descent, some of them recent immigrants. Unassuming general manager William Garriock, a Vancouver native, cites his diverse staff as one reason for the Miles success there. Canada had sales of more than $23 million in 1978 and marched into the Centennial year with an annual volume (including Cutter) of around $72 million.

Heading into the 1980s, the Canadian subsidiary was taking over the Bayer AG pharmaceutical line. "This is an exciting development," Garriock explained. "It represents a real commitment to become a significant force in the ethical drug market in Canada." In early 1981, a beefed-up sales force,

including 40 new representatives, met in Toronto to map expanded marketing endeavors.

Going into Latin America

After Canada and England, Miles gave its keenest attention to building an international business in Latin America. It discovered quite early that Alka-Seltzer, when astutely promoted, was well accepted. The next step was to build production facilities that could enhance sales and profits.

Mexico seemed the first logical choice, even though Alka-Seltzer had been ably handled by L. G. Aguilar, S.A. A small plant was built, with the first tablets rolling off the line on July 4, 1953. This modest structure was to expand several times.

Next came Brazil, with ground broken that same year in São Paulo, and with the first packages appearing in drug stores in May 1954. Within a decade, Brazil had become one of the largest subsidiaries. It took a bit longer before a plant could be built in Argentina—long a top priority country—because of import restrictions on machinery, but building started in 1956 in a suburb of Buenos Aires. Manufacturing began in 1955 in Cali, Colombia; and in 1966 in Venezuela and Guatemala.

It takes adroit management to function profitably in Latin countries. Unbridled inflation has fettered operations for many years, as have price controls, restrictions on products and political instability. Nevertheless, Miles has steadily built its business in these tough and varied markets.

Employees in Brazil celebrate
the 10th anniversary of the São Paulo factory.

Even now, Alka-Seltzer remains popular in the Latin culture after 30 years in first place among products of its kind. Manny Perez gives much credit for that success to the Robert Otto Advertising Agency, which cleverly adapted material from domestic efforts. He recalls that many imitations of Alka-Seltzer were launched in Latin America, but all of them failed miserably within a short time due to poor manufacturing or packaging. One of them was Sterling's Sonrisal. Aware of its introduction, Miles in Mexico quickly started a new advertising campaign. Sonrisal made little headway there, nor did it in Colombia. Although it would have been much more economical to have manufactured Miles' products in one or two sites for all of Latin America, local laws and restrictions made this impossible.

Moving into Europe

In 1960, European Common Market headquarters for Miles were established in Lausanne, Switzerland, and the company moved more or less conventionally into the major continental countries.

The Miles network first began in Paris at about that time. In a few years, these small quarters were outgrown. In 1969, a new plant was built at Epernon, 40 miles from Paris, and another was acquired at Vinay.

A local marketing and distribution entity was formed in Milan, Italy, in 1963, with a staff of three that grew to more than 200 under the astute guidance of Marcello Costi. A Spanish operation in Madrid followed suit in 1967, almost faltered into bankruptcy in 1971, but recovered under Costi's stewardship, and was later ably managed by J. A. Perez-Espana.

Expansion came less easily in the tough German market in the 1960s. In 1972 Miles GmbH formed a joint venture with Kali-Chemie AG in Hanover to produce enzymes for the food and beverage industries. That same year, Miles began a joint venture with Fortia in Scandinavia in order to get into the food business. Fortia's Meda Company became an excellent outlet, not for the food business, but for Ames and Dome.

In 1962, Miles built a plant to make citric acid at Haifa, Israel. It underwent several expansions in the next decade and a half. During that time there were cooperative arrangements with the Weizmann Institute of Science and with Hebrew University. In 1978, Dr. Compton was presented with the prestigious Weizmann Medallion Award in New York City in recognition of Miles' activities in Israel.

Chief architect in developing Miles in Italy was Marcello Costi. He started with a staff of three, built it to more than 200.

An Ambitious Global Reach

The ambitious reach of Miles in the 1960s and 1970s was indeed global. In 1969, for example, it purchased Seravac Laboratories (Pty) Limited of Cape Town, South Africa, a maker of biochemical products including enzymes.

Although the products of Ames had been distributed "down under" for some years, remote Australia, with New Zealand, did not become a part of the Miles family until 1964. The first manufacturing plant was built near Melbourne in 1969. It had 140 employees as early as 1970. It serves some 50 countries in Africa and Asia.

The Australian operation illustrates another challenging facet of selling American products around the world—a facet largely unconnected to wars, revolutions, and volatile governments. It concerns the practical matters of names, the symbol, size, shape, and color of packaging and point of sale material.

As Trevor Foustie of Australia said in 1971, "Selling Alka-Seltzer in the Philippines with its 12 major dialects, presents a verbal communications

Alka-Seltzer is sold in more than 100 countries around the world, including South Africa, above.

problem equal to selling in 12 countries, each with a separate language...then in Africa you not only have superstitions regarding colors but a fondness for products that are believed to produce virility...."

Establishing a Foothold in Japan

Japan posed different challenges to Miles, as it has to other U.S. firms. In the postwar period, it easily supplanted England as the second largest drug market in the world, reason enough for it to be eyed with envy.

Walter Compton impatiently wanted Miles to establish a foothold in Japan. When he became chief executive officer in 1963, sales in that booming land actually amounted to a miniscule $17,000. He asked Bob Schlegel to do something about it, and he did,

primarily by introducing Ames' diagnostics into the Japanese market. By 1966, sales jumped to about $4 million. By 1983, with several joint ventures (Miles-Sankyo and Miles-Kyowa) and with Cutter sales, volume exceeded $118 million. Outlets also served Okinawa, Taiwan, and Korea. (Negotiating with the Japanese is different, retired Miles president Bob Rose notes. "They gladly socialize in English but in formal business matters insist on speaking Japanese, and agreeing on points on the basis of long translations takes a lot of concentration and patience." On one occasion, a team in Tokyo had to return to Elkhart but tireless general counsel Adrien Ringuette stayed on and hammered out final negotiations.)

Distant India entered the Miles fold in 1974 for the production of Ames' line. It was the first facility in that country to make urine test strips. Walter Beardsley echoed the Miles philosophy at a plant dedication at Baroda on February 22, 1976, calling attention to the Miles goal of "improving the quality of life in different parts of the world through better health and nutrition."

Inroads into the Socialist World

Miles, then, has overlooked few opportunities in the Free World and it has made inroads or overtures, as well, into the socialist world. In 1973, it concluded an agreement to package and market Ames diagnostic strips and tablets through agencies of the Hungarian government. In 1976, a similar arrangement was made with Czechoslovakia, and it entered into collaborative agreements with Yugoslavia and Poland. In 1977, it joined a Yugoslav consortium to provide enzyme and high fructose syrup technology to Eastern Europe. Sales have since been made to those countries.

The first commercial discussion with Russia took place in 1975. At the time, Miles' scientists Robert Erickson, Ph.D. and Robert Boguslaski, Ph.D., presented papers at a scientific symposium in Moscow. There have been further scientific and research exchanges. The Soviet Union imports some Miles products through Vienna. The Biostator glucose controlled insulin infusion system and Dextrostix reagent strips have had particular appeal.

China remains an intriguing possibility. Miles has long felt its highly technological product lines, notably those of Ames, would be of special interest in that mammoth land. The strategy, under the guidance of such experts as China-born Ed Hou (who left mainland China for Taiwan in 1949 and came to the

United States in 1959), has been to adapt to Chinese health-care traditions and peculiarities.

"Ames fits ideally into the Chinese structure," Hou explains. "Our products are suitable to a lower technology as well as to a higher one in major hospitals. We have a working relationship with the Ministry of Health and have been asked to help organize its clinical and diagnostic areas."

Employing Nationals—A Proud Policy

In its aggressive outreach to the world, Miles has consistently maintained certain policies and principles. It is most proud of its employment of nationals overseas, a practice pretty much followed by a good many pharmaceutical companies, but not by all.

No one has been more dedicated in this approach than Dr. Compton. "When we sell in a foreign country, we are privileged to be there, and we should look at ourselves as guests," he said flatly many years ago.

In 1971 he said, "We are strongly committed to a program of local domestication, going far beyond the hiring of local nationals.... Many corporations do that.... But to inculcate a concept of global participation.... In which each general manager considers that he is operating the company to the benefit of his fellow citizens."

Given these convictions, an early objective was to replace some country agents, or hire the best ones, and to establish indigenous operations managed and manned by the people of that country.

Clearly, the system has worked well in developing both local leadership and local skills. The list of general managers and executives who have risen to the top in their native land is imposing. The 20 general managers have an average tenure of 17 years with Miles; the average tenure in their present positions is nine years.

Some have gone on to top posts at headquarters in Elkhart. Take Australian-born Tom Black, a pharmacy graduate of the University of London, who went to work for Miles in the Ames Division in 1959. He rose to head the Miles operation in England, came to Elkhart in 1969, and by 1971, as mentioned earlier, had been named head of all International Operations. He retired in 1978.

Another was steady Mike Dashwood. Born in what was then Ceylon, he joined Miles in Britain in 1958. Four years later he was promoted to Elkhart, and before his retirement in 1978 had served as a vice president in International Operations.

George Davy, a buoyant Canadian, started at Miles as advertising and promotion manager for the Canadian subsidiary, later became general manager. His outstanding record there brought him to Elkhart in 1974 as president of the newly formed Consumer Products Division. Shortly thereafter, he was named to the Miles board of directors and elected an executive vice president.

Efrain Pardo, M.D., was an area vice president for Latin America until his retirement in 1982. He started with Miles in 1961 as head of its modest research labs in Mexico City. He became general manager of Mexico in 1968, while at the same time doubling in brass as director of the Miles Research Division in Elkhart. He excelled in both posts.

Attuned to Worldwide Involvement

These and other examples are hardly given a second thought in the hierarchy of Miles, simply because its policies and traditions have been attuned to worldwide involvement, with people judged by their ability and dedication, not by their national or racial origins. It is estimated that people of at least 50 different nationalities worked for Miles worldwide at the inception of its second century.

Reliance on nationals, of course, did not mean loose ties between parent and child. Since all of the subsidiaries started small, they needed infusions of money, moral support, and specialized advice and technology from Elkhart.

That kind of help is typified by the career of Lloyd T. Johnson, a proficient 44-year veteran, who retired in 1978. A graduate in chemistry from Cornell, he was first assigned to aspirin and Alka-Seltzer related matters under Maurice Treneer. Then Lloyd and one associate gravitated into Quality Control when the company moved from the old Franklin Street building to the new quarters in 1938.

The need for quality assurance soon burgeoned, not only in the United States, but abroad. So in 1966, Johnson went "international," being appointed head of quality assurance for overseas plants. The intent: make Miles' quality standards uniform worldwide. He eventually audited some 30 different sites in more than a score of countries, helping to bring their technology up to desired levels.

In his final three or four years, working out of the Austrian office in Vienna, he audited plants in Czechoslovakia, Hungary, and Yugoslavia. "These people were difficult to work with because of their political environment," he recollects. "They would

Epernon, France, 1976

Toronto, Canada, 1959

Mexico City, 1958

Bridgend, Wales, 1950

Buenos Aires, Argentina, 1975

Cali, Colombia, 1955

Only a trickle of products found their way overseas during the company's first half century. Then the success of Alka-Seltzer spurred an interest in world markets, and in 1935 Bill Koerting was hired to set up an export operation. From that modest start, Miles International grew to where it accounted for nearly a third of total corporate sales, with plants in some 30 countries and entities in several score others. Products now go into some 140 markets, including those behind the Iron Curtain.

Madrid, Spain, 1976

Cavenago, Italy, 1975

Caracas, Venezuela, 1965

over-estimate sales, and products would linger in the warehouse beyond expiration dates. They would destroy older stocks only with great reluctance. But we could develop a rapport with their scientists."

Dr. Walter Goldstein, now vice president for research and development in Biotechnology, recalls an amusing incident in Yugoslavia, when he was monitoring the start-up of what was probably the first enzyme fermentation operation in Eastern Europe. For several days he deferred his starting signal, to the dismay of the workers. Finally satisfied that all was in order, he gave the go-ahead. "The staff cheered and started singing partisan songs from World War II. Then they began drinking to celebrate the event. It was a long time before we could get anybody back to work."

Challenges to Management

No challenge has surpassed that of how to create, organize, and monitor international operations. No drug firm has done this task with anything like perfection, and the records are studded with change and floundering, even amidst overall success and rapid growth. Miles, too, has experienced its share of evolution from the simple, crude agent system to the present diversified, complex, tightly organized, yet far-flung structure.

The early leaders, like resourceful Bill Koerting and his ebullient aide Manuel Perez, could succeed because of their forceful energy and their ability to work in a spirit of camaraderie with individual entrepreneurs. The job called for tireless travel, and they loved it. For its time it worked, and for that matter, it set the stage for elaborations to come in even more complicated times.

Little purpose would be served by attempting to detail these changes, but the general outlines show a high sense of resolve and close attention to varied views and alternatives.

Some sort of general manager system was the natural rung up the structural ladder as soon as manufacturing commenced, particularly in Latin America, so the new system was loosely in place by the early 1960s. It cannot be said that it did not work, for the nationals appointed to these posts were by and large able men, and they used line authority and directions from Elkhart effectively.

There were complications, since corporate representatives also played a role in running international business. Along with the general managers, some reported to an able but overburdened executive vice president of the corporation, at that time Vincent Romeo, who had joined Miles as a lawyer.

The trauma over how to administer the international business rocked management in the 1960s. Many people felt it was time to more fully recognize that the world of Miles wasn't all Alka-Seltzer. Ames was eager to exploit the Alka-Seltzer network, which by that time reached into some 130 countries. In 1965 the general managers met in Elkhart with the division heads and Charlie Owens, later to head all of International, recalls that "a bloody battle" ensued. On a Friday there was an International Division, on Monday it was organizationally dissolved.

Never one to shrink from difficult decisions, Dr. Compton decided it was time for stronger experimentation. As a result, product line responsibility abroad went to the operating divisions. The key here was Ames, given two years to see how it could really do overseas. Ames went virtually from zero to full-scale operations everywhere, and it succeeded in penetrating or expanding foreign markets.

The Matrix System Begins

As more or less expected, problems persisted with the operating divisions going their own way, with country coordinators seeking to mesh with headquarters and country managers. In 1967, another debate shook the walls in Elkhart. Out of it came the beginnings of what was known for a decade and a half as the "matrix" system.

More power, so to speak, went to the general managers, with responsibility for the profits of all product lines. It meant no more unilateral responsibility. There was some disgruntlement in the belief that a certain amount of conflict was healthy, that "kinetic equilibrium" stimulated ideas.

In another major action, Dr. Compton brought Tom Black over from England in 1969. One of the first things Black did was to run annual seminars for general managers, "to try and improve the skills of these chaps," as he said. The seminars drew deserved praise.

Black, among others, thought that any continuing "kinetic" conflict was wasteful, "resulted in the improper utilization of resources." With the encouragement of Compton, Black worked with Owens and others and put on paper a well-drawn program which attracted notice even beyond Miles. A summary was printed in the magazine *International Business*, and other articles about the plan appeared.

With this paper as groundwork, Miles moved

closer to the matrix system. In broad terms, it strengthened and clarified the role of the general manager in running concise operations, while at the same time giving the divisions ample opportunity to provide their expertise, and, if need be, their authority.

In 1971, the company's global effort reached more maturity with the new post of vice president, international operations, to which Black was appointed, and with the establishment of regional vice presidents for Europe-Africa, the Far East, and Latin America.

The System Has "Worked Like a Charm"

"The matrix system, like any other, is not perfect," Dr. Compton once said. "Points of dispute can arise, but policies can be set by agreement between the general manager and the corporation. Any real disagreement can go to the Executive Committee. I can't recall any getting that far. Overall, the matrix system has worked like a charm."

It clearly led to crisp decision-making, closer control of inventories, improved technical and marketing services to subsidiaries, and the overall better use of human and corporate resources. It is synergistic rather than kinetic. Perhaps, in the eyes of the international managers, there has also been an intangible asset—the appropriate weight given to business overseas in the corporate scheme of things—no small matter.

Reflecting on the system, Owens admits it violates the textbook system of accountability. "It doesn't work well if it's overbalanced, as it has been at times," he acknowledges. "It has required a new kind of manager overseas who can efficiently handle up to 10 product lines, who can use his resources wisely. It takes a long time to develop such managers for a high-technology company."

Owens also thinks that Miles has contrived to steer the matrix constructively, which he considers a major achievement. "It is very, very difficult to do this," he says, "and experimentation must go on. But profits and market penetration, I am convinced, will continue to be based on the matrix and its modifications from country to country."

Changes in Global Business

Earlier annual reports, and more especially reports to shareholders in recent years, have underscored management's concern over swift changes—social, political, regulatory, environmental, economic—in the whole complicated latticework of global business.

In 1964, for example, Dr. Compton warned that everywhere "the machinery of public health and medical care is under constant heavy pressure and intensive scrutiny, and only those companies which are looking strongly to the future instead of merely profiting from the ingenuity and efforts of the past can hope to swim through this torrent."

The torrents kept surging, especially in the 1970s. In 1973, George Orr, then executive vice president, analyzed charges made against multinational corporations, by then a fraternity to which Miles clearly belonged.

A decade ago, critics commonly charged—as they still do—that global companies cause U.S. unemployment by exporting capital, damage the U.S. balance of trade, undermine U.S. technology by transferring it abroad, manipulate transfer pricing, and take advantage of tax loopholes.

"Careful research...proves all the charges are fallacious." Orr told shareholders, and he went on to explain why, in the company's first detailed defense of multinationals.

Orr described the technology flow as a two-way street. "Our own company has derived new products and technology from our overseas operations," he said. He listed the host of reasons production plants had to be built abroad, among them tariffs, regulations and protection of local industries. "They prohibit imports through every trick in the book," he pointed out. "Low wage rates are a factor in only a few cases....A major reason is ever-growing nationalism...."

Orr explained the value of joint ventures where "only in a very small percentage of instances are products imported back to the United States." In addition, he declared, "The very large investments made by multinational corporations abroad are now producing many billions of dollars in the way of dividends, royalties, and technical services, materially helping our balance of payments...."

Finally, he pointed to the auditing operations of both the United States and other governments as precluding illegal tax manipulations.

Orr asserted that Miles was importing nothing from its plants abroad and had an average positive balance of payments of $6.5 million (or $11 million by another calculation) over the previous four years.

The 1973 Report to shareholders also dealt in some detail with growing international problems, first on the question of foreign investment controls, then on broader fundamentals.

International managers came together in this 1974 gathering of area vice presidents: Left to right, Robert H. Simon, Far East; Marcello Costi, Europe and Africa; Thomas C. Black, then international vice president; and Efrain G. Pardo, M.D., Latin America.

The Miles Mission Abroad

This time, Dr. Compton eloquently proclaimed reasons for the Miles mission abroad. "Human health and human nutrition cannot be geographically quarantined," he declared.

"The one single fallacy which infects many (legislative) proposals is the belief that markets in other countries can be served by exports from the United States. This simply ignores the economic facts of life.... We and other multinational corporations have found through experience that we must invest abroad in order to develop and retain markets which otherwise would be relinquished to foreign competition...."

Dr. Compton stressed that overseas jobs created jobs in this country. "For example," he said, "many hundreds of our employees in the United States have their jobs directly dependent upon... our overseas operations." He forthrightly sounded an alarm about "the deceptively attractive trap of economic isolation," which "does not recognize the fact that security... is only protected by a willingness to remain competitive."

Again, in 1974, Dr. Compton turned to the international scene, and once again proudly pointed to the fact that of some 3,000 Miles employees overseas, only 10 were U.S. citizens. He deplored "local nationalism" as "corrosive when it degenerates into... economic conflict." He praised the company's joint ventures as the best means at the time for using both capital and human resources "more rapidly and broadly than we could otherwise manage...."

With the acquisition of the company by Bayer AG, the flow of traditional annual meetings, in the old sense, came to an end. But for informative and cogent comments, those gatherings, especially in the 1970s, impressively document how a growing and diversified company not only evaluated its performance at home and abroad, but expressed social concerns as well in a turbulent world.

Promotion Overseas Also Sprightly

A book could be written about the story of Miles' promotion abroad—much, but by no means all of it, related to Alka-Seltzer and Ames diagnostics. The ingenuity of agents, distributors, and managers knew few bounds.

In the early 1960s, because of heavy traffic in San Jose, Costa Rica, that branch resorted to push carts that wended their way through the snarled streets faster than delivery trucks. A cart, emblazoned with Alka-Seltzer signs, held 332 cartons of the product packed 50 to the package.

In Colombia, an all-girl troupe promoted the product door-to-door, and in one year, rang an estimated 100,000 doorbells. In Ecuador, Speedy—or Pron-tito—became a sort of mascot for a soccer team, with a float carrying Alka-Seltzer slogans. In Switzerland, a promotion once included free balloon rides for participating pharmacists.

Various kinds of laws and controls affected the product. At one time, a package cost 2¢ in Mexico but 8¢ in Guatemala, Raul Ochoa recalls. So peasants would buy it in Mexico and carry cases across the border to sell in Guatemala. The same "contraband" practice prevailed in Colombia to meet demand in Ecuador.

With Indian cultures only partly assimilated in such countries as Ecuador, Peru, and Bolivia, Ochoa hired Indians as advisers on copy, posters and so on.

Regardless of the market, Pron-tito remained popular wherever Alka-Seltzer was sold in Latin America. Parents named children for him, and "Pron-tito" bars were not unknown.

In countries where the product could only be sold in pharmacies, peculiar problems would arise. The small size of Japanese drug stores, for example, made adequate display space difficult. So a display contest was organized and kits of materials distributed. The contest improved product exposure.

Through the years, from world capitals to remote hamlets, Alka-Seltzer posters and displays have decorated everything from shack stores to elegant shops. But probably no Miles executive ever went as far afield as Herbert C. Beulke, a sales and advertising director in Latin America. In 1959, he ventured into the Peruvian part of the Upper Amazon—to what *The Alkalizer* called "the most uncivilized outpost of Alka-Seltzer." Beulke got the witch doctor of a local tribe to try the tablets. When they saw the bubbles, the natives got a bit restless, and Beulke feared for a moment that they might resort to their blow guns. At any rate, he never went back!

The familiar effervescence of the product led to parts of the Pan-American Highway being referred to as Alka-Seltzer Canyon because, from a distance, it looked as if the sandy terrain was bubbling.

Through these years advertising awards kept rolling in after the pattern of the United States. A "stomachs" ad, for instance, was voted the best commercial of 1967 in Australia.

Export Volume Climbs

Even during World War II, overseas volume, as already mentioned, began climbing. It has done nothing else ever since. When these sales rose to $1.7 million in 1945, the annual report boasted, "Our foreign business is splendid." By 1953, volume reached almost $6 million, close to 15 percent of the total business; then it more than doubled in the next five years. In 1965, the international portion amounted to $30 million, or 23 percent of the corporate total, and by 1971 had more than doubled again to more than $60 million. In the early 1970s came additional spurts (sales up 20 percent and profits 33 percent in 1972, for example).

By 1974, Miles was selling in 130 countries. It had 58 different entities, including manufacturing plants in 27 nations. That year, sales abroad soared past the magic $100 million mark to $115 million.

The following year saw another hefty gain to $128 million. Then overseas business settled down for a few years. It did not rise as steadily as it had in the past, but with its diversity and scope, Miles International was well poised for the opportunities it expected to burgeon in the 1980s.

Meeting Third World Needs

Social and economic problems cluttered the international scene for the drug industry in the 1970s and into the 1980s. Years ago, nobody had even heard of the Third World; today, any school-age child can explain how it represents scores of countries and vast populations struggling for a better life. Third World aspirations in the medical field alone jolt the imagination. Peoples and governments avidly seek modern drugs, equipment, and services.

American and European firms have made efforts to meet these needs and demands. It's not especially lucrative. One U.S. Dept. of Commerce 1981 publication shows that subsidiaries of U.S. companies in Third World countries earned a 3.1 percent return on assets—due to higher manufacturing costs and price controls—compared to 8.1 percent for overall operations abroad.

Nevertheless, the obligations and long-range prospects are there, etched boldly on the horizons of human need.

As Tom Black perceptively said in a 1980 interview, "Companies are starting to recognize they can't regard themselves any more just as economic units. They have to recognize the impact on the ecological sphere.

"If you go to these countries with a project," he continued, "it's no use coming just to expand the market. To make them really believe...you've got to show what this project will do for them.

"The basic problem in the Third World," Black noted, "is that people always think that money is going to do it; it isn't. What is really needed is the way to improve the health and nutrition of the rural poor. There are a billion people in the world who are not properly fed. You cannot expect them to be productive; they are going to be apathetic and indolent...."

Beguiling Third World Views

Black firmly believes that the very survival of our society depends ultimately upon the development of

Miles' products aid the sick in major cities around the world as well as in more remote places, such as Zaire.

Third World countries and that Miles, through the nature of its products and services, is singularly equipped to improve health and nutrition in those tormented lands. That belief has been echoed for some years throughout the entire corporation.

Some Third World views around the turn of the 1980s were based on beguiling assumptions that companies were dumping inferior or outdated products on poor lands. Some countries, and particularly the World Health Organization, looked to international drug lists, or formularies of a limited number of low-priced drugs, as panaceas. Only drugs on those lists, under price controls, would be eligible for government purchase.

Marketing practices came under more frequent fire. In short, the competitive free market, in which the American pharmaceutical industry works best, both for its own ends and for those of sick people, ran counter to the rigid socialistic structure of many governments that could not provide even minimum medical care for their impoverished people.

In this kind of environment, the inability to raise prices to meet rising costs put dampers on expansion abroad. The wonder is that Miles and its sister drug

firms have done as well as they have against these uncomfortable odds. Price controls in the early 1980s were not confined just to the less developed world. They also crimped progress in all of Western Europe and in markets elsewhere.

New Trends for the Second Century

Nevertheless, product lines signaled overseas opportunities for Miles in launching its second century. So did other trends as well.

Miles management believes that the sheer enormity of health needs—and the costs—even in advanced nations, makes more self-medication a must in coming decades. It has mapped its strategy accordingly. It expects the worldwide proprietary drug market, which was valued at $6.1 billion in 1975, to reach $14.8 billion by 1990, with $5.3 billion of it in Western Europe, $3.9 billion in Japan, and $2.4 billion in the rest of the world.

Consequently, at a general managers meeting in 1982, new priorities were set, first for nutrition support. Miles obviously feels it has ideal products to prevent and cure deficiencies and assure optimal nutrition. Here it expects to assume an even stronger leadership role.

Next comes what is loosely called cough-cold with products for the relief of the symptoms of cold, flu, sore throat, cough, allergy, and asthma. Here, too, a simmering trend to convert more prescription items to over-the-counter sales could be helpful to the self-medication tide.

In the areas of cough-cold, gastrointestinal and topical remedies, the goal would be to solidify established positions. Finally, analgesics would get selective but less intensive opportunities. Another trend seemed obvious as a bulwark to the global future of Miles—the swift growth of high technology medicine. Here, of course, the products and services of Ames are splendidly relevant. Such was the overall assessment in the early 1980s.

Restructuring for Growth

In the first years following the acquisition by Bayer AG, international operations felt little direct impact. The parent, with its vast experience, had far too much discernment to move too abruptly or

incautiously into a complex network. As a result, it imposed no harsh demands, set no impossible goals. It relied on encouragement and generalized support.

Pressures for cost control, for reduced expenses, for less red tape intensified—as they would have anyway. When he addressed the general managers at the February 1982 meeting, chief executive officer Heinrichs did not tread delicately. "Change is forcing us to restructure the way we are doing business. We are in one cosmopolitan world."

He stressed that the challenge must be met by "high performance," by instilling team spirit in one basic family, by realigning the organization to fundamental precepts and to balance. He said the primary aim would be to concentrate on the United States and seven to 10 other countries, but with emphasis the same, even in minor markets.

Heinrichs made it clear that it was time for Bayer AG and Miles to move closer together. "We have reached the point where we know each other," he said. "Basically, there is tremendous good will on the part of Bayer. Miles must nourish its century-old culture, must retain its pride and identity. At the same time, each operation abroad should take positive

Alka-Seltzer became a big seller in the Pharmacia Nifo in Alges, Portugal, as well as in pharmacies elsewhere.

advantages of the Bayer presence in individual countries. That presence is strong. It can be very helpful at a time when resources get more scarce and we are in danger of being spread too thin."

At that agenda-jammed meeting, Owens avowed that the time had passed for business as usual, or for following old textbooks. He pointed to factors beyond corporate control—corrosively high interest rates, the plight of the dollar in competing against foreign currencies, and volcanic social change.

"As far as we can see into the future, we are going to have very tough times," he said. "So we have no choice except to become more streamlined and efficient, to tightly control expenses, to hold down inventories, to be innovative—all very pragmatic but critically essential."

An Organized System of Sharing

Two-score country managers left snow-banked Elkhart that February day in 1982 with reasonably sure directions, and each with his own ideas, no doubt, as to how to achieve the goals in his own domain.

At Centennial time, then, the company was well into a new chapter of its history based upon Miles-Bayer coordination—an organized system of sharing technology, resources and facilities that by 1983 exceeded 50 projects. In Australia, for example, the Miles plant was producing and packaging drugs for Bayer's Pharma Division. In Peru, where Miles had no plant, the Bayer AG local subsidiary was making Alka-Seltzer. Another was marketing the famous product in Argentina. As already mentioned, with no pharmaceutical subsidiary in Canada, a prescription drug line had been installed in Toronto. In August 1982, Cutter Canada and Miles Canada were administratively merged.

The parent company had been using contract manufacturers in Venezuela where it had no facilities, either, so Miles took over Bayer AG manufacturing there. The field sales forces of Bayer and Miles had been consolidated in the United Kingdom. This kind of blending, wherever it promised cost savings, market expansion and efficiency, would naturally magnify in the 1980s. A new and almost tantalizing era had begun.

PART III

IN PURSUIT
OF EXCELLENCE

CHAPTER 15

People—The Priceless Ingredient

If you were to look at the payroll records at Miles, you'd find they go back to the late 1880s. During that time, the number of workers varied from 19 to 28, and most of them were women who worked 10 hours a day, six days a week. These early employees had several days off over Christmas, but without pay, then a common practice.

The women usually earned from $.66 to $1 a day, while the men were paid from $.75 to $1.25. A glance at the 1890 ledger shows one worker losing at least a day's pay for "error," while some others had "tardy" notices next to their names.

Later payroll ledgers reflect the wages and working conditions of the time. Although they may seem grim compared to today's hours and benefits, Miles' employees were probably better off than most others of their day. Even in the early years, they worked in well-lit rooms, unlike most people who labored in the cramped, squalid sweatshops and factories of the new Industrial Age.

Early Hiring Practices

An 1897 letter offering William E. Root a job as chemist and superintendent of the Compounding Department gives a glimpse of some early hiring practices. Root could expect to earn $.25 an hour while learning to make tablets. He could even earn a premium of $120, provided he could "make our tablets and do other work to our satisfaction." The offer concluded, "We agree to give you work every working day.... Should business be slack in your department, you are to do such other work as we may direct." He was even promised two weeks' paid vacation.

By 1903, employees were assigned to separate departments. During one 60-hour week, three "office personnel" and their weekly pay are listed as: Fernald, $15; Berhous, $15; and Gampher, $14.12. There is even some mention of Sunday overtime. Unlike the

Miles of today, only six of 60 employees worked in the "Medicine" Department. Even at that early stage, product promotion was important, with nine employees listed as working on the newspaper, 56 on wrapping, 8 on the press, and 15 on composing.

Many Elkhart women spent their lives performing routine tasks at Miles. For example, in 1890, Mary Durham began at $.66 a day when she was 20 years old. She was still on the job in the Newspaper Department 29 years later in 1919, but by then had been raised to $13 a week.

"A Nice Place to Work"

You can see what it was like to be a Miles employee in its formative years by reading the recollections of Frances Meiser. At the age of 17, when she began work in the Order Department, she earned $11 a week. Within a month her pay was raised to $14. Even in 1919, she says, it was a nice place to work. At

Frances Meiser, second from left, was honored at the 1971 Quarter-Century Club dinner for her 47 years of service. Others pictured, left to right, are Marguerite Strong, Maxine Schmidt, and Marie Mitchell.

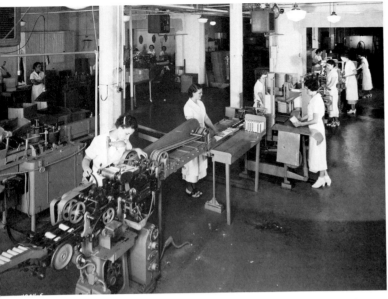

By the 1930s, when this photo was taken, Miles was well established as "a good place to work."

18 she was promoted to the "front office." Arthur Beardsley came to work at the same time, telling her, "You're new here, I'm new, we'll learn together."

Office rules were strict, Frances remembers. Being two minutes late meant losing a half-hour's pay. By then, the work week was down to five and one-half days, but with no paid holidays. "In those days," she says, "you really worked."

Frances talked of the strong family feeling that was always evident among Miles employees. Occasional staff parties were managed by Harry Beaver, the popular chief pharmacist. In the spirit of sharing with their employees, the Beardsleys generously let women workers use their Eagle Lake cottage in the summer.

The Managing of Human Resources

In more recent times, the company has moved vigorously toward the new corporate concept of managing people as "human resources."

The term "human resources" readily fits personnel concepts and practices that are now familiar parts of corporate life. It covers a great deal more than in the past, when the function involved little more than hiring, firing and retiring employees.

When Paul Campbell, long the head of personnel activities at Miles, suggested to Dr. Compton more than a dozen years ago that "human resources" reflected more accurately than "industrial relations"

the value of people and all programs pertaining to them, Compton promptly agreed. Campbell was then named vice president of human resources, the position he held until he retired in late 1982. He guided a corporate program that compares favorably not only with other health-care companies but with industry in general.

An often-repeated saying in the business world is: A company's greatest resource is its people. It also happens to be true, and few companies have believed in it more fervently than Miles. Employee relations from the earliest days testify to the company's belief in caring and sharing.

Charles Reed, retired sales executive, remembers that Hub Beardsley loaned him money to go to college and hired him as a salesman for the Chicago area at $40 a week, which he soon raised to $45. "Strange as it may seem, I could save money on that," Reed remembers, "even though I had to drive my own car and buy my own gas. We were like a big family in those days. We used to come to sales meetings and bring our wives and even our children. They would arrange baby-sitters. One year we went out to Walter Beardsley's and had an afternoon outing. Another time we had a pig roast, or ox roast, at Ed Beardsley's."

Why Miles Will Continue to Grow

Retired distribution manager Joe Rowe, after a career of 40 years, thinks the same quality of people work at Miles today as in earlier years. "I see no difference," he says, "which is why Miles will continue to grow and grow. It will always be an excellent place to work."

First impressions on being hired at Miles invariably stood the test of time. Horace "Ike" Moyer, an engineering specialist, recalls that he came under contract and was interviewed by Fred Lobley, Bim Compton, and Lem Beardsley. "This was a treat in itself," he says, "because I don't think we overlooked anything in our understanding of the relationship before I came with Miles, and afterward, I found that everything fell into place."

Retired president Rowland G. Rose, former W. R. Grace executive, well remembers being talked into moving to Elkhart in 1958 from New York City. "What swung me was the warmth and consideration of top management people. I recall being entertained at dinner but couldn't quite understand why people kept popping into and out of the room. Then I learned the Indiana State Basketball Championship was on. They were checking scores on a TV outside

Company picnics were a tradition well into the 1960s. This one took place in 1955.

The Miles Activities Association was well-known for its shows in the 1960s.

the dining room. Somehow that gave me a sense of small town atmosphere that I liked."

"Those initial feelings never changed," Rose says. "The founding families, and those closely associated with them had, if it can be summed up in one word, *class*. That genuine concern for people has never flagged, even with the pressures and problems of recent years."

Pride in Performance

Both at Elkhart and overseas, there was always a sense of pride in performance. Scientist Ray Snell cites the Mexican citric acid plant as an example. "They took a very intense pride in the place, and guys who had no previous industrial experience whatsoever learned how to operate the plant."

Raul Ochoa, a retired 22-year veteran of both domestic and overseas operations, says he was never asked to do anything illegal or unethical—something he couldn't say about his earlier employment in other companies.

An Enormous Humanity

Perhaps few people are more vehement about the company's attitude toward people than Marcello Costi, a 20-year veteran who now heads the U.K. operation. "The company has had an enormous humanity," he says, "and I am not talking about money. There is no limit on its human generosity. I know personally of many examples where people were taken care of as part of the family."

A typical example of concern for employees can be found in the Union Starch case. Acquired in 1966, the Illinois-based company appeared to be a good buy with a promising future. Unfortunately, it did not work out that way. Union Starch became a drain that

153

no corporation could tolerate. Miles reluctantly closed the plant in 1972, cutting more than 700 jobs.

While it had no legal obligation to these employees, generous severance pay was arranged, and a strenuous attempt was made to find them jobs, personnel manager Len Conches recalls. About 100 were relocated to Elkhart.

Despite the fact that, according to the terms of the plan, many of them could have been terminated without a benefit, Miles "vested" all those on the payroll when the plant closed. This caused the pension plan to be underfunded. Miles then voluntarily put $1 million into the fund to ensure that retirees would receive what they were entitled to.

Taking Care of Their Own

In one way or another, Miles' people have always taken care of their own. For example, in 1954, Ray Snell's wife became seriously ill and for the next year, Opal Gunter, secretary to Dr. Compton who later became his administrative assistant, spent hundreds of hours helping to care for the Snell children.

Despite the extensive benefit programs at Miles, prolonged and unusual illness can still cause hardships. In 1981, employees contributed $3,600 at a bingo and dance benefit for a co-worker stricken by cancer. A year later, they put on a country music show to collect $2,500 for another employee whose wife had died after a long illness.

This softball team won the city championship in 1937—a feat that was to be repeated time after time.

Women's basketball teams were popular in the 1920s and 1930s. This one captured the area championship in 1931.

A mustache derby was run in 1940, and nearly every executive participated. Walter Beardsley even brought in a "bum" from the street as a "dark horse" entry, who proved to be the winner!

So, in these and other ways, the Miles spirit of "small-town" sharing has survived the supposedly impersonal character of the modern corporation.

Getting Along with the Unions

Labor relations sharply measure the degree to which companies get along with their workers. A notation in the archives suggests that employees may have begun to organize as early as 1904. Not much else happened until the 1935 Wagner Act spurred the union movement's massive organizing efforts. In 1941, District 50 of the United Mine Workers of America convinced Miles production workers that they should petition for the union's recognition.

Few companies in U.S. history have voluntarily embraced unionism, and Miles is no exception. When the UMW effort was under way, company President Arthur Beardsley wrote to employees in an effort to persuade them to reject the union.

Beardsley raised the usual questions covering membership dues and benefits, then told employees that "the extent of benefits will be determined by the company's ability to give them and not by the fact that they are requested by a labor union."

"This company," he promised, "is now considering the adoption of retirement with a pension plan, and a hospitalization plan." He said that, "No employee will ever be required to buy his job... by belonging to a labor union."

Labor relations have been unusually good in Miles' first century. Shown below, Elkhart negotiating team from sometime in the 1950s.

First Union Organized in 1941

The letter no doubt swayed many employees, but enough signed the petition to create Local 12273. No fewer than five Beardsleys plus Harry Gampher, Fred Lobley, and W. H. Denison signed the original contract in 1941. Signing for the union were Durward F. Gardner, Charles R. Glase, Ross Kauffman, Delos T. Thrapp, and Louis F. Melkus.

That same union, covering production and maintenance workers at Elkhart, was still functioning in 1983—although now as part of the United Steel Workers of America.

With the diversity of its products, operations, and locations, it is hardly surprising that five unions exist in six of the 25 plants. Two of them were inherited when the plants were acquired by Miles: the Paperworkers International Union at West Haven, and the Oil, Chemical, and Atomic Workers Union at Clifton, New Jersey. The Paperworkers also represent people at the citric acid plant in Dayton, while the International Chemical Workers Union is in place at Kankakee. The newest is the International Longshoreman's and Warehouseman's Union, Local 6, at Cutter in Berkeley.

"We have had an extremely good relationship," says Francis Terrell, the head of Labor Relations who learned his trade in the strife-torn auto industry before coming to Miles in 1966. In recent decades only three strikes have marred a long and relatively harmonious labor-management record—in 1964 at Elkhart, in 1967 at West Haven, and in 1983 at Elkhart.

"Few people have wanted to join the union after starting to work at Miles," Terrell emphasizes. "But whether an employee belongs to a union or not, we have concentrated on building good will, and we think we have been successful. We spare no effort in getting along."

The Labor Record Speaks for Itself

John Bergeron, a carpenter with a 30-year service record at Miles, has been a union steward for 25 years and president of Local 12273 since 1976. "The labor record speaks for itself," he says. "While management and the union may have somewhat different philosophies, they have learned to sit down together and find a happy medium."

Bergeron assesses the some 950 union members (including 190 skilled trades) as open-minded and willing to help solve company problems. "They understand the tough competitive situation," he says, "and the importance of such factors as automation in staying competitive."

To a large degree, the union president attributes stable union relations to the quality of people hired at Miles. "The company has always aimed at getting the cream of the crop, and it makes quite a difference," he says.

Real confrontations have been rare in the labor history of Miles, but occasional albeit minor, incidents occur. Once, women on the Alka-Seltzer production line were asked to insert a reminder slip in the bottles of 25 tablets. It was an extra chore and they refused. Ed Beardsley, then in charge of manufacturing, appealed to them in person. They wavered, but held fast. Finally, a compromise was reached—a $.10-an-hour pay increase.

By early 1983, growth and diversification had generated disagreements over work rules. Union and management could not get together on changes. So in March, some 950 union members struck the seven plants in the Elkhart area. The strike was settled seven weeks later on a "mutually responsible basis," Terrell noted, with a new contract to run until March 1986.

With the settlement, Dr. Geks visited plant sites, shaking hands with hundreds of union workers—a gesture that clearly demonstrated management's intent to reassure employees and to maintain harmony.

The Women of Miles

The women of Miles have always been the backbone of the production lines, as in virtually all pharmaceutical companies. Many made their mark as dedicated supervisors. Luella E. Horn, Idella Sensenbaugh, Dorothea Bowers, Marie Kelly, and scores of others are remembered for exceptionally long and faithful service.

It would be impossible here even to begin to name the loyal and capable secretaries and assistants who for a full century helped their bosses function successfully in the diverse world of the executive suites. When Opal Gunter, administrative assistant to Walter Compton, retired in 1982 after 44 years of service, Lem Beardsley said, "We are extremely proud of our long-service employees, and you are one of those at the top of that honorable list."

Others at the top include Frances Meiser and Virginia Parkhurst, both secretaries to Walter Beardsley, and Elinore Martin, first secretary to Charles Beardsley and later to Lehman Beardsley. Elinore wrapped up 46 years of service in 1982, having worked only for these two men. Reviewing advertising copy in the 1930s and 1940s and traveling between the Wade Advertising Agency in Chicago and Elkhart are among her happiest memories.

First an assistant to Walter Lerner, corporate secretary, Isabelle Hollingsworth, as personnel manager, helped build the modern Miles.

Walter R. Lerner, a company stalwart, started in the consignments area in 1935 and succeeded his father-in-law Harry Gampher as corporate secretary, retiring in 1965.

Doris Corey, who began at Miles in 1936, worked her way up into accounting management before retiring in 1976. Isabelle Hollingsworth, first an assistant to Walter Lerner, probably hired at least 1,000 persons before retiring in 1976 after 41 years in personnel.

Wilma Williams, as a junior in high school, worked part-time on the packaging of K-Rations in 1944. She eventually became an administrator in Employee Services before retiring in 1982. "I was

Helen Free accepts the 1980 Garvan medal awarded by the American Chemical Society.

promoted before the big push came for putting more women in executive positions," she emphasizes. "So management felt I could do the job, not because I was a woman."

The company thought many others could also "do the job." A number of them made their mark with Ames.

Helen Free, A Garvan Medalist

Certainly the most honored is Helen Free, who spent more than 38 years with the company before taking early retirement in 1982 to become a consultant.

Upon graduating from college as a chemist in 1944, Helen joined the small quality control staff of Ames. She soon moved toward higher responsibility, becoming over the years new products manager, senior new products manager and director of specialty test systems. For about five years at the end of her fulltime employment, she was marketing services director for the Research Products Division.

She and her husband, Al, whom she met at Miles, were deeply involved in development of all of the first dry-reagent-strip urine tests in the Ames line. They are co-authors of two books on urinalysis, one of them a classic in its field, and each has written or co-authored more than 100 scientific papers.

In 1980, Helen was the recipient of the Amer-

ican Chemical Society's prestigious Garvan Medal, awarded annually for distinguished service to chemistry by women chemists. In 1982, she was elected to the ACS Board of Directors to represent a 12-state region. She and her husband have always traveled extensively, demonstrating Ames tests to physicians and technologists at medical meetings on every continent.

Another Ames achiever is the gifted Mary Sproull who worked in Quality Assurance at Miles from 1946 to 1963, left for a stint in Washington, D.C., then came back in 1969 to help direct Ames' planning and organization. She was named Elkhart Businesswoman of the Year in 1980. Carol Miller, Ph.D., and Jean Safdy, Ph.D., distinguished themselves in immunological chemistry research leading to development of Ames Therapeutic Drug Assays. Judy Cromer has served as senior financial services accountant in the Ames Division for many years.

Two Entrepreneurs Build Pentex

Without Trudy Dickinson and Jean Thomas, Miles certainly would not have the long line of biochemicals it sells to universities, hospitals, and other companies for research purposes.

Trudy and Jean were two of five founders of Pentex Incorporated in Kankakee, Illinois, in 1953. As research chemists in Chicago, they knew how exasperating it was not having ready access to raw materials needed in their work. They spent hours at the Chicago stockyards each week procuring animal blood and internal organs. Conceived out of frustration, Pentex was born as a hobby as Trudy and Jean began preparing supplies of bovine albumin and blood fractions for their friends.

"We thought we could do this for our contacts on a part-time basis," Trudy says, "but by 1955 it became clear we had to give full-time attention to our business." The ladies took business courses and hired Haskins and Sells to tutor them in finance. Trudy served as president and Jean as executive vice president and treasurer until the company was purchased by Miles in 1968. When acquired, Pentex was making several hundred research chemicals in a 8,500 square-foot building in Kankakee and marketing them worldwide.

These two female entrepreneurs could have retired easily on what they made from the Miles acquisition. Instead, they chose to work in what they looked upon as "the big corporation," shuttling back and forth between Kankakee and Elkhart several times a week. At this writing, Trudy holds the title of

Dr. Dorothy Carter, the only woman to be named a vice president in the company's first century.

director, manufacturing biological enzymes, while Jean is director, marketing services, Miles Scientific Division. Their influence goes well beyond their titles. The name Pentex has carved out such a niche with researchers that Miles has continued to use it as a brand.

Dr. Carter Holds Key Posts

Dr. Dorothy L. Carter joined the company in 1958 as research and medical director in what was then the Miles Products Division. Born and medically trained in England, she was married to Dr. Kenneth Carter, who joined Ames as scientific director in 1957. Soon after moving to Elkhart, she began applying her medical background to consumer products, particularly Alka-Seltzer.

By 1963, when other corporations had few women in key positions, Dr. Carter was promoted from director to vice president within the division. She remained in this position until 1966 when she went to The Interpublic Group of Companies, Inc., then handling Alka-Seltzer advertising, as vice president and senior medical consultant.

As a consultant in the 1970s, Dr. Carter provided

testimony of inestimable value on the safety and efficacy of Alka-Seltzer to regulatory agencies in the United States, the United Kingdom, and Australia.

Dr. Carter holds the distinction of being the only woman ever to achieve a vice presidency in the company's first century. There were, however, an increasing number of women named director, especially at the division level.

Perhaps the real pioneer was Treva Van Solingen, who worked for Miles 43 years before she retired in 1966 as director of marketing research in the Consumer Products Division. She illustrates the company's early willingness to recognize talent and promote from within. Her contributions and achievements are described in Chapter 17.

The Information Explosion Brings Change

Library services are a key element in pharmaceutical research, and it was Charlotte Mitchell who organized and brought them to life at Miles. With an M.A. degree in library science from the University of Chicago and after having worked seven years at the Michael Reese Hospital School of Nursing Library, she was eminently qualified when named head librarian at Miles in 1951.

During the "information explosion" of the next 25 years, Mrs. Mitchell and her very professional staff worked diligently and graciously supplying the needs of a rapidly diversifying company. With consolidation of the Corporate Libraries and the Scientific Information Services in 1972, Mrs. Mitchell was promoted to director, library resources and services, the position she held until her death in 1979.

The first professional public relations director was Doloris Cogan, hired in 1972. She and Charlotte Mitchell were the only women with a director's rank at the corporate level of Miles throughout the 1970s. A graduate of Columbia University Graduate School of Journalism, with nine years of writing and editing experience in Washington, D.C. and seven years with Pepperidge Farm before joining Miles, she handled public relations during the Bayer AG–Miles acquisition. She is responsible for both internal and external corporate communications, and planning for the Miles Centennial was initiated by her, including establishment of a corporate archives and historical exhibits. Active in community affairs, Mrs. Cogan was named Elkhart's first Businesswoman of the Year in 1977.

Professional home economist Helen Horton made her mark helping develop the Morningstar

Doloris Cogan, left, corporate director of public relations, and Helen Horton, director of consumer service for the Grocery Products Division, often worked together during the 1970s at medical and trade shows, here shown at the Golden Anniversary Gala for Home Economists in Business, where Morningstar Farms products were just introduced. Both hold several "firsts" at Miles and in their professions.

Farms line of cholesterol-free frozen meat analogs. For more than 10 years, she worked with the American Heart Association, the Society of Nutrition Education, newspaper food editors, grocery chain home economists, and other influential consumer groups in getting these analogs accepted for their nutritional value. Mrs. Horton was named Home Economist of the Year by the 3,000 Home Economists in Business in 1981, bringing honor to Miles as well as herself.

The Women's Committee

The Miles Women's Committee was organized in 1979 by the women themselves as a networking support system. Presiding during the organizing was Jane Moffitt, a staff attorney, who often represented Miles at the FDA; the first elected president was Mary

Ann Osuch, Ph.D., marketing manager in the Research Products Division. Approximately 100 Miles employees (including a few men) are members.

Cogan, Mitchell, Sproull, and Free were especially active in the 1970s supporting the Equal Rights Amendment and helping to assure that the Indiana State Legislature ratified it. Also active in ERA rallies were Dr. Aurora Fernandez DeCastro, of Cuban origin, and Dr. Alice Janik, who was born in Czechoslovakia. Both are highly respected scientists.

Husband and Wife Teams Play Vital Roles

By the 1980s, more and more women had begun joining their husbands in the corporate structure. But in the 1950s, when Al and Helen Free began working together at Ames, the phenomenon was relatively new. Other husbands and wives at Miles have included Ann Cocks, librarian, and her husband, Richard, an engineer assigned to long-range property management; Adrien Ringuette, corporate secretary and general counsel, and his wife Celeste, scientific information specialist; Peter Chang, vice president for the Ames' Quality Assurance, and his wife Eppie, a scientist holding a number of patents; Judy and Steven Doan, both marketing executives; and scientists Jean and Max Safdy. Other couples include John and Karen Bergeron, Betty and Robert Boussom, Joan and James Copsey, Jr., Helen and Francis McKee, Eleanor and Stephen Menhart, Marjorie and Harold Meyer, Joe and Norma Papa, Tyron and Aileen Schuler, Phil and Marianna Steele, Sally and Gil Stump, and Phyllis and Dick Winchell. The list could go on.

The history of Miles would be incomplete without mention of a mother-daughter combination, that of Manila Boyer and Marie Sunday. Manila went to work for advertising expert O. B. Capelle in 1936, and subsequently helped with everything from radio scripts to writing items for *The Alkalizer*. She retired in 1965.

Her daughter Marie began at Miles as a typist in 1956. Within a few years, she had become a budget analyst, an assignment she has seen grow from "simple concepts to complex worldwide cost control." Marie has been a profit planning analyst since the late 1970's.

Promoting Minorities

Among blacks holding executive posts at Centennial time were Max Abernathy, supervisor of customer service for Ames, also known for his radio show, "NAACP Outreach"; Donna Smith, chewable vitamins product manager, Consumer Healthcare;

Franklin Breckenridge, the first member of a minority to be named assistant secretary and assistant counsel, holds both state and national honors for his work with the National Association for the Advancement of Colored People.

James Pyles, manager of sales promotion, Consumer Healthcare; Curtis Brown, corporate senior placement representative; Leslie Sudbury, quality assurance manager, Miles Scientific Division; and Franklin Breckenridge, assistant corporate secretary, who in 1981 received the NAACP's William Ming Advocacy Award, a national honor.

Over the past 10 years, the Miles record in hiring and promoting women and minorities has advanced sharply. There were only a few women in the sales force in 1970. By 1981 there were 121, and the hiring of minority salespeople had doubled. The number of professional women during that time climbed from 9.7 percent to 22.2 percent.

Helping the handicapped has been something of a Miles mission, too. Dr. John J. Gavin, allergy specialist in Hollister-Stier, who is deaf, originated the first symposium on "The Physically Disabled Scientist," at the AAAS meeting in 1975. Paul R. Filpus, once a civil engineer who learned to be a computer programmer at Miles in Elkhart after going blind, also spoke at that program.

Benefits Go Back to 1918

The benefits program that envelops Miles employees would startle both the company's founders and its first workers. It covers nearly every eventuality of a complex age and a demanding society. If the Miles program is not unique, neither has it been parsimonious or lax by any standards of the past half century.

The company's formal concern for the welfare of its people surfaced early—in March 1918, when it established a group life insurance plan. Modest as this plan may now seem, it nevertheless set a pattern for employee welfare that has been adhered to through the years.

In fact, the company entered its second century with an improved comprehensive packet of benefits, including a savings plan where Miles would add one dollar for every two dollars an employee would save, up to three percent of an employee's pay.

Dictums Old and New

Times change. When the new administrative offices opened in 1958, Charlie Beardsley took a look at the open, spacious area and wondered if it would ever be fully used. Within a few years it was crammed with desks and people.

At that time, neatness was demanded. Only men could smoke, and they had to wear suits, as Marie Sunday recalls. Each new employee was introduced to top management. The policy manual dictums, probably carried over from earlier days, still had rather quaint overtones. "All conversations are to be con-

Paul Campbell became the company's first vice president of Human Resources in 1971.

This very first Quarter-Century Club dinner was held in 1966 in the Athenian Room of the Hotel Elkhart.

fined to company business.... Personal animosities are not to be tolerated.... Do not ask questions of the one sitting near you.... Unnecessary loud noises [are] forbidden.... It is not permissible to eat, to read magazines or newspapers during working hours.... Running in the office is not permissible as this may result in serious injury...."

This slim booklet is a far cry from the current policy manual covering more than 60 subjects—from such simple items as "signing authority" to such complex matters are "divestiture of assets," "improper foreign payments," "joint ventures," "conflict of interest," and "investment capital."

The Barometers of Success Are Manifold

There are various barometers of Miles' success in human relations. One is its Quarter Century Club. Such clubs are commonplace enough in American industry, and that of Miles may be no more significant than that of scores of others. At the same time, it probably would not have to take a back seat to any of them. By 1983, the Club mustered 838 members worldwide—656 in the Elkhart chapter with 296 still actively employed.

Not to be overlooked among employee programs is a federal credit union. It is popular, and with reason, since it provides employees opportunities for savings and investment at rates that equal or exceed those available on the "outside." In April 1982, EFCU President Melvin Thompson reported that the credit union had doubled in size in just four years, its assets

burgeoning from $10.4 million to $19.1 million in 1981. By 1983 they had reached $28 milliion. Its membership exceeds 6,000.

Another notable barometer is Miles Activities Association, whose inception goes back to 1936, when it was organized as the Miles Athletic Association, with Mark Hess as its first president. It soon had 500 members, with a $.50 fee. (It is only $3.00 today.)

After almost half a century, the M.A.A. still fills a real need, notes the 1983 President, Marie Kelly, a production area veteran of 41 years. She works with an average of about 25 volunteers in planning and implementing a host of activities. The original emphasis was on sports—softball, bowling, basketball, and golf—and much of that emphasis remains, having been extended to sports whose popularity has grown, such as tennis and skiing. But social events also play a big role, from bingo, dinner theatre, and Las Vegas nights to shopping trips to Chicago. Dancing was once well attended (370 persons showed up for one dance in November 1936), but as a group activity, that no longer fits most life styles.

The Alkalizer—One of the Best

Part and parcel of Miles for almost half a century has been its employee publication, *The Alkalizer*. That was its first and only name. Even a contest for a new one failed in 1974.

Its origin goes back to March 1936, when at a staff meeting, Fred Lobley recalls, someone suggested publishing a company magazine. Grover Mishler, the printing foreman, picked the name and offered to print it with blue Alka-Seltzer ink on some discarded paper trimmed from larger sheets. When President Arthur Beardsley saw the small first issue, he said, "I think that's a fine idea."

At the beginning, *The Alkalizer* concentrated on sports and recreational and social activities. The first issue urged that "an additional span of chicken wire be put on the backstop to frustrate some of Bill Rich's high balls. This would save the boys a lot of trouble crossing the tracks to find the ball. . . ."

Through the decades, *The Alkalizer* often had such "homey" touches. But it also moved with the times, its coverage expanding, its sophistication and usefulness growing. Nor has it ever lost sight of the fact that it is "published for employees." This has been true from the days of its first editor, W. H. Denison, down to Bob Pattillo and Roger Snow of more recent times. Today it ranks with the best corporate publications of its kind.

Commitment to Safety and Health

On the morning of October 12, 1977, Dan Wessley, a superintendent at the Marschall Division's culture plant, walked into a cooler, unaware that a malfunctioning compressor had depleted the room's oxygen. He quickly collapsed.

Luckily, his office phone rang at almost the same time. Since he did not answer his page, two fellow employees, Wayne Kuenzi and Kermit Hermanson, went looking for him. Kuenzi glanced through the cooler window and saw the unconscious superintendent. He quickly flung the door open and dragged him out. Kuenzi and Hermanson then took turns giving Wessley mouth-to-mouth resuscitation. By the time paramedics arrived, Wessley was again breathing comfortably. He fully recovered.

This incident was unusual if only because it was the kind of thing that hardly ever happens at Miles. For in its concern for its human resources, Miles has paid great attention to health and safety. It has never had a major industrial accident, serious injuries to workers have been rare, and no one recalls any accidental deaths on the job.

Such a record, however, did not happen by accident. Evidence of early interest goes back a long way.

Occupational Health Interest Escalates

During World War II, the company had a medical facility run part-time by Dr. R. L. Conklin,

Richard L. Conklin, M.D., a popular Elkhart physician, began a health care program for Miles employees in the 1940s. He is shown here with Carlene Thornton, left, and Ruth Maxon, company nurses.

a popular Elkhart physician. With so many doctors in military service, Conklin worked exceedingly long hours to minister to patients, whether Miles employees or not. For this reason, he kept a cash register in his Miles office; he dispensed drugs and accepted payments for treating illnesses that were not job-related.

Interest in occupational health escalated after World War II. So Miles hired an industrial hygienist, Joel Charm. Then, in 1965, Dr. Charles Martin set up a full-fledged medical department. Dr. Donald Harrell followed him and started new programs such as hearing tests for people working in high noise areas. He also established programs in other Miles plants.

This effort expanded further when Dr. Bill Himmelsbach joined the company in 1972. With production lines often running 24 hours a day, the nursing staff had to be expanded to three full-time and three relief people. Retired head nurse Roberta Kennedy says the company has been fortunate to have had such "fine doctors as Martin, Harrell, and Himmelsbach." The company has been fortunate to have nurses as dedicated as Mrs. Kennedy, too.

One barometer of the times is the array of company programs to aid employees with drug or alcohol problems. Himmelsbach feels, though, that both are less of a problem at Miles than in the population at large.

Working Together for Safety

The first formal safety programs, managed by John Bennett, began in the 1960s and 1970s. Since

William A. Himmelsbach, M.D., joined Miles in 1972 and developed a companywide health program that measures up to the standards of a modern health-care corporation.

1977, John Polhemus, manager of corporate safety and health, has headed a comprehensive effort that extends to every facility of the company. He conducts seminars on dozens of safety topics. He prepares a monthly health and safety bulletin covering safety factors not only within the plant but also for the home, highway, and elsewhere. Virtually every manufacturing employee attends a monthly safety meeting. Each plant is closely audited annually to ensure maintenance of safety standards. The company involves the unions in safety planning, too, and the cooperation is excellent, Polhemus stresses.

By controlling hazards in the workplace, Miles has won many awards from the National Safety Council. It had no difficulty in meeting OSHA (Occupational Safety and Health Administration) standards.

"The source of an accident involves unsafe conditions only about 10 percent of the time," Polhemus points out. "People failure accounts for 90 percent, so we concentrate on personnel training. Where we do well, the credit belongs to the plant managers and plant people."

To underscore the importance of safety, Miles established the President's Safety and Health Award in 1972. The Clifton plant won it in 1972 and 1977. Other winners include: Elkhart, twice; South Bend,

twice; Bedford Park, Kankakee, Lab-Tek, Dome, and Worthington, once each.

Such programs, Polhemus says, take the positive approach. He believes the working environment is gradually getting safer, but that the job is never finished. "When you have safety, you don't think you need it," he says. "That's when you have to watch out."

People Approach

In its people approach, Miles is like most other great pharmaceutical houses, where concern for workers, whether unions exist or not, is traditional. Even in the last several decades, when pressures to maintain satisfactory earnings have mounted in the business world, putting severe demands on performance, these firms have persevered in caring for their people and in recognizing them as the most valuable of all corporate assets. Few industries have been as attractive to employees in the 20th century.

"Consequently," points out John Gildea, vice president of administration, "leading companies such as Miles have been able to recruit and keep top level individuals—especially in the critical scientific and technological areas, where success has to come if it is to come at all. Ultimately, only the skills and dedication of people make companies work."

John Gildea, an Elkhart native and University of Notre Dame Law School graduate, was named vice president of employee relations and public affairs in 1981 and vice president of administration in 1983.

CHAPTER 16

R&D—The Boundless Quest

At Miles nothing engenders a greater sense of hope, and sometimes even excitement, than the boundless quest for new and improved products. Research and development skips on many waves of a restless tide, constantly moving and shifting from the routine and practical to ill-defined and almost remote shores—from such seemingly simple matters as better-flavored vitamins to genetic engineering that, in seeking to unravel the mysteries of biochemistry, tracks close to the secrets of life itself.

The sheer versatility of R&D at Miles is remarkable. When combined with that of Bayer AG, the scope becomes almost staggering, yet inevitable in a science and technology pervaded by the computer and the laser and by the onrush of knowledge. Company leaders time and again sturdily affirm that the key to the future is research, and as Miles wheeled into its second century that commitment had not only been made, it was unassailable, expressed in every approach and attitude—and budget.

"We want to build Miles into an even stronger research-based company," Dr. Franz Geks, for many years head of all of Bayer AG's pharmaceutical operations, said without equivocation in 1983. "We can only be successful if we get new products. So we are prepared to invest even more in research."

It's as simple as that. Except that carrying it out is complicated indeed.

The Key—Interlocking Technologies

The strands of research running back and forth from parent to subsidiary, from division to division, from small projects to major programs form a most complex lattice-work. Somehow it's all interlaced. The popular term for it is "interlocking technologies." And so they are, and to a degree not easily matched even in other multinational corporations.

The R&D budget at Miles for many years was not large by the standards of some research-based companies. It didn't get above $50 milllion until 1981.

But it has climbed steadily under the aegis of Bayer AG to more than $85 million annually, enough to support 1,200 scientists and technicians in the Miles/Cutter network by 1984.

Miles scientists reconnoiter many frontiers, ranging from fermentation and enzymology and diagnostics and animal health to such exotic areas as recombinant DNA. No attempt will be made here to encompass the full range of their complicated handiwork. Some scientific accomplishments are described in other chapters. Again, it cannot be said too forcibly that no part of Miles' operations looms larger than R&D. Nor does anything set the stage more suitably for the coming decades. After all, it took a long time to build the framework of 1984.

Alka-Seltzer—An Early Research Triumph

For the company's first half century, the research story can be briefly told. It amounted to little. It was similar to that of other pharmaceutical firms producing home remedies. True, the formulation of Alka-Seltzer in 1931 was a research triumph representing a unique method of mixing chemically incompatible ingredients. The inventiveness of Maurice Treneer in putting together an effervescent tablet was quite an exploit for its time.

But otherwise, until the 1940s, R&D was primarily product development performed by manufacturing chemists and pharmacists, who would take a concept directly into manufacturing. Basic investigation barely existed.

It is difficult to state how swiftly a bona fide research function would have come to Miles without Walter Compton. Unquestionably, it came much faster with him. He was its guiding spirit. He first championed the modernization of an inconvenient test (Benedict's method) for urinary glucose by combining the test reagents into a single tablet, Clinitest. Further improvements he suggested led to the

CHARLES SUMNER BEARDSLEY
RESEARCH LABORATORY

DEDICATED MAY 15, 1962, IN MEMORY OF

Charles Sumner Beardsley

1875 – 1962

PRESIDENT AND CHAIRMAN OF THE BOARD OF DIRECTORS

MILES LABORATORIES, INC.

Clinistix reagent strips and a new line of diagnostic aids.

Even earlier, Dr. Compton had initiated some important basic studies on sedative drugs. For hard on the heels of the Federal Food, Drug, and Cosmetic Act of 1938, drug manufacturers began to make changes, essentially the first since 1906, and long-smoldering questions regarding the safety of well-known compounds were fanned into public controversy. In particular, the "coal-tar" preparations containing acetanilid and the bromides came under suspicion.

Founding a Research Institute

In 1938 the young Dr. Compton had already formed the ambitious idea of organizing an industry-wide research network to investigate the medical safety and effectiveness of several compounds, including the aspirin so vital to Alka-Seltzer, Miles' Nervine, and Miles' Anti-Pain Pills. Little clinical research had ever been done on these drugs. Dr. Compton felt it was time to begin. So it was that on November 16, 1938, Miles was one of six companies that met with Dr. F. C. Cullen of the Proprietary Association. They decided to pool their research and to launch a comprehensive investigation of the drugs in question.

At the first meeting of the Institute for the Study of Analgesic and Sedative Drugs in New York City in December, a research committee, which included Dr. Compton, recommended a review of all scientific papers published in the last 20 years with the goal of sorting out the contradictory evidence and paucity of clinical findings on acetanilids and bromides. Miles became a charter member of the Institute, helping to fund its operations, and Miles attorney John A. Cawley became its secretary.

Over the next two decades, the Institute sponsored many basic research programs and published valuable monographs on long-neglected drug topics.

A high point in the Institute's history was a 1951 symposium which dealt with N-acetyl P-amino-phenol, the analgesic compound later marketed by another company with great success as Tylenol.

Not to be forgotten among the mounds of reports and clinical studies is the personal role that Dr. Compton and others at Miles took in the Institute's affairs. Charles S. Beardsley's presence at the annual meetings added a particularly human aspect, and a store of good sense and homely humor, to the august

Research began in earnest when Walter Compton, M.D., having graduated from Harvard University Medical School, returned to his hometown and was named the company's first medical and research director.

proceedings. In 1939, he stood up among the learned doctors and had this to say:

"I will make a motion. I think you are entitled to a vote of thanks, but the direct benefit that comes to a company such as ours, and every other company in an institute of this kind, just can't be measured in dollars and cents. It is measured in the number of years you live as a result of this type of work. Dollars are not under consideration at all, but when you come to make pure research, as this organization is organized to do, it benefits the whole drug industry, and for a company's board of directors, organized for profit, to enter into an altruistic effort of this kind, it takes some imagination.

"We have felt for a long time that this is true, and when Dr. Compton came into the organization, he had the same idea. Maybe that is the reason why he has spent so much time on his work, and maybe a motion of this kind is rather inappropriate. I hate to see the meetings run into sugaring of each other—like the Scotchman's family. He said if they came down in the morning fighting and quarreling, he knew they were all right. But if they were sugaring each other, he gave them a physic because he knew that they were sick. However, I will make the motion that the original companies and their executives who organized the Institute and who have had an active part in it (and that will cover the entire group) be given a vote of thanks for their cooperation up to this time."

The Charles Sumner Beardsley Research Laboratory
was dedicated in 1962.

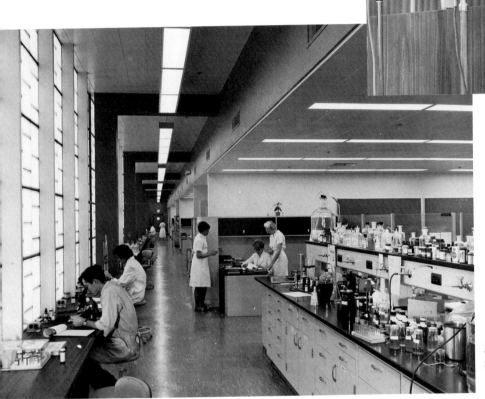

Large, open work areas characterized the
new corporate research facilities.

Centralizing R&D in the 1940s

Soon after returning from wartime service, Dr. Compton, as newly named vice president of research and development, organized a centralized R&D group. This made sense. The company was still small enough for such a unit, even as more biochemists, pharmacologists, microbiologists, and chemical engineers filled the laboratories.

Early on, too, Dr. Compton had pinpointed a need for a reliable source of high quality citric acid, a key ingredient of Alka-Seltzer. He led the search toward a new means, i.e., large-scale submerged fermentation. The 1956 acquisition of Takamine Laboratories enlarged the capability to produce by fermentation an array of enzymes useful in the food and other industries. Also captured was valuable technology and talent in microbial biochemistry that resulted in early involvement in molecular biology—when the term was little known and even less understood.

The Miles entry into this newly emerging field rates special attention. In 1959 the Takamine plant was making bacterial catalase by a process patented by consultant Roland F. Beers, M.D., Ph.D., with improvements developed by Dr. Leland A. Underkofler's staff. Dr. Beers had observed that the cellular debris, a waste product in the early stage of catalase production, was a rich source of enzymes involved in nucleic acid metabolism. From this debris he isolated large quantities of a chemical with the forbidding name of polyribonucleotide phosphorylase. In essence, he turned it into polyadenylic acid. With other steps, one involving the forming of proteins from amino acids, Dr. Beers enlarged on his research in such a way that Miles became the first commercial source of several polyribonucleotides used by investigators to study the structure and function of RNA and DNA. Shortly thereafter, an explosive growth in the functional studies of these two substances matured into what has been termed "the era of molecular biology" and stimulated the 1964 formation of Miles Research Products.

During the expansion of R&D, Miles reaped other valuable benefits from the 1956–1972 consultive services of Dr. Beers. For in addition to the specific technologies transferred to the company from his laboratory, he provided counsel on other exciting new elements of biomedical research such as immunology and genetic engineering, to name a couple, that became embodied in R&D programs of that and succeeding periods.

Dr. Harry Collier's research in the United Kingdom earned him a worldwide reputation.

The Golden Age of the 1960s

If there is a golden age in the variegated story of Miles research, it has to be the decade of the 1960s. To meet expanding needs, the centralized R&D structure early in the decade was split into the four units of Chemical Therapeutic Research, Ames Research, Miles Chemical, and Miles Research Products. Valuable products and systems emerged. Acquisitions and new ventures spurred diversification and growth. Veteran scientists carried work to fruition, and new ones made worthwhile contributions.

The acquisition route proved to be fortuitous. By buying Dome Laboratories in 1959, the Atomium Company and Lab-Tek Plastics Company in 1964, and Pentex, Inc. in 1968, the company expanded into anti-allergens and dermatologicals, life science instruments, clinical laboratory hardware ("the shaking, rattling, and rolling of specimens," as Ames' Jim Murphy says), and research biochemicals for internal use and external sales. R&D was basic to exploiting the know-how of the acquisitions.

In this decade research took on a more international flavor with the 1962 establishment of a research laboratory at Stoke Court in England under Dr. Charles Dagliesh. His successor, Dr. Harry Collier,

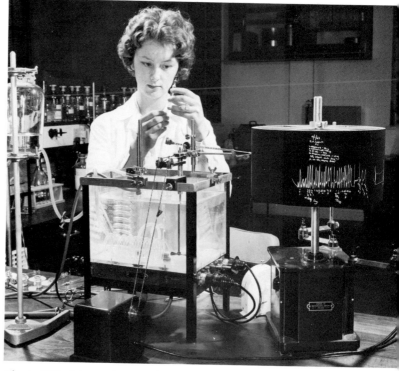

Also in 1962, laboratories opened in the United Kingdom for the testing of new pharmacological substances.

set up programs on bronchodilators, anti-allergenic agents, and drug addiction. Within a few years, fruitful research on prostaglandins—whose therapeutic potential was recognized by Charlie Owens among others—was conducted under Dr. Collier. He had observed that aspirin and aspirin-like compounds blocked the formation of prostaglandins in human tissue and thus provided a major research basis for the efficacy of Alka-Seltzer.

Another element of Miles' international research also began operating in 1962 through a pharmacology facility in Mexico City under the able guidance of Dr. Efrain Pardo and Dr. Julian Villarreal. A collaborative effort between scientists there and at Elkhart led to four promising drugs, two of which were still in clinical trials in 1984. The mid-1960s also saw joint ventures in Israel with heavy R&D overtones, some of which led to improved products for Ames.

There was no letup in advancing the technology of fermentation in the 1960s, especially with citric acid, and improved enzyme strains kept the company cost-competitive in a tough commodity market. Enzymology, too, was a key to new products in the Marschall Division.

The Dominant Thrust of Ames

But perhaps the dominant thrust of the 1960s came from Ames as it broadened its vistas, under Dr. Henry Wishinsky, from the urine strip products (which in themselves came of age in those years) to

Having served as director of biochemistry in the laboratory of a large hospital, Henry Wishinsky, Ph.D., brought both vision and pragmatism when he joined Ames in 1964. He became vice president of Ames R&D in 1968.

Efrain G. Pardo, M.D., joined Miles in 1961 as director of the research laboratories in Mexico City. In addition to being general manager for Mexico, he served for a time as president of the Miles Research Division.

A pharmacologist in Miles' research laboratory in Mexico, opened also in 1962, tests a new compound that may be useful in controlling hypertension.

skillfully contrived systems in the field of blood chemistry. Ames scientists utilized the physical sciences to develop new analytical techniques employing instruments. Thus the concept of a total *in vitro* system found full acceptance—blending tests with instruments—by providing first the means to measure, and then quick and convenient answers for patient and doctor, and for the hospital and clinical laboratory.

All this formed a checkered skein. One interesting thread winds back to the relatively obscure but important work of Drs. Sergio Mannucci, G. Linoli, and Carlo Bergonzi, all Italian scientists. First in Switzerland, then in Italy (the present laboratory is in Cavenago) they developed a unique system for immobilizing materials on plastic—an alternative to the paper matrix first used in the famous strips.

This was a sort of companion effort to the pioneering work done by Drs. Al Free, Ernest Adams, and Chauncey Rupe. Their concurrent testing on plastic strips reinforced the practicality of the concept. John Rebar then choreographed investigations that led to the advanced multistix. Dextrostix, for instance, which detects glucose in whole blood, was one of the research conquests of the 1960s. Another was the reflectance meter, the first of the sophisticated "answer" instruments.

The field of immunoassays had an early fascination for Ames. Dr. David Medley, for example, showed that ultraviolet wave length detection of reactions occurring on a paper matrix was possible. So, again in the 1960s, it was determined that in the long run there were advantages in getting away from radioactivity in the development of new assay systems. This was a prescient decision, although it may not have appeared to be one at the time. In any event, such researchers as Drs. Robert Boguslaski, Nagesh Mhatre, Chester Sutula, and James Christner, among others, charted various advances.

Again, enzymes played a memorable role. In this instance investigators had discovered a system called enzyme amplification. They adapted it to enhance, via fluorimetry, the read-out of immunochemical tests. Another methodology successfully exploited was chemiluminescence. It took the hazards out of isotopic clinical assays. In doing so, Miles served medical science, patient welfare, and its own long-term marketing interests.

Leaving no related field uncovered, Ames in the mid-1960s moved into hematology with a stainer device for reading white blood cells. Again, lab convenience was an objective in furnishing histologists and cytologists with new instruments.

A Salute to the Miles International Symposia

One more company program that began in the luminous 1960s warrants a salute. It's the Miles International Symposia, 14 of which have been held since 1967.

The concept evolved from a research promotion proposal of Jack Carlin, who once headed Miles Chemical in Israel and later the Research Products Division. Dr. Compton and Dr. Beers liked the concept but not the promotional aspects. So all symposia since the first one have had no product mentions or other commercial overtones.

Roland F. Beers, Jr., M.D., Ph.D., succeeded Dr. Pardo as head of the Miles Research Division in 1973. He had been a consultant on enzymes since 1955 and left his mark on Miles' history through the organization of 14 international symposia dealing with molecular biology.

An original purpose was to follow and record the evolution of the science of molecular biology into the technology of molecular biology. The meetings and published proceedings have done just that. Subjects have centered around research that was peaking in interest. In 1968, for example, speakers dealt with the synthesis, structure, and function of transfer RNA. The 1976 symposium, "The Impact of Recombinant Molecules on Science and Society," was held just a month before the National Institutes of Health issued guidelines on genetic engineering. Other subjects have included immunology, oncology, viral infec-

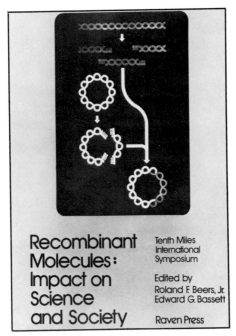

One of many books resulting from the Miles International Symposia.

tions, hormones, mechanisms of pain and analgesia, and cell fusion.

All this focusing on research frontiers enabled Miles to build contacts with academic investigators. Many Nobel Prize winners and other scientists of renown have served as speakers or session leaders.

Much of the credit for the success of these symposia goes to Dr. Beers as its organizer and chairman. He has edited all the proceedings, since 1972 with the aid of Edward G. Bassett, Ph.D., who has served as coordinator. And supporting these forums with his presence, speeches, and approval has been Dr. Compton, proud that the printed proceedings comprise a significant part of the scientific literature of the day in fields critical to the advancement of science and, ultimately, of health care.

Versatile and Esteemed Scientists

Behind all these accomplishments of the 1960s stands a band of diverse and esteemed scientists. One was Dr. Kenneth Carter, an early vice president, who succeeded Dr. Lathan Crandall. Another was Dr. Otis Fancher, a first-rate basic researcher. Dr. Willard "Whitey" Croxall, a chemist, with Drs. L. B. Lockwood and L. B. Schweiger, pioneered explorations in citric acid. Dr. Underkofler, a superb enzymologist and head of research at Takamine, using Dr. Beers'

laboratory findings, began the first basic program in molecular biology. Dr. C. J. O'Donovan, an erudite physician, served a successful stint as Ames vice president for research and medical affairs before moving up to be corporate vice president for medical affairs.

For several years, C. J. O'Donovan, M.D., served as Ames' vice president for research and medical affairs.

Dr. Wishinsky expanded Ames R&D. His predecessor and an intuitive genius, Dr. Alfred H. Free, stamped his name indelibly on the origin of the Ames "dip and read" reagent strips. Dr. John Rebar had much to do with the developmental aspects of Ames research. Others—Dr. John Mirza, Dr. John Gavin, Chester Sutula, Nagesh Mhatre, and Blaze Palermo— bequeathed legacies of distinction to the scientific annals of the company.

Perhaps the most appealing story is that of Robert Kho-Seng "Bobby" Lim, M.B., Ch.B., Ph.D., D.Sc. He proved to be a fine scientist, but his life could easily have been the theme of a sweeping historical novel. Born in Singapore, educated in Scotland, he served in a Scots regiment, kilts and all, in World War I. He went to China in 1924 to do research in gastroenterology and related fields. His work brought him recognition far beyond China.

Compton persuaded R. K. S. "Bobby" Lim, M.D., ChB., Ph.D., D.Sc and surgeon general of Chiang Kai-shek's army, to join Miles in 1952 and continue the research on pain and analgesics for which he was world-famous.

With the Japanese invasion of China, war dictated Lim's life for some years. He became head of the Chinese Red Cross and eventually surgeon general of Chiang Kai-shek's army. As Dr. Compton once remarked, "not bad for an academic bloke."

Compton described a wartime episode as follows: "Assigned in 1942 to the Chinese forces in Burma under U.S. Army General Joe Stilwell, this research man with four degrees, at age 45, led the remnants of Chinese army hospital units, some 3,000 men, on a 26-day march through the roadless jungles of Burma back to China—and he didn't lose a man."

Later, in World War II, Lim visited Fitzgerald Army General Hospital in Denver where he met Dr. Compton, who decided such a promising scientist would be quite a man to have at Miles. This took some time and persuasion. But in 1952 Lim joined the company.

In the 15 years he carried on basic research at Elkhart, Lim left a conspicuous imprint on the scientific escutcheon of the times. His classic explorations into the physiology of pain led to his election to the prestigious National Academy of Science. He proved that aspirin acts peripherally, and not in the brain, and that morphine and narcotic analgesics act on the central nervous system. He showed that many chemical agents can produce pain anywhere in the body without physical injury. Among other things, he devised a system for screening compounds for tranquilizer effects in animals. It is still used today. Named the first Senior Miles Laboratories Fellow in 1962, he retired in 1967 and died in 1969.

Research Reorganizes and Matures

R&D in the 1970s and early 1980s matured, building steadily on the previous decade. Dr. Earl Dearborn, Dr. Efrain Pardo, and Dr. Beers successfully led organizational changes, with shifts in emphasis due to new technologies and with a reinforcing of the multidisciplinary team approach. In 1976, Dr. Richard Falb, a talented scientist-administrator, came to Ames as director of research. Within a few years he was the division's president.

Every area of research scored distinctive gains, some of them in high technology rather than in pure science, but notable nonetheless.

At Ames in the 1970s additional tests bolstered the "Stix" line, so that by 1982 up to ten tests could be included on a single strip. Reaching that number took intricate, creative craftmanship. Instruments became more important in Ames' various programs. In fact, a major new plant had to be acquired in Mishawaka for their research and production.

New trademarks, with measures of glamor, crept into Ames' product line—Biostator GCIIS, Seralyzer, Optimate, and Glucometer reflectance photometer. Synergism between diagnostics and therapeutics intensified.

In other areas, more advanced instruments for histology strengthened the Lab-Tek line, and Marschall added to its Superstart brand of cultures for cheesemaking, introducing five new ones in 1981 alone. Enzyme technology expanded into more food, industrial, and agricultural areas. Work continued on the classic *Aspergillus niger* and on other microorganisms involved in fermentation. Cutter brought into the R&D network fresh dimensions in blood fractions and animal health research. New formulations enriched the vitamin line. And with Bayer's leadership, pharmaceutical research became a primary domain.

Enzyme Research Brings Gains

Dr. Compton always insisted upon establishing Miles as a company with a sophisticated technology. How well he succeeded can be measured in many ways, one of them involving enzymes. Early in the 1970s a group from the Research Products Division produced the first commercially available "restriction" enzymes—a feat that had much to do with the worldwide growth of genetic engineering. Vital to this program were the studies of Dr. Robert J. Erickson, who, at the behest of Dr. Beers, had started an active recombinant DNA project. Dr. Erickson's successor, Dr. Gary Wilson, now directs this activity, the applications of which hold promise in several parts of Bayer-Miles operations. (Restriction enzymes cleave a strand of DNA from a living cell at a constant and specific site, enabling the insertion and functioning of a segment of "foreign" DNA. That alters, by design, the recipient cell's genetic machinery. Ultimately produced are proteins not usually generated by that cell.)

Besides that bit of scientific legerdemain, Miles was as early as anyone in coming up with immobilized enzymes. Attached to inert substances, these enzymes react with a desired substrate, perform their catalytic function, and can then be recovered for subsequent use. Both restriction and immobilized enzymes kindle more efficient processes.

The Growing Network of the 1980s

By the 1980s, Miles R&D strategies and programs had become well-defined. In broadest terms, they embrace the research phase that aims at new products, the development phase that takes them through to marketing, and the supportive phase that maintains marketability. All are included in the Bayer-Miles-Cutter mosaic. The first two are obvious and well understood conceptually. The third is less appreciated, possibly, but no less paramount. Some call it "defensive" research. Dr. Karl Meyer, a Bayer AG veteran and the first vice president of research and scientific affairs after the acquisition, much prefers the more positive "supportive," because it involves, as he sees it, vital steps— "the upgrading of product quality, process improvement, applying new technologies, better delivery systems, and bringing computer controls into various operations."

Whatever the commitment and pace, as Dr. Meyer emphasizes, Miles is increasingly a "technologically-driven company with innovation and the development of new technologies going at a much faster pace than in the past."

R&D strategy for the 1980s deploys in three major areas—biotechnology, diagnostics, and pharmaceuticals. There are some ancillary fields, as in consumer products and in the Cutter lines.

Biotechnology Has Its Share of Glamor

No word has more glamour for the 1980s than biotechnology. Its various R&D segments did not come together until it was formally organized as a group effort in 1979. First under Dr. Blake Ingle, then Dr. Erickson, and now under Dr. Walter Goldstein, a chemical engineer, it sifts into many developing fields and calls upon a host of experts, from microbial geneticists to computer specialists.

As vice president of research and development in the Biotechnology Group, Walter Goldstein, Ph.D., a chemical engineer, leads teams probing the many newly developing uses of industrial enzymes in the 1980s.

Within biotechnology's sphere lies recombinant DNA. Initial work in that field focused on *E. coli*, but Miles scientists weren't comfortable with it because as a part of intestinal microflora in humans, it had the potential of creating health problems. By the early 1980s a shift had been made to *Bacillus subtilis*, a bacterium which does not affect man. It can be grown in massive quantities by deep-tank fermentation, and it has GRAS (generally recognized as safe) status from the FDA. *E. coli* does not.

So Bayer AG and Miles scientists in recent years began exploring gene sequences, isolating DNA molecules and fragments thereof for a variety of purposes. It's wily scientific business, but a good many Miles researchers know how to do it, and they know what they are seeking. And there are commercial goals, such as the production of specific polypeptides and proteins not obtainable in practical quantities by conventional processes.

In fact, the manipulation of DNA could be a doorway to a host of new products and processes. The application of nucleic acid derivatives and their role in the synthesis of proteins and other metabolites now is a central element in the projects of the Biotechnology Group—which is in a footrace with other firms engaged in genetic engineering. Still, no one expects a quick revolution. DNA chemistries are highly complex, and it may take a long time for pilot programs to supplant classical fermentation and become commercially feasible.

Still another goal isn't easy either. It embodies an analytical system that could be applied to the diagnosis of disease. Here the tool is a gene probe, identifying whether a certain disease-causing gene is present in a particular organism or human cell. Such a probe might even detect genetic deficiencies or abnormalities in babies before they are born, enabling an earlier use of therapeutic measures.

Another esoteric program, involving monoclonal antibodies, is no stranger to Bayer-Miles investigators. Although only research tools in the early 1980s, they could lead to the diagnosis and/or treatment of disease. An early finding is that the monoclonal antibody, since it is specific—unlike whole antisera containing a mixture of antibodies—and recognizes only a single antigen, can be utilized for new diagnostic tests. Long range there's the chance that such substances could fight viral diseases and other ailments, even cancer.

As has been apparent time and again, enzymes preoccupy researchers in the Biotechnology Group—and in other groups as well, since life itself, and nearly all reactions in living organisms, depend upon the action of enzymes. Hence an ongoing research objective continues to be the improvement, through genetic manipulation, of enzyme-mediated reactions. Obviously, one goal is increased yields. Another is better quality for a given product. In the delicate interplay of the fermentative process, improved microbial strains hold out hopes for a new generation of products in ever-widening commercial channels.

This recounting by no means exhausts the range of projects under Biotechnology with its intertwined fields that at any time might point to clues for new products and processes. The prospects on the threshold of Miles' second century were indeed rife with promise.

A gene machine, installed in the Biotechnology Laboratory in Elkhart in 1983, gives evidence of the company's pioneering research. David Leland, a biochemist in the Biotechnology Group, studies results.

Alford L. Williams, senior research scientist in the Biotechnology Group, studies the yield and efficiency of a substrate being used in the production of citric acid.

Blending Diagnostics with Instruments

The research of Ames, as often cited, surges along the concurrent streams of diagnostics and instrumentation. The record glistens from the first Clinitest tablet to the Multistix products that can simultaneously test nine components in urine, and from the original Biostator system for hospital use to the ingenious Glucometer for patient use—with their momentous impact on diabetes. Yet all this in 1984 seems only a prelude to what could come in the next decade.

"After all, Ames pioneered diagnostics when others were giving it short shrift," Dr. O'Donovan once noted. Hence the clear-cut strategy of Ames research is to stay in the forefront that it so ably carved into a critical area of medicine. It won't be easy. The field is cluttered with as many as 450 competitors. A major new drug normally may last profitably 10 to 12

years; a new diagnostic instrument will be fortunate to last half that long.

New advances often bring gradual or abrupt changes. Bayer AG's own Agfa-Gevaert, for instance, is exploring multi-film systems, extensions of its expertise in photography, that could lead to novel adaptations for diagnostics.

Joseph Rosloff, executive vice president in charge of Professional Products, and Dr. Falb, Ames' Division president, view the United States as the core of diagnostic technology, with Ames at the center of the core. Down the road they foresee a whole new range of improved diagnostics with methodologies based on the chemistry of genes and how they affect organs and tissues. They admit that all this will take time, insight, experience, and money. Gene probes remain in an early phase and many technologies must be pulled together if "true elegance" is to be achieved. "In one sense," Rosloff asserts, "we are still at the level of the wheel. We must design the racing car."

"Making Blood Talk in Minutes"

If the "dry chemistry" concept of reagents stands out as a lasting triumph of Miles technology, hardly less lasting is what has been accomplished with instruments. The early Biostator system still has the admiration of many people. Dr. Meyer calls it an "exciting and far-out instrument considering that it was available for research back in 1972."

A real commercial advance came with the Seralyzer reflectance photometer—not unrealistically described in its product literature as "making blood talk in minutes, not hours." This versatile tool utilizes the dry chemistry of impregnated reagent strips to perform tests—via a microcomputer—for various body substances contained in serum or plasma. In 1982 Ames marketed another exotic piece of equipment, the Optimate instrument, which moved the company deeper into the field of therapeutic drug assays. This instrument can determine drug levels in body fluids; it can analyze up to 90 samples in an hour and store the results as patient profiles in its computer memory. The Seralyzer and the Optimate are strong testaments to cohesive research teamwork.

By the early 1980s the pattern for Ames was sharply inscribed: to concentrate on the methods of identifying clinically significant substances, to measure them in blood and urine, then to devise instruments that could monitor the course of various ailments, assay therapeutic agents, and determine risk factors that predispose disease development.

So Ames is poised not only to push forward its

reagent systems but its instrument line as well. For if one thing really stimulates its researchers, it is the synergy of diagnostics and therapeutics. Every top executive hammers home its significance. Clearly, it makes sense to integrate new, and for that matter, old tests into apparatus that can provide the answers to diagnosis. For instance, sensitivity to an antibiotic could be accurately measured by an Ames instrument—a finding that would assist the physician as to which Bayer AG antibiotic to use. In addition, the readings could forestall a toxic dose while establishing an effective one. Or a test revealing a cardiac disorder could perhaps help decide selection of a Bayer AG cardiovascular agent. That would be synergy with solid medical, company, and patient values.

Literally corralling instrumentation, of course, is the world of electronics, zipping along at a frenetic pace in the early 1980s. Hugo Gauss, head of the complex research and production operations at the Mishawaka plant, says that all this augurs well for diagnostic products by decreasing microprocessor costs, boosting reliability because of fewer components, smaller size, and lower power consumption. Such factors, he predicts, can open markets "that no one could even have dreamt of several years ago...such as very sophisticated applications for diagnostics in the home environment."

A Dramatic Shift to Pharmaceuticals

While Biotechnology and Ames research have roots deep in the Miles past, that of Miles Pharmaceuticals and its predecessor, the Dome Division, had no major thrust until the merger with Bayer AG. Then the shift became dramatic. No one is more aware of this than Dr. Paul Spiekermann, a 25-year Bayer veteran in charge of medical R&D at West Haven as well as at the corporate level. As a physician-scientist, he knew where the future lay, knew how Bayer AG worked, and how functions and goals could be meshed to accelerate the Bayer entry into the United States prescription market.

The strategy is direct and logical. Candidate drugs for the American market, either established ones being sold overseas, or new compounds, are carefully selected. The first choices, the antifungal, Mycelex, and the antibiotics, Mezlin and Azlin, had gained recognition throughout the world. They proved themselves in the United States, too, with strong sales.

With its extensive resources, Bayer AG does the early work on promising new agents. West Haven handles the clinical testing and regulatory requirements. For this purpose, it swiftly expanded its scientific staff from a bare baker's dozen to more than 350 by 1983.

The research areas had been clearly drawn soon after Bayer AG's acquisition of Miles. They were broad and flexible, some geared to the most urgent needs of medicine—at least for the rest of this century—that is, finding and marketing superior antimicrobials, cardiovascular agents, and cures for metabolic diseases. This does not mean that other targets are being overlooked. Bayer's arsenal, broad and deep, includes geriatric studies in recognition of America's aging society. Its R&D pipeline can be expected to discharge many a good clinical candidate for the United States, perhaps antiarthritic and anticancer drugs among them.

Building on a Great Strength

Concentration on infectious diseases stems, of course, from one of Bayer AG's great strengths—its armamentarium of antimicrobials. For even with steady incremental gains in antibiotics, infectious diseases stubbornly persevere. There are still some 500 of them, each with a causative agent; only some 200 are treatable or preventable. Viruses resist antibiotics, and some bacteria thwart them as well. So the microbial and viral armies persist in conducting guerrilla warfare, and the Bayer-Miles products stay in the thick of the battleground.

There's hardly a major pharmaceutical firm that doesn't have an interest in the cardiovascular arena. Few fields of study offer more promise, even with the current array of effective therapeutic agents. Hypertension itself remains a mystery, with only theories as to its underlying causes. Heart attacks and strokes are still major killers and cripplers. So Bayer AG-Miles can be expected to augment the quest for better medications.

Entities that could combat metabolic diseases would also be a tremendous boon to mankind. Here special interest naturally centers on diabetes, where the Ames record in diagnosis and patient service towers proudly.

For some time, Bayer AG has had a large R&D staff in Germany: at Elberfeld alone there are some 1,200 scientists. "We would eventually like to have additional research centers, and for that the United States would be a prime location," Spiekermann says. "It's too much to expect Europe to carry the full load, even though we must have a unified and integrated system, directed from Leverkusen, but oriented to worldwide objectives, and with data generated at any of the research centers applicable to regulatory agencies anywhere."

The research at Miles Pharmaceuticals is based not only on internal resources but on links to academe. Besides providing generous research grants to dozens of leading universities, Miles has always encouraged researchers to get baccalaureate or advanced degrees, either by part-time or full-time study. And a large number of them have. It is estimated that at one point, 40 to 60 percent of R&D staffers were going to school part-time, some with direct company aid.

The Miles Science Forum

Assisting in the personal and professional development of the many scientists at Miles is the Miles Science Forum, a group of 23 representatives drawn from various sectors of the Elkhart, Mishawaka, and South Bend operations. Training and refresher courses conducted by the Forum combat technical obsolescence. Functions providing peer review of varied research and development projects on a quarterly basis are also sponsored. A unique publication, "Miles Analecta," furnishes some 1,200 readers at Miles and Bayer with articles of professional journal quality about investigations conducted by Miles' scientists. Briefly, the Forum's *raison d'etre* is enhanced communication throughout the R&D community.

The scope of research today is such that it would be prohibitively expensive to set up in-house clinical or other facilities for every desirable project. So by the 1980s Miles either had, or was working on, arrangements with scores of medical schools. The breadth and complexity of Bayer-Miles research programs ordain such connections.

Quite visibly, then, by Centennial time Miles was moving with speed and zest in its search for products of the future. The strands of research wound intricately throughout the company. Take animal health. It is a cornerstone of Bayer's business and vital to the Cutter Group. A new Cutter facility at Kansas City is occupied solely with veterinary medicine, seeking better drug dosage forms and vaccines for cattle, swine, and other animals.

Cutter scientists are engaged, for example, in sophisticated studies of blood. Their research has already led to the commercial production of Factor VIII, a protein whose absence causes hemophilia. Factor VIII can be tediously isolated from human blood, but research could lead to making it through genetically engineered fermentation.

There is an R&D base, too, for consumer products, although it is small by comparison and largely lodged in the development labs. Requirements for over-the-counter remedies are considerably less rigorous than for prescription drugs. As long as vitamins, for instance, are sold as nutritionals and not as drugs, regulatory constraints pose few problems. It would be another matter for new therapeutic claims in the self-medication field. The sheer growth of the need for OTC products, which Dr. Compton predicted decades ago, could assure more R&D for new or revamped consumer items.

From about 1977 to 1983, 28 ingredients and dosages had been switched from prescription to OTC status, with another 16 awaiting FDA decisions. Such a trend holds opportunities for Miles.

Given the diversity of its product lines, then, Miles can have it both ways: Miles Pharmaceuticals can take the prescription avenue; Consumer Products has an enviable background in assessing consumer demands. It's a nice combination. Such a common condition as osteoporosis provides a good example. Should a calcium preparation to counteract it be prescription or OTC? Either way, Miles could move expeditiously, and did. Early in 1984, BioCal tablets were introduced as an OTC product.

By 1984 the scope, purpose, and efficiency of R&D had reached a high plateau. Solidly in place was the multidisciplinary approach. Interlocking technologies assured synergism throughout the fundamental areas of biotechnology, diagnostics, and pharmaceuticals. Better instruments were speeding the evaluation of compounds and systems. Data processing was automating the laboratory, cutting project time and cost. Such programs as SCOUT (Scientific Council—Outside Unique Technologies) were helping to keep the company at the leading edge of science. The scientific and financial resources of Bayer AG were backstopping an imposing effort whose imprint was only beginning to be seen at Centennial time.

CHAPTER 17

"Zip" Is Still The Word In Marketing

When he was nearly 80 years old in 1954, Charlie Beardsley gave a rousing talk on "zip" at the national sales convention.

"I feel this company has had zip during its entire history," he claimed. "Dr. Miles...had this vital quality....A. R. Beardsley and George Compton also had zip. And as to my older brother, Hub, who would say he didn't have zip?"

The still lively "Uncle Charlie" spurred on the sales representatives. "Of what value is the most useful and wonderful formula for the benefit of health...unless it is exploited by the man who knows how to see it? When he is not abroad in the land, there is not much doing....Just in proportion as he succeeds, the tide of prosperity flows."

Selling with "Zip"

Thus did he enthusiastically reinforce that year's theme: "Zip up your sales for a brighter future."

Earlier, in 1948, he had said that "he would like to confer a degree upon any man who continues as a salesman for 10 years with the same company in the same line....", a suggestion he would repeat on other occasions.

Thirty years ago, a typical sales meeting at Miles seldom lacked flamboyance. Lengthy exhortations—the "pep talk" approach, often enlivened with verse and song—were aimed at inspiring the sales force. To a considerable extent, they undoubtedly did; cama-raderie and conviviality always ran high.

At the 1954 meeting, Tom Keene, publisher of

Early sales representatives, vintage 1912, had great confidence in the remedies of Dr. Miles, third from left in this photo. Note the assortment of hats and baggy pants.

Newspaper ads, free samples, eye-catching labeling, drugstore displays featuring paper dolls, oversize apothecary display jars, Little Books, testimonials, pamphleteering even in foreign languages, premium offers of gold-framed pictures of "Sweet Sleep"—all of this and more was part of the promotion of Dr. Miles' first products.

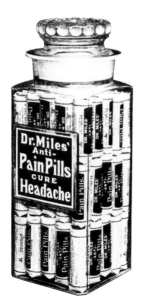

The Elkhart Truth, composed a bit of doggerel that went as follows: "We're feeling mighty zippy, oh boy, are we alive! We'll sell like hell and ring the bell in 1955." Tom was wildly applauded.

Today, the typical salesperson may find the old style less appealing. Sophistication has come to sales and marketing as it has to other corporate areas. A sales representative is more apt to study a marketing computer print-out than listen to product "pitches." Probably there will never again be anything like the lively 1955 sales convention skit, with Virginia Parkhurst playing the role of "Mother Nervine."

A Colorful Record of Dedication

Still, the record of dedication to selling Miles' products is colorful, whether it applies to old-timers or the newer breed. Both in length of service and in performance, salespeople have forged a sterling link in the history of Miles.

Herb Thompson liked to recall "a fellow named Walter Lawton who covered a Michigan territory by auto, in an open car with side curtains and no windshield wipers at a time when there were few improved roads. He would sometimes get stuck in the mud and have to trudge to the nearest farm house to get a team of horses to pull him out."

Thompson, who started at Miles in 1920, was continuing to entreat the "troops" in the 1950s in this fashion: "Boys, when things seem to be going wrong...when you feel in the dumps, don't let it get you down. Say to yourself, 'Yes, it's tough but it's not as tough as it used to be. If those old boys could overcome what they had to overcome and still come out on top, so can I.'"

National sales meetings throughout most of the company's history were major events. At the 25th convention in 1948, the line-up of speakers included Charlie, Ed, and Walter Beardsley, Frank and Chuck Miles, Walter Compton, Bill Koerting, O. B. Capelle, John Cawley, Walter Lerner, Herb Thompson, and Perry Shupert. That was quite a Who's Who of Miles!

Perhaps no one more typified the attitude and energy of a successful sales manager than Shupert, who began learning the drug business as a Walgreen delivery boy in Chicago in the early 1920s. He joined Miles in 1929 to help trim drugstore windows and put up road signs in Indiana, Michigan, and Wisconsin. But then he got a chance at a sales territory in Michigan. With that "break," Shupert was on his way. He opened the first Chicago sales office in 1935

Always looking for new ways to promote its products, Miles ventured into the relatively new medium of motion pictures in 1921. Here ad manager Herb Thompson and Mrs. Thompson meet with members of the cast in "The Curse of Carthis."

and was division manager there until 1942, when he was promoted to Elkhart as assistant sales manager. Next came three big January firsts, for on those dates in 1944, 1950, and 1952 he became successively sales manager, vice president in charge of U.S. sales, and vice president in charge of sales and advertising. He retired in 1968.

Charles Beardsley, second from left, was an advertising genius. Here he confers with John Daly of radio fame, surrounded by top executives, left to right, Ed Beardsley, Oliver Capelle, Perry Shupert, and Walter Beardsley.

Perry L. Shupert, left, was the first to sell Alka-Seltzer to the trade in 1932 and later introduced the theme of "Zip" in marketing as vice president-sales and advertising. At right, Bob Campbell, Portland Division sales.

Selling Consumer Products

A lot of crack salespeople had a hand in building strong consumer sales, going back as far as Shupert's predecessor, Hal McCann, and later including Bob Wallace, Lou Bonham, "Red" Kennedy, and Don Bryant, all talented future heads of the Consumer Products Division. Long timers became commonplace. Fred Lean, a 43-year veteran, was in charge of the California branch of the company (a separate entity) when it was finally dissolved in 1971. In some 30 years with Miles, Fred DiOrio rose from salesman to president of Nutritional and Hygiene Products Division before retiring in 1974.

At a sales meeting in Bermuda in 1976, Miles president George Orr said, "In this division there resides one of the greatest reservoirs of consumer products marketing skill in the entire world. Your competition knows this and respects you for it. Have you forgotten it? Have you forgotten 1966 when you beat off the challenge of Bristol–Myers? Have you forgotten that you taught the people of this country to take vitamins, almost single-handedly?"

Those were sharp reminders and they have borne fruit. In 1977, sales achievements were praised, since a division goal of $120 million was exceeded by $2.4 million. In 1978, five challenges were listed: to make budget, to increase trade merchandising with fewer promotional dollars, to improve business with the drug trade, to heighten professionalism, and to make training and development a reality.

See if you can find four Beardsleys (Arthur, Charles, Ed, and Walter), Harry Gampher, "Tommy" Thompson, Oliver Capelle, Georgia Compton Walker, and Bill Koerting in this 1936 sales convention photo.

Division sales rose again in 1979, to over $129.5 million with the San Francisco Region under Peter L'Amoreaux taking top honors for the second straight year.

National sales manager from 1976 to 1982 was R. L. "Rich" Novak. In 1978, he summed up "realities" in blunt terms: "The race becomes one of the Sales Department working to keep our trade franchises in good stead as the advertising builds the all-important consumer franchises," he said. "Doing better in sales volume doesn't just happen of itself. It's the culmination of a heck of a lot of planning, determination, commitment, discipline, execution, ingenuity, and good old hard work."

By the 1980 meeting, the sales force was accustomed to getting plenty of hard data and realistic projections. Speakers exhaustively discussed retailing, and a Nielsen Report dealt in detail with sales volume, market shares, and inventories.

Steve Reim, vice president of Consumer Healthcare Division marketing for the past several years, who has an advertising budget of nearly $50 million annually, warned that in the 1980s "an avalanche of parity products will hit the marketplace, abetted by half a million commercials cluttering the media." Against these odds, he said, "we have to be cunning and clever...to outgun our competition...to think more about superior strategy and tactics...."

National sales meetings by the 1980s gave way to regional gatherings, while the emphasis on professionalism increased.

The pretty "Miles girl" from the 1921 silent film, "Danger Ahead," smilingly demonstrates a nightly dose of Nervine in her boudoir.

Sales Training Is Important

Sales training in the Consumer Healthcare area is no longer the casual briefing of years ago. Instead, it's a six-weeks formal program for a newcomer; other elements over a two-year span include everything from behavioral training to a detailed review of performance. "Our efforts are people-oriented," explains Bob Foyle, field sales manager. "Our goal is to make people aware of the division's objectives, so we work hard at communicating. And we have developed a sales incentive program that seems to be working well."

Organizational efficiency, of course, is another objective. People in the field make use of a computerized reporting system. It saves a lot of paperwork and leaves more time for calling on customers—food and drug chains, drug and food wholesalers, mass merchandisers, and so on.

Products go on a 12-month promotional cycle, with flexibility for individual accounts. More than 100 salespeople in the division, called key account representatives, encourage stores to promote in ways they think best, whether by print advertising in small or large newspapers, by store displays, by price reductions—or perhaps by a combination of all three. "We look on our people as sales consultants to their accounts as well as being salespeople," Foyle notes.

John Howell, national sales manager, looks for the Consumer Healthcare Division to strengthen its presence in over-the-counter drugs "where the self-medication field is expected to expand."

George Davy, executive vice president in charge of the Consumer Products Group during the 1970s heartily agrees. As chairman of the Proprietary Association in 1980, he organized and led a national symposium on "Self-Medication: The New Era."

To announce the Consumer Healthcare Division's growth plans for the 1980s and celebrate Miles' 100th birthday, marketers chose for the theme of the 1984 national sales meeting, "The Best Is Yet To Come." As at the 25th annual sales meeting held in 1948, the lineup of speakers constituted a "Who's Who" of Miles.

Ed Gustafson, division president, pointed out that "sales of Alka-Seltzer, One-A-Day vitamins, Flintstones, Bugs Bunny, and Bactine account for a major portion of Bayer AG's worldwide sales of self-medication products. Few other companies in the health-care field have the breadth of strong consumer franchises that Miles has. All the hard work the Sales Department has put into these businesses stands the company in good stead for the future. The 1980s will be marked, we hope, by several new, strong products

Miles Learning Centers in some 300 hospitals in the United States have helped achieve awareness of the "new Miles" and its growing line of prescription drugs.

feeding into this pipeline. Certainly that will be one of our major objectives."

Consumer Healthcare Products hold the most historic portion of the sales story, but the total tale is far more than that, since the other divisions, each an offshoot of a new technology or new effort, have their own selling operations. Aside from Consumer Healthcare, six different sales groups serve the traditional Miles divisions, not counting those in the Cutter Group.

The Sales Team at Miles Pharmaceuticals

In late March 1979, some 160 salespeople assembled in Miami, Florida, for the first general sales meeting of the Dome Division, now Miles Pharmaceuticals.

It was an historic moment for several reasons. First, half those present were newcomers to Miles, since the sales force had doubled in a matter of months. Second, the meeting literally launched Miles into the "big time" U.S. prescription drug market, with the introduction of marketing plans for Mycelex and Mycelex-G, the broad spectrum antifungals from Bayer AG.

Enthusiasm prevailed. Dome president John Paolo predicted that within the framework of the German Bayer groups, Dome would "turn into a dynamic enterprise." The goal, he said, was to drive Dome eventually into the top 10 drug firms, "and who knows, maybe one day we'll be number one."

Other steps were taken with relative speed to build the marketing strengths required to reach physicians. In May 1981, for example, in New York City, Miles Pharmaceuticals sponsored the first part of a major conference on "Gaps in the Therapy of Infectious Diseases," with such authorities as Maxwell Finland, professor emeritus of medicine at Harvard, among the speakers. The conference then shifted to Leverkusen, in Germany, with European speakers. It was estimated that the proceedings reflected 2,500 collective years of experience with anti-infectives. Highlights were published in the *Journal of Infectious Diseases.*

Rolf W. Buell, then the division's new president, described the objectives of the conference. He said they were to introduce the company as a "new force in drug therapy" for North America, as a "new entity dedicated solely to developing major new ethical compounds," and to "create credibility" by showing the resources of both Miles and Bayer Leverkusen.

Technology armed the effort with new tools.

One was the setting up of Learning Centers, with self-instructional equipment for medical and nursing education. They are computer-based, of course, with videodisc playback units, TV monitors, and hand-held remote control devices. The 12-inch videodiscs, scanned by a laser beam, provide up to 54 minutes of motion picture with stereo sound. By late 1983, some 300 had been placed in hospitals and other sites as a major contribution to continuing medical and nursing education within the United States health-care system.

With its growing sales force thoroughly schooled in new products, and with its physician-targeted programs, marketing for Miles Pharmaceuticals quickly came of age.

Selling Diagnostics Takes a Different Approach

Selling Ames products began as a hybrid, blending diagnostics with therapeutics. That never worked too well. George Orr, a veteran of another drug firm before coming to Elkhart, recalls that it took him quite some time to recognize that, at Miles, there were two distinctive markets and that they should be treated accordingly. Informing a doctor about a drug and a hospital about a testing device required quite different approaches.

Actually, this dichotomy was recognized fairly soon, and after the Dome purchase in 1959, detailing of drugs gravitated to the new division, while Ames began specializing in a direction mandated by its own chain of breakthroughs, largely in the diabetic field. Technical diagnostic information became a critical component in medical practice and a build-up of the sales force began in earnest by the early 1960s. Its number reached 150 by 1969 and has steadily increased to more than 1,000 today, making it the largest in the field of diagnostics.

Ames recruits both college graduates and sales personnel experienced in the diagnostic area. Its training program is intensive, reflecting the need for highly technical expertise. Ames has a complete Education Center in Elkhart, with video network and playback facilities in 40 U.S. locations. This network reaches around the world, with international managers translating the English audio portion into their native tongues. Becoming a qualified Ames representative takes a full year.

Ames is committed to supporting clinical chemistry and medical technology. It exhibits at more than 30 annual national scientific society meetings and

More than 700,000 diabetics subscribe to "Diabetes in the News," published bi-monthly by the Ames Division.

sponsors numerous scholarships and awards to society members. Its technical service experts include a good many professions: chemists, biochemists, toxicologists, immunologists, and microbiologists among them. They furnish a wide range of assistance both to sales personnel and customers and are "indispensable to the business," according to James Lavery, director of U.S. sales.

Some diversity in methods applies to Ames overseas, under the tutelage of Roy Wakeling, a veteran international marketing specialist. In major markets, salespeople are hired and trained by Ames and integrated into Miles' operations. In small markets, distributors are retained, and they sometimes direct Ames' own personnel. Elkhart-generated formal courses and training programs on product areas are now standardized worldwide. Basic training is in English, but the salespeople overseas speak the language of their markets—close to 50 different tongues in all.

Selling Soap Pads

Selling the company's household products requires operations that differ markedly from those in other divisions.

"*Big Blue*" *made his own appeal
on behalf of S.O.S soap pads.*

Thanks to Robert J. Wallace, the first Household Products Division president, a smooth transition took place when Miles bought S.O.S from General Foods, which had a well-placed national network of 64 food brokers, each responsible for a specific marketing area. This network served 35,000 supermarkets. Miles simply supplanted General Foods, and the system continued like clockwork.

"It has worked almost flawlessly," reports Henry Fitts, who has served both General Foods and Miles in top marketing positions. "Our sales costs are highly predictable, with a set commission, and we avoid the sales expenses of hiring, training, and providing automobiles. The brokers call on customers, get the orders, handle promotion, and maintain close relations with the trade. They have some 1,200 people calling on supermarkets—far more than we could afford ourselves—and while they sell other products, of course, S.O.S has for many years been consistently among the top 10 accounts for each broker."

Household Products can direct the whole operation with a small headquarters staff and only four regional managers. "Not only Miles but the brokers wouldn't have it any other way," John Grant, division president asserts. "It's the way we keep efficient controls on marketing." He calls attention to another plus—strong advertising. The same agency widely known for its creativity—Doyle, Dane, Bernbach—has been coming up with first-rate advertising ever since S.O.S steel wool pads became part of the Miles family.

Selling to Cheesemakers

As with so many other Miles products, skillful promotion has had its role in boosting Marschall sales, profits, and prestige. The sales force is quite small, and some "double in brass" by calling on customers who buy more than Marschall products—industrial enzymes and so on.

College graduates in dairy and food science and people already knowledgeable in such areas as food biochemistry are sought as representatives. They get training so intensive, both at headquarters and in the field, that they know their jobs fully in six months.

Integral to marketing in such a specialized area is the Technical Service Department. It is responsible for literature, for providing complete information on new products, and for problem-solving in close coordination with sales.

About half the sales force of 20 or so spends its time exclusively with the dairy industry. All this is extremely effective. Division president Verle Christensen says marketing vice president "Viv" Rowley has always had a "great knack for hiring the right people."

Marschall promotion goes off on tangents unique to Miles and to marketing situations. More

*Stan Ferris, originator of the Annual Italian Cheese
Seminars, receives the Man-of-the-Year Award from the
National Cheese Institute in 1982.*

than 20 years ago, Stan Ferris, an imaginative marketer, suggested sponsoring an annual seminar for American makers of Italian cheese. The first gathering drew only a 100 people, but it soon became the nation's premier event for that portion of the industry, its popularity climbing year after year. By 1982 attendance surpassed 750.

Expanding on the success of the Italian Cheese Seminar concept, the company held its first Biennial International Cheese Conference in Madison in 1979 with 2,500 people in attendance. Later ones, in the early 1980s, attracted as many, along with some 100 exhibitors. In Madrid in 1980, Marschall sponsored its first Symposium for Spanish cheesemakers.

Selling to Clinical Laboratories

Miles Scientific Division, a consolidation of Lab-Tek and Research Products, has its own singular marketing strategies. When Lab-Tek was purchased in 1964, its small sales organization was pretty much rolled into Ames. Separation came about three years later, with a sharpened selling plan for petri dishes and the other plasticware.

There were only three or four salesmen at the time, but between 1968 and 1975, the number went up to about a dozen. Sales training techniques were adapted from Ames. A technical services function was tacked onto marketing. In the late 1970s, reorganization and growth were led by such experts as Shirley Johnson, Ray Szafransky, James Ogle, and Bill Williams.

Most importantly, Bob Myers ushered in the major expansion overseas. Lab-Tek indeed became global. The process had started with the introduction of Tissue-Tek in Japan in 1972 and by 1978 was moving fast. Sales in Europe, Australia, and Brazil climbed from $3 million to $10 million in four years.

Wherever Miles has a presence anywhere in the world, so does Lab-Tek. With formation of the Miles Scientific Division in 1982, the Lab-Tek sales force of about 30 people took over selling the line of more than 1,000 research biochemicals as well. Direct sales still play their part, with three or four mailings of a catalog going out annually to various disciplines, some 75,000 in the United States and another 25,000 abroad.

Selling Citric Acid

A mixture of marketing approaches marks citric acid and sodium citrate sales, even though there is essentially only one product with an enormous number of applications. The Biotech Products Divi-

Harold Stalter, left, vice president of marketing, Biotech Products Division, and Robert McGrath, division president, bring Leland Underkofler, Ph.D., developer of many of Miles' industrial enzymes, back to Elkhart for Centennial-year honors. Underkofler is featured in publications being used at meetings of the International Food Technologists.

sion has its own highly trained sales representatives, most with backgrounds in chemistry and engineering. Their diverse selling job is heavily oriented to service, to working with production and lab managers. In the words of Biotech Products Division president Bob McGrath, the sales reps are the "tip of the spear" in projecting the technology of citric acid across scores of industries.

Participation in trade shows, trade journal advertising, pinpoint mailings, and other promotions supplement an effort bolstered by marketing research, especially in such major areas as the beverage industry. As Harold Stalter, division vice president of marketing, explains, citric acid is not sold in small quantities; the average order runs 110,000 pounds. It is these large orders, to such companies as General Foods and Lever Brothers, on which the salespeople focus.

Less than truckload quantities are handled by distributors serving hundreds of locations in the United States.

Tied closely though it is by experience and expertness to citric acid, the division's sales outlook will not always be locked into a single item. For one thing, citric acid and enzymes have been combined under one division president. For another, there is constant examination of chemicals from Bayer Leverkusen as sales possibilities in the United States. In coming years, then, the division's sales will probably expand far beyond the present products.

Trouble-Shooting with Enzymes

No Miles salesperson needs a more exacting background than a seller of enzymes. A very modest number, usually only four to six people, sell to some 100 market segments, and they must understand the role of enzymes in all of them. They work closely with customers, often being on hand for plant trials and laboratory tests. The typical enzymes sales specialist works about two years in the technical services labs before going to the road.

"Our people must know how to put enzymes into any applicable system," Marketing Director Bill Allen explains. "They become trouble shooters. When the customer has difficulties, and since he is dealing with the unseen, he tends to blame the enzymes, which is rarely the culprit. So the Miles representative must get at the real source of the problem."

As Allen notes, "Our job is to maintain momentum in a rapidly changing technology, to identify markets and opportunities in a fluid industry, and at the very least to maintain our leadership position in the ever-growing enzyme field."

It's a stiff challenge, and one that Miles has full confidence in meeting for decades to come.

Marketing Research Gets Its Start

The enthusiasm and capability of salespeople at Miles has long been bolstered by marketing research of a high order. In the days before Alka-Seltzer, it may have been a bit primitive and intuitive, based on limited surveys and crude statistics, not to mention the hunches of such individuals as Charlie Beardsley. That was all to change in the 1940s.

There is no particular hero in the story of Miles marketing research, but there is a heroine. In 1923, a young woman named Treva Van Solingen went to work for Harry Gampher. After years of clerking, she began putting together rudimentary sales statistics. "There was a complete vacuum in the compiling of such statistics when I started at Miles," she says. "This gave me a great opportunity to utilize my creative talents with figures."

Van Solingen became an expert statistician, and set up a graphic charting service and the first key-punch tabulating department. Meanwhile, Miles moved propitiously into state-of-the-art marketing research. In 1932, it became a pioneer subscriber to the renowned firm of A. C. Nielsen. Miles has been one of its best customers ever since.

Van Solingen and her staff also traveled coast to coast, meeting often with Ernest Dichter, who was retained to handle motivational research; Horace Schwerin, who tested commercials; and the advertising agencies doing the radio and TV spots and print ads. "We got the best of whatever was needed," she says.

In August 1946, a formal Marketing Research

Treva Van Solingen virtually originated market research in the 1920s. She became the company's first woman executive when named director of the newly organized Department of Market Research in 1946. Here she discusses sales trends with Bill Copenhaver in 1952.

Department was established in the Consumer Division, with Van Solingen as its first director. She developed the most sophisticated practices, always employing the latest techniques in analyzing the motives and attitudes of consumers, advertising effectiveness and so on. Her forecasts at sales conventions received rapt attention; one prediction came within one-tenth of one percent of eventual final figures, so the advertising agency presented her with a crystal ball.

This enterprising woman's pioneering opened gateways to the advanced, computerized services that now characterize marketing functions in every division. She retired in 1967, her place secure for all time as a marketing "trail blazer" and as Miles' first woman executive.

In the Consumer area alone, it is not unusual to have ongoing some 150 marketing research projects, covering everything from name-testing to product satisfaction to advertising effectiveness and to concept-testing in the search for new products. About 70 percent of the work delves into new product ideas, according to Bruce Godfrey, head of Consumer Market Research at Centennial time. Consumer products have always been rigorously tested. The thoroughness of the research embracing them can be illustrated by an example, picked more or less at random from scores of excellent studies. This one was done in November 1968. Its purpose: to find a shape most liked by children for Miles' chewable vitamins. What did they prefer—circus characters, toys, or the Flintstones?

Child Research Service, Inc., conducted sessions lasting one and one-half hours in groups of 10 to 12, half boys, half girls. Flintstones vitamins easily conquered, with two thirds of the youngsters, aged five to 10, preferring them as "the brand they would like mother to buy for them." Barney and Pebbles and other cartoon characters were favored by much higher percentages over competitive brands. So Flintstones chewable vitamins were introduced in 1969 and Bugs Bunny, the runner-up, in 1971.

Rigorous Sales Training

While disparate markets make different demands, sales training and standards are uniformly high throughout the company. All told, about one out of every nine employees sells products and services. With rich traditions to uphold, with individual talent to be expeditiously used, and with the high promise of growing markets, Miles' sales forces in 1983 were poised and eager for the remainder of the century.

Their job will be difficult; it always was. So Charlie Beardsley's saying, "All honor I say to the man who sells things," is still most befitting.

Finding a Corporate Logo

A corporation is known by the trademarks it keeps—and that begins with its logo. Back in the 1960s, Miles was tired of its old one; in 1968, it found a new one. The design did not come from an advertising agency or from corporate identification experts who had been struggling to replace the old-fashioned logotype with something more representative of a modern corporation.

The double profile, used on Dr. Miles' earliest products, seems a world away from the "Miles M", the corporate trademark for the last 15 years.

Dr. Compton happened to spot a somewhat crude "homemade" logo on a map of the West Haven property. "That's it!" he said. He felt instinctively that the search had ended. The mark consisted of a capital M with the word "Miles" in capital letters across the middle. It had been sketched by a young engineering draftsman, Robert Pherson, not for anything as grandiose as a new corporate mark, but simply to identify the various properties of Miles in a convenient way. Chief draftsman Ben Pethe had liked it and ordered that it be used on similar assignments.

The mark was given to Thompson Arts Studio in South Bend, which made some minor modifications of Pherson's original drawing. Miles then had a unique "M" that Dr. Compton ordered placed on everything from business cards to tank trucks worldwide. Application of the mark was uneven, however, and in the mid-1970s the Public Relations Department began a review. More than 2,000 uses were studied by a Public Relations Advisory Committee, headed by Doloris Cogan, and a corporate identification manual was developed with the help of Robert Stanley Associates. Accepted for use in 1979, at Centennial time the program was again undergoing review.

Protecting Trademarks

All kinds of attempts to take advantage of its famous trademarks, especially Alka-Seltzer and One-A-Day vitamins, have cluttered the legal history of Miles. Importantly, defense of those names has steadily been successful.

The early success of Alka-Seltzer prompted imitators by the score. As early as 1935, Miles stopped one company from using "Premo-Seltzer," another "Foamo-Seltzer," still another "Healtho-Seltzer." The company won similar infringement cases against firms trying to get by with such names as "Vita-Seltzer" in 1943, "Aphco-Alkaline-Seltzer" in 1953 and "Carba-Seltzer" in 1955.

Other products, of course, have had to be defended from time to time. A European chemist once sued both Pfizer and Miles, claiming he had a patent controlling the presence of assimilable phosphate in the making of citric acid.

It is true that phosphate was utilized very efficiently in the manufacturing process, and even residual amounts could be detected by analytical methods. But the complainant didn't really know all that much about citric acid, at least as it was made at Miles. Evidence showed that by restricting trace elements, the phosphate did not hamper production at all, no matter how much of it was present. This matter was favorably settled.

Unexpected conflicts can develop in trademark choices. In 1975 Dome selected Exzit for its medicated cleanser for acne. It discovered another company was using Exit "for relief of the itching of dogs." The conflict was settled on the basis of different uses for the respective products. So Exzit survived!

Speedy—A Prime Target

Much of the trademark story is more amusing than significant. Many entrepreneurs sought to capitalize on Speedy Alka-Seltzer, seeking to put his name on such items as racing motorcycles, Mexican food, dog food, hair-thinning shears, helmets, shirts, utility masks, belt buckles, race horses, and carpet cleaners. All were denied, but permission was granted for Speedy to appear in a trademark "hall of fame" TV

Display advertising near check-out counters in drugstores proved invaluable.

Speedy Alka-Seltzer appeared in more than 100 commercials, not to mention print ads, and became one of the best-loved product symbols of all time. Here he is introduced to the retail drug trade in 1952.

One of the most powerful incentives for the Miles salesmen was Mr. Rosebud, a deodorized skunk that had to be kenneled by the lowest division. He is shown here with the Chicago sales manager, Kendall McKee.

spot when Standard Oil introduced its new name of Exxon.

Attorneys sometimes had fun with tongue-in-cheek responses. In 1966, John Gildea denied a request from a musical trio to be called "Speedy and the Alka-Seltzers," but he wrote that "since we know that any venture of this sort encounters some headaches, we are enclosing an Alka-Seltzer credit card to assist in alleviating these difficulties."

Mel Silver responded in a similar fashion to a report of a dancer in Philadelphia "bubbling over with sex," to be known as "Elke Seltzer." Mel wrote that "she is in a line of business so unrelated to ours that no confusion is likely. On the other hand, her stage name might be considered disparaging to our trade reputation, and thus actionable under a state's unfair competition laws." He recommended that "no objection be made in this matter as 'Miss Seltzer' would be the only one to benefit from the consequent publicity," but said "he would be happy to investigate the matter further."

There are in the records two remonstrances to the name Speedy. "This is my husband's name," one woman wrote, "and we are the only family in the United States with the right to use it." Another objected: "You have taken a great liberty.... To think my husband, a very nice looking man, has to have his memory abused with his name on a dummy."

Dick Beals, the radio and TV voice of Speedy, once asked permission to paint the name on his new airplane. The response was speedy; his wish was granted.

Americans are bombarded by some 1,500 trademarks every day. Some of Miles' are among the best known. One proof: in 1982 on a Johnny Carson show featuring the 100 best commercials of our time, five of them, all emphasizing the trademarks, came from Miles—more than from any other single company.

Silver wrote in a 1980 *Alkalizer* article, "imitation is the sincerest form of flattery, but imitation of our trademarks is something we would rather do without." Miles does not want them to go the way, for example, of cellophane, escalator, linoleum, yo-yo, and zipper—all once treasured but now in limbo as generic words. Given the record of Miles in safeguarding its "most valuable assets," it seems that this danger is relatively remote.

CHAPTER 18

Keeping Quality High

At a seminar for quality control managers in 1975, President George Orr wanted to impress them with the importance of a name change for a critically essential function. He asked them to remove their badges, and below the word "quality" strike the word "control," write in "assurance," then sign and date the badges.

That's how quality *assurance* replaced quality *control* as a more positive phrase and became the official designation for the company-wide task of maintaining consistently high standards for every product. As a symbolic action, Orr's request brought into focus the full maturity of a concept and of a whole range of technologies.

Obviously, no program carries a higher priority if a company is to succeed and grow in the marketplace. No more exacting penalty swoops down when a product fails to meet the expectations of buyer and user. Nothing gets more attention at Miles, both formally and informally, than quality assurance.

Lloyd T. Johnson, hired in 1937, was "Mr. Quality Control" for many years.

Lloyd Johnson, a Legend

Probably the first true quality control scientest at Miles was a chemist, Lloyd T. Johnson, who was hired in 1935. Maurice Treneer wanted him to "look after" the manufacturing of Alka-Seltzer. This was significant since moisture in the bottle would destroy the effervescence. The product stability of Alka-Seltzer thus was the first major quality control problem that confronted Miles in its first half-century. The problem was managed with packaging that provided the critical moisture protection.

Following on the heels of Treneer, Fred Lobley ably developed standards for maintaining low humidity in the compounding and compressing areas. Richard S. Reamer also did much to develop better controls, as did Treneer's son-in-law, R. S. Nicholls. What had started out as a department with Johnson and a technician eventually grew into a force of hundreds. In 1966, Johnson went into International Quality Control. He had set standards that served as a foundation for a thorough quality assurance program.

This development can be traced by looking at the small notebook Johnson kept, which detailed specifications and procedures. In it, he also began keeping batch records. His dittoed instructions to supervisors were precise enough for the time. In about 1950, his notebook was not more than three inches thick. In contrast, by 1982, the Quality Assurance records took up 24 feet of file cabinets, although they would soon shrink spectacularly with the computer transforming them into microfiche storage.

More Extensive Quality Assurance Since 1962

Quality Assurance has been more extensive at Miles and elsewhere since 1962, when the government began requiring more batch records. At Miles, these Good Manufacturing Practices posed no special problems. "We had to make only one change in procedures," Bill Hendershot, corporate director of quality assurance, remembers.

Meanwhile, sophisticated instruments, bearing such designations as high pressure liquid chromatograph and gas chromatograph, with the inevitable aid of the computer, have come along to carry much of the quality burden. Vibration tables even check packages by shaking them. There are pallet shakers, too, for as Gordon Hostetler, director of QA for the Consumer Healthcare Division, explains, "We have to make sure that everything from vitamins to complicated Ames instruments will withstand shipping."

A Finicky Lot of Perfectionists

The Quality Assurance people march painstakingly to the beat of their own technology. They are, in one sense, a finicky lot of perfectionists who, in the minds of some employees, take actual glee in finding defects. But their iron-clad resolve protects the company, the health professions, users, and patients. Management wants it no other way.

Above all, Hendershot emphasizes, quality assurance pervades everything Miles does. "Testing the

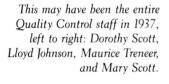

This may have been the entire Quality Control staff in 1937, left to right: Dorothy Scott, Lloyd Johnson, Maurice Treneer, and Mary Scott.

Joining Miles in 1962, William F. "Bill" Hendershot, Ph.D., became corporate manager of quality control development in 1967 and succeeded Ollie Vaughn as top man in 1968. Bill now has eight employees in corporate Q.A. and another 800 quality assurance people work in the divisions.

ment standards, but our own." Back in 1971, Lloyd Johnson felt that Quality Assurance had already come a long way, and he proudly proclaimed the function at Miles as "second to none in our industry any place in the world."

Worldwide Quality Assurance Seminars

A few years before that, Hendershot had been seeking ways to expand and coordinate programs. He suggested seminars every other year for all Quality Assurance managers worldwide. The first was held in August 1971, with a satellite gathering in Cali, Colombia that fall. At these meetings, subsequently held in 1973, 1975, 1977, and 1979, no aspect of quality went unexplored, from fundamental management and regulatory requirements and recall case studies to the most esoteric of topics, such as computer applications and assay reliability.

finished material is only the last step," he says. "We are kidding ourselves if we believe otherwise. We can only verify what manufacturing has done. Thus, process control is essential day by day, on a consistent basis. Call it a cliche if you will, but Quality Assurance has to be everybody's business.

"Today it goes beyond the classical concept of control," Hendershot says, "to embrace every prescribed process and procedure, all in place and properly used in conformance not only with govern-

From products and processes in trial stages to field sampling of items already on the market, the

In 1942, Isabel Chester, left, and Beula Copher help keep track of products under a "central numbers" system provided by this equipment.

patient and thorough pursuit of quality never ends—whether it concerns the stability of Alka-Seltzer tablets, One-A-Day vitamins, Bactine, or the performance of instruments as sensitive as the Seralyzer or Optimate.

As trends and directions go, the computer, not surprisingly, will no doubt be more heavily engaged.

Peter Chang, vice president of Ames Quality Assurance, cites an intriguing example involving a glucose monitoring and feedback system that relies on a sensor—a complex electrode that transmits responses from physical stimuli. It is not easy to develop tests in such a device built around a delicate membrane. It takes a highly skilled laboratory worker an entire day to examine one electrode with manual procedures. However, a fully automated, computer-controlled system can test a dozen electrodes in two hours and provide hard copy documentation as well.

Chang notes that computers "may actually be better suited than humans to perform certain functions...since human memory is time-oriented and computer memory is list-oriented and capable of total recall independent of experience or mood...." He sees a combination of "human and computer intelligence being brought to bear on the key Quality Assurance problems of the future."

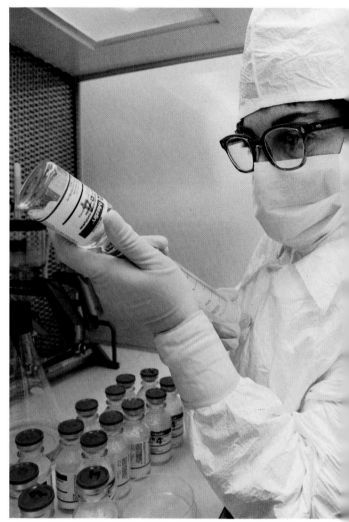

A microbiologist at Miles Pharmaceuticals tests Mezlin (mezlocillin) for sterility.

Ames instruments get rigid inspections before being shipped to customers.

For example, in the Blood Chemistry Q.A. lab, as many as 12 Seralyzer instruments are interfaced to a single HP85 computer which collects the data from the instruments as it is generated. The technician does not have to record any numbers. This eliminates transcription errors and frees him for more productive work. The data are transmitted to the Miles main frame computer for analysis and storage. Other departments, such as R&D, have access to the Q.A. data at any time via their own computer links to the main frame.

Further attesting to Dr. Chang's vision of computers in Q.A. is the first laboratory robot in the entire Bayer complex. Installed in 1983 in the South Bend Q.A. area, the Zymark Robot has been programmed to automatically carry out the physical testing procedures for Ames TDA products and analyze the data needed for release of these products. Other robots are planned for other Q.A. areas as well.

In the Diagnostic Systems Validation Department within Ames, computers find still more use. DSV conducts the clinical field testing of all new Ames products to validate that they will work as intended in the customer's laboratory. Richard N. Phillips, Ph.D., director of DSV, has installed a computer in his office to receive daily data transmitted by clinical investigators. It saves time and money.

Joe Brady, director of Q.A. for Biotechnology, and John Cherry, director of Q.A. for Cutter Laboratories each have incorporated the use of computers in their operations wherever possible. Cutter's infusion solutions and plasma fractionation operations, for example, are computer-controlled for increased accuracy and precision, as well as for time and dollar savings.

Quality Assurance at Miles is a vibrant operation. Extensive use of computers has helped make it that way.

When Miles introduced the first urine test strips in India in the 1970s, it applied the same rigorous Q.A. standards there as elsewhere.

The pursuit of quality assurance goes on at the same high level worldwide, as in this Miles-Sankyo plant in Japan, where employees inspect Clinitek reagent strip urine tests.

CHAPTER 19

From Bookstacks To Bytes

In 1940, Miles Laboratories decided that the world of science had advanced to the point where a trained librarian was needed at Elkhart to organize a medical, chemical, and business library. A modest ad was placed in the *Washington Star*, and more than a score of qualified applicants responded.

That quest for a librarian with "some typing necessary," seems quaint indeed by the standards of the 1980s. Today at Elkhart the single librarian of 40 years ago has been replaced by a number of librarians and information scientists with links to other specialists at Cutter in Berkeley, at Miles Pharmaceuticals in West Haven, at Stoke Court in England, and, of course, to the vast resources of Bayer. Their developing network serves both corporate and local needs with unique internal databases.

It is the virtual magic of the computer that has transformed library science. In effect, the full range of the world's scientific, technical, and business information is at the electronic fingertips of the library professional. It would boggle the mind of Elizabeth Weissinger who got the job at Elkhart in 1941. She would be totally bemused if she did not understand how to use a computer terminal for database searching.

Dedicated Traditional Librarians Hired

Perhaps the Miles library is as good an example as any in delineating the computer's role in a modern corporation. For all its proficiency, the system in

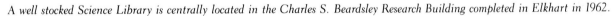

A well stocked Science Library is centrally located in the Charles S. Beardsley Research Building completed in Elkhart in 1962.

Charlotte Mitchell, left, named head librarian in 1951, and a large staff of professionally educated librarians, including Margaret Clark, guided Miles through the "information explosion" of the postwar years.

place today did not come all at once. The stage was set in a sense by the dedication of such head librarians as Charlotte Mitchell, from 1951 to 1979 and Ann Cocks, who retired in 1980 after 23 years of service. Another pioneer was Margaret Clark.

The Miles library had access to the first databases in the early 1970s. They provided only lists of relevant citations. But as the databanks multiplied, they could include article abstracts along with the citations. Now some systems can even speed full texts to users. At Centennial time the number of databases exceeded 1500. Their value is evident in the example of Medline, the database of the National Library of Medicine, which was started way back in 1879. It stores more than a quarter of a million articles drawn from some 2,500 journals.

Computer Resources Added

Dr. Alan Hagopian, head of library services, almost nonchalantly lists four reasons for using both internal and external computer resources. First, speed in getting answers, even to complicated questions, from the already vast storage in databanks. Second, improved productivity made possible by sharing catalog information with other libraries. Third, electronic mail techniques for borrowing books, obtaining cop-

ies of articles from other libraries and maintaining journal subscriptions. Fourth, setting up unique in-house databases for sharing within an organization.

The key to effective use, of course, is the library staff which must not only be qualified in specific academic disciplines but in knowledge of the burgeoning variety of data collections.

The technology of information handling and retrieval is advancing rapidly. As Miles edged into its second century, the "dumb" terminals used for database searching were being replaced or supplemented by multifunctional desk top microcomputers. They can do lots of things, such as word processing, the capturing and manipulating of data, and electronic mail.

As Dr. Hagopian emphasizes, computerized databases are not magical. Their value is limited by the quality of data put into them and by the expertise of the searcher. But as a tool the computer has clearly revolutionized information storage and retrieval. As it continues to improve, the Miles network of libraries will take full advantage of each new step.

A Gradual Entry into the World of Computers

Miles' entry into the domain of the computer goes back to its relative infancy in industry, 1959. The company installed what today seems little more than a fast-moving, intricate punch-card tabulator to handle consumer product billing and the payroll. The first computer was about 10 feet long, four feet wide, and five feet high, a real behemoth by today's standards. Now its power could be contained in a single printed circuit the size of a nickel.

Step by step, the company kept up with computer technology, acquiring its second Univac in 1962 and an IBM second generation solid-state unit in 1966. By then, some 35 people worked in the computer center, and its functions had expanded into inventory, sales and marketing, financial, and so on. In 1970 came the IBM System 360 Model 50, which could be hooked up to computer terminal data centers in Chicago, Granite City, Toronto, and West Haven, and to 19 separate warehouses from California to Connecticut.

Carl Shouse, then director of management sciences, knew it would not be the ultimate machine, but he did know that it would produce twice the work of the replaced Model 40. By that time, the staff numbered 50.

One of the first jobs given the new model was, as *The Alkalizer* put it, "helping to determine how closely Alka-Seltzer commercials follow the pattern of upset stomachs across the United States." "As a result," Shouse explained, "Alka-Seltzer commercials are shown more often in those parts of the country where our computer-produced analysis indicates greatest potential for sales growth." Thus a new technology came to the aid of a classic product.

Uses kept growing. For example, in 1978, a computer-to-computer link between Miles and the Dauphin Distribution Services Company in Harrisburg, Pennsylvania, began helping speed consumer products to grocery stores. Video display units started to appear around 1974, permitting people at office terminals to "talk" to the main computer. More than 500 now chatter away at various company plants and points. This "on-line" advance clearly boosted efficiency.

In June 1978, came a formidable new central unit—the Amdahl 470V5, a machine with the capacity for 5 million memory "characters." In contrast to the 1966 computer, which could handle only one job at a time, Amdahl could run 18 separate jobs at once.

Management Sciences Department

By this time, too, with its myriad functions cutting across so many activities, the computer had created its own bureaucracy—a management sciences department organized into six separate sections with a staff of 120, including 60 programmer-analysts. Staff responsibility ranged widely from the routines of data entry and control to systems design and programming, to evaluating computer hardware and software, to procedure writing and medical support services—and to literally dozens of other tasks.

One of these was materials management, including purchasing, which did not become a full beneficiary of the computer until 1979. It took time to perfect the purchasing function, beginning with a concept study in 1975. Sadly, Craig Bishop, corporate director of purchasing, a key innovator in developing the system, died just before it went into operation.

Four data bases shore up this particular operation. In its first year, operators handled 37,000 purchase orders, 7,000 more than in the previous year. The new system cut purchase order copies from as many as 13 to three. As warehousing foreman Jim Gunter expressed it, "It's a Godsend to us. It has cut down on paperwork, it has cut down guesswork, it has cut human error to nearly nothing, and it has reduced problems by 95 percent, since we can track down information from the system."

By the late 1970s, the computer had become pervasive in operations ranging over every aspect of corporate life. Here, William E. McGuire, supervisor data coordination/documentation, and Melinda Karavan, medical research associate, coordinate data on the clinical evaluation of a potential new drug at Miles Pharmaceuticals.

Making Miles More Efficient

The lengths the computer will go to in making Miles more efficient and effective stretch almost to infinity. Human beings seem intent on making its miniaturized circuits superior to the 10 billion neurons in their own brains. That brain took many millenia to develop; the computer has been forged in a wink of history. One of them, the BKG98, has already whipped the world's backgammon champion, seven games to one, and may do the same to the top chess masters by the time this book is published. Computers even buttress the artistic world; painters and musicians now extract data from chips to help work up their own creations.

The computer already speaks in more than 150 programming languages. Its sheer miniaturization through "magnetic bubble" memories bewilders the imagination. A million such bubbles can be stored in a single chip half the size of a match box. Computers talk to and test each other, along with their human monitors.

The Latest Computer Technology

Miles will move along computer frontiers wherever they are. Its impressive Amdahl 470V5, for all its power and versatility, had been outgrown by 1982 and was shoved aside by the IBM 30-33, a much smaller but much more powerful model. It cannot, of course, be expected to do the job for more than a few years without being displaced.

The new IBM is a truly central processor, where all computation and sorting takes place. It is connected to all internal points and to Miles plants throughout the country. It can run 15 jobs at once, and operators can interrogate it and get responses if something goes wrong. And things inevitably go wrong.

At the big data processing room at Elkhart, an average of four to five problems are logged each day at the telecommunications control desk—the nerve center of the system. Most of them are quickly solved, and most involve smaller telephone companies around the country that had been denied access to Bell technology as a result of the classic AT&T divestiture decision of 1981.

The Miles computer network entered the early 1980s with about 165 specialists. Its output goes to users in two forms—by print and by the less expensive microfiche, which enables 250 pages of print-out to be read on a desk-top instrument through magnification. In a typical month, about 31 million lines become available on microfiche, about 36 million lines in hard print-out copy. Does this optional system have a "candy store syndrome"? Not necessarily, since users' departments are charged for the services rendered.

A Dual System of Storage

A dual system provides storage. A library contains some 12,000 reels or tapes, catalogued as to be instantly on hand. More startling to the uninitiated is the Memorex 3676—rows of desk-high consoles holding magnetic discs. Each segment has about 20 discs layered like pancakes, and each disc can store about 6,250 characters. The system even maintains its own index.

For all its wondrous capabilities, the computer demands intense application if it is to be cost efficient

Facilities throughout the world, like this one in Cavenago, Italy, are now linked by computer, bringing the resources of Bayer and Miles ever closer.

and productive. "In earlier years we probably had too many technicians," Ray Johnson, vice president of management information services, says. "Today we realize that to make good use of data processing, you must know how the business operates. Fortunately, it's easier now; you don't have to be a mathematician. In fact, most of our people have at least some business background along with specialization. About a dozen are highly trained statisticians."

Now Coming—The Electronic Office

"Clearly, all managers today must have some working knowledge of the computer," Johnson asserts. "For in the 1980s we are seeing the merger of classical data processing with telecommunications and office automation, the so-called electronic office."

Johnson looks back on the 1970s in one sense as not all that great. "We had a relatively information-poor management environment," he says. "Now, with the torrents of data that can be generated in the 1980s, we believe we are information rich." A challenge, he believes, will be how to use this data, how to organize and structure databases for better decision making and to integrate data retrieval into every area to cut costs and improve performance.

A True Handmaiden

Johnson estimates that directly or indirectly, the computer affects the jobs of 50 percent of all employees; so Miles in the 1980s will leave no chip or byte or fiche or screen unchecked in a quest to make the computer a true handmaiden of its operations.

For that matter, it already performs that role. The system in the pilot plant of Biotechnology links computers that talk to each other. As Steve Schlager explains it, "There are 17 different computers in this system. One computer checks another one, and if something goes wrong, another takes over. We have never been down; with one computer we talk to the corporate computer. We save all the data, and we can access that and do experimental studies. We also have remote hookups that go into our plants. I even have a computer at home and I can see what's happening in the plant."

The flashing language of the computer, expressed in black, green, red, and yellow figures and symbols, permeates corporate life. To the highly trained and mostly young people pushing buttons and flipping switches and calmly watching messages blink

Joe Dregits, lead computer operator in the Data Center, welcomes Dr. Gerhard Dittmar, member of the Bayer board, and Dr. Walter Compton, then Miles chairman, to the computer tape library during the historic 1978 visit.

Ray Johnson, vice president of management information services, center, introduces Prof. Herbert Gruenewald, chairman of the Bayer Board of Management, right, to Jack McCray, supervisor of computer operations in Elkhart.

rapidly on the screens in the giant center at Elkhart, the meanings are clear. For the messages do nothing less than help to chart and direct the every-day tasks of business in ways few dreamt of a generation ago.

One of Industry's Oldest Archives

Alongside its libraries and computers, Miles has long nurtured an important planning and information resource in its Corporate Archives. Firestone Tire and Rubber is generally credited with the earliest business archives, established in 1943. Yet the Miles collection of historic documents, records, products, and memorabilia began to take shape as early as the 1930s. A sense of history seemed to crowd in on those who witnessed the first phenomenal decade of Alka-Seltzer sales.

Company secretary Harry Gampher deserves credit as the unofficial first archivist. During his 45-year career, beginning in 1898, he put the company in the vanguard of record-keeping and made possible the breakthrough development of marketing research under Treva Van Solingen, hired by him in 1923. He built a makeshift platform for corporate historical records halfway up the wall of the Shipping Department in the company's cramped Franklin Street offices. For years, the archives were divided between this single shelf (which Gampher nicknamed his "pigeon's roost") and the quaintly-decorated vault now in Ruthmere Museum. In 1938 Miles moved to its new building on Myrtle Street and a vast "File Room" was set aside for the growing collection of corporate records. No one dreamed it would ever be filled. In a year it was bursting at the seams.

A solid, meticulous series of records—indispensable for charting trends—came together thanks to the unusually long service of such people as Harry Beaver (production), Charles S. Beardsley (marketing), Doris Corey (treasury), and an honor roll of dedicated secretaries who saw Miles catapulted into history. A certain historical perspective grew out of Miles' professional relationships—its 60-year association with the law firm of Pattishall, McAuliffe & Hofstetter, successor to Reed and Rogers, its 50-year-old account with A. C. Nielsen, and a 40-year span with Wade Advertising.

In the 1940s, Gampher's successor, Walter Lerner, instituted the first records retention system, further developed by library director Charlotte Mitchell in the mid-1960s. Today over 6,000 drawers of records extend, row upon numbered row, in the basement location of the old "File Room." As 1984 approached, the long-slumbering collection of historic records stood ready to be moved into a modern depository in the new Miles Centennial Center being built under the auspices of the Public Relations Department. Its organization and use are being directed by Donald N. Yates, Ph.D., who was named corporate archivist in September of 1983, and who has also developed a program of corporate exhibits and guest relations.

CHAPTER 20

Designed For Productivity

It was the first major award under the company's new Suggestion Award Plan, begun in February 1982, and it was worth $4,225 to Russell Gullett, a machinist on a production line in Elkhart. He had proposed an extension of the vitamin filler process to increase output. Supervisor Bill Shively and others thought the idea would save about $21,000 in the first year.

This wasn't the only time Gullett had made suggestions to improve the efficiency of the line, but as he said, "It's really nice that the company encourages and recognizes employee ideas."

The Suggestion Award Program, common to many companies and industries for years, had been a long time coming at Miles. It wasn't that employees had not been innovative in turning up ideas to improve all kinds of processes and operations over the decades, or that they had been unrewarded in one way or another.

It had, however, been a bit haphazard. So a formal program of direct payment for worthwhile suggestions was not launched until February 1, 1982.

Russell Gullett, a machinist in Elkhart, receives the first major award under the company's Suggestion Award Plan. Fellow employees on hand, from left: Cliff Metzler, Theodor Heinrichs, Bob Markley, Max Lund, Gullett, Larry Richmond, Bill Shively, Dick DeCraene, and George Davy.

Striking the Right Chord

Well drawn and fully publicized, it seemed to strike the right employee chord. Within six months, 1,200 suggestions poured in from Miles' workers at facilities from West Haven, Connecticut, to Berkeley, California. These early awards ranged from a minimum of $50 to Gullet's $4,225. In the plan, awards of up to $20,000 per suggestion could be granted.

The booklet explaining the program said employee ideas and contributions would be a "key element of our productivity improvement strategy."

For of all the words of the 1970s that bounced to the forefront of American industry—and throughout the industrialized world, for that matter—none was more loudly heard than "productivity." Under it, or after it, trailed a stream of analysis, interpretation,

statistics, approaches, and strategies; it virtually developed a philosophy of its own.

What happens to productivity in the 1980s is starkly fundamental to corporate success or failure—to innovation, market positions, human performance, use of resources, environmental needs, public support, and so on. Every employee will either contribute to or detract from it. Real earnings clearly depend on it. In short, productivity has become an inherent part of the new "bottom line."

In attempts to achieve better productivity, Miles wanted first of all to increase employee awareness, to get people involved in finding ways to improve their job performances. The Suggestion Award Plan was the first step.

A Productivity Services Department was estab-

Whether selecting manufacturing supplies from an automated carousel, as Norm Duel and Alice Ward are doing in the Ames Instrument Plant, or holding down inventory in some 90 warehouses across the United States, Miles today relies heavily on computers to keep tight control.

lished to serve as a focal point. One of its primary goals was to seek new approaches. Jerry Carmichael, experienced in employee relations, was appointed manager. Thus, a new and in some ways revolutionary venture was on its way.

To launch this effort, all personnel were shown a film highlighting the relationship of employee input to efficiency and job satisfaction in Japan. The message hit home. Afterward, a survey of 1,200 people who had seen the film disclosed their interest in improving productivity, provided they could take part in the process and not just be "told" what to do. Thus in forming the department, it was decided early that while top management would be committed to the program, it would not be imposing it by edict.

"The effort and ownership of ideas does not represent a corporate program but something that originates in plants and divisions," Carmichael says. "Consequently, we have structured the effort around local productivity action teams serving as suggestion committees for their respective units. Strong up and down communication is essential in a problem-solving team approach."

Management at Miles, as elsewhere, then, is striving to establish ways to measure productivity, surely a must for corporate success in the 1980s.

Logistics Management: A New Buzzword

The 26-acre Mishawaka plant, housing the Ames Instrument Division, has no typical stockroom. For one thing, it has to handle some 12,000 parts and speed them to where they are needed, mostly on very short notice. A small staff does this with precision, making the job a model of sorts under the heading of an important new corporate "buzzword" created in the 1970s called Materials (or Logistics) Management.

It is part of an even broader term, "integrated management logistics" which includes order entry, production inventory control, purchasing, transportation, and distribution/warehousing.

The shipping room in 1913, when Miles, as the biggest postal patron in Elkhart, was already sending its products overseas.

Members of the first quality circle in a Miles plant meet to discuss guidelines. From left: Ed Klimek, administrator, Corporate Productivity Services; Bob Flood, Walter Bohlman, Roger Heiser, Bob DeBroka, Bob Whitson, and Jack Zuidema, all in the Ames Instrument Plant in Mishawaka, IN.

Collecting, storing, and distributing of the huge parts inventory in Mishawaka exemplifies modern materials management. For a stockroom's efficiency can be just as critical as that of a research lab or production line. In this instance, the stockroom's flow of materials depends on three basic elements: an automated floor-to-ceiling parts carousel, parts trays that can be stacked in special carts for density storage (they eliminate conventional skids and tow motors), and the inevitable computer that enters the movement of each part and maintains a complete inventory.

Other elements are important, too, such as prepackaging as soon as receipts arrive, and even industrial tricycles for rushing needed items from storage to production points. Nobody waits very long for a part at Mishawaka.

Just the Right Blend

Management professionals look upon highly integrated logistics control as an ultimate weapon in maintaining low inventories, moving goods efficiently, holding down fuel charges and labor intensity, and otherwise slashing costs.

Over the decades, Miles has employed both integrated and decentralized control of materials management. In December 1981, overall functional control of all logistics was assigned to a corporate vice president with worldwide responsibility. The job went to a respected Miles veteran, Donald R. Lohr. Under him, the company overlooks no opportunity to cut costs. It saves in purchasing by buying from the same vendors whenever possible and holds inventories to the lowest practical levels at the 90 distribution centers and warehouses, mostly publicly owned, that store and move products to customers.

Lohr sees distribution patterns tied closely to productivity. "Every dollar in sales is going to be

harder to come by in the 1980s," he says. "We will have to concentrate on basics, on improving operations." Obviously, wisely managing logistical change had become paramount at Centennial time.

The Start of an Engineering Epoch

In 1926, a young Englishman, Fred Lobley, who had served on ships in World War I and afterwards as an engineer, came to Elkhart as a consultant to supervise the installation of a new four-color rotary printing press, then the fastest and largest of its kind anywhere. Given those huge almanac, calendar, and Little Book orders, it made sense to have the biggest and the best. At that time, at the old Franklin Street plant, the printing operation occupied two floors, requiring as much space as the medicine manufacturing on the other two floors!

Lobley watched over the functioning of the mammoth press until 1928. Then Arthur Beardsley asked him to stay on permanently. He did, and soon set up the first Engineering Department—and in doing so inaugurated an enduring epoch in engineering at Miles.

The role of professional engineers in the company's history interlaces all the essentials, from maintenance to capital expansion—but most significantly, it forged a chain of achievements in productivity beginning pretty much with the advent of Alka-Seltzer.

Laurels for Innovation

Lobley got the title of chief engineer in 1935, and until his retirement in 1965 had prime responsibility for scores of projects that earned Miles laurels for innovation in manufacturing processes. Robert Huber, current head of the department, is rather

One of the company's most valued long-term employees, Fred A. Lobley, came to Elkhart in 1926. He became chief engineer in 1935 and vice president of engineering in 1951. He retired in 1965 after 39 years.

typical of Miles' engineers in the scope and diversity of his assignments. He spent his first dozen years under Merrick Shepard helping to solve problems in the production of citric acid, went international for a few years, then formally joined Engineering in 1964. His department embraces about 40 professionals and some 220 maintenance and operating craftsmen at Elkhart alone.

Today's engineering staff is called upon to help shape facilities as diverse as the new enzyme plant at Elkhart, the recently completed allergen plant at Bridgend, Wales, and the new wastewater treatment plant scheduled for completion in Elkhart by 1986.

No capital expansion nor production improvements have taken place—nor can they take place—without the endeavors of engineers. Scores of outside firms, of course, have contributed to the story. Miles' own specialists, however, have usually been more important than outside vendors and have been conspicuously sharp in adapting the equipment of others to the needs of Miles.

Bright Lights on the Drawing Boards

Many names brightly illuminate Engineering's drawing boards. Wendell E. "Bim" Compton came to the company fresh from Purdue University and eventually succeeded Lobley as vice president of Engineering. He skillfully guided many key programs.

In 1926 Miles installed this four-color press to print calendars, almanacs, and Little Books. It was the fastest and largest of its kind anywhere.

Wendell C. "Bim" Compton, grandson of one of the founders and brother of Dr. Walter Compton, helped build the main plant in Elkhart as a graduate engineer from Purdue University. He joined the company in 1938. He was elected to the Miles board in 1951, and as vice president, Corporate Engineering, in 1962, he succeeded Fred Lobley. He retired in 1977.

Albert C. Buffum is remembered for accomplishments in citric acid and at other production points. Few did more to bring advanced techniques to the Alka-Seltzer and Ames reagent strip lines than Horace B. "Ike" Moyer, who retired in 1980 after 27 years of employment. Ron Hansing and Alex Karay both gave 30 years of exceptional service. Accolades could go on for quite a while and would include such experts as Art Butler, Donald Barto, and James Nelstrum.

The first major victory for production in which Engineering played a signal role was almost "forced" by a compelling need to make enough Alka-Seltzer for a mounting demand—and to make it more efficiently.

A Victory for Productivity

Up to 1953, Alka-Seltzer tablets were compressed with single-punch presses, each of which would turn out about 200 tablets a minute. Volume then required 85 such machines, each manned by one person. Eagerly sought was a rotary press, with its promise of much faster tableting.

After long testing, a machine called the Colton 260 was brought to a practical stage, partly because Miles perfected central lubrication. That was the real beginning of a lubrication system for all rotary presses.

Company engineers provided another "first" with a vanadium-plated punch and die, which enabled proper pressing of the tablets without letting powder stick to the punches. The Colton 260 created the desirable high-speed compression—up to 2,600 tablets a minute. (Today about 2,200 a minute is considered to be the most suitable rate.) "The history of the Colton 260 is probably the most outstanding in the world when it comes to rotary presses," Moyer insists.

A Packaging Triumph Adds Luster

Another technical triumph for the Alka-Seltzer line had to do with packaging, since, in the 1960s, marketing studies showed a need to diversify from bottles into foil pouches. Pin-holes had long been a

The speed of modern-day Alka-Seltzer lines goes back to the ingenious engineering of the 1940s and 1950s.

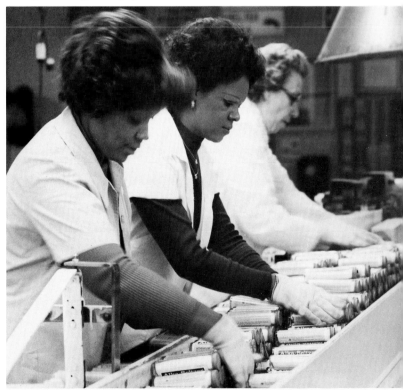

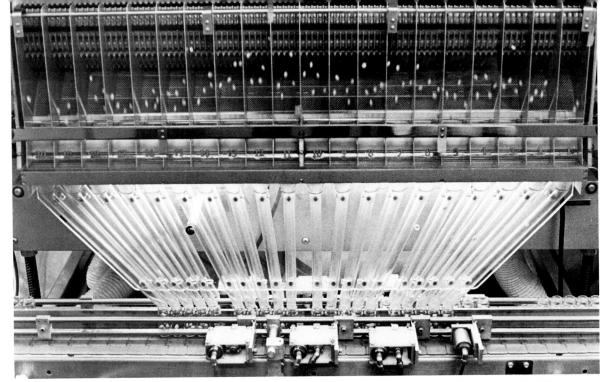

A vitamin tablet counter-filler is but one of the complicated pieces of equipment installed and maintained by Miles engineers.

problem with aluminum foil, and a better substance, made by DuPont, was finally found. This, in turn, led to the admirable megapack sealer—which took the tablets from the Colton machine and sealed them in foil.

Impeccable quality assurance steps, using such devices as microswitches and laser beams, make certain that each megapack carton has perfectly packaged tablets, encased in the foil so familiar to countless Alka-Seltzer users.

By devising apparatus—automatic stackers, filling machines, various types of sealing systems, bottle-cleaning equipment, a "Rube Goldberg" contraption to prevent breakage, plastic-insert machines to replace cotton, even by adapting a self-winding fishing reel for one operation—Miles has remained a leader, quite possibly *the* leader, in high-speed tablet production lines.

Close Teamwork Brings Success

As Moyer recalls, this success would have been impossible without close teamwork among engineers, machinists, and manufacturing specialists. He praises the cooperation of union workers, too, remembering that when new Alka-Seltzer procedures were being considered, he "told them exactly what I was going to do, how many people I was going to replace, and they accepted it."

Reams of engineering specifications have gone

Fermentation processes, like those being built into this citric acid plant in Dayton, Ohio, in 1975, are constantly being improved by Miles engineers.

into other operations. Reagent strips provide a good example. There, oddly enough, much was learned from the automobile industry's weaving of paper for car seats. That provided clues to handling paper for the strips. Ames contributed its own unique dryers and worked unceasingly until it found a plastic material to replace paper. All kinds of ingenuity had to go into determining ways to take rolls of filter paper, put on a "barrier," and then print and finally

impregnate the reagent. Just the cutting and slitting procedures, and the automatic filling of bottles with strips, took years of engineering inventiveness. Today, with speed and precision, a filling machine can automatically take, cut, and insert into a bottle, 50 or 100 strips. It's all cost-effective, and a testament to the discernment of Miles' engineers for more than half a century.

Ames Division, in Elkhart, IN

Miles Pharmaceuticals in West Haven CT

Corporate headquarters in Elkhart, IN

CHAPTER 21

Reaching Out Into The Community

In 1831, Havilah Beardsley (A. R. Beardsley's uncle), an early settler and physician, obtained a deed, later ratified by the President of the United States, for a full section of land belonging to a Pottawatomi Indian chief named Pierre Moran. Beardsley paid $1,500 for the 640 acres. He promptly had them platted and built a gristmill. The site was soon called Elkhart.

Apocryphal or not, the name supposedly derives from the Indian legend that the island formed by the confluence of the St. Joseph and Elkhart Rivers has the shape of an elk's heart.

Water assured the settlement's early growth, first with the keel boats that enabled goods to be shipped on the St. Joseph River to Chicago, giving Elkhart some importance as a river port. Waterpower for grist and sawmills gave the town an industrial start, and the coming of the railroad between Toledo and Chicago, around 1851, hastened its development. Railroad shops came in the 1870s; by 1880, Elkhart boasted a population of close to 7,000 people.

Dr. Miles Leads the Way

Elkhart was a thriving town when Dr. Miles began his practice and founded his company, and launched as well a full century of congenial and beneficial relationships between city and company. This linkage deserves mention as a model of its kind and as an integral part of the corporation's life.

Even as a young physician, Dr. Miles closely involved himself with the day-to-day affairs of the town, serving on its Board of Health, urging its citizens to guard against such killer diseases as diphtheria and to practice good hygiene.

The creation of a city museum was one of his fond projects. He was named vice president of The Elkhart Academy of Natural Sciences, which was instrumental in making the museum a reality. The Museum Associates then asked him to head its

Archeology Department. He did more than that; he contributed shells, coral, and lava most likely sent by his father from Hawaii, fossil vertebrae, and other items, including a mastodon's shoulderblade from one of the earliest excavations in Indiana.

The Beardsleys' Influence Strong and Broad

Even more active in Elkhart affairs was Albert Raper Beardsley, who took to politics early, probably spurred by his cousin, J. Rufus Beardsley, for many years an influential figure in local and state Republican circles. As noted earlier, A. R. Beardsley was elected city clerk and city treasurer and served on the city council. With service in the state legislature added, his civic record was exemplary indeed.

He left his mark on the city in many ways. In 1914 he proposed a new $100,000 municipal building that still serves as City Hall. In his obituary, *The Elkhart Truth* cited "his immense desire to promote the commercial prosperity of the town." "Whatever labor or material you buy, first try to secure it in Elkhart," he would say. Many of his efforts gained no publicity. "Among his intimates...he had an abhorrence of letting his benefactions be known," the paper reported.

Following the example of his uncle, Andrew Hubble Beardsley played a brisk role in civic affairs. From 1926 to 1934 he served on the county council, and he labored with distinction in the state legislature from 1916 to 1924. As a state senator, he championed women's suffrage, good roads, and the early gasoline tax. He was so active in Boy Scout work that he became known as the "father" of the movement in Elkhart.

The Legacy of Mrs. A. R. Beardsley

Mrs. A. R. Beardsley also left a notable legacy of public service. She was the first woman school board

Walter R. Beardsley (1905–1980), combined a love of art and public service. Beside him in his office stands a Rodin sculpture, and behind him, a Georgia O'Keefe painting.

member (1919–1923), and the first state president of the League of Women Voters. In 1923, she donated the Baldwin House, later called the Four Arts House, the original home of A. R. Beardsley, to the local League for its headquarters.

Two other past presidents, Edward Huggett Beardsley and Walter Raper Beardsley, were extremely active not only in local and state political circles but on the national scene. Their staunch Republicanism became legendary. Walter, a frequent White House visitor, earned the sobriquet of "Mr. Republican," and was a delegate to every G.O.P. national convention from 1948 through 1972. He was an Indiana State Senator from 1936–1940. In the 1939 session of the Indiana State Legislature, he sponsored the first uniform state Pure Food and Drug Act in the United States. This act set a precedent for other states, which later passed similar bills. First elected to the Proprietary Association's Board of Directors in 1946, Walter Beardsley served as president from 1948–1950 and as an honorary vice president from 1971 until he died in 1980.

Donating Time and Money

Ed Beardsley served as a State Senator from 1941 to 1945. Both Ed and Walter donated time—and money—to various local groups and causes, including the hospital and the YM-YW building. Still another Beardsley, Charles Sumner, was a leading Republican activist.

Certainly the steadfast support given Elkhart by the five Beardsley presidents was extraordinary by any standard. It must have encouraged many others to "go

In 1942, Lieutenant Walter R. Beardsley, on behalf of Miles, presents a check for its first ambulance to the city of Elkhart. Left to right, Arthur L. Beardsley, Francis E. Compton, Charles S. Beardsley, Lieutenant Beardsley, Fire Chief Ed Clark, and Mayor Clyde Paxson.

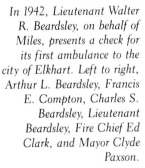

For years Miles executives have served on the board of Elkhart General Hospital. Lehman F. Beardsley, hospital board president, recognizes 25-year hospital employees.

and do likewise," not the least of them being another Beardsley, Lehman F., known to all as "Lem," and without doubt one of the most popular executives in the history of Miles. A warm and outgoing man, he made his mark with the company in such fields as plant management, administrative services, and public affairs before retiring as a senior vice president in October 1982. He distinguished himself in Elkhart through a lifetime of civic service on important boards, committees and commissions, including the Indiana Airport Authority, the Elkhart General Hospital Association, where he served 12 years, the United Way Board, Associated Colleges of Indiana Board, and others too numerous to mention. He was instrumental, for example, in campaigns for a new hospital addition and for an expanded airport.

The Comptons, too, have a long history of public involvement. A full page was required to list Dr. Walter Compton's board and committee memberships in the 1970s. They included medical associations at all levels in the United States and some abroad; the National Advisory Food and Drug Committee of the Food and Drug Administration; the Board of the Pharmaceutical Manufacturers Association; Honorary Vice President of the Proprietary Association, the Board of the Indianapolis Museum of Art, and many others.

"K-Rations" for Servicemen

Little wonder, then, that Walter Compton and Walter Beardsley, before they enlisted in the armed forces during World War II, went to Chicago to see what Miles could do to help the war effort in its own plant and community.

They discovered that one deplorable Army item was powdered coffee that would quickly become hard and resinous in its tin container. They realized at once that an answer to this dilemma lurked in the technology of Alka-Seltzer. Several years prior to the war, Miles had devised a hermetically sealed Alka-Seltzer package. It was designed to maintain solubility and flavor under any weather conditions for two years. Maurice Treneer adapted the same technique to seal in five grams of coffee.

With the plant on three shifts under the dedicated direction of Bill Rich, deft women workers, aided by high school boys and girls, produced an astonishing 384 million packages of soluble coffee in the next four years.

The scope of Miles' wartime activity was not fully apparent until the autumn of 1945 when the Chicago Quartermaster Depot awarded the company its "Certificate of Meritorious Service" for "outstanding performance in producing and supplying foods

The technology developed for packaging Alka-Seltzer in water-tight foil packs was applied to millions of K-rations, soluble coffee tablets, bouillon powder, and other rations for the armed forces during World War II. Employment, mostly women, nearly doubled.

and equipment to the Armed Forces of the United States."

In addition to the coffee, the list included some 25 million K-ration units; 102 million aspirin tablets; 19 million bouillon powder packages; 143,000 chili powder packages; 110,000 earth packages (a filter for producing potable drinking water); 189 million tablets of sodium chloride for various uses; 168 million lemon powder packages and 24 million orange powder packages (not too popular, but good for cleaning mess kits, Dr. Compton remembers); 6 million vitamin tablets for use in life raft kits; and 4 million phenacetin tablets for the U.S. Navy.

Perhaps the most exotic item came under the heading: 455,704 pounds of chemical pellets. Turned out for the Navy under the tightest secrecy, the pellets were used in prime ammunition to retard powder flashes from naval guns, thereby making it difficult for the enemy to determine the source of the firing.

Using its then largely idle printing equipment, the company also produced 450,000 booklets for the Office of Price Administration. It even provided patriotic posters to druggists, extolling the K-ration. The total value placed upon the products produced for the Armed Forces during the war came to almost $10 million—no mean sum for that time.

Largely because of these new activities, corporate sales rose steadily from $8.6 million in 1941 to nearly $19 million in 1944.

A Spirit of Community Involvement

No Elkhart resident speaks more highly of the company's community role over the years than Jack Dille, who came to the city in 1951 as the new publisher of the *Elkhart Truth*.

"A corporation's philosophy and performance reflect those individuals who run it," he says. "In Miles' case, it has been run by men who believe they owe something to the community. The three founding families succeeded remarkably well in getting along, so they were extremely effective in helping the city."

Support of the Elkhart hospital has been a primary interest from the earliest days. In 1910, the company pledged $10,000 toward construction of a hospital, provided an additional $30,000 could be raised. It was, and the donation was made in 1912. In 1950, Miles pledged $100,000 toward a $750,000 renovation program. It funded a research laboratory for the 322-bed hospital in 1963. Not only the Beardsleys, but many other employees have served on its boards and committees and have otherwise helped to make it an outstanding small-city institution.

College scholarships have been part of Miles' community relations program for decades. Past and present winners and alternates are brought together in 1965. Seated, from left: Ruth Shank, Brenda Cocanower, Janet Moore, Constance Post, Myrna Miller, Kay Freeman, Joan Lee Fisher, Charlene DiCamillo, and Jennifer Prugh. Standing, from left: John Zience, Eric Johnson, Dana Ackley, Mitzi Sarantos, Mary Ellen Pletcher, Ann Kalman, Nancy Cripe, Richard Davis, Stuart Pickel, Dennis Huff, Serge Krauss, Andrew Pike, and Tom Gamble.

Aiding Elkhart's Youth

Another field of special interest focuses on youth. In 1962, the company began sponsoring two Junior Achievement companies annually. When the economy warranted it, the "summer hire" program gave jobs to a total of 350 young people beginning in 1958. Many of these youngsters later were hired as permanent employees.

Every year a $1,500 Miles Merit Scholarship is awarded to the son or daughter of a Miles employee, and additional smaller scholarships are awarded to honor students at each of the Elkhart high schools. Minority student scholarships are granted through the Elkhart Urban League.

Whenever something is needed, Miles people are there, from United Way participation to civic projects. Employees and the company gave strong financial support to the building of a new YM–YWCA building in 1972. In 1975, for example, 50 company volunteers participated in one night of a five-day auction for the local educational TV station and raised $62,000. In 1978, Miles donated four lots for a new fire station.

Soliciting funds at the auction on behalf of Elkhart's public television station, Channel 34, becomes a fun-thing-to-do during the 1970s.

Helping the Park System

In 1922, a strip of valuable land sloping to the St. Joseph River by the North Main Street bridge was given to the city for park land. In 1957, it was appropriately named Beardsley Park—since it had been donated by Andrew H. and Albert R. Beardsley. In his will, Walter Beardsley gave $125,000 to the park system, the largest donation it had ever received. The company's gift to the community commemorating its hundredth birthday will be the Miles Centennial Footbridge over the St. Joseph River, connecting Island Park with Pulaski Park, valued at more than $100,000 counting landscaping at both ends of the bridge.

For the Elkhart Centennial in 1958, Charles Beardsley was made Honorary General Chairman. The Miles float in the memorable parade was a spectacular, over-sized Speedy surrounded by giant Alka-Seltzer packages. In the nation's Bicentennial in 1976, Miles donated a plaque mounted on a boulder in a city park and a time capsule containing both Miles and city memorabilia to be opened in the year 2027.

Well-known company names literally encumber the civic, educational, and business history of the community.

For example, way back, George Compton was part of a group that obtained a Carnegie Library for Elkhart.

The founder's grandson, Franklin B. Miles, ably served as president of the Airport Development Corporation and as president of the Elkhart Health and Welfare Corporation.

Charles Miles, another grandson, and retired Miles executive, was chairman of the building committee for the First Presbyterian Church in Elkhart, a member of the President's Advisory Council of Goshen College and a National Associate of the Boys' Clubs of America.

Renewing the Downtown Area

In the late 1960s, the Elkhart business community had problems. Like most small cities in America, it nervously watched its downtown area stumble downhill. For this reason, Dr. Compton and Lehman Beardsley, along with Jon Armstrong, chairman of what was then the St. Joseph Valley Bank, took the lead in the 1970s in forming a study committee to reinvigorate the area. Dr. Compton and Beardsley represented Miles.

Out of this effort in 1979, came the razing of a whole downtown square block to make way for the

Generous contributions by employees and a substantial corporate gift have helped put the United Fund "over the top" in plant communities year after year. Charles R. Ver Berkmoes, Mary Burmeister, and Charles F. Miles accept the 1957 award.

146-room Midway Motor Lodge. Importantly, the motel is flanked by a large parking lot within walking distance of most downtown stores. The project was accomplished smoothly, spearheaded by Armstrong, Compton, and Beardsley with city supervision by community development director Jane Roberts. As Bill Miller, 1981–83 president of the Elkhart Chamber of Commerce, pointed out, it was done "with reasonable purchase prices, no lawsuits, and satisfactory relocations of merchants."

In the opinions of Dille and Miller, the company has enhanced the community overall with the caliber of its people from the assembly lines to the executive suites. "The types of management men and women who have worked at Miles have been highly educated and sophisticated, more often than not oriented to the international scene," Dille emphasizes. "So they have added breadth and interest. And from my observations, the work force in general merits the highest praise for its skills and performance."

The crowning individual contribution of the Beardsley family to the area has to be Ruthmere, the magnificently renovated Indiana limestone mansion built in 1908 for Arthur and Elizabeth Beardsley and named for their only child, who died in infancy. "It had fallen into a disgraceful condition," Miller recalls, "so the money that went into its restoration was staggering."

It was worth it. With its walnut woodwork, antique furniture and silk wall coverings and draperies, Ruthmere is a resplendent private home restoration. Credit goes to Robert B. Beardsley, son of Walter R. Beardsley, who personally supervised the work.

Environmental Concerns at the Forefront

Harmony today is linked closely to the environment. "A health-care company, perhaps more than most others, has to demonstrate that it cares about the world in which it operates," Paul Turpin, environmental director from 1978–1984, says. "Miles has proved its concern by spending millions of dollars in recent years on environmental controls. And millions more must be spent in the coming years."

For example, company plans for a new $15 million wastewater treatment plant in Elkhart began in earnest in 1982. When completed in 1986, it will cap a half century of projects revolving around efforts to manage waste, to maintain the quality of water and air, and to enhance the appearance of facilities in every community where Miles has plants or offices.

Miles has always been aware of environmental realities. What it invested in and around its new Elkhart plant way back in 1938 still looks impressive today. A $300,000 parking lot with unique landscaping and $250,000 for a chlorinated private well system were among major items.

Since that auspicious start, scores of additional projects have embellished the record. Costly cooling towers constructed in 1956, 1959, and 1965 reduced demand for water used in processing citric acid and allowed its reuse. Various scrubber, vacuum, and dust collection systems have controlled emissions into the atmosphere. A fuel conservation program began as early as 1940. Noise control was started in 1938 with acoustic ceilings being installed at a cost of $400,000. Some $100,000 worth of carpeting was laid for better working conditions. Hefty sums for the times—and spent long before anyone had ever heard of "environmental concerns."

Wastewater Disposal

With the expansion of manufacturing and general growth over the years, emphasis on the

environment intensified and Miles became more entwined with Elkhart's wastewater disposal problems.

In 1980 the city began to renovate its inadequate wastewater treatment plant and Miles stepped in, willing to do its share. It urged the City Council to fund a new plant, knowing it would be costly to the company. This was followed by studies leading to the $15 million pretreatment plant mentioned earlier.

The modern phase of environmental control at Miles began in 1972 when Elmer Hartgerink—once manager of the Zeeland, Michigan, plant—was given responsibility for it. He did his job skillfully at a time when environmental fervor almost inflamed some communities. Hartgerink retired in 1979. His successor, the energetic Turpin, belongs to the new generation of environmental engineers with few links to old traditions. In early 1984, when he was appointed to a position in Leverkusen, the company turned this responsibility over to Bruce Carter, who had been Elkhart city engineer.

"This company means business when it comes to waste and pollution control," Turpin says, "not only in its technical aspects, but in the broad concept of social responsibility. We will do what has to be done in the most cost-effective manner, whether it's controlling air emissions from the drying of S.O.S pads at Bedford Park, eliminating any danger from the disposal of radioactive or chemical materials, working on emergency response procedures, or whatever."

While the quantity of hazardous wastes generated by Miles plants is not large, the company has implemented a vigorous waste control program to insure compliance with State and Federal hazardous waste regulations. Seven facilities were registered with the Environmental Protection Agency in order to conform with new standards in November 1980.

Turpin emphasizes that industry would never consider doing things today that were done with impunity, or at least casual disregard, 20 or 30 years ago. "The state-of-the-art has advanced," he says, "and we are using it to the maximum in every area, not the least of which is saving energy through tight monitoring at every Miles facility."

By the early 1980s, energy was getting far more than passing attention. Some 75 Miles and Cutter specialists spent a week in Elkhart in November 1982, exchanging their experiences. In his message to this pioneering seminar, CEO Heinrichs said that to create more energy awareness, he was designating November as "Energy Conservation Month," and he noted with satisfaction that almost 200 suggestions on saving energy had been submitted. He also wryly observed that "Many times in the evening, I have had to shut off lights neglected by other managers."

The central monitoring system for energy, as you might expect, relies on a computer, installed in 1974, to dispense data on temperature, static pressure, steam pressure, relative humidity, running time, and startup and shutdown times. At Elkhart alone, information darts into the computer from more than 2,000 control points. By 1980, it was estimated that the system was saving more than $1,000 per day in electrical and fuel costs.

Landscaped Parking Lots

Perhaps the most pleasant visible aspect of the Miles environment is landscaping, including the parking lots. In 1958, Miles won a national "Plant America" award from the American Association of Nurserymen—one of only 15 industrial firms chosen. In 1961, Dr. Compton, then vice president of medical and research affairs, sketched a parking area for the new Charles S. Beardsley Research Laboratory. It wasn't the standard kind of lot. It conserved existing trees and ground water, with drainage strips of permeable soil. It provided for new shade and ornamental trees, graveled medial strips, islands of trees and grading to keep the lot "puddle free."

William Crain, senior project engineer, guided the concept into reality. *The Alkalizer* described it as "concrete proof that beauty and utility can coexist."

That concept has prevailed ever since at Miles' facilities, all under the watchful eye of Wendell "Bim" Compton, now retired vice president of engineering, a stickler for making sure that nature's handiwork beautified every bit of land in and around the lots and buildings. His crew developed three different parking lot designs, all unique enough to warrant detailed articles in trade journals. As the September 1971 issue of *Grounds and Maintenance* editorialized, "Miles proved that it is possible to have a parking park rather than just a parking lot."

On its almost impeccably landscaped grounds at Elkhart, several hundred varieties of trees, shrubs and flowers bud, bloom, and flourish. Not only at spacious West Haven, but at such restricted sites as Bedford Park, trim landscaping prevails as a symbol of regard for the surrounding community. Miles has its environment, both the visible and invisible, under control.

"That's the way it will stay," Turpin predicts, "since management recognizes its responsibilities. Fortunately, too, we have available to us the enormous environmental technology and resources of Bayer."

Norman Stamm works with a computer as part of a system that monitors energy use in the Elkhart complex.

Attractive landscaping has long prevailed at Elkhart and other sites, both to provide relaxing vistas for employees and as a symbol of regard for the community.

Even the parking lots in Elkhart have ornamental trees, drawing attention from the citric acid pipes overhead.

McNaughton Street at the main plant in Elkhart.

Planting gardens at Miles Pharmaceuticals in Connecticut.

PART IV

FOUNDATIONS FOR THE FUTURE

CHAPTER 22

Joining Hands Across The Atlantic

It all began with dyes.... In 1856, the Englishman William Henry Perkin had been successful in obtaining synthetic dyestuffs from coal tar, thus enlarging the very narrow palette of natural and also expensive dyes. His discovery was one of the greatest pioneer achievements of chemical research.

News of Perkin's breakthrough spread to the center of the German textile industry in Elberfeld and Barmen on the river Wupper. In 1963, Friedrich Bayer, a merchant well-versed in the natural dyestuffs trade, and the dyer Johann Friedrich Weskott founded the company of "Friedrich Bayer et Comp." in Barmen, which is now a part of Wuppertal. Aided by a single worker, they started producing aniline dyestuffs, also called coal tar dyes, in earthenware pots on Bayer's kitchen stove.

A History of Scientific Achievement

In the early days, very little was known about the chemical reactions taking place during the production of dyestuffs. The industry based its innovation on trade skills. A new dyestuff was even discovered now and then by purely empirical means. But during the latter half of the 19th century, when economic crises riddled Europe, Friedrich Bayer's son-in-law, Carl Rumpff, made a decision which changed the course of the company.

Realizing the importance of research, he hired three young chemists in 1883 and had them trained at his own expense for a further year at various universities. Within a short time these scientists successfully produced new and better dyestuffs unequalled by competitors. This transition to a firm whose activities are centered around scientific achievements of its own marked the beginning of Bayer's impressive development. The first pharmaceuticals and agricultural chemicals, or in short, all of organic chemistry developed out of this dyestuff chemistry.

A Wide Ranging Company

Today, Bayer Leverkusen is one of the world's

The original location of the Bayer enterprise in Barmen-Rittershausen in the Ruhr Valley around 1863, the founding year. This was the birthplace of today's Bayer.

largest chemical companies with 180,000 employees in Germany and abroad. Around 400 affiliated companies and more than 100 production plants on five continents contribute to world sales of over $14 billion. The heart of this worldwide organization is Bayer AG with its headquarters in Leverkusen, Germany. Situated on the Rhine River, the main Leverkusen factory alone covers 840 acres and has more than 600 buildings. Other German production facilities are located in Dormagen, Uerdingen, Elberfeld, and Brunsbuettel.

Ownership of the company is now widely dispersed, and 30,000 of the 350,000 shareholders are Bayer employees. With capital stock of DM 2.53 billion, Bayer AG is the largest publicly held company in Germany.

Laboratory work on Lazarin dyes, Leverkusen. Spacious laboratories like this assured the future of chemical research in the first decades of the twentieth century.

Perhaps the most striking fact about the company is its product range. From its modest dyestuff business, Bayer AG has branched out into all fields of chemistry with a sales program now consisting of 6,000 products. Bayer AG supplies industry with a total of 1,500 dyestuffs and textile auxiliaries; 2,800 industrial chemicals including specialized intermediates and plastics as well as synthetic rubber; 600 pharmaceutical, dental, and veterinary products; 9 synthetic fibers; and 1,000 crop protection and pest control products. When the consumer products of the affiliated companies are added, such as the photographic articles, cosmetics, dietetics, and the rubber product line, Bayer's total sales assortment includes more than 10,000 different items.

A Variety of Research Areas

Bayer AG research is inseparable from the history and progress of chemistry. It has been a major factor contributing toward the status the company now enjoys throughout the world. More than 125,000 patents and 26,000 trademarks in Germany and abroad are evidence of the work done in the interest of scientific progress.

Specialized facilities are available for the various types of research: central scientific laboratories in Leverkusen and Uerdingen, laboratories for organic-analytical problems and applied physics, technical service departments for textile dyeing and plastics applications, development laboratories for synthetic fibers, a technical center for processes of organic chemistry, a pharmaceutical and veterinary medicine research center, and an isotopes laboratory. Soon a new agricultural chemicals complex will be completed in Monheim.

Research—The Key to Success

In 1883, the company hired three chemists. Today Bayer AG employs over 6,000 chemists, physicists, engineers, doctors, biologists, and other scientists. The annual research budget for Bayer worldwide exceeds DM 1.7 billion or $665 million.

Behind the growth of the chemical industry were organic and inorganic intermediates produced by the firms themselves and used as raw materials for products lying outside the classical dyestuffs field. The first of these were synthetic pharmaceutical products.

The first to be developed at Bayer AG was the pain-reliever phenacetin, in 1888. With its discovery the company established its own Pharmaceuticals

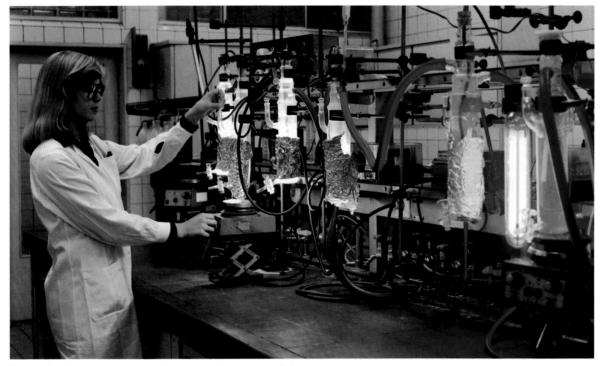

In search of new connections—basic research in a Bayer laboratory.

Department. Then in 1899 came what was destined to become the world's best-known drug: aspirin.

In the years to follow, Bayer AG research developed drugs against sleeping sickness (1923), against malaria (1927), and against the tropical disease bilharziosis (1929). In 1935, the first sulfonamide appeared under the name Prontosil. The Bayer AG scientist, Gerhard Domagk, discovered it while testing a chemical in an azo dye. He was awarded the Nobel Prize in 1939 for coming up with the first drugs for causal therapy of bacterial infectious diseases. His work with sulfonamides opened the doorway to antibiotics.

Shortly after its introduction to the market, news of Prontosil's wonder-working qualities reached the United States. President Franklin D. Roosevelt's son was suffering from a serious streptococcus infection of the throat. In a last attempt to avoid the dangerous operation necessary to save his life, Prontosil was rushed to the States. Young Roosevelt recovered completely and was spared the operation.

Over the years the company's pharmaceutical research has made notable contributions to world health. Major emphasis was—and still is—on heart and circulatory diseases, disturbances of the metabolism and mycoses, as well as infectious diseases and cancer.

Professor Gerhard Domagk (1895–1964) a bacteriologist in the Bayer Pathology Laboratory in Elberfeld, won the Nobel Prize for Medicine and Physiology in 1939 for his discovery of the therapeutic effects of the sulfonamides.

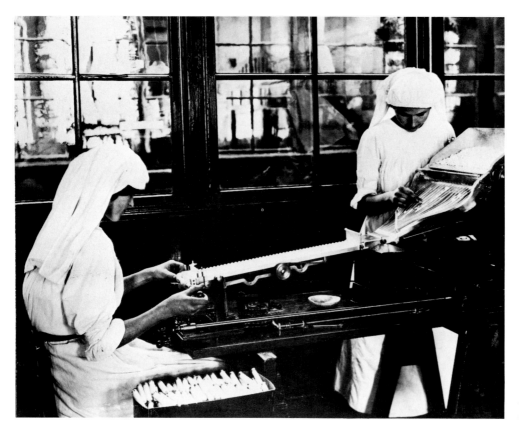

Aspirin—today as yesterday, man's favorite medicine—is mechanically packed into glass tubes at Bayer's factory in Elberfeld sometime at the beginning of this century.

Serving Humanity

Chemistry saves lives, and it helps to feed the world's growing populations. Research on pest control products began only a few years before the turn of the century. Bayer AG produced the first synthetic insecticide in 1892. The range of achievements in crop protection have continued to the present, and Bayer is now the leading world producer of agricultural chemicals.

And the list goes on and on. Bayer was a pioneer in the field of engineering materials and synthetic rubber and man-made fibers. One of the company's greatest chemists, Professor Otto Bayer, was the founder of polyurethane chemistry in the 1930s. He received numerous honors and awards. For example, he was the first person to be elected to the Polyurethane Hall of Fame of the American Plastics Society, in 1983.

Environmental Awareness

With the product range in a state of constant renewal, higher and higher demands are being made on the accompanying environmental research to

Polyurethane is formed in a Leverkusen production area. Dr. Otto Bayer, who died in 1982, developed polyurethane as a base for high performance chemical engineering materials in 1937.

make sure that processes, products, and technical applications have a minimal impact on the environment. Bayer is justly considered a pioneer in new environmental protection techniques and instruments.

As astonishingly early as 1901, Bayer set up a wastewater commission to regulate plant effluent. From 1913 onwards, waste gases from smokestacks were subjected to systematic control. The double contact process developed in 1964 reduces the sulphur dioxide content in the waste gases of sulphuric acid factories by 90 percent. The most recent result of environment research is the Bayer Biology Tower, internationally recognized as an excellent step in treating biological wastewater.

Diversification—A Watchword

Products and processes, the results of over a century of chemical research, are represented in almost all branches of Bayer. Diversification and specialization safeguard against economic crises in various market sectors.

The company philosophy which has led to its international standing is based on this principle of diversification. Not only is the wide product assortment remarkable, but of equal importance is the regional diversification. The company boldly seeks the opportunities which the world market offers. This strategy applies above all to the largest chemical market—the United States.

Bayer's presence in the United States goes back to 1865, when the firm of Friedr. Bayer et Comp. participated in the first production of aniline dyes in Albany, New York. Carl Rumpff played an important role in setting up the company's business in the U.S. before he became a partner in 1872.

The Bayer Cross

In 1904, Bayer began to market its products worldwide under the Bayer Cross, a trademark consisting of horizontal and vertical displays of the name Bayer which cross within a circle. This trademark quickly gained international prominence. During World War I, however, the assets of Bayer's U.S. subsidiary, Bayer Co., Inc., New York, were seized by the U.S. Government which later sold them to Sterling Drug, Inc., including the registered rights to the Bayer and Bayer Cross trademarks. These are still used by The Bayer Company, Glenbrook Laboratories, a division of Sterling Drug, Inc., New York, for its aspirin products in the U.S. and Canada. Bayer AG is the exclusive owner of the Bayer and Bayer

Bayer's commitment to the environment may be seen in the constant control checks to which its treated wastewater is subjected in the laboratories.

A forerunner of the famous "Bayer Cross" was this trademark alluding to the coat of arms of Bayer's original hometown, Elberfeld—a two-tailed lion with the grill on which St. Lawrence was roasted as a martyr.

Cross trademarks, including their use for aspirin products, in all other countries of the world. Bayer AG, Germany, and Sterling Drug, Inc., U.S.A., are not connected by any corporate relationship and do not pursue any common corporate policy.

In a Bayer development laboratory new applications for existing chemicals are investigated.

Bayer Leverkusen did not return to the U.S. until 1954, when a joint venture with Monsanto under the name of Mobay Chemical Company was established with the aim of introducing the new polyurethane chemistry to the American market. Bayer bought Monsanto's shares in 1967.

Today, Mobay Chemical Corporation, with its headquarters in Pittsburgh, Pennsylvania, employs about 5,800 people and has five major manufacturing sites. Mobay not only has become America's largest and most diversified manufacturer of polyurethane raw materials and polymers, but also has expanded into broad new areas of agricultural chemicals, dyestuffs and pigments, plastics and coatings, industrial chemicals, and textile fibers. Total annual sales are now well over $1 billion.

Other long-standing affiliated companies in the U.S. are Haarman & Reimer Corporation, Springfield, New Jersey, manufacturers of fragrances, flavors, and aroma chemicals; Helena Chemical Company, Memphis, Tennessee, which formulates and markets crop protection products, and Agfa-Gevaert, Inc., Teterboro, New Jersey, whose parent company is the second largest producer of photographic products in the world and, since 1981, a wholly owned subsidiary of Bayer AG. At the beginning of 1982 Agfa-Gevaert acquired a majority interest in the Compugraphic Corporation of Wilmington, Massachusetts, the world's largest manufacturer of computerized photo-composing systems.

The re-entry into the American pharmaceuticals market after World War II was more difficult, especially with the handicap of not being free to use the company trademark, Bayer, and the Bayer Cross.

The first step came in 1967 when Bayer formed a joint venture with Schering Corporation. Named Delbay, it obtained FDA approval in record time for Bayer's clotrimazole, the first broad-spectrum antimycotic agent. Although the joint venture was successful, the possibility for major expansion was limited.

In 1974 Bayer AG took a further step to establish its presence in the United States with the acquisition of Cutter Laboratories, an old and respected healthcare firm based in Berkeley, California. It had long specialized in intravenous solutions and disposable equipment, but in recent years had intensified efforts on plasma products, anti-allergy agents, sophisticated apparatus for parenteral administration (feeding by vein) and animal health products.

Cutter had another plus—the requisite infrastructure for working with the Food and Drug Administration. Cutter grew solidly under the aegis of Bayer. Sales surpassed $200 million by 1977 and continued to nearly $350 million by 1983. Still, Cutter was not in prescription drugs.

Bayer management felt very strongly that a pharmaceutical company could retain international status only if it had an appropriate presence in the U.S. market. There, Bayer AG had scarcely made its mark in what was considered its most truly representative field, that of ethical drugs. In 1977, the corporate strategy was to build up an ethical drug business in America through the introduction of Bayer's existing drug specialties and, at the same time, to expand the total pharmaceutical research program. In addition, Bayer AG sought to enter the rapidly growing market for diagnostics. And so the search began for an experienced and well-established partner.

But Why Miles?

Miles had been groping toward some kind of merger but for different reasons and under different circumstances.

Why would a substantial Midwest company, diversified with a sound reputation, want to become part of one of the world's greatest corporations—and a foreign one at that—with $13 billion in annual sales? What would be the benefits to shareholders, employees, and plant communities?

Few people were asking such questions in the late 1960s or the early 1970s.

Given its success from the 1950s, and into the 1970s, Miles did not appear to be a likely candidate for acquisition or merger. Alka-Seltzer and the vitamins continued to flourish. Diagnostics had grown impressively. Profits had fueled diversification into enzymes, citric acid, cheese cultures, and S.O.S. Markets had been expanded overseas. In many ways, things had never looked better.

But the overall picture was deceptive. Retired president Bob Rose, a realist, says "By the mid-1970s it had become apparent that, to be successful, the strategies of Miles were beginning to require resources considerably in excess of those readily available to it."

Difficulties began harrowing Miles from the start of the decade. A scarcity of funds hampered research efforts and the development of an ethical pharmaceutical business. The attempt to build a market for vegetable proteins proved to be ahead of its time, demanding more resources than Miles could provide to make it succeed. The diagnostics area,

Bayer's main administrative, research, and manufacturing facilities in Leverkusen, West Germany, spread along the Rhine River. Some 42,000 persons work here in about 600 buildings.

becoming more and more a major growth element, needed funds for research and expansion.

The weakening economy didn't help at a time when even major drug firms had trouble maintaining satisfactory profits. Stock prices and investor confidence languished, while interest rates crept upward.

Still, with its traditionally strong marketing, Miles kept posting hefty sales gains. They rose from $142.8 million in 1970 to $449.6 million just a year before the merger. Profits fluctuated, but Miles remained an attractive "plum" during an era when mergers had become quite commonplace.

No one better analyzed the future than Compton and Rose. Even when Miles stock stood at $75 a share in 1972 (it was to hit a low of $13 a few years

later) they began talking to suitors, and there were plenty of them, some ardent indeed.

So Compton and Rose did a lot of listening, not only to U.S. but to foreign companies as well, seeking a proper fit. For a time, sometimes aided by John Buckley, the two men explored the joint venture route because it was one way of obtaining additional resources that would, at the same time, have retained the independence of the corporation. Nothing quite jelled.

All this led back to Bayer Leverkusen. The quest that took the German company to the doorstep of Miles can be traced to the early 1970s. Bayer and Miles officials held some amicable conversations. Nothing much happened; interest on both sides had been tentative. By 1976 the urgency at Miles for greater resources had not lessened. In fact, it had increased. So had the desire to protect employees, shareholders, and the economies of plant communities. That concern kept sharpening. So in 1977 conversations between Bayer and Miles not only resumed, but they intensified.

By the summer of 1977, negotiations reached a serious stage in various meetings in New York City. Of course, tight secrecy had to be maintained because of stock market and legal considerations.

Philosophy is not just the province of the academic world. It occupies, or should occupy, quite a niche in the business world, too. In the Bayer-Miles negotiations it played a significant role. Miles had a half dozen key points that it felt had to be satisfied if a merger could come to fruition. Bayer was fully aware of these points and dealt with them candidly.

Moving Toward Merger

First, Bayer realized that Miles wanted to maintain its own identity as a solidly-based U.S. enterprise. That was really no problem at all. As Bayer's chairman Prof. Herbert Gruenewald has often said, "We enjoy the American way. It's the essence of the free enterprise we all believe in."

Next, Miles needed assurance that Bayer would commit resources to support existing businesses and fund enough research for new products. As Bayer could point out, research, deeply rooted in its history, has been at the heart of its growth, and it would surely bolster Miles' quest for new products and markets.

The U.S. firm felt that especially in the early years, Bayer AG should rely on the long experience and expertise of Miles' veterans in their various specialized fields. That, too, posed no problem for a company with such diverse and broad backgrounds in research, production, and marketing. It would rely on Miles' best.

Bayer also was most conscious of Miles' wishes to keep its strong links to Elkhart and to its other plant communities. Miles found that Bayer had the same feelings about its own larger, plant community at Leverkusen. That was reassurance enough.

Perhaps most of all, Miles wanted to understand the people approach at Bayer AG as well as the Bayer attitude toward the health-care system and quality of life both at home and abroad. As Bob Rose said, "An unexpected dividend was that the operating philosophies of the two companies were very similar as to their social responsibilities and their concern for the well-being of their employees." He concluded that the

The Elkhart Truth, *naturally, gave page one coverage to the story of the acquisition of Miles by Bayer AG in 1977–78.*

combination of the two companies "satisfied to an astonishing degree the needs of each principal and carried the promise of a considerable synergism for the future."

Finally, neither side had any interest in an adversarial takeover. There would be a really friendly tender offer or there would be none at all.

With both companies finding themselves in full agreement on operating philosophies, the merger moved swiftly toward consummation. Miles had set a purchase price a bit above what Bayer had first wanted to pay. To resolve that issue, Dr. Gruenewald flew to New York. A quick compromise was reached at $47 a share. It seemed to all concerned to be a good price. The timing was crucial. "If the Bayer offer had fallen through, we would no doubt have had to settle for a lower price with a less desirable suitor," Dr. Compton explains. "We could delay no longer without truly jeopardizing the future. We would have been torn apart and submerged." On September 26 and September 27 press releases reported that discussions were under way.

Merger Becomes a Fact

On October 17, 1977, Bayer's tender offer was unanimously endorsed by the Miles Board, and the merger announcement was made on the same day. By November 9, 81 percent of the shares had been

Bayer visits Miles, January 17–18, 1978. From left: Dr. Gerhard Dittmar, Dr. Franz-Josef Weitkemper, and Dr. Franz J. Geks, members Bayer Board of Management; Professor Herbert Gruenewald, Bayer chairman; Dr. Walter A. Compton, Miles chairman and chief executive officer; Rowland G. Rose, Miles president.

tendered. The offer was extended to January 5, 1978, by which time 97 percent of the shares were tendered at nearly double the market price.

Some employees, naturally, may have preferred to merge with an American company. Others felt that it was time to "shake things up," and thought that Bayer AG, with its resources in research, production, and marketing, would be a spur to superlative growth within a decade.

An acquisition may be harder on the acquired company, but it also concerns the acquirer. The parent has the obligation to be even-handed across a diverse spectrum of activities, all the while dealing with the sensitivities of the people involved. It has to make judgments of many kinds, few of them easy, some bound to be resented, particularly those that do not turn out as expected.

Even so, the parent company has no choice; it must provide the direction and allocate the human and material resources. It must make tough decisions about people, programs, goals, budgets, and profits. People at both Miles and Bayer recognized and accepted this reality.

Gruenewald Welcomes Miles Into Bayer Family

As early as January 17, 1978, only a couple of weeks after 97 percent of Miles' stock had been tendered, Prof. Gruenewald, and several other members of the Bayer AG Board of Management visited Elkhart. More than 200 Miles managers were invited to hear addresses by Prof. Gruenewald, Dr. Gerhard Dittmar, spokesman for the North American Region;

Dr. Franz J. Geks, head of the Pharmaceuticals Division, and Dr. Franz-Joseph Weitkemper, responsible for financial matters.

"With Elkhart as the center of Bayer's pharmaceutical interests in the United States, you—the people in Elkhart—assume a particularly important role," Prof. Gruenewald said.

"You must preserve your identity in the United States and in the community," he continued. "It is not Bayer's policy to infringe on the rights and the responsibilities of an affiliated company to serve its community, through its employees and as a corporate body.

"Getting to know one another is particularly important . . . for it is only when we know more about each other that it will be possible to establish a relationship based on confidence.

"Perhaps the term 'family' is the best word to describe this kind of relationship. The members support each other and the family as a whole. Individual members have a personality and an identity that is unique to each. . . . Bayer strives to model

the relations with its worldwide affiliated companies after a good family unit. We are here in Elkhart today to welcome you as the newest members of this worldwide Bayer family."

Dr. Dittmar Explains Importance Of U.S. Market

Dr. Dittmar summarized the scope of Bayer's activities in the United States. He touched on a few of the management principles practiced by Bayer to achieve the best use of its resources and to assure the distinct character of the many companies that together form the Bayer family.

"Very basically," he said, "there are two principal avenues available to a foreign company to do business in the United States: one is to serve the market by importing products; the other is to establish business enterprises and production sites here. We have used and continue to use both. Normally, we first enter a market by importing products, but as our growth potential by this route becomes limited, we gradually

Professor Gruenewald, Bayer AG chairman, meets officers of United Steel Workers of America Union Local #12273. He is shaking hands with John Albrecht, financial secretary. Others, from left, are: Francis L. Terrell, director labor relations and security; Duane Cable, vice president of the union, and John Bergeron, president of the union .

build up production facilities. Today our main emphasis is on the latter, not only for such practical reasons as the problems and costs of duties, freights, currency fluctuations, and the need for quick market response, but also because of the growth strategy discussed by Professor Gruenewald, the striving for product as well as for regional diversification. This, we believe, is particularly true in a demanding market such as the U.S. where from our experience only true participation, and that includes local production, can provide the basis for an integrated program of technology and, ultimately, the opportunity for success."

Dr. Dittmar went on to describe the Bayer AG affiliated businesses in the United States. He stated, "In the year just completed, total net sales of the Bayer affiliated companies in the United States have reached about $1.2 billion, having achieved satisfactory profits. Eighty-five percent of the total U.S. sales which, by the way, are about 14 percent of Bayer's worldwide sales, is accounted for by products manufactured here. All in all, our American subsidiaries without Miles provide about 12,000 jobs. Not including Miles' prospects, we anticipate sales in this country to reach the $2 billion level by 1980. This cannot be accomplished without considerable capital investments. We are now at the early part of a five-year, half-billion dollar program to build production and supporting facilities in this country—again, this is before consideration of Miles."

These figures proved that Bayer AG had singled out the United States for a major effort of its business activities. They further demonstrated Bayer management's belief that the company had operated successfully in the U.S. In Dr. Dittmar's words, "It is and will continue to be our basic goal to participate adequately in the largest and most progressive market of the world." Bayer management was convinced that Miles could contribute substantially to this development.

Dr. Geks Describes Pharmaceuticals

Dr. Geks then provided further information on the pharmaceutical activities of Bayer AG—the division into which Miles would be integrated.

The range of products was described as "broad and diversified." World sales would exceed $1 billion in 1977, he said, roughly 60 percent of which would be accounted for by the ethical business. Bayer AG's pharmaceutical business ranked among the largest in the world.

"There is still plenty of room for innovation in the pharmaceutical sector," Dr. Geks continued,

"witnessed by the fact that only about half of all diseases can presently be treated by medication. Yet, suitable treatment with drugs is more economical than any other form of therapy."

"In your Dome Division laboratories we saw an adequate base for the introduction of our ethical products into the U.S. market," he said. "The Ames Division, of course, is the leader in the diagnostics markets. Miles also possesses a research organization that is well ahead in certain significant areas that show tremendous potential for the future."

Bayer was not strong in the diagnostics field, he went on, yet "the therapeutic and diagnostic fields considered together form the two pillars of medicine," presenting a whole range of new possibilities for research.

"We fully recognize that Miles is much more than Ames and Dome, and we see a great potential for synergy in the other areas as well," he said, concluding that it would take "time, investment, and cooperation—elements well known to each of us."

Dr. Weitkemper Forecasts Capital Investments

Discussing financial realities, Dr. Franz-Josef Weitkemper said Bayer's total assets then amounted to approximately $9 billion, which would "put us number 14 among the largest industrial corporations in the U.S."

"It is our aim," he said, "that Miles should have a strong capital structure and also that there should be new investments which bring their returns."

Speaking of policy applying to all 400 subsidiaries, Dr. Weitkemper said, "Our major aim is integration and, parallel to this, the individual expansion of each separate company into a highly profitable unit—and this must also apply to Miles."

These statements from the Bayer board members were reassuring to Miles managers and welcomed by more than 2,000 employees in the Elkhart area who heard and saw through videotapes what had been presented. Copies of the tapes were soon distributed to other plants in the United States and abroad.

Gruenewald Addresses Elkhart Chamber Of Commerce

On January 18, the day after addressing Miles managers, the Bayer board members met also with the Elkhart Chamber of Commerce and the local press. Professor Gruenewald addressed a standing-room-only audience at the Chamber's annual meeting.

"Our knowledge of Miles as a worldwide operating company with an excellent reputation has convinced us that this affiliation will benefit both our firms and the city of Elkhart as well," he said. "Cooperation between Miles and Bayer must be supported by the people *and* by the community...."

"An essential basis for our relationship is the preservation of Miles' identity," he continued. "Miles will remain Miles. In fact, we see Miles' role as the center of Bayer's pharmaceutical operations in the United States.

"If we succeed in establishing a fruitful cooperation on all levels, we will have a guarantee that both firms set in motion a development which will lead to growth, more jobs, greater job security and prosperity, which will also benefit a state like Indiana. Traditionally, Indiana is a state which has encouraged progress and, at the same time, respected free enterprise. This is exactly *our* philosophy, which is why we feel in good hands in Indiana and particularly in a city like Elkhart." These were reassuring words, indeed.

Collectively, the Chamber of Commerce breathed a figurative sigh of relief. Instinctively, they knew Miles management would not sell out to a company that would seriously disrupt the economic base of Elkhart. But they needed to hear it. And they applauded warmly when John Gildea, then corporate secretary of Miles as well as president of the Chamber, said, "I think, Professor Gruenewald, that as you

John Gildea, then Miles corporate secretary, and president of the Chamber of Commerce, welcomes Bayer AG to Elkhart after the acquisition in 1978.

come to know the people of Elkhart, you will find them to be *progressive*, I hope you will find them *productive*; but I know you will find them to be *proud* of their community and what they mean in it."

These addresses, then, set the scene for what was to come in the years ahead.

Bayer's pharmaceutical research center is situated on a green suburban campus in Wuppertal-Elberfeld, West Germany.

CHAPTER 23

Since The Acquisition

Synergy is a word often used by corporate managers involved in acquisitions. Bayer AG executives were well aware of its meaning. Dr. Geks had told Miles managers at their historic first meeting in January 1978, "We all have a lot of work ahead of us to see that the results of our efforts will not obey the ordinary laws of arithmetic.... That one and one will make more than two." Literally hundreds of opportunities lay ahead. Good communications would open the way to those opportunities and the synergism that would result. Lines were opened with deliberate speed.

Federal regulations prevented Bayer AG from becoming involved in the day-to-day business of Miles until the acquisition was approved by the Federal Trade Commission, and this did not come about until February 8, 1979. In retrospect, this may have been a very stabilizing factor. It provided more than a year for the two companies to become better acquainted before any significant management changes would take place.

Four Bayer executives, including Theodor H. Heinrichs, then president and chief executive officer of Cutter Laboratories, Inc., were elected to the Miles board April 25, 1978. The others were Dr. Dittmar, Dr. Geks, and Dr. Weitkemper, all of whom had addressed Miles managers in January. They could help set policy, but until the acquisition was complete they could not get into operations. Strategic studies could be initiated, and they were, but implementation would not be undertaken until a later date.

A New CEO at the Helm

It was at their April meeting in 1979, nearly three months after the acquisition was complete, that the Miles board accepted the request of Dr. Walter Compton, then 68, that he turn over the duties of chief executive officer to Mr. Heinrichs. Two years later, on March 11, 1981, Dr. Compton also relinquished to him chairmanship of the board.

Future Miles chief executive officer Theodor H. Heinrichs gets acquainted with Louise Ergle, left, and Dorothy Suggs in the Consumer Products Packaging Department during the historic visit of Bayer executives to Miles in January 1978.

Heinrichs accepted his election as CEO as an honor and challenge, telling the board in an address later printed in *The Alkalizer* that it meant a great deal to him "to follow in the footsteps of one who has set high standards of ethics and equally high standards of personal performance."

As CEO he said it would be his "prime objective to assure that a solid framework is established that will lead to a new order of magnitude for the Bayer AG health care presence in the United States, and wherever else affected by the U.S. presence.

"Even now," Heinrichs continued, "cooperative efforts are under way to identify, analyze, and effectuate the areas of synergy we all know to exist. I mention this to emphasize the different sources of the many impulses that can be channeled together to achieve new plateaus of accomplishment."

In 1979, the Miles Board of Directors (and their wives) met Bayer Board of Management members in Leverkusen for the first time.

He went on to say that the business philosophy developed under the leadership of Dr. Compton and Walter Beardsley at Miles was very similar to that prevailing at Bayer. Concern for people would continue to underlie any changes.

Areas for Synergistic Growth

What were some of the areas that would lend themselves to synergistic growth? Pharmaceutical re-

search, obviously, with a very large research center well established by Bayer in Elberfeld, West Germany, and several smaller Miles research groups, primarily in Elkhart, West Haven, Mexico City, and outside London. Diagnostic medicine, with Miles being a world leader in the field. Over-the-counter drugs, with Bayer AG making a number of intermediary chemicals and Miles having unusual marketing acumen. The whole range of Cutter and Miles health-care products. To scientists in both groups working with blood fractions, the future of cellular diagnostics loomed especially bright.

The technology of fermentation presented still more opportunities. Antibiotics made by fermentation were part of Bayer AG's product line, but not Miles'. On the other hand, Miles was a leading world producer of citric acid and industrial enzymes, both products of fermentation. Additional biotechnology research on both sides of the ocean could prove fruitful.

One of the first jobs would be to set priorities, to decide where the companies could accumulate "critical masses" worthy of investment and exploitation. Strategic studies that had been started by Bayer/Miles/Cutter groups working together were accelerated under the leadership of Richard J. Koerting, vice president of planning, son of the fabled Bill Koerting. Research was also undertaken to see where activities could be combined or sometimes even eliminated in order to reduce overhead expenses. The world had just been through one crippling recession in 1973–1974 and it would encounter a second even before the decade of the 1970s ended.

Communications were opened through periodic senior management meetings in Elkhart. Repeatedly, Heinrichs invited questions and comments, urging the 200 to 300 present to pass along to their staffs the information imparted to them. Heinrichs also initiated a bimonthly management newsletter, sent to some 600 executives worldwide.

New People Bolster Management

In his second *Newsletter*, on September 4, 1979, Heinrichs spoke of people as communications links, stating, "Certainly, the technologies, successful business strategies, and even the history of a corporation are carried forward by its people. And when companies merge, there is a need to build bridges in many directions."

That, he said, was what was behind the personnel changes made by the Miles board at its August meeting. At that time, Dr. Karl Meyer, of Bayer AG, had been named senior vice president of science and technology; W. F. "Bill" Ausfahl, of Cutter, senior vice president of finance; Rolf W. Buell, of Bayer AG, president of the Dome Division; and Ray Johnson, of Miles, vice president of corporate management information services for both Cutter and Miles. In addition, Wolfgang Schmidt, of Bayer, was appointed international liaison for management information services. Computers, Heinrichs went on to speculate, "can serve as the most profound communications links of the twentieth century."

This selection of outstanding individuals to fill key positions was a harbinger of things to come. Henceforth, top executives would be chosen on the basis of expertise, not nationality. This was to be even more clearly seen on January 1, 1984, when Bayer set in place its initial Health Care Sector management, consisting of Germans, Americans, and a Dane.

Facilities Expand Swiftly

Even in its first few months of ownership, Bayer AG was assessing its new daughter-company's capital needs. Among the first expenditures approved was a $5 million addition to the West Haven facilities,

providing drug development laboratories and offices. The first employees moved to the new facility were 20 or so people from Delbay, Bayer AG's former joint venture with Schering-Plough.

Other projects approved in 1979 included doubling the capacity of the $25 million citric acid plant in Dayton that had gone on stream just a year before, installation in Elkhart (at a cost of around $20 million) of a new method of citric acid processing designed to increase the yield while reducing the load to the city's wastewater treatment plant, a $12 million addition to the Ames building in Elkhart for R&D, and acquisition of a 250,000-square-foot building in nearby Mishawaka for Ames instrument manufacturing. A final allocation, perhaps the largest of all, went for a new industrial enzymes plant in Elkhart at a cost in excess of $20 million.

With commitments like these, it was clear that Bayer AG was fulfilling its promise to develop many lines of Miles' business, not just pharmaceuticals. The amount of construction in Elkhart underscored the parent company's concern for the long-standing headquarters community.

Within the next few years, several other capital projects were approved and completed, among them a sterile manufacturing plant for antibiotics in West

It was a happy occasion and symbolic of Bayer AG's expansion program when Miles president Bob Rose (center) and Rolf Buell, president of Miles Pharmaceuticals (second from left) cut the ribbon for the formal opening of the new addition at the West Haven plant. Others shown are West Haven mayor Bob Johnson (left); Bob Huber (center, rear), director of Miles' Corporate Engineering Department; Dr. Paul Spiekermann (second from right), vice president of medical research for Miles Pharmaceuticals, and Ed Stockton, commissioner of the Connecticut Department of Commerce.

Ames' R&D expanded laboratories in Elkhart were another aspect of Bayer's capital investment program for Miles in 1980.

Haven, a new plant for freeze-dried cultures to be added to animal feed in Madison, biotechnology research labs in Elkhart, and offices and labs for the Scientific Division in Naperville and Lisle, Illinois.

New Products

Meanwhile, new products were reaching the North American markets from both Bayer AG and Miles. These advances have been described in other portions of this book, but their scope and importance deserve a summary here as integral to the basic strengths of the company at the dawn of its second century.

Bayer AG's first drug to be cleared by the FDA after the acquisition was clotrimazole, a broad-spectrum antifungal product sold as Mycelex, for topical use, as Mycelex-G for vaginal application and, most recently, as Mycelex Troche for thrush. The first of these reached the market in the spring of 1979.

The antifungals were followed by Mezlin (mezlocillin sodium), a new-generation broad-spectrum semisynthetic penicillin, Niclocide (niclosamide) for treatment of tapeworm infestations, Biltricide (praziquantel) for snail fever, in 1982, and Azlin (azlocillin) for fighting hospital infections in 1983. Also, nifedipine, Bayer AG's drug for treatment of angina in cardiovascular disease, was approved for sale by Miles in Canada in 1982. Prior to the acquisition of Miles, it had been licensed to Pfizer for

sale in the United States. The U.S. sales force at Miles Pharmaceuticals was increased from about 80 representatives at the time of the acquisition to 160 in 1979 and roughly 300 in 1983. Plans call for doubling the size again by 1985 or 1986.

New diagnostic products since the acquisition have included 17 Ames therapeutic drug assays, beginning with a test for gentamicin (an antibiotic) in 1979. Both that test and one for theophyllin (an asthma drug) now contain monoclonal antibodies making them slightly more specific and therefore more reliable than tests with conventional antisera. These Miles diagnostics are among the first to use monoclonal antibodies, and well they should since Miles Scientific Division was among the first to list these substances in its catalog.

Two new instruments have been developed for use with the therapeutic drug assays: the Optimate and the Seralyzer. Both may also be used for routine blood tests. Introduced in 1982 after many years in development, the Seralyzer has been widely acclaimed for its convenience and precision.

The Glucometer reflectance photometer, a portable electronic instrument used by insulin-dependent diabetics in the monitoring of their blood sugar, is also a new Ames instrument and one of its most successful, opening the way to more home-use tests. Visidex glucose strips, for the visual monitoring of blood sugar without instrumentation, were introduced in 1982 and also exceeded sales forecasts.

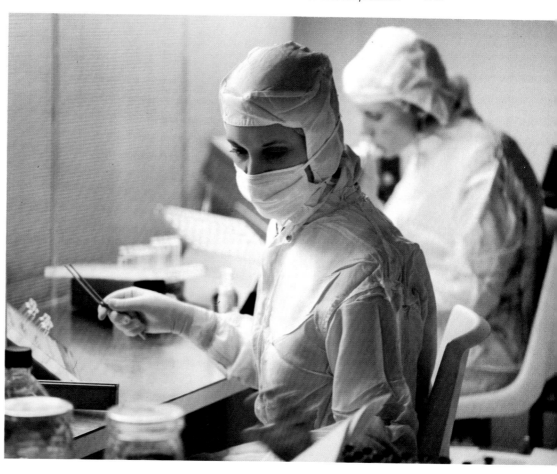

*New prescription drugs are
the key to Bayer's expansion
of pharmaceutical operations
in the U.S.*

Another of Ames' most successful products is N-Multistix SG reagent strips, which added a test for specific gravity in urine to eight other tests on the single reagent strip. It was introduced in 1981.

To assure that these new medications and diagnostic aids would be developed as quickly as possible, Bayer AG encouraged the addition of a large number of scientists to the R&D staffs both in Elkhart and West Haven. Research expenditures, $26 million in 1977, the year of Bayer's tender offer, exceeded $85 million in 1983.

An Institute for Preclinical Pharmacology was established in rented space at Yale University in 1980. Headed by Alexander Scriabine, M.D., it now has research on new compounds under way in 150 university and hospital laboratories throughout the United States.

Meanwhile, clinical studies in man, under the supervision of Paul H. Spiekermann, M.D., have been thorough, expeditious, and well documented, moving through the FDA ahead of many others.

Near the end of 1983, Rolf Buell became head of marketing and sales for the Ethical Products Business Group at Bayer's world headquarters in Leverkusen. Horst Wallrabe, most recently chief executive of the Bayer Pharma Division in the United Kingdom, succeeded him as executive vice president of the Miles Pharmaceuticals Group. Buell will also chair the Health Care Sector's Coordination Committee for Commercial Activities, obviously a critical function.

Entry into the vast North American prescription drug market that Bayer AG targeted through Miles has been realized. A solid organization, able to adapt and expand, is in place, and new products are in the pipeline.

Cutter Becomes Part Of Miles

With the merger into Miles of Cutter Laboratories, at the beginning of 1983, the allergen extracts of Hollister-Stier came under the Pharmaceuticals Group. That Group now supervises both domestic and international marketing of the allergens.

Blood plasma fractionation is monitored at the control center of Cutter's Clayton, NC, plant.

The merged companies, Cutter and Miles, had much in common. To begin with, both had strong individualists as founders. E. A. Cutter, Sr., a self-trained pharmacist, started the Cutter business in 1897 in the central valley of California primarily to provide biologicals to cattle ranchers. He moved his small operation to Berkeley in 1903.

The company grew modestly for the next quarter of a century with a variety of human and animal immunological products. When the founder passed away, his son, Dr. Robert Cutter (always to be known affectionately as Dr. "Bob") took over the management.

The doctor and his colleagues originated an early method of administering intravenous solutions. The product was a success, enabling the firm to reach

The Cutter portfolio of plants at the time of the merger with Miles.

Covina, California

Clayton, North Carolina

$1 million in sales by 1937. It then went into processing blood plasma for the Armed Forces.

In 1955 came fame of an unwanted sort. Its polio vaccine caused problems, even though government regulations had been painstakingly followed. After that, Cutter diversified into the veterinary and allergen businesses, and both did well.

Companies producing intravenous solutions ran into a chain of contamination problems in the early 1970s. Cutter had to recall supplies and shut down its Chattanooga plant for a time. Losses were severe, so David Cutter, president, began conversations with Bayer AG in November 1973. Bayer Leverkusen made a friendly tender offer, and Cutter became part of the German company in January 1974. The effect was salutary; sales rose from $90 million in 1973 to $348.4 million in 1982.

The Merger Brings Advantages

The Miles-Cutter merger had been contemplated for several years on the basis of logical business premises. The management of Bayer and of the two companies saw advantages in consolidating their United States-based health-care business under one roof. It would increase the influence of their "critical mass" in research, production, and marketing.

The companies had been growing together for some time anyway. They had had, since 1979, the same chief executive officer—Heinrichs.

At the time of its total integration with Miles, Cutter had five divisions that would become known as the Cutter Group, under the leadership of Wilhelm F. Schaeffler, Ph.D., who had served as president

David Cutter, grandson of the founder, was president of Cutter Laboratories when Bayer AG acquired the family firm in 1974.

since 1980. Those five divisions were, and are, Cutter Biological, which concentrates on products derived from blood plasma and blood collection and storage products; Cutter Medical, which focuses on liquid nutrition administered in hospitals, fluid filters and control devices; Bayvet Division, which embraces animal health and veterinarian medicine; Cutter Biomedical, which is a leader in the synthetic cast

Shawnee, Kansas

Berkeley, California

The Cutter Tower in Emeryville, housing the executive offices, overlooks San Francisco Bay.

Wilhelm F. Schaeffler, Ph.D., became executive vice president in charge of the Cutter Group effective January 1, 1983.

market, and Cutter Dental, which provides specialized equipment for dentists. Cutter Consumer, noted for its insect repellent products, had previously been transferred to Miles' Household Products Division in the Consumer Products Group.

At merger time Cutter products were sold in more than 100 countries. Its international business accounted for 31 percent of the total. It employed some 4,000 people, thus becoming the largest of the five operating groups at Miles both in number of employees and sales.

The other Miles operating groups at Centennial time were Consumer Products, headed by George E. Davy and second only to Cutter in annual sales; Miles Pharmaceuticals, headed by Horst W. D. Wallrabe; Professional Products, led by Joseph H. Rosloff who succeeded Robert P. Schlegel; and Biotech Products, guided by Richard B. Kocher, now also corporate president, who has spent more than 40 years in the biotechnology field.

Other Management Changes

Several other management changes should be noted as Miles moves into its second century.

246

Konrad M. Weis, Ph.D., whose background is in organic chemistry and who has been president and chief executive officer of Mobay Chemical Corporation since 1974, was elected to the Miles Board of Directors March 17, 1981. Dr. Weis, a native of Germany, began his professional career with Bayer AG in 1955.

Three others were added to the Miles board at its March 23, 1983, meeting: Kocher, of Miles, and two long-term Bayer executives, Wilhelm C. Ostern, executive vice president of Mobay and its chief financial officer, and Prof. Dr. Ernst Schraufstaetter, head of the Bayer Health Care Sector.

At the same time, the board elected Dr. Geks chairman and chief executive officer, succeeding Heinrichs.

In his four years as head of Miles, Heinrichs had broadened communications and put in place the basic structure that would carry the organization forward. He had encouraged German language instruction for Miles employees while constantly improving his already excellent English. He had announced the first exchange of delegates between Bayer AG and Miles. Most of all, he had encouraged synergy at all levels and successfully merged the operations of Cutter and Miles. After years of boarding planes flying between Berkeley and Elkhart, not to mention overnight flights to Leverkusen, and after moving his family 16 times on three continents (including Africa), he chose early retirement in 1983. He remained, however, on the Miles board.

Dr. Geks came to Elkhart in the spring of 1983 full of enthusiasm for his new assignment and determined to see that Miles would succeed. After all, hadn't he, more than any other Bayer board member, influenced the choice of Miles as Bayer's corporate bride?

Dr. Geks was faced with a seven-week strike almost before he got started. But that left him undaunted. For as a "people person," he shook hands with more than 500 workers on their return.

In the spring of 1983, Bayer AG, like Miles before it, was reaping the results of its strategic studies. Far-reaching changes would touch all parts of the parent company, tightening its organization, yet leaving it flexible.

As early as May, Dr. Geks told senior managers at a meeting in Elkhart that the old Pharma Division of Bayer AG would be dissolved in favor of a new concept—the Health Care Sector.

"And what is unique in that?" he asked rhetorically. "That it is 'rooted' in two different cultures.

Dr. Geks welcomes Edna Usery of the Ames Reagent Manufacturing plant back to work following a seven-week strike. In an all-day tour of the seven Elkhart plants, Dr. Geks personally welcomed more than 500 union members back to their jobs. Here he is accompanied by Plant Manager Dale Pfingst.

This is the first real trans-Atlantic venture. Half of it is rooted in Europe, half in the United States. And I don't know of any pharmaceutical company that is so broadly based."

As later explained, the Health Care Sector consists of six business groups, three headed by Americans and three by Europeans. Those managed from America are Diagnostics, by Joseph H. Rosloff (American); Hospital, by Dr. Wilhelm F. Schaeffler (German by birth but long an American resident); Biotechnology, by Richard B. Kocher (American). Those managed in Europe are Ethical, by Prof. Siegismund S. Schuetz (German); Self-Medication, by Dietmar Gronenborn (German), and Consumer, by Hans-Juergen Jensen (Danish). An impressive blend!

The Health Care Sector, headed by Prof. Schraufstaetter, is one of six new Bayer business sectors, reduced from nine. The others are: Plastics, Rubber, and Fibers; Organic Chemicals and Dyestuffs; Inorganic Chemicals, Polyurethanes, and Coatings; Agriculture; and, finally, Agfa-Gevaert, which makes photographic products.

"This new organization will serve to achieve delegation of authority and decentralization," Dr. Geks said. "Each business group will be run as a profit center. Thus, the decision-making process is shortened and flexibility to adapt to our constantly changing environment is improved."

In June, the Miles board elected Kocher Miles' twelfth president. He had moved to Elkhart in 1966 as executive vice president of the Marschall Division, which he had joined in Madison, Wisconsin, in 1950 when he was a research chemist just starting out, long before it was acquired by Miles. He had served in a number of key posts and had been named executive vice president of Miles in charge of the Biotechnology Group in 1982.

In September 1983, the board elected Klaus Heinz Risse, Ph.D., vice chairman of the board and chief executive officer-elect, to succeed Dr. Geks July 1, 1984. This action recognized that Dr. Geks would reach retirement age in 1984 and gave Dr. Risse time to become familiar with the people and spirit of Miles before assuming his full duties.

Partners in Marriage

Speaking to the Rotary Club in Elkhart August 1, 1983, Dr. Geks summarized what the affiliation of Bayer and Miles had meant.

"You might say that our merger in 1978 was a bit like a marriage between Bayer and Miles, and like any successful marriage, both partners together accomplish more than each separately, and each partner contributes to the marriage.

"What has Miles contributed? Miles offered Bayer AG the entrance into the American pharmaceutical market. It was a company with management, production and research facilities, and with a broad, well-known product line. For instance, Miles was the leader in the diagnostic business. Bayer was not in that at all. Miles was in the biotechnology business on a much larger scale than Bayer. Miles was in the consumer business, which Bayer AG covered in the rest of the world, but not in America. As you may derive from that, Miles activities were complementary to Bayer activities.

"What has Bayer contributed? Bayer merged Cutter into Miles, a company with a broad product line and more than $300 million sales volume and good profitability. Bayer brought products of its extensive research into Miles, which are now being introduced in this country.... With new products in the Bayer pipeline, we are confident that we will grow even faster in the future. Bayer AG also invested an additional $170 million over the past five years, which

In 1983, Klaus Heinz Risse, Ph.D., was elected vice chairman and chief executive officer-elect to succeed Dr. Franz J. Geks, July 1, 1984.

enabled the pace of capital investments to double during this period. Of this total, about $75 million have been right here in the Elkhart area."

Dr. Geks went on to say that Bayer's total sales volume in the United States in 1982 was $3.3 billion and that the U.S. now accounts for over 20 percent of Bayer world sales, up from 14 percent when it acquired Miles.

"Bayer is the largest German investor in this country and one of the largest from any country," Dr. Geks said. "This large investment in the Health Care Sector of Miles with its headquarters here in Elkhart gives, in my opinion, a very positive outlook for the future."

No one could disagree. Bayer AG had put into Miles not just money but imagination and foresight, and an intensive resolve to make the company grow and prosper. As the curtain came down on Miles' first hundred years, its employees could look back with pride on what had been accomplished. Even more important, they could look ahead to advances in products and systems that Miles would surely achieve as its second century unfolded.

CHAPTER 24

Growth Through The Decades

Few if any documents more tellingly elucidate corporate progress—or the lack of it—than annual reports and annual meeting statements. Those of Miles are no exception. In fact, their style and candor have been good enough to have earned several awards from *Financial World* magazine. What follows here is material from these reports—a brief stitching together of key facts from about 1930 to mid-1983.

With the explosive growth of Alka-Seltzer in the early 1930s, decades of relative lethargy ended. The Depression that strangled most of business and industry was, for Miles Laboratories, an era of prosperity. Sales doubled between 1933 and 1934, then rose from $3,271,000 in 1934 to $5,867,000 in 1935, with profits climbing from $402,000 to $607,000.

Alka-Seltzer sales alone escalated to $8.7 million in 1937, slumped slightly for a few years, then got back on track, reaching $13 million in 1946.

Few complaints sprinkled the sparse Annual Reports of the 1930s, but it was observed that the 1938 drug amendments had led to a relabeling of all products "four times in the past year." In May 1940, the first accounting of the "Scientific Department" appeared, prepared by Dr. Compton. His incisive statements of stewardship would follow for almost 40 years.

Weathering the 1940s

For all the problems of manpower and material shortages, the company weathered World War II with relative ease—except for reluctant abandonment of the classical almanac and calendar printing operation. That vacant space, however, became available for production of the coffee tablets and K-rations for the Armed Forces.

A 1944 report noted that the reconversion problem "would not be as great as those in the mechanical industries." It wasn't.

Even then, the need to diversify did not go unrecognized. In 1946 Charlie Beardsley outlined that desire at the annual meeting. The search for acquisitions began seriously in the following year.

In June 1947, Miles purchased Chemical Specialties, Inc., a small manufacturer of intermediate chemicals in Zeeland, Michigan. It was renamed the Sumner Chemical Company in honor of Charles Sumner Beardsley. Although never a major force, it long remained a part of the chemical production network, with some 125 employees producing 30 organic chemicals, such as sodium and potassium citrate, for use in consumer products. It was sold to the Hexcel Corporation of Dublin, California, in March 1977.

By 1947 Miles ranked 13th in size among the 20 leading drug firms, with sales of close to $20 million. The original four stockholders had grown to 153.

Management sensed that fortune beckoned in 1948, with an opportunity to buy Schering-Plough from the Alien Property Custodian. But in the end the idea had to be abandoned; the company could not afford the $20 million plus needed for purchase. Since Schering-Plough went on to become an industry colossus, one wonders how drastically the course of Miles would have changed if such an acquisition had materialized!

At the mid-point of the 20th century, Miles' sales had climbed to $26 million, 73 percent of it due to Alka-Seltzer. In 1951, with the Korean War, the company went back to producing some soluble coffee tablets for the Armed Forces. A $765,000 sales item was listed under that heading.

In the early 1950s a few more acid comments about government appeared. "Politics has entered business, therefore, business is forced to enter politics...." management said, "and over everything hangs the pall of confiscatory taxation and the vast uncertainty of the smoldering cold war."

1950s—Good to Miles

In 1949 came the first printed Annual Report, a plain, spartan black-and-white booklet—almost a deceptive forerunner of the polished professional accounts soon to come. In 1957, the report featured a single theme—quality, "a watchword which must be forever held inviolate." Happily a fine year could be reported, too—an 18 percent gain in sales and a whopping 52 percent jump in net income. Foreign sales rose 21 percent. In 1959, the Diamond Anniversary year, gains continued.

In retrospect, the 1950s, if unspectacular, were still good to Miles. Sales almost tripled from $26.2 million in 1950 to $72.2 million in 1959. Earnings climbed from $1.8 million to $4.4 million. The Ames Division, first under "Chuck" Miles and later under George Orr, had boomed, and its innovative Stix reagent line heralded a lasting dominance in the diagnostic field. International, under Bill Koerting, had advanced steadily, and the persistent popularity of Alka-Seltzer and the vitamin line had been encouraging. Promotion moved cautiously but smoothly from radio to TV.

Citric acid sales had grown, too; consequently a new $4.1 million addition to the citric plant at Elkhart was completed. Also, the purchase of Dome Chemicals, Inc., in 1959 promised reinvigoration of the ethical drug market.

A Festive Air for the 75th

As a result, a festive air marked the 75th anniversary. An open house for employees and townspeople was held in June. Expected to draw some 8,000 people, it attracted 10,749.

At the shareholders meeting on April 28, 1959, Walter Beardsley proudly summed up the first 75 years.

"We have survived wars and panics, almost unbelievable changes in medicines and medical practices, chemistry, nutrition, communications, and advertising," Beardsley said. "We have changed from a privately held, small company to a publicly held, medium-sized company. I hope that the founders and early developers are able to look down and see where their labors have led."

The new decade of the 1960s started well enough with sales up 14 percent, but earnings slipped slightly due to start-up costs of new plants in Argentina and France and to loss of the profitable Cuban business—a fate shared by other leading drug manufacturers. In 1961, earnings reverted to a more desirable pattern, climbing 30 percent.

Moving into the "Big Time"

By then Miles was moving into the "big time." In 1958 it had wedged into *Fortune's* list of 500 largest U.S. corporations; it was slotted 463 in its Diamond year. In July 1961, Walter and Ed Beardsley and Dr. Compton gave the company's first formal presentation to the New York Society of Security Analysts. Walter still proudly proclaimed Miles as a "Hoosier Company," but he did not neglect describing it as a versatile domestic and international firm, either. In October came a three-for-one stock split. In February 1962, the stock began trading on the New York Stock Exchange.

The determination to pursue the pathways of research became more than evident with the May 1962 dedication of the $4 million Charles S. Beardsley Research Laboratory. Research centers were established in Mexico and England. By then, the research and medical staffs had grown to 380, with 83 holding doctorates. Prophetically, the annual report said that the new federal drug legislation (the historic 1962 Amendments) "will cause greater delays in new drug applications and in the introduction of new products."

Commenting in the annual meeting report, Walter Beardsley said that "no one challenges the need of some improvement in our laws. Basically, the industry is clean, highly competitive, oriented to the public interest, and has been most productive in advancing the quality of medical care. It is carrying on a very large amount of scientific research. It is relatively young, aggressive, and its personnel are well above the average in education and scientific achievement. . . . It would be a catastrophe for the future of medicine and the public health to clamp too smothering a government control on this industry."

A Sales Milestone: Passing $100 Million

In 1963, sales reached a milestone, surpassing the $100 million mark for the first time, at $107.8 million. This was the 18th consecutive year of increased sales. By that year, the preoccupation to diversify once again strongly surfaced. A chart showed that since 1954 chemicals and professional products had grown from 12 percent of volume to 29 percent. It was a valiant gain but not really enough. There was no denying that the consumer line—

notably Alka-Seltzer and the vitamins—still bulwarked the business.

Diversification in the 1960s

Diversification did come with the acquiring of Lab-Tek in 1964, of Union Starch and Marschall Laboratories in 1965, S.O.S and Pentex in 1968, and finally of Worthington Foods in 1970. This was ambitious action and taken in the decade that saw Miles march firmly toward higher sales and earnings.

The 1960s overall were even more successful than the 1950s. It had taken 79 years to reach the $100 million level in sales. But it took only five years to surpass $200 million, and then by a wide margin, reaching $228 million in 1968. Net earnings had almost doubled. The final year of the 1960s closed impressively with sales soaring to almost $280 mil-

lion, up 23 percent, and as the Annual Report said, "far surpassing the quarter-billion dollar sales goal we had set for ourselves for 1970!"

Earnings surged also, to $14.3 million, but had to be reduced $1.5 million by an "extraordinary" item—"losses caused by the government banning of cyclamate, the non-caloric sweetener, which had been used extensively in vitamin formulations." The report echoed quiet confidence in the "dynamic growth of the company." Major capital ventures at Elkhart, West Haven, and virtually every Miles plant had geared operations for further gains. International expansion had proceeded rapidly with new or enlarged plants in a score of countries and with sales expanding into more than 100.

In retrospect, progress had been relatively smooth in the 1950s and 1960s. The 1970s were to be

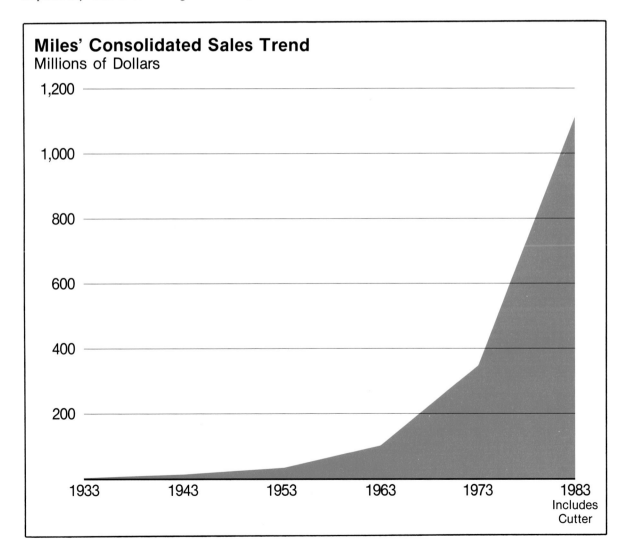

Miles' Consolidated Sales Trend
Millions of Dollars

different, the circumstances and challenges tougher, the change more rapid. Sales rose in the first year of the decade, but earnings dipped in 1970 and again in 1971. The shutdown of the corn wet milling plant of Union Starch in Granite City didn't help. Neither did an economic downturn.

Sales and earnings normalized once more in 1972, with volume moving over the $300 million mark to $319 million and earnings increasing to $15 million. Thus it had taken only four years to climb from $200 million to $300 million!

Defending Business

Compton and Beardsley in 1972 spoke out forcefully on international and regulatory problems. They attacked the "simplistic jingoism" of those criticizing international expansion as causing job losses in the United States.

"Experience shows," they wrote, "that foreign industry simply fills...(any) vacuum with resulting increased competitive disadvantage to American industry and labor." They expressed confidence that the FDA review of over-the-counter products was a "constructive step," and that it would find Miles' products safe and effective.

The 1974 report could react happily to the recommendation of the Antacid Advisory Review Panel, confirming Alka-Seltzer "for headaches, body aches and pains, and for acid indigestion, heartburn, or sour stomach."

Confronting Consumer Advocates

Bitingly, the report deplored "the meddlesome and distracting activity of a relatively few individuals who have noisily attempted to substitute their judgment for that...of a panel of experts," an obvious reference to Ralph Nader and Dr. Sidney Wolfe. "We object to these headline-seeking tactics of harassment...based on "strained and superficial analysis of data...we in business feel entitled to the same level of responsibility and integrity from self-appointed consumer advocates as they rightly expect from us."

The difficulty of maintaining good profit levels became more apparent in the mid-1970s. The 1975

Annual Report, for example, referred to a drop in earnings, as "costs for raw materials, services, media, and borrowed funds have all risen rapidly in unpredictable patterns."

There were bright spots, though, the report noting that international volume had risen 18 percent, representing 31 percent of total corporate sales, compared to 21 percent five years earlier. Leadership was being provided for 3,250 employees overseas by 17 general managers—a far cry from the early Bill Koerting and Manny Perez days! Sales in 1976 hit $450 million, with earnings from continuing operations up 24 percent. Net earnings, however, showed only a 5 percent increase, rising to $16.2 million from $15.4 million the year earlier.

Sales forged ahead in the late 1970s—from $479 million in 1977 to $743 million in 1982. Stringent economies led to a 1982 profit before tax of $2.3 million, and net earnings in excess of $10 million, in spite of a one-time write-off relating to divestment of the vegetable protein business.

Changes in the 1980s

The 1983 performance, including the Cutter Group, resulted in net sales of $1,115 million, 4 percent above the previous year, and profits before taxes of $66.5 million, 34 percent above the year before. Net income was $35 million.

Capital expenditures soared, too, as Bayer, the new parent, was intent on rearing a "lusty" child. Investments from 1979 through 1983 totalled $230 million, quite a commitment in view of corporate, national, and world conditions.

The new era that had come with the Bayer AG purchase would not bring drastic change all at once. For one thing, Miles took a lot of absorbing. By 1984 it had roughly 12,000 employees worldwide, 3,200 of them in the Elkhart area. There were 61 plants around the world in 21 countries producing more than 2,000 products. Its diversity matched, in fact, well exceeded, that of most broad line pharmaceutical-chemical firms. How to manage that diversity and build on it posed a challenge to Bayer, but one that was being met boldly and confidently.

CHAPTER 25

The Eras In Retrospect

Much earlier in this accounting it became evident that singular individuals had made an everlasting imprint on the history of Miles. Hundreds, if not thousands of them, had done so if you count all the men and women who worked with skill and dedication through the rolling decades.

From the standpoint of leadership, the century can be classified into four eras under the headings of Miles, Beardsley, Compton, and Bayer.

The Doctor and His Grandsons

The Miles era starting in 1884 might be said to have ended when Dr. Miles began spending time in Florida after 1906. But this was not entirely true, for he still had influence and he did have three grandsons who became active in the business. Their solid performances in prominent posts added up to 94 years of service—and much longer if board membership is included.

Franklin B. Miles, the eldest, born in 1905, was a Yale graduate who started with Miles in 1933 by demonstrating Alka-Seltzer at the World's Fair in Chicago. He next worked in sales out of Boston, then went into the financial side of the company at Elkhart. He became treasurer in 1944, retired in 1962, and continued to serve on the Board of Directors in the 1980s.

As noted earlier, Charles F. Miles, born in 1907, started as Ames' first salesman in 1931, when he was fresh out of Yale University. Eventually he became its able president and a senior vice president of the corporation. He also headed public relations at one time and was a board member for 44 years, until 1978. He retired in 1967.

Edward L. "Ned" Miles, the youngest of the brothers, was an Ames vice president in charge of public relations and marketing before retiring in 1961 after 30 years with the company. He also served on the Board of Directors.

Dr. Franklin L. Miles founded the firm in 1884 and played an active role in company affairs until 1893, when he moved with his Grand Dispensary, an independent concern, to Chicago. He returned to Elkhart in 1902 and was president continuously until his death in 1929.

Three grandsons of Dr. Miles, children of Charles Foster Miles and Rachel Beardsley, entered company affairs in the 1930s and played key roles for many decades.

Franklin B. Miles, who retired in 1961, started with the company in 1933, demonstrating Alka-Seltzer at the World's Fair in Chicago. He became treasurer in 1944 and today sits on the Board of Directors.

Charles Foster "Chuck" Miles, who retired in 1967, started in 1931 as the first salesman for Effervescent Products, later Ames Division. He became president of Ames in 1947 and served as a Miles Board member until 1978.

Edward L. "Ned" Miles, who retired in 1961, began as a salesman in the Chicago office in 1934 and later ran Ames' public relations and marketing. He also served on the Miles Board of Directors.

Lehman F. "Lem" Beardsley represents the fourth generation of Beardsleys involved in Miles management. Taking early retirement in 1982, he ended 34 years of active service in plant management, administrative services, and public affairs as senior vice president.

The Beardsley Dynasty—Long and Distinguished

Next came the Beardsley era, or it might be more aptly called a dynasty. It has few, if any, parallels in American business history, at least among the top 500 corporations. For practical purposes, it lasted longer than the bare figures show. That is, Dr. Miles, as noted before, had little interest in running the company on a day-to-day basis, and he was not often seen in Elkhart after 1912.

For this reason, the Beardsleys guided Miles from around the turn of the century (and to some degree as early as 1889) until 1964 (when Dr. Compton was elected president.) They continued to have a strong influence until Walter Beardsley retired as chairman of the board in 1973. For that matter, Walter, as a board member and chairman of the finance committee, played a key role at the time of the Bayer acquisition. And Lehman, his cousin, also a member of the board at that critical time, has continued to serve with distinction on the board, contributing particularly to good community relations.

"A.R.," "Hub," and "A.L."

The records of A.R. and Hub Beardsley have already been described. Since Dr. Miles was nominally president until his death in 1929, Hub was formally president only from that year until 1936. Then Arthur Lehman Beardsley, who had joined the company in 1920, took over until 1941. He served through the pivotal Alka-Seltzer years as a skilled administrator able to keep things on an even keel.

"Uncle Charlie's" Lasting Influence

The achievements of Charles S. Beardsley as president, from 1944-1947, and as chairman from 1947-1961, withstand the sternest scrutiny of time. A law school graduate of the University of Michigan, he started with the company in 1926 after practicing law for 10 years. His influence extended through his long years of retirement, for as honorary chairman, he lived to be 87. He was, as an admirer put it, "one strong man."

Charlie Beardsley's flair for promotion bordered on genius. Without his insistence on greatly expanded advertising, Alka-Seltzer might well have slipped into oblivion. He had to fight for advertising expenditures, sometimes over the objections of other executives.

That kind of vigor didn't always win the admiration of the board of directors. They put him on "probation" in 1933, then hastily rescinded that action within six months!

Clearly, during the span of "C.S.B's" influence, Miles grew from a small mid-western firm into a major corporation. He was a dominant figure with great force and judgment, and not without a great measure of self-confidence and charisma as well.

Walter Beardsley's Durable Career

Walter Beardsley, son of Hub, served as president from 1947 to 1961, and as chairman of the board from 1961 to 1973. He had worked for the company since 1930, with time out for the war years. He was a graduate of Princeton University and the London School of Economics. Sophisticated, urbane, and oriented to the political and world scene, he wasn't particularly fond of administration, but he could always impress the financial community. He pushed hard for international growth, and was an effective "balance wheel" through critical years. He saw Miles grow from $19.5 million in sales in 1947, when he was elected president, to $348 million in 1973, when he retired as chairman of the board. He died in 1980 on his 75th birthday.

Beardsley's interest in politics has already been noted. He was also more than willing to serve his industry. For example, he was most active on behalf of the Proprietary Association, including a stint as president.

A man of wide-ranging interests, he became an avid collector of first-rate modern art. He started this avocation in 1960, and although he insisted he knew little about it, which may have been true at the outset, he eventually knew a great deal about it. Some of this collection graces the walls of Elkhart headquarters; some is housed at the Walter R. Beardsley Gallery of 20th Century Art in the Snite Museum at the University of Notre Dame.

Ed Beardsley, the Engineer

Edward Huggett Beardsley, a son of Arthur L., was an engineering graduate of the University of Wisconsin. He joined the company in 1930, serving in purchasing, production, and administrative posts before becoming president (1961–1964). He had an aptness for management, with a special affinity for the technical and manufacturing areas and a warmth for people. He knew hundreds by their first names.

Miles went on the Big Board of the New York Stock Exchange February 5, 1962 under the symbol MIL, here held by Ed Beardsley, president.

Hub—1929–1936

Arthur—1936–1944

Walter—1947–1961

Edward—1961–1964

Charles—1944–1947

*Five Beardsley presidents followed the founder
from 1929 to 1964.*

He made sure the company was up to snuff on its
production lines. During his years as president, the
sales curve went up from $82 million in 1961 to $143
million by 1965. That alone is a testament to his
leadership. Ed Beardsley continued to serve with
distinction on the board of directors until 1978. He
died in 1980 at the age of 81.

The Beardsley years stand as a remarkable record
of consistent service and of talent and dedication
faithfully applied decade after decade by individuals
who felt not only a responsibility to their own families
but to hundreds and eventually thousands of people
whose jobs depended on the company.

The Towering Compton Years

The Compton era also remains unique for all
time. It embraced, of course, the years 1964–1981,
when Dr. Walter Ames Compton served as president
and chairman. But its roots go back to the forceful
role of George E. Compton in the early years of the
company.

George's pioneer wife, Lizzie P. Ames, a patient
of Dr. Miles, treasured a long interest in the Miles
company until her death in 1952 and played a spirited
role on an early Board of Directors. It was she who
urged her grandson Walter Compton to go to work for
Miles. Three of her children also served as able
members of the Board: Herman, the chief financial
officer of the Compton Investment Company, which
he inherited from his father, Herman; Francis E.,
who carried on the banking and development tradition of Herman, and Georgia Walker, the fourth
woman to be a Miles director. Herman died at 45 in
1933, and Francis served for 30 years, until his death
in 1962. The engineering achievements of Bim
Compton, Walter's brother, also helped to create
modern Miles. And the era has not ended, since
Gordon Compton, Walter's son, holds an important
marketing post.

Dr. Compton's towering role in the story of
Miles can only be described as awesome in its
dimensions. In the breadth and depth of his vision
and intellect, he certainly had few peers in the
American business community. Eventually, he had to
cope with more intractable problems than his prede-
cessors, such as rampant inflation and international
difficulties. He met them head-on with skill, judgment, fervor, and integrity.

His part in various activities marking the company's progress has been described in other portions of
this book. No facet of the company was beyond his
reach or acumen, so he played many diverse roles,
some in areas as varied as bench research and promotion. In all, he gave 43 years of service from the time
he was hired as the first medical director in 1938 to his
retirement as chairman in 1981. Without his zeal and
foresight, Miles' commitment to research would,
without question, have been delayed and less intense.
He took the company into the modern world of
science.

Often that risky domain did not achieve what he
had hoped for or had in mind. Still, he never flagged
in goading decisions that would lead to a higher
research capability. He felt Miles was otherwise
doomed to fail or limp along on a treadmill of

Walter Ames Compton, M.D., succeeded a long line of
Beardsleys as president and chief executive officer, serving
as president, 1964–1973, and chairman, 1973–1981.

George W. Orr, Jr., president, 1973–1976.

mediocrity. As Roger Snow wrote in *The Alkalizer*, on
the occasion of Dr. Compton's retirement, "It was
largely his vigorous enterprise that thrust Miles
beyond the sphere of patent medicines and imbued
the company with a new scientific character."

Any recounting of the Compton era must include the accomplishments of Rowland G. "Bob"
Rose, who earned a lofty niche as Miles' ninth
president from 1977 to his retirement in early 1981.
His financial and administrative sagacity in both the
international and domestic arenas was critical to
company progress. But far more than that, his was a
steady hand on the tiller, always calm, yet energetic
and forceful. His judgment and good sense prevailed
in times of both triumph and tribulation. He was
known for his candor and courtesy to all around him.

"Insight, Breadth of Knowledge, and Moral Philosophy"

At that same time, in 1979, Dr. Geks paid
generous tribute to Compton's long list of contributions: "As a scientist...at a time when the 1938 Food
and Drug Act imperiled much of the product line ...
as a creator of new products, the chief expression
being reagent products...as a physician, preoccupied
with the medical quality and usefulness of the company's products...as a visionary who perceived the
need and foresaw the ultimate acceptance of vitamin
supplementation, citric acid fermented from a variety
of raw materials, diagnostic reagents and instruments,
enzyme modulated chemistry, and an entire concept
of biochemical relationships, including the derivation
of protein direct from vegetable sources."

"But perhaps most of all," Dr. Geks said, "Miles
has benefited from his insight, breadth of knowledge,
and moral philosophy."

Outside the company, Compton's contributions,
too, are lengthy: he served often on industry trade
groups, university advisory councils, museum
boards, medical institutions, and governmental
bodies.

Dr. Compton had other special interests; one of
them had nothing to do with industry, medicine or
science, but rather with culture. Something his father
had given him to read ignited a fascination for

Rowland G. "Bob" Rose, president, 1977–1981.

Theodor H. Heinrichs, CEO, 1979–1983, and president, 1982–1983.

Japanese swords, especially the exotic and graceful samurai. As a youth, he spotted one in a Chinese laundry in New York City and bought it for six dollars. That was the start of what has grown into a world famous collection, most of which will be bequeathed to the Boston Museum of Fine Arts. Not surprisingly, Dr. Compton was elected an honorary Fellow of the Society for the Preservation of Art Swords. His interest in Japan and the Orient, for that matter, goes well beyond the romantic samurai. For returning a sword that was considered a national cultural treasure to Japan, he was presented in 1963 with the Order of the Rising Sun.

The Ambitious Heinrichs Years

With the retirement of Dr. Compton in 1979, Theodor H. Heinrichs, head of Cutter Laboratories since the acquisition in 1974, also became chief executive officer of Miles.

Tireless, tough-minded, and forthright, Heinrichs began shuttling between Berkeley and Elkhart, guiding both companies toward integration.

Heinrichs was a determined leader with a clear idea of the responsibility his new position held. By the time of his retirement on April 1, 1983, he had achieved his major objective: "To assure that a solid framework is established that will lead to a new order of magnitude for the Bayer health care presence in the United States."

In his last speech to senior management, Heinrichs described his feelings: "In beginning a different future, I am somewhat in the position of an architect and builder, who has helped to complete the design, to build the foundation, put the walls in place, and who has just put, with the completion of the merger of Miles and Cutter, the last tile on the roof."

Dr. Geks' Zest and Zeal

The new "Elkhart man" succeeding Heinrichs was no stranger at all, since it was Dr. Geks, head of Bayer's Pharma Division and a frequent Miles visitor and interpreter of Bayer planning and philosophy, as well as an active planner and negotiator in Bayer's investment in Miles. As a member of Bayer's Board of

Franz J. Geks, M.D., CEO and chairman, 1983–1984.

Richard B. Kocher, president, 1983 to present.

Management since 1977, Dr. Geks had been actively engaged in the affairs of Miles, including membership on its Board. For this reason, when he bought a house in Elkhart, he was in familiar territory.

Dr. Geks is a quarter-century veteran of Bayer. A thoroughly schooled scientist to begin with, he received his medical education at universities in Cologne, Munich, Innsbruck, and Dusseldorf. He also took post-graduate studies in economics.

Dr. Geks plunged into his assignment with unquestioned zest and zeal, telling employees he was depending on them to operate Miles successfully and to make it a "cornerstone" of the Health Care Sector. He said he expected 1983 to be a year of "consolidation" and of "concentration on achieving goals," with full confidence in Miles' "people, products, ideas, and determination" to find "the place in the health care industry that we deserve. I want to help you to get there."

Dr. Geks sums it up this way: "We want to establish the Health Care Sector of Bayer as an international, broadly-based, highly diversified, excellently-managed trans-Atlantic health care business which can smoothly operate across two cultures."

Since Dr. Geks would be reaching Bayer's retirement age in 1984, it was announced in mid-1983 that Klaus Heinz Risse, Ph.D., would succeed him on July 1, 1984.

Dr. Risse was no newcomer to America. He had joined Bayer AG in 1955 after obtaining his doctorate in organic chemistry and had worked in both the pharmaceutical and the agricultural chemicals divisions. From 1971 on, he had been head of agricultural chemicals worldwide and had played an important role in the establishment of Bayer/Mobay's agricultural chemical business in the United States. He was looking forward to doing the same for the pharmaceuticals business.

"This action by the board recognizes that I will be reaching retirement age next year and assures that... Dr. Risse be given full opportunity to become familiar with the people, the business, and most importantly, the spirit of this company," Dr. Geks said.

And what is that spirit? As viewed over the long first century, it is one embodied in good people—people interested in the welfare of others around them; people innovative enough to create new prod-

The Miles Board of Directors on April 18, 1960. Seated, from left: Georgia C. Walker; Walter R. Beardsley, chairman; Charles S. Beardsley, honorary chairman; Edward H. Beardsley; and Dr. Walter A. Compton. Standing, from left: Granville W. Keller; William E. Koerting; Edgar Kobak; Franklin B. Miles; Lewis F. Bonham; Dr. Maurice H. Seevers; Howard F. Roderick; Walter R. Lerner; Charles F. Miles; and Wendell C. Compton.

The Miles Board of Directors on the eve of the Bayer acquisition in 1977. Seated, from left: John B. Buckley; Walter A. Compton, chairman; Walter R. Beardsley; Rowland G. Rose; and George E. Davy. Standing, from left: George J. Vojta; Franklin B. Miles; Dr. Theodore B. Van Itallie; Charles F. Miles; Wendell C. Compton; Henry M. Schachte; Richard C. Gerstenberg; Lehman F. Beardsley; and John R. Gildea, secretary.

261

ucts and willing to take financial risks; people grateful for the opportunity to work and work hard; people who honestly believe that the world is enriched by ethnic differences that can be blended into common purposes.

This story of Miles had to wind down on the eve of the Centennial. The milestones of its first century had been passed; the records had been inscribed. Of course, a great many people who created those records are gone, but a surprising number still live with rich memories of their services in the building of the company. Perhaps at the 150-year mark, if not sooner, another historian will write sparkling new chapters of other times and other eras in this continuing saga. We wish him or her Godspeed!

APPENDIX

THE MILES BEHIND US

A Chronological Overview of the First Century of Miles Laboratories

The Founding Years

1875   Franklin L. Miles, M.D., establishes a practice in Elkhart, Indiana.

1882   Dr. Miles sells the first bottle of Nervine, a calmative formulated in his Jackson Street office dispensary.

1884   Dr. Miles launches the Miles Medical Company (stationery order, March 7).

Dr. Miles' *Medical News* appears.

Dr. Miles' Restorative Nerve and Liver Pills (to 1949) are introduced.

1885   Articles of association are filed and first stock issued on capital of $1,000.

Dr. Miles' Restorative Tonic (to 1938) and Dr. Miles' Restorative Blood Purifier (later Alterative Compound, to 1937) are marketed.

1887   Investor George E. Compton and businessman A. R. Burns become associated with the company.

Dr. Miles' New Cure for the Heart (later Cactus Compound, to 1938) is introduced.

1888   Company expands to 110 High Street in the former office of the *Independent* newspaper.

1889   Manufacturer Albert Raper Beardsley becomes a partner in the business.

1890   Andrew Hubble "Hub" Beardsley joins the company.

Dr. Miles founds the Grand Dispensary diagnostic service (to 1922).

1892   New building at 117 W. Franklin Street is occupied.

1893   A three-story printing plant is added.

The Grand Dispensary moves to Chicago, returning to Elkhart in 1902.

Dr. Miles' Anti-Pain Pills (to 1973) are introduced.

First dividends are declared.

1897   Franklin Street plant expands.

Cutter Laboratories founded in Fresno, California, drugstore.

1898   Number of employees passes 100.

Sales reach $400,000.

Harry B. Gampher is hired, later becomes company secretary and office manager (to 1943).

1902   Dr. Miles starts Almanac (to 1942).

1903   Franklin Street plant adds four stories.

"Miles Plan" of fair trade for druggists is instituted (to 1917).

1904   Number of employees reaches 200.

Print shop votes for first recorded labor organization.

1906   San Francisco earthquake destroys Cutter records. Company provides vaccines.

Dr. Miles retires to Ft. Myers, Florida.

1908   A. R. Beardsley and wife, Elizabeth Baldwin, build Ruthmere residence on Beardsley Avenue.

State Street warehouse is erected.

1910   George Compton dies.

1911   U.S. Supreme Court rules against price fixing in the Dr. Miles Medical Company vs. John D. Park Sons & Company case.

Company re-organizes as a co-partnership (to 1922).

1912   Company donates $10,000 toward Elkhart's first hospital.

1915   First motor truck replaces dray.

1918   Company adopts first group life insurance plan.

Sales surpass $1 million.

1920   Arthur Lehman Beardsley joins company in Purchasing.

Production of almanacs, calendars and Little Books attains major importance, with distribution running to 40 million per year.

1924   A. R. Beardsley dies.

Franklin Street Plant adds fourth floor.

1925   Pura-Laxa is picked up as first product developed outside the company and first to become effervescent.

1926   Effervescent product development begins under British-born chemist, J. Maurice Treneer.

Charles S. Beardsley joins management in Advertising.

1927   Dr. Miles' Aspir-Mint is introduced (to 1949)

1928   Franklin Street plant adds westside addition.

1929   Dr. Miles dies in Florida.

Radio advertising premiers on WSBT, South Bend, Indiana.

Hub Beardsley is elected president.

$200,000 of preferred stock is issued.

The Alka-Seltzer® Era

1930   Effervescent Products, Inc., is formed to market Aspir-Vess, Cinsa-Vess and Bromo-Vess.

1931   Alka-Seltzer® effervescent analgesic antacid tablets make first appearance.

1932   Company updates name to Dr. Miles Laboratories, Inc.

Radio advertising for Alka-Seltzer is launched on WLS, Chicago, with "Songs of Home Sweet Home."

1933   Alka-Seltzer-sponsored broadcast of the National Barn Dance makes debut February 4.

1934   Sales jump to $3.3 million from $1.6 million.

1935   Company changes name to present form, Miles Laboratories, Inc.

Export Department is formed under William Koerting.

Honeywell plant on Myrtle Street is purchased for Printing Department.

1936   Walter A. Compton is elected to the Miles board of directors.

Andrew Hubble Beardsley dies.

Arthur Lehman Beardsley is named president.

First *Alkalizer* is published.

First foreign plant is established in Toronto for Alka-Seltzer production.

1938   Company moves into new building on Myrtle Street.

Dr. Walter Compton is engaged as first medical and research director.

Miles products are sold in 45 foreign countries.

1939   Number of employees nears 600.

Vitamin research begins.

Company drops Alka-Seltzer claims for "acidity" following Federal Trade Commission charges.

1940   One-A-Day® A and D Vitamins are marketed.

Scientific Department is established.

Citric acid research is inaugurated.

Fuel conservation program is placed into effect.

1941   Miles enters the diagnostic field with Clinitest® tablets for testing sugar in urine.

First retirement plan is adopted.

First labor contract is signed with Local 12273, U.M.W.

Factory begins production of coffee tablets for Armed Forces.

1942   Sales surpass $10 million.

1943   One-A-Day® Multivitamins are marketed.

1944   Number of employees surpasses 1,000.

Effervescent Products, Inc., becomes Ames Company.

Last edition of Dr. Miles' weather calendar appears.

Charles Sumner Beardsley becomes president upon death of Arthur L. Beardsley.

Miles Scholarships begin.

Growth and Diversification

1945   Miles Laboratories, Ltd., is started in Bridgend, Wales, U.K.

Riedel-de Haen, producer of Decholin®, becomes Miles' first acquisition through the Ames Company.

"Certificate of Meritorious Service" is conferred on Miles for wartime contributions.

1946   Dr. Walter A. Compton organizes R&D group.

Market Research Department is established with Treva Van Solingen as director.

Alka-Seltzer sales reach $13 million.

1947   Charles Sumner Beardsley becomes chairman and Walter Raper Beardsley, president.

Chemical Specialties (later Sumner Division) of Zeeland, Michigan, is purchased.

1949   Advertising is largely switched to TV.

First printed Annual Report is published.

1950   Bactine®, non-sting antiseptic and Tabcin® anti-histaminic products are introduced.

Thin tablet coating of vitamins is initially developed.

Pilot plant for production of citric acid for Alka-Seltzer goes on stream.

1951   Research space doubles.

Miles Laboratories Pan-American is formed.

1952   Elkhart citric acid plant becomes operational.

Speedy Alka-Seltzer® first appears in journal ads.

Mexico City and São Paulo Alka-Seltzer plants are established.

1953   Three-story addition to Elkhart plant is completed.

1955   Earnings surpass $2 million for the first time, reaching $2.4 million

Ernst Bischoff Company of Ivoryton, Connecticut, is acquired.

Company goes public, offering 106,962 shares of common stock.

Alka-Seltzer plant in Cali, Colombia, is built.

1956   Takamine Laboratories of Clifton, New Jersey, is bought for enzyme know-how.

Production of enzymes is undertaken at Elkhart.

Clinistix® test for glucose in urine inaugurates dip and read "Stix" line.

Buenos Aires plant is established.

1957   Sales pass $50 million to $56.3 million.

Number of employees reaches 2,000.

Albutest®, Albustix®, and Ketostix® reagent strips are introduced.

1958   Company forges onto *Fortune 500* list.

Uristix®, Combistix® join "Stix" family.

Elkhart site landscaping wins national award.

1959   Company marks 75th Anniversary with huge open house.

Dome Chemicals, Inc. of New York, manufacturer of dermatological products, is purchased

Stoke Court research facility is established in England.

Stilphostrol®, Phenistix® are introduced.

A hospital insurance plan is adopted.

Data processing system is installed.

1960   Chocks® children's vitamins are introduced.

Miles California is merged with parent.

Citric acid is first produced for outside sale.

1961   Number of employees attains 3,000.

Walter Raper Beardsley becomes chairman, Edward Huggett Beardsley, president.

Stock is split.

Destrostix®, Bactine® Skin Creme, Nervine® tablets are introduced.

Net earnings surpass $5 million for the first time.

1962   Charles S. Beardsley Research Laboratories are dedicated in Elkhart.

Research laboratories are dedicated in Stoke Court and Mexico.

Company stock is traded on "Big Board" of New York Stock Exchange.

Citric acid production begins in Israel and in Mexico.

"Diabetes in the News" appears.

Research is split into four groups: Corporate, Ames, Miles Chemicals, and Consumer.

1963   Sales pass $100 million.

Ames acquires Atomium Corporation, Billerica, Massachusetts, maker of Volemetron® and Gammacord® instruments.

Allpyral® allergenic extracts are introduced.

Business in Japan is built up.

1964   Corporation purchases Lab-Tek Plastics Company, Woodmont, Illinois, and introduces disposable laboratory equipment line.

After an association dating back to 1892, the Wade Advertising Agency is dropped and Interpublic Group signed on.

Dr. Walter A. Compton becomes president.

Specialty biochemicals began to be developed.

1965   One-A-Day® Multivitamins with Iron, Chocks® Plus Iron and Labstix® are introduced.

Plant is finished in Venezuela, and others acquired in Epernon, France, and Guatemala City.

Elkhart citric acid and enzyme plants are expanded.

International operations are restructured.

1966   Marschall Dairy Laboratory, Inc., of Madison, Wisconsin, and Union Starch Company, of Granite City, Illinois, are acquired.

Joint program with Yeda, Israel, on immunochemicals is begun.

Miles enters dairy food technology field with Marschall's Marstar®.

1967   Ames enters markets in Japan and Spain.

New corporate identity symbol is adopted.

First Miles International Symposium is held.

Matrix system for international operations begins.

1968   Sales soar to $228 million.

S.O.S soap pad business of General Foods and biochemicals of Pentex, Inc., Kankakee, Illinois, are purchased.

Dome moves to new plant in West Haven, Connecticut.

Two plants begin operating in Canada.

Interpublic Group advertising is dropped and Doyle, Dane, Bernbach ad agency is retained.

Disease Detection Information Bureau is founded by Ames.

1969   Flintstone® Vitamins, Alka-Seltzer® Plus Cold Tablets are introduced.

Cyclamates are removed from Miles products.

New or expanded plants go into operation in Elkhart, Madison, Australia, and Canada.

1970   Worthington Foods, Inc., of Worthington, Ohio, is acquired to bolster entry into vegetable protein business.

Miles Research Division is formed.

New plant opens in Melbourne, Australia.

Flavor Department is started.

1971   J. E. Siebel Sons Company of Chicago is purchased.

Historic Franklin Street building is razed.

Tridesilon® and Clinilab® are introduced. Bugs Bunny® joins vitamin team.

Doyle, Dane, Bernbach is replaced by Wells, Rich, Greene agency for Alka-Seltzer advertising.

First of five major Quality Control Seminars is held.

1972   Sales reach $319 million.

Thin film-coating for vitamin tablets is perfected.

Alka-Seltzer studies are submitted to FDA panels.

Marzyme® and Tek-Check® are introduced.

Union Starch plant is closed.

Joint ventures are started in Germany and Scandinavia.

New plant for Lab-Tek is occupied at Naperville, Illinois.

More extensive environmental program begins.

1973   Earnings reach new high of $17 million.

George Orr becomes president and Dr. Compton chairman and CEO as Walter R. Beardsley retires.

Multistix® and Microstix® are introduced.

Vitamins are reformulated to meet FDA standards.

Company parries criticisms of Alka-Seltzer in Congress and elsewhere.

Morningstar Farms line of cholesterol-free meat substitutes is placed on the market.

Ames enters the diagnostics market in Hungary.

1974 FDA Antacid Panel rules favorably on Alka-Seltzer.

Legal victories are scored over vitamin imitators.

Cutter Laboratories, Inc., of Berkeley, Calif., acquired by Bayer AG, of Leverkusen, West Germany.

Tissue-Tek® and Biostator® are introduced.

New Worthington plant at Schaumburg, Illinois, opens.

Corn wet-milling joint venture is entered into with CAR-MI at Dayton, Ohio.

Number of employees reaches 8,650.

1975 Sales reach $413.8 million.

New Ames plant opens in Elkhart.

Production of citric acid at Dayton begins.

DTIC-Dome®, N-Multistix®, Exzit®, N-Uristix®, Mecostix,® and Kernkluete® are marketed.

Plants are opened in Italy and Spain.

Negotiations to enter Russian market start.

1976 George Orr retires, succeeded by Rowland G. Rose as president.

One-A-Day® Vitamins Plus Minerals and Alka-2® Chewable Antacid are introduced.

New Marschall plant is completed for production of Superstart Cheese cultures.

More key evidence on Alka-Seltzer is submitted to FDA panels.

Ames Elkhart plant is expanded.

The diagnostic market in Czechoslovakia is tapped.

Bayer and Beyond

1977 Bayer AG of West Germany makes tender offer to acquire Miles stock.

Major citric acid plant at Dayton goes on stream with new extraction system.

S.O.S business is extended to Japan.

Joint venture for medical instruments is started in Ulm, West Germany.

Miles joins Yugoslavian consortium for producing enzymes.

Marzyme, enzymes for processing sweet acidophilous milk and high fructose syrup are introduced.

1978 Sales reach $537.0 million and earnings hit a new high of $18.1 million.

Miles and Bayer executives exchange first visits.

Theodor Heinrichs is named CEO.

Alka-Seltzer is successfully defended in England.

Clinitek® and Pacer® instruments are introduced.

Fire destroys much of Stoke Court.

1979 The Bayer-Miles merger is finalized.

Major pharmaceutical sales effort is launched at West Haven.

Delbay Division of Schering-Plough moves to West Haven.

Capacity of Dayton citric acid plant is doubled.

Nervine is reformulated without bromide.

Large plant is acquired in Mishawaka, Indiana, to produce diagnostic instruments.

Institute for Preclinical Pharmacology is founded in laboratories at Yale University.

Mycelex® and Mycelex®-G are introduced.

A major study on diabetes is launched.

Biotechnology Division is formed.

1980 Capital expenditures attain a record $62.8 million for added facilities at Elkhart, Kankakee, Dayton, West Haven, England, and Brazil.

Lux Scientific Corporation, Newbury Park, California is acquired.

Biostator®, Dextro-System®, Bactine® Hydrocortisone, Tissue-Tek® III, Seralyzer, S.O.-Ezy® are marketed.

Dome name is changed to Miles Pharmaceuticals.

Massive documentation on Alka-Seltzer is submitted to FDA.

1981 Mezlin®, Glucometer®, N-Multistix® SG are introduced.

Ames and citric acid plants at Elkhart are expanded.

Calcium sulphate extraction process is started at citric acid plant in Elkhart.

Marschall introduces five new Superstart cultures.

R&D budget reaches $50 million.

1982   Miles-Cutter merger plans proceed.

Worthington Foods divestiture ends involvement in protein food business.

Haifa citric acid operation and J. E. Siebel are sold. Ames-Yissum is closed.

New enzyme plant opens at Elkhart.

Stressgard®, Azlin®, Visidex®, Optimate®, Nicloside®, and Biltricide® boost product lines.

Adalat® is marketed in Canada.

New antibiotics filling plant is completed at West Haven.

Miles Learning Center program expands to 275 hospitals.

Research Products and Lab-Tek merge into Miles Scientific Division.

Cutter IV plants at Chattanooga, Tennessee, and Ogden, Utah, are closed.

President R. G. Rose retires.

Bayer purchases major share of Molecular Diagnostics.

Suggestion Award Program is implemented.

1983   Miles-Cutter merger is completed on January 1.

Five business groups are established: Pharmaceuticals, Professional Products, Consumer Products, Biotechnology and Cutter (including Medical, Biological, Bayvet, Biomedical, and Dental).

CEO Heinrichs resigns and Franz J. Geks, M.D., becomes chairman and CEO as Klaus Heinz Risse, Ph.D., is named vice chairman and CEO-elect. Richard B. Kocher elected president.

First labor union strike in Elkhart since 1964 lasts seven weeks, settled amicably.

Sales exceed $1 billion for the first time.

Corporate Officers

President

Franklin L. Miles, M.D.	1885–1929
Andrew H. "Hub" Beardsley	1929–1936
Arthur L. Beardsley	1936-1944
Charles S. Beardsley	1944–1947
Walter R. Beardsley	1947–1961
Edward H. Beardsley	1961–1964
Walter A. Compton, M.D.	1964–1973
George W. Orr, Jr.	1973–1976
Roland G. Rose	1977–1981
Theodor H. Heinrichs	1982–1983
Franz J. Geks, M.D.	1983
Richard B. Kocher	1983–

Chairman

Andrew H. "Hub" Beardsley	1925–1936
Arthur L. Beardsley	1936–1944
Charles S. Beardsley	1947–1961
Walter R. Beardsley	1961–1973
Walter A. Compton, M.D.	1973–1981
Theodor H. Heinrichs	1981–1983
Franz J. Geks, M.D.	1983–1984

Chief Executive Officer (CEO)
Same as President until 1973

Walter A. Compton, M.D.	1974–1979
Theodor H. Heinrichs	1979–1983
Franz J. Geks, M.D.	1983–1984

General Manager

Albert R. Beardsley	1890–1922
Arthur L. Beardsley	1922–1937
Edward H. Beardsley	1937–1960
Lehman F. Beardsley	1960–1962

Corporate Secretary

Norris E. Felt	1885–1887
A. R. Burns	1887–1890
Albert R. Beardsley,	1890–1891
Andrew H. "Hub" Beardsley	1891–1925
Harry B. Gampher	1925–1943
Walter R. Lerner	1943–1965
John B. Buckley	1965–1969
Adrien L. Ringuette	1969–1975
John R. Gildea	1975–1979
Adrien L. Ringuette	1979–

Corporate Treasurer

Hugh McLachlan	1885–1887
George E. Compton	1887–1890
A. R. Burns	1890–1891
Albert R. Beardsley	1891–1924
Arthur L. Beardsley	1924–1944
Harry B. Gampher	1943
Franklin B. Miles	1944–1961
Robert L. Grant	1962–1964
Rowland G. Rose	1964–1967
Merlin D. Knispel	1967–1978
Rowland G. Rose	1978
Donald R. Lohr	1978–1981
Jon R. Wyne	1981–

THE BEARDSLEY, MILES AND COMPTON FAMILIES IN ELKHART
(SIMPLIFIED GENEALOGY)

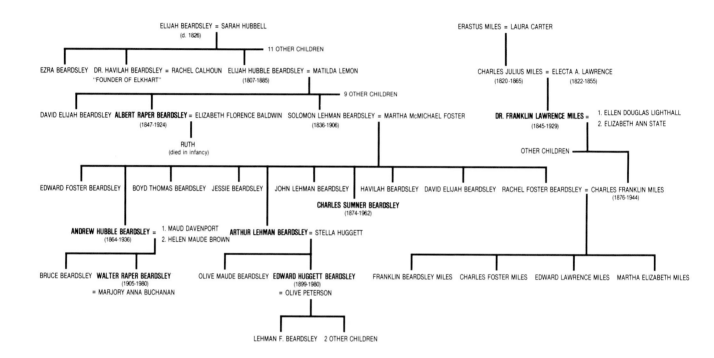

ELIJAH BEARDSLEY = SARAH HUBBELL
(d. 1826)

11 OTHER CHILDREN

EZRA BEARDSLEY   DR. HAVILAH BEARDSLEY = RACHEL CALHOUN   ELIJAH HUBBLE BEARDSLEY = MATILDA LEMON
"FOUNDER OF ELKHART"   (1807-1885)

9 OTHER CHILDREN

DAVID ELIJAH BEARDSLEY   **ALBERT RAPER BEARDSLEY** = ELIZABETH FLORENCE BALDWIN   SOLOMON LEHMAN BEARDSLEY = MARTHA McMICHAEL FOSTER
(1847-1924)   (1836-1906)

RUTH
(died in infancy)

EDWARD FOSTER BEARDSLEY   BOYD THOMAS BEARDSLEY   JESSIE BEARDSLEY   JOHN LEHMAN BEARDSLEY   HAVILAH BEARDSLEY   DAVID ELIJAH BEARDSLEY   RACHEL FOSTER BEARDSLEY = CHARLES FRANKLIN MILES
CHARLES SUMNER BEARDSLEY
(1874-1962)

ANDREW HUBBLE BEARDSLEY =   1. MAUD DAVENPORT   **ARTHUR LEHMAN BEARDSLEY** = STELLA HUGGETT
(1864-1936)   2. HELEN MAUDE BROWN

BRUCE BEARDSLEY   **WALTER RAPER BEARDSLEY**   OLIVE MAUDE BEARDSLEY   **EDWARD HUGGETT BEARDSLEY**
(1905-1980)   (1899-1980)
= MARJORY ANNA BUCHANAN   = OLIVE PETERSON

LEHMAN F. BEARDSLEY   2 OTHER CHILDREN

ERASTUS MILES = LAURA CARTER

CHARLES JULIUS MILES = ELECTA A. LAWRENCE
(1820-1865)   (1822-1855)

DR. FRANKLIN LAWRENCE MILES =   1. ELLEN DOUGLAS LIGHTHALL
(1845-1929)   2. ELIZABETH ANN STATE

OTHER CHILDREN

CHARLES FRANKLIN MILES
(1876-1944)

FRANKLIN BEARDSLEY MILES   CHARLES FOSTER MILES   EDWARD LAWRENCE MILES   MARTHA ELIZABETH MILES

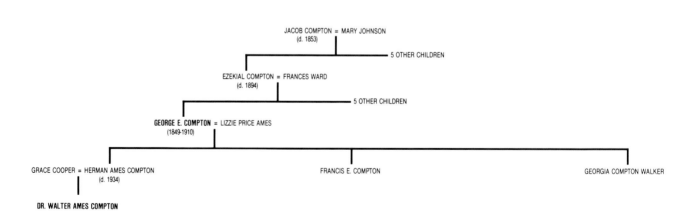

JACOB COMPTON = MARY JOHNSON
(d. 1853)

5 OTHER CHILDREN

EZEKIAL COMPTON = FRANCES WARD
(d. 1894)

5 OTHER CHILDREN

GEORGE E. COMPTON = LIZZIE PRICE AMES
(1849-1910)

GRACE COOPER = HERMAN AMES COMPTON   FRANCIS E. COMPTON   GEORGIA COMPTON WALKER
(d. 1934)

DR. WALTER AMES COMPTON

272

Index